*M*c

MW01283583

THE COSTS OF COALITION

The Costs of Coalition

Carol Mershon

STANFORD UNIVERSITY PRESS

STANFORD, CALIFORNIA 2002

Stanford University Press
Stanford, California

© 2002 by the Board of Trustees of the
Leland Stanford Junior University

Printed in the United States of America on acid-free,
archival-quality paper

Library of Congress Cataloging-in-Publication Data

Mershon, Carol.
   The costs of coalition / Carol Mershon.
      p.   cm.
Includes bibliograhical references and index.
   ISBN 0-8047-4083-6 (cloth : alk. paper)
1. Coalition governments.   I. Title.
JF331 .M47 2002
321.8'043'094—dc21   2001008283

Original Printing 2002

Last figure below indicates year of this printing:
11   10   09   08   07   06   05   04   03   02

Designed by Sandy Drooker
Typeset by BookMatters in 10/12.5 Sabon

To my father
Lyle Mershon
and to the memory of my mother
Harriette Cochran Mershon

Contents

Tables and Figures

FIGURES

Preface

A book is a journey, not only for its readers, but also, and above all, for its author. In the years that I have worked on this book, I have traveled both figuratively and literally. I have moved between theory and data, from observation to inference, and from new findings to new questions. I have also left one university for another, and I have crossed the Atlantic many times to participate in conferences, buy books, and gather data.

To view this book as a journey is especially appropriate given the assumptions at the base of its argument. I assume that political actors—parties, party factions, and individual politicians—exercise some degree of discretion in charting their courses of action. The paths they travel are influenced, but not dictated, by such features of their environment as political institutions and economic resources. The journeys they take are also journeys they *make*. Political actors are able to choose, and change, direction. Their choices in navigation will depend on their reading of the costs and benefits of moving one way or another. Searching for advantage, actors will not always shun a route that seems to carry some risk; at times they will follow that route and try to lower the costs of doing so. These assumptions undergird my analysis of coalition governments in parliamentary democracies.

I divide the book into three sections. Part I identifies a puzzle about coalition governments and develops a general argument to solve the puzzle. It outlines a design for appraising the explanation as well.

Part II is devoted to an intensive study of coalition politics in Italy, the country whose politics I know best and a country whose coalition governments are widely known to be unusually short-lived. I hope to cast Italian politics in a new light. I also hope to cast coalition politics in a new light, which means that my research moves beyond Italy.

Part III examines coalition politics in nine other parliamentary democracies. My treatment of evidence from, say, Denmark, Germany, Belgium, and Sweden cannot be as fine grained as it is for Italy. I must trade depth for breadth in Part III. Of course, Part II achieves depth at the expense of breadth. The point is that each trade-off balances and eases the other. The concluding chapter discusses additional trade-offs in the study of coalition politics at the same time that it discusses the place of this research within contemporary political science.

Put briefly, the research tackles big questions of enduring interest in real-world politics and in political science. The substantive aim of the book is to understand and explain who governs, and for how long, under the institutions of parliamentary democracy. The analytical purpose is to insist on asking, How do we know that what we believe (or want to believe) is in fact right or wrong? In other words, the book seeks to reorient thinking about the relationship between theoretical and empirical research on coalitional behavior.

All of the chapters that follow are needed to elaborate fully the substantive and epistemological themes. For now, the substantive argument may be summarized in three sentences. The composition and duration of national-level executives depend on both the environment facing, and the actions of, political parties. The environmental factors of greatest interest here are electoral and parliamentary institutions and the array of parties and voters in policy space. Beyond reacting to their environment, political parties also act to affect the costs and benefits of governing, and thus help to determine cabinet composition and duration. The epistemological message of the book, in a nutshell, is that theoretical and empirical studies of coalition politics need to be brought into closer conversation with each other. On the one hand, game-theoretic research should be more attentive to identifying propositions capable of being assessed against evidence on actual coalitions. On the other, empirical research should insist on the importance of tapping and tracing causal mechanisms.

The substantive theme will be obvious to the reader from the very first pages of Chapter 1. The epistemological concern will be developed more gradually and may even seem to disappear occasionally under a mass of detailed findings; it is present throughout, nonetheless, and the conclusions will drive it home.

Scores of people have contributed to the book I have written. I owe them all a great debt of gratitude. Many colleagues read portions of the manuscript in various guises and at various stages. My sincere thanks go to Janet Adamski, Gerard Alexander, Barry Ames, Chris Anderson, Glenn Beamer, Shaun Bowler, Greg Caldeira, John Echeverri-Gent, Lee Epstein, David Farrell, Ada Finifter, Rob Franzese, Paul Freedman, Peter Hall, Kerstin Hamann, Will Heller, Steve Hellman, John Huber, Piero Ignazi, Junko Kato, Dick Katz, John Kautsky, Jack Knight, Michael Laver, Michael Lewis-Beck, Web Marquez, Gianfranco Pasquino, Ted Perlmutter, Simona Piattoni, Bingham Powell, the late Barbara Salert, Norman Schofield, Herman Schwartz, Serenella Sferza, Ken Shepsle, Kaare Strøm, John Sprague, Sid Tarrow, George Tsebelis, David Waldner, Brantly Womack, and Alan Zuckerman. I am especially grateful for the generosity and good judgment of Peter Hall, Michael Laver, Gianfranco Pasquino, and Norman Schofield, who read the entire manuscript in near-final form and who offered me sharp, sympathetic, and extraordinarily thoughtful criticism. I also thank a number of political scientists who have kindly given me data and/or responded to the country-specific questions I needed to clarify in order to compile the data sets for the book: Chris Anderson, Alice Cooper, Herbert Döring, John Huber, Erik Jones, Paulette Kurzer, François Pétry, Bjørn-Erik Rasch, Susan Scarrow, Mary Volcansek, and Matti Wiberg. I have learned much from discussions with seminar participants at Harvard University, Indiana University, the University of Notre Dame, the University of California at Irvine, the University of Virginia, Virginia Polytechnic Institute and State University, and Washington University. I thank Muriel Bell at Stanford University Press for her faith in this project and for her advice, encouragement, and expert handling of the manuscript. I am grateful, too, to Matt Stevens, production editor for the book at the Press, Julie Du Sablon, who copyedited the manuscript, and Lillian Ashworth, who prepared the index.

I am lucky to have been able to rely on the talent and hard work of twelve research assistants: Kerstin Hamann, Bill Hixon, Karl Kaltenthaler, and Barbara Sgouraki-Kinsey at Washington University in St. Louis; and Shawn Aaron, Janet Adamski, Rob Martin, Stacy Nyikos, Haiyan Qu, Sally Roever, Judson True, and Scott Woodard at the University of Virginia. I am equally fortunate to have been awarded financial support from several sources: a Fulbright-Hays Faculty Fellowship; Rowland Egger Grants, Department of Government and Foreign Affairs, University of Virginia; and a Sesquicentennial Research Leave, University of Virginia. Funding from the National Science Foundation (SBR 9320666) indirectly contributed to this research by allowing me to compare the development of data sets in the field of American judicial politics and in the field of coalition studies.

I have tried the patience of more than a few librarians and public officials in my search for data. I would especially like to thank the staff of the Institut Belge d'Information et de Documentation, Brussels; Annelise Quistorff in the Archives and Information Department, Library of the Folketing, Denmark; Lea Vatanen in the Office of the Prime Minister, Finland; Marianne Purtinger at the German Information Center, New York; Ray Henry in the Government Secretariat, Department of the Taoiseach, Ireland; the staff of the Press and Cultural Section, Royal Netherlands Embassy, Washington, D.C.; Øivind Østang in the Office of the Prime Minister, Norway; and Rune Hedman in the Archive and Information Department, Central Services Office for the Ministries, Sweden.

Early versions of portions of the book manuscript were published in the *American Political Science Review* and *Comparative Political Studies*; in Norman Schofield, ed., *The Theory of Coalition Governments* (1996); and in Shaun Bowler, David M. Farrell, and Richard S. Katz, eds., *Party Discipline and Parliamentary Government* (1999).

As I wrote the final version of the manuscript, I re-read the auto-biography of Rita Levi Montalcini, *Elogio dell'imperfezione* (1987). A neurologist, Levi Montalcini moved from Italy to St. Louis and worked at Washington University, where she discovered the nerve growth factor. She won the Nobel Prize in medicine in 1986 for that discovery. The title of her memoir expresses Levi Montalcini's conviction that locating imperfection, and probing what lies beneath it, is what scientific research is all about. Scientists should praise and prize imperfection. It is the imperfect match between theory and data that keeps us going, that gives us an idea of what to do next, that guides us toward cleaner data, better theory, and fuller understanding. As Levi Montalcini (1987, 11) recalls a lifetime of research, she observes: "The fact that activity carried out in such an imperfect fashion has been and still is for me an inexhaustible source of joy, makes me believe that imperfection in executing the task that we have set ourselves or have had assigned to us is more consonant with human nature, which is so imperfect, than is perfection." (This and all other translations in the book are mine.) Political methodologists and philosophers of science have taught me much, but I owe above all to Rita Levi Montalcini my assurance that achievement in science is inescapably accompanied by imperfection. Thankfully, work in science is never really complete.

I owe to Doug Loyd the fact that my work on this book has come to a close. Doug has seen me through the last years of writing the book, and he has helped me to let go of it. He has encouraged me, cooked dinner for me, and argued with me over semicolons; he uses more than I do. He has also rescued my computers, restored files, and otherwise fended off impending electronic chaos. Through it all, he has helped me to work, and to live, better, and I thank him with all my heart.

I dedicate this book to my father, Lyle Mershon, and to the memory of my mother, Harriette Cochran Mershon. Even after her death, my mother has inspired me. Even during his grief, my father has expressed joy in my life and work. For these gifts and more, I am deeply grateful. The book would not be here without them.

To the readers of my book: Explore its imperfections and appreciate them. I have tried hard, but you might well think of something I could have done better. You will increase the likelihood of coming up with ideas for improvement if you read not only the main text but also the endnotes and appendices (I wrote them for a reason!). You may access the database constructed for the book at the following Web site: http://www.faculty.virginia.edu/cmershon/. To let me know your reactions, E-mail me at cam6m@virginia.edu. I hope you enjoy the journey through the pages ahead.

THE COSTS OF COALITION

Part **One**

THE PUZZLE, ITS PIECES,
AND A SOLUTION

1 *How Can Governments Fall at Low Cost?*

Common sense holds that the fall of a government is likely to cost politicians something they care about, such as office, policy influence, or votes. The rules of the game in parliamentary democracies reinforce the point. In parliamentary regimes, the executive is drawn out of the legislature and depends on legislative support. If the cabinet loses the support of a legislative majority (for instance, if a motion of no confidence is approved in parliament), the cabinet must resign.[1] Bowing to inevitability, governments often resign when they anticipate defeat on a confidence vote or on major legislation. Executives relinquish office in these circumstances precisely because they have the constitutional right, duty, and authority to direct public policy. Cabinets unable to muster a legislative following deserve to end, and do. These procedures and practices mean, among other things, that the content of policy tends to flow from the party composition of governments (e.g., Laver and Budge 1992). Of course, not only office and policy are at stake when a cabinet is dissolved. Votes hang in the balance as well. Parliamentary elections afford voters the opportunity to pronounce a verdict on erstwhile incumbents. Given the institutional design of parliamentary democracy, then, governments that fall are exposed to the possibility of punishment: replacement by an alternative cabinet that is able to command a parliamentary majority; a reduced capacity to shape policy from the opposition bench; or even a setback in the next round of elections.

This conventional wisdom would be upset if, despite numerous cabinet collapses, a governing party were to resume positions in the executive, wield substantial influence over public policy, and retain electoral support. Just that scenario materializes in Italy.

The Puzzle

The record of Italian governments displays a pattern that is deeply perplexing. As Figure 1.1 shows, from 1946 to 1992 cabinets in Italy both

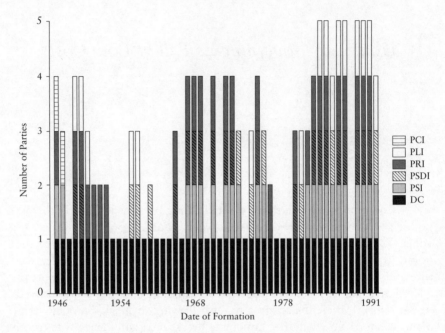

FIGURE 1.1. The Composition of Italian Governments, 1946–92.
Note: Governments are ordered chronologically on the horizontal axis, with tick
marks representing separate cabinets. For simplicity, this figure always depicts the
Socialists (PSI) and Social Democrats (PSDI) as separate parties, even though they
were united before 1947 and between 1966 and 1969. Other party abbreviations
are defined in the text and in Appendix A.

changed and remained the same. The Christian Democratic Party (Democrazia Cristiana, DC) always held governing power. But almost no government managed to stay in office for more than a few years, and many governments collapsed after only a few months. Italy exhibited the lowest rate
of turnover in government of any parliamentary democracy (Strøm 1990b,
128)[2] and yet had, except for the defunct French Fourth Republic, the most
short-lived cabinets (King et al. 1990, 867).

How can instability coexist with stability in this way? How can governments break up at such low cost and with so little impact on alternation?
These are the key questions that animate this book's comparisons of Italy
and other parliamentary democracies.

In posing and pursuing these questions, I am guided by the game-
theoretic literature on coalitional behavior. My question about (in)stability
reflects a central—perhaps *the* central—result in this literature: that voting
games in multidimensional policy space under simple majority rule are sub-

ject to endless cycles among alternative decisions. Voting generates a sequence that theorists label "chaos," in which one majority backs a decision
and is overthrown by a second majority endorsing a second decision; that
decision yields to a third, then to a fourth, and on and on (e.g., McKelvey
1976, 1979; McKelvey and Schofield 1987; Schofield 1983; discussion in
Riker 1980; Shepsle 1986). Given these predictions, it is a mystery why real-
world legislative decision making exhibits substantial stability. Efforts to
comprehend the inconsistency between predictions of chaos and empirical
observations of decisional stability have stimulated the development of entire schools of spatial theory (for reviews, see Schofield, Grofman, and Feld
1988; Strom 1990). Such efforts inform my study. But I move beyond extant
theoretical and empirical research in order to deal with an anomaly that to
date has not been adequately explored and understood: the combination of
decisional stability and instability found in Italy.

My question about costs, too, is rooted in the body of work on coalitions. An implicit but widely shared assumption of coalition theorists is that
government coalitions, once installed, can withstand much internal tension
because their members want to avoid the costs associated with destroying a
coalition. (Echoing the conventional wisdom summarized earlier, the reasoning often runs that, in interactions among parties, politicians fear the
loss of office or a diminished influence on policy and are so deterred from
undoing governments. Some analysts posit that parties risk electoral punishment in interactions with voters.)[3] As Figure 1.1 suggests, however, such
costs seem to be very limited in Italy before 1992. Why? The available literature clarifies the question but does not answer it.

The Argument

The answer offered in this book is that politicians' purposive actions
can reduce the costs of coalition. I argue that the costs and benefits of making and breaking coalitions depend on political institutions and on the array
of parties and voters in policy space. Institutional and spatial conditions[4]
structure politicians' opportunities and attempts to lower costs. Under some
conditions, as I demonstrate, coalitions are cheap, and politicians can easily make coalitions even cheaper.

Such conditions, I contend, are not unique to Italy. Figure 1.2 (see pg. 5)
illustrates the broad correlation between cabinet duration and alternation
in office.[5] Governments in Italy, the French Fourth Republic, Israel, and
Portugal (and to a degree Finland and Belgium) last a short while and are
subject to limited turnover. Ireland, Iceland, and Norway (and to some extent Canada and the United Kingdom) evince long duration and high alter-

nation. In Sweden, Spain, Denmark, and the Netherlands, cabinets attain an average duration resembling that of the second group, but experience fairly restricted turnover. Italy is an extreme case, then, and looks anomalous in light of coalition theories. But it is not *sui generis*. Scrutiny of this case gives special leverage, for Italy's extremity points up that a common, key assumption among coalition analysts—the notion that coalitions are costly to build and break—fails to hold under certain conditions. I reason that in Italy (and France, Israel, Portugal, Finland, and Belgium), institutional and spatial conditions curb the costs of coalition and allow politicians to try to lower costs further.

Such conditions are not impervious to change. The logic presented here implies that if political institutions or configurations of policy space are redrawn, then changes in patterns of coalition politics should ensue. Intertemporal comparisons admit tests of this implication. Belgium provides one particularly apt setting for probing change over time. The activation of a long-dormant linguistic cleavage redefined the Belgian policy space in the early 1960s, and institutional reforms were enacted in 1970 and 1980. I document in Chapter 7 that each of these shifts left an imprint on governing coalitions in Belgium.

Other compelling intertemporal comparisons involve Italy. The Christian Democrats dominated the Italian policy space from 1946 to 1992. From 1976 to 1992, however, electoral outcomes rendered the Socialists (Partito Socialista Italiano, PSI) the essential component of any DC-led coalition able to control a majority while excluding the Communists (Partito Comunista Italiano, PCI). The costs of coalition from 1976 to 1992 thus should have differed from costs incurred earlier. Differences do appear, as detailed in Chapter 5. Moreover, recent events furnish clinching evidence on variations across time. The 1992 elections registered far-reaching change in both spatial and institutional conditions in Italy. Consequently, coalition politics was transformed.

It merits emphasis that my argument has two related, but distinct, parts. First, the costs of assembling and dismantling governments vary across different types of party, types of party system, and types of institutional context. Given exogenous forces, some players have more to lose, and some less, from making and breaking coalitions. To illustrate: Where parliamentary rules require that the final floor vote on bills be held by secret ballot (as in the Italian Chamber of Deputies until 1988), legislators can sabotage government legislation—and the government itself—without worrying about antagonizing their electorate or endangering their careers. Second, some of the parameters of coalition politics that are often assumed to be fixed, *ex ante*, are in fact at least partially endogenous. Through strategic action, politicians can modify the costs of coalition. For example, as noted in the

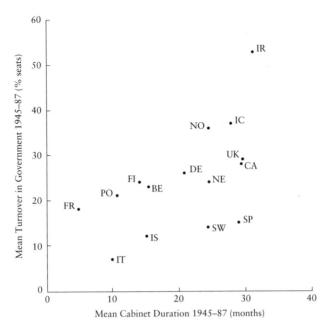

FIGURE 1.2. Cabinet Duration and Alternation in Office
in Fifteen Parliamentary Democracies.
BE = Belgium; CA = Canada; DE = Denmark; FI = Finland;
FR = Fourth Republic France; IC = Iceland; IR = Ireland; IS =
Israel; IT = Italy; NE = Netherlands; NO = Norway; PO =
Portugal; SP = Spain; SW = Sweden; UK = United Kingdom.

next chapter and examined more fully in Chapter 5, the Italian Christian
Democratic Party limited the number of offices it surrendered in multiparty
executives—that is, it cut the office costs of building coalitions—by increasing the total of governmental portfolios. The DC paid a relatively low
office price to rule in coalition as a result of the sort of party system found
in Italy and also as a result of that party's own deliberate effort. The sources
of variations in costs are both exogenous and endogenous to the process of
coalition formation and dissolution.

Plan of the Book

I develop the argument as follows. Chapter 2 assesses the treatment
of costs in the literature on coalition bargaining. In doing so, it drives home
the challenge to coalition theories posed by the conjunction of brief duration

and low alternation. Put differently, the chapter buttresses the claim intro-duced here that the Italian record contains a puzzle worthy of investigation.

Chapter 3 distinguishes several kinds of costs attached to coalitions and advances an explanation for variations in those costs across party systems. The central hypotheses, as already sketched, are that political institutions and configurations of parties and voters in policy space shape the costs of coalition that politicians face; and institutional and spatial conditions struc-ture politicians' efforts to deflate those costs. The third chapter also outlines the rationale for evaluating this framework through broad cross-national comparisons and an in-depth study of Italy. A multicountry comparison maximizes variation in explanatory variables but relies on fairly sizable leaps in inference about the causal mechanisms linking one aggregate indi-cator to another. Intensive examination of one country enables the analyst to trace processes and tap diverse data sources in ways not possible in cross-national research. A focus on the Italian anomaly holds particular theoret-ical promise.

Chapters 4 through 8 implement the two-pronged research design. Chapters 4 and 5, which constitute Part II of the book, carry out numerous comparisons of costs and strategies within Italy—comparisons across par-ties, across sets of governments, and across time. The evidence indicates that given the spatial and institutional conditions in postwar Italy until 1992, parties paid low prices in coalition politics; and parties easily set prices even lower, through the successful pursuit of cost-containment strate-gies. When policy space and institutions were redefined in the early 1990s, as noted earlier, costs and outcomes in Italian coalition politics saw radical change.

In Part III, Chapters 6 through 8 extend the empirical analysis to coali-tions in nine other parliamentary democracies. The findings suggest that my explanation comprehends Italy's extremes and the degrees of stability found in other parliamentary democracies. For example, the country that most nearly resembles Italy in spatial terms, the Netherlands, displays relatively long-lived governments and fairly ample turnover. Dutch institutions, working through their influence on the costs of coalition, account for the difference in outcomes.

The analysis in Part III parallels, but does not fully replicate, that in Part II. The range of evidence on Italy is richer than that on the nine other coun-tries. For Italy, I marshal abundant qualitative and quantitative data. This in-depth approach permits me to ascertain and plumb Italian politicians' in-tentional attempts to manipulate the costs of coalition. In the cross-national comparisons, quantitative data and methods predominate, so that most of the analysis in Part III is devoted to establishing the fact that different types of party, competing in different types of party system and under different institutions, do incur different costs of coalition. To recall language used earlier, for Italy I appraise both the exogenous and endogenous components of the book's central argument, whereas the ten-country analysis addresses exogenous forces most thoroughly. The two-pronged research design fits the twofold argument: An intensive case study is needed to get close to strategic behavior, and cross-national comparisons increase the variation in the environmental conditions also posited as influences on coalition politics.

Chapter 9 discusses the implications of the argument for research on coalitions. Since the explanation I develop accommodates what is otherwise an anomaly, it advances the general understanding of coalition bargaining. Indeed, the book as a whole underscores the importance of organizing research around anomalies. Another basic message of the book is that hypotheses about coalitions can be tested in more ways than are often imagined. Two prominent contributors to the field have lamented that virtually all empirical analyses of coalition politics chase after the same body of data—the "same rather small fixed universe of post-war European governments" (Laver and Schofield 1990, 9). This problem can be greatly alleviated, if not overcome, by redefining units of study and reconceptualizing research designs (King, Keohane, and Verba 1994, ch. 6). Attributes of governments aggregated over the postwar period do not represent the only observations relevant to the theory here. Variations across parties and across time bring crucial evidence to bear on my hypotheses. To show that still more observations may be acquired, Chapter 9 extracts additional hypotheses implied by the framework and moves beyond the data sets created for Chapters 4 through 8.

In emphasizing the place of the book within social science, I by no means wish to obscure its concern with real-world politics. The book grapples with some of the most fundamental issues in democratic political life: who governs and for how long.

2 Costs in Coalition Theories

Chapter 1 introduced an intuitively puzzling phenomenon: short-lived cabinets staffed by perpetually governing parties. The chief aim of this chapter is to show that what common sense identifies as a curiosity also constitutes an anomaly in the current political science literature on coalitional behavior. Despite the elegance and analytical purchase of theories of coalition, they do not offer a clear solution to the problem at the heart of this book: how instability and stability could coexist as they do in Italy.

In what follows, I outline predictions from four schools of research on coalitions and weigh the discrepancies that emerge when each prediction meets the record of coalition governments. The extensive cross-national aggregate evidence already accumulated by other analysts enables me to devote special attention to Italy, an outlier in study after study. A repeated theme in my survey is the costs and benefits of erecting and undoing coalitions. The chapter concludes by reevaluating the puzzle and taking stock of what it reveals about studies of coalitions.

Predictions and Outcomes in Coalitional Behavior

I distinguish schools of research here by the assumptions that researchers make. The first school considered was founded by William Riker in his pioneering work, *The Theory of Political Coalitions* (1962). Whereas Riker assumed that an undiluted desire for office motivates politicians, much of the contemporary literature incorporates policy motivations in some way. Whereas Riker depicted cooperative games, several prominent noncooperative theories have recently been developed. And whereas Riker, like many analysts after him, envisioned bargaining in an institution-free environment, an influential school has focused on the ways that institutions structure the strategies available to political actors.

OFFICE-DRIVEN, INSTITUTION-FREE,
COOPERATIVE THEORIES

Riker (1962) predicts the formation of minimal winning coalitions, which would lose their parliamentary majority if any member party were to withdraw from them. Riker assumes that politicians seek power above all else and share power only to enhance efforts to win, and that office provides fixed rewards. His argument is that coalitions do not expand beyond minimal winning size because no ally wants to hand over slices of power to a party superfluous to the majority. Pushing the logic of power maximization as far as it can go, Riker reaches the prediction of minimum winning coalitions—the subset of minimal winning coalitions with the narrowest possible majority in parliament. Thus, this model highlights the costs of enlarging coalitions and operationalizes costs in foregone cabinet portfolios. By implication, the desire for office motivates politicians to do what they can to prevent cabinet collapses.

Theories closely related to Riker's classic work envision costs entailed in launching and keeping up coalitions. Leiserson (1968) predicts as most likely those minimal winning coalitions that have the smallest number of parties. He reasons that the fewer parties there are, the more readily they strike agreements to coalesce and stick to agreements once allied. Axelrod (1970) predicts minimal connected winning coalitions, which join parties adjacent to each other on a policy spectrum and would either slip below a majority or stop being connected if any party were to withdraw. The logic here is that internal policy conflicts threaten unconnected protocoalitions and coalitions, whereas policy compatibilities make connected coalitions easier to erect and then maintain. In different ways, then, bargaining is pictured as a costly activity. Politicians save on such costs if they minimize the number of partners they have (for Leiserson) or span differences in policy across partners (for Axelrod). Both views suggest that politicians first figure out how to attain office via a minimal winning coalition and next think about bargaining simplicity, applying either a numerical or a policy criterion (Taylor 1972).

Tests of these theories indicate that the minimal connected winning prediction performs most successfully, and the prediction of minimal winning coalitions ranks second (e.g., Franklin and Mackie 1984, 676; cf. Browne 1973; De Swaan 1973; Lijphart 1984; Taylor and Laver 1973). The performance of these predictions varies markedly across countries, however. For example, only one Italian government from 1946 to 1992—of 52 total—unambiguously qualifies as a minimal winning coalition, and even that cabinet contradicts the logic of minimal winning theory.[1] More broadly, a recent twelve-nation study finds that the minimal connected winning prediction fares least well in Denmark, Finland, Ireland, Italy, and Norway (Laver and Schofield 1990, 100). Similarly, the minimal winning prediction is least often fulfilled in Denmark, Finland, Italy, Norway, and Sweden (ibid., 71). Table 2.1 reports that result and the incidence of minimal winning coalitions in the fifteen-nation data set created by Strøm (1990b). (Because the Laver-Schofield and Strøm data sets use different criteria to define the start and finish of a government, they register somewhat different counts of cabinet types for the same country.[2]) The table illustrates further that surplus coalitions (larger than minimal, containing one or several parties not needed to command a majority of seats) appear above all in Finland, Fourth Republic France, Israel, and Italy. Minority cabinets (smaller than winning) are quite common in Denmark, Finland, France, Italy, Norway, and Sweden.

In a moment I take up theories that predict minority and surplus governments. For now, it is worth reflecting on the mechanisms that are supposed to produce the minimal connected winning and minimal winning outcomes. One study shows that the level of internal policy conflict differs little between minimal connected winning coalitions and other types of coalitions (Browne, Gleiber, and Mashoba 1984). A search for policy-based bargaining simplicity, then, does not seem to generate the coalitions that fit the minimal connected prediction. By the same token, policy compatibilities (and conflicts) may not be the only determinant of cheap (and costly) coalition bargaining. Hence, "[minimal connected winning] theory may predict the right coalitions for the wrong reasons" (Laver and Schofield 1990, 102).

According to minimal winning theory, surplus coalitions are costly because office benefits are assumed to be fixed. The ten-nation database compiled for this book tracks office benefits, among other things. In Belgium, minimal winning coalitions contain 17.7 ministers on average, and surplus coalitions, 23.5 ministers. In Italy, 38 junior ministers served in the single straightforward minimal winning coalition before 1992, whereas surplus coalitions average 47.5 junior ministers. The more flexible offices are, the more obscure the causal mechanisms underlying the expected coalitions become, and the more the ostensibly "right" minimal winning coalitions originate "for the wrong reasons." The pressing task is thus to discern the conditions under which offices can be manipulated more or less flexibly. Chapter 3 addresses that task.

POLICY-DRIVEN, INSTITUTION-FREE,
COOPERATIVE THEORIES

Whereas office-driven predictions deal primarily with coalition size and are often fulfilled by coalitions of different parties, policy-driven theories predict policy outcomes that are often consistent with coalitions of different sizes. Theories based on the assumption of unidimensional policy

TABLE 2.1.
Frequency of Cabinet Types, by Country

| | MAJORITY SITUATIONS[a] | | MINORITY SITUATIONS[b] | | | |
| | Single Party | Surplus Coalition | Minority Cabinet | Surplus Coalition | Minimal Winning Coalition | Percent Minimal Winning Coalition in Minority Situations |
Country						
	LAVER-SCHOFIELD DATA SET (1945 TO 1987)					
Austria	4	2	1	—	6	86
Belgium	1	—	2	4	15	71
Denmark	—	—	18	—	2	11
Finland	—	—	10	17	5	16
Germany	—	2	—	—	10	100
Iceland	—	—	2	2	10	71
Ireland	4	—	5	—	3	38
Italy	—	4	14	14	3	10
Luxembourg	—	—	—	1	9	90
Netherlands	—	—	3	8	6	35
Norway	4	—	8	—	3	27
Sweden	1	—	10	—	5	33
	STRØM DATA SET (FIRST POST–WORLD WAR II ELECTION TO 1987)					
Belgium	3	—	3	9	15	53
Canada	10	—	7	—	—	0
Denmark	—	—	22	—	3	14
Finland	—	—	11	18	3	8[c]
France IV	—	—	16	11	3	10
Iceland	—	—	4	1	14	74
Ireland	5	—	9[d]	—	3	25
Israel	—	—	5	19	5	17
Italy	—	5	20	19	4[d]	9
Netherlands	—	—	3	9	7	37
Norway	6	—	12	—	3	20
Portugal	4	—	2	3	4	31[c]
Spain	2	—	3	—	—	0
Sweden	2	—	14[d]	—	5	26
United Kingdom	16	—	2	—	—	0

SOURCES: Laver and Schofield 1990, 71; Strøm 1990b, appendix A. Strøm lists majority governments without distinguishing between surplus and minimal winning coalitions. I identify such coalitions for the Strøm data set by using seat data in Mackie and Rose 1991 (for all countries but France) and MacRae 1967 (on France).

[a] Majority situations are defined as those in which one party controls more than half of parliamentary seats.

[b] Minority situations are those in which no single party controls more than half of parliamentary seats.

[c] Included in the calculation of this percentage are 7 non-party governments in Finland and 4 non-party governments in Portugal. Other columns do not report non-party governments.

[d] Includes 2 one-party cabinets controlling exactly half of seats in Ireland; 3 coalitions controlling exactly half of seats in Italy; 2 one-party cabinets controlling exactly half of seats in Sweden.

space (De Swaan 1973) predict that the party containing the median legislator will control policy and can govern alone, even in a minority cabinet. Multidimensional models predict that a party will control policy and will govern if it occupies the core—a policy position that cannot be overturned, given the overall configuration of actors' sizes and positions.

For readers unfamiliar with spatial theories of voting, a brief discussion of the concepts of median and core is in order. As Black's (1948, 1958) famous median voter theorem shows, the key characteristic of the median voter on a single spectrum of policy (such as the left–right dimension) is that his or her vote can transform either left-leaning voters or right-leaning voters from a minority bloc into a majority bloc. Since the median voter's most preferred policy lies "in the middle" of all voters' best alternatives, the median voter's favored outcome is the only one capable of attracting majority backing. In the legislative setting, then, the party containing the median legislator dictates outcomes.

In two-dimensional policy space, a core party—if it exists—also has the capacity to transform minorities into majorities. To grasp this capacity, imagine a median line drawn in a two-dimensional space that demarcates two alternative majority coalitions: one on the line and to the right, and the other on the line and to the left. If all median lines that can be drawn intersect, the point of intersection is the core of the policy space. The core party is a member of all possible majority coalitions, in other words. The problem is that under simple majority rule a core is unusual in two dimensions and quite rare in three or more. In essence, as the number of dimensions increases, the chance that the median lines meet at one point drops away.[3]

Under simple majority rule in two dimensions, a core is unusual, and only the largest party is able to occupy a stable core (e.g., McKelvey and Schofield 1987; Schofield 1986, 1993). For a core party, allies represent no gain in policy (which the core party already dictates). A core party is thus likely to form a minority cabinet (e.g., Schofield 1993, 8). For parties outside the core, a coalition with the core party exacts the lowest possible price in policy terms. The coalition follows the preferred policy of the core party, which is the best the non-core allies can hope to achieve. In the absence of a core, the cycling of coalitions—in a word, chaos—is costly to all: "Policy cannot be intelligibly formulated or intelligibly implemented" (Schofield, Grofman, and Feld 1988, 207). This school expects lasting governments only in the presence of a stable core (ibid., 206).

These theories plainly pass one vital test, that of identifying incumbents. More than 80 percent of all governments in twelve parliamentary democracies either incorporate or are supported by the median party on the left–right spectrum (Laver and Schofield 1990, 113–19). Table 2.2 details that finding and documents the success of the median party prediction in a sec-

TABLE 2.2.

Performance of the Median Party Prediction, by Country

	Percentage of Governments Joined or Supported by Median Party (Laver-Schofield Data Set, 1945–87)	Percentage of Governments Joined by Median Party (Laver-Budge Data Set, Mid 1940s–Late 1980s[a])
Austria	71	—
Belgium	82	85
Denmark	60	40
Finland	97	—
France IV	—	90
Germany	90	93
Iceland	78	—
Ireland	40	82
Israel	—	77
Italy	100	100
Luxembourg	90	87
Netherlands	100	100
Norway	94	60
Sweden	94	54

SOURCES: Laver and Budge 1992, 416; Laver and Schofield 1990, 118.

NOTE: Entries in the left column show the percentage of governments that included, or drew support from, the median party. Entries in the right column show the percentage of governments that included the median party. Dashes indicate a country omitted from the data set.

[a]Refers to time coverage for most countries; some exceptions appear (e.g., coverage is 1957–88 for Ireland).

ond data set (Laver and Budge 1992). (In Table 2.2, as in Table 2.1, differences across data sets reflect differences in the criteria used to define governments.)[4] The median party prediction is quite successful, but it is not efficient (Budge and Laver 1992), for many hypothetical governments include the median party and only a few of those actually form.

Party systems in Italy, the Netherlands, and several other countries are best modeled as two-dimensional, so that locating the unidimensional median does not suffice (Laver and Schofield 1990, 136, drawing on Budge, Robertson, and Hearl 1987). In Italy, the two-dimensional configuration of parties' sizes and positions qualifies the Christian Democrats (DC) as a core party from 1946 through 1992. The prediction is thus that the DC should always govern, and this has been true. Likewise, Dutch Christian Democracy (the KVP/CDA), another strong core party in another fragmented system, has ruled without interruption. It is reassuring that the incumbency prediction performs so well—indeed, perfectly—in the only two-dimensional systems in postwar Europe with strong core parties.[5]

These models not only predict which party governs but also bear on cabinet duration, size, and policy, as outlined earlier. To assess the latter three hypotheses, it is instructive to continue scrutinizing the highly similar systems of Italy and the Netherlands. It would be inexplicable within this reasoning if two fragmented party systems with strong core parties featured cabinets with substantially different average durations—which is in fact the case. Why do Italian governments display shorter tenures (King et al. 1990, 867; Laver and Schofield 1990, 152) and yet also lower turnover in office (Strøm 1990b, 128) than do Dutch governments? If the balance of costs and benefits brings core parties to form minority governments, why are minority cabinets much less common in the Netherlands than in Italy? Given the spatial similarities between Italy and the Netherlands, the explanation for differing outcomes in the two cases is unclear. The contrasts in outcomes become more baffling, not less so, in light of evidence that both core parties mold government policy, as posited. Content analyses of party manifestos and government programs disclose that, in both Italy and the Netherlands, the mean distance between party policy and government policy is smaller for the core party than for any other party (Mastropaolo and Slater 1992; Tops and Dittrich 1992). With the mechanism of policy control running smoothly in both cases, what accounts for the contrasts they exhibit?

POLICY-DRIVEN, INSTITUTION-FOCUSED, NONCOOPERATIVE THEORIES

A third school examines how institutions restrict the alternatives open to politicians and thus shape the coalitions that politicians build (Austen-Smith and Banks 1988, 1990; Baron 1991; Baron and Ferejohn 1989; Shepsle 1979, 1986; Shepsle and Weingast 1987). Laver and Shepsle (1990a, 1990b, 1990c, 1994, 1996, 1999) have developed the most ambitious institution-focused model to date. Their starting point is the observation that institution-free theories, when applied to parliamentary regimes, "implicitly assume that parliamentary democracies are governed directly by their legislatures" (1996, 9). Laver and Shepsle explicitly model how executives are installed by legislative parties and implement policy. Before a cabinet can be installed, portfolios must be assigned to parties, the nominated parties must accept the portfolios, and a legislative majority must endorse or at least tolerate the cabinet. Once in office, cabinet ministers enjoy discretion in framing and carrying out policy and strive to realize party ideals within the jurisdictions they control. Under this institutional design, "the policy outcomes associated with any given government (and thereby payoffs to legislators) can be forecast from the policy preferences of those nominated to hold key cabinet portfolios" (1990c, 4). The costs (or benefits) of building a coalition depend on actors' calculations of policy distance (or nearness), are communicated through portfolio allocation, and are expected to materialize since prospective ministers work to enact their party's preferences in office.

Whereas institution-free theory isolates a policy position (held by the core party) that cannot be overturned, the Laver–Shepsle institution-focused model isolates two types of portfolio allocations (one held by a single party, termed a "strong" party, and the other constituting a coalition) that cannot be overturned. Laver and Shepsle define a strong party as "one that can veto any alternative cabinet that is preferred by a legislative majority to the cabinet in which the strong party gets all key portfolios. . . . [T]here can be at most one strong party in any party system, but . . . there might be no strong party for particular configurations of parties" (1999, 34). Where a strong party does exist, it should govern and is able to govern even as a single-party minority cabinet. Laver and Shepsle define a dimension-by-dimension median (DDM) cabinet as one in which the key portfolio on each dimension is awarded to the party containing the median legislator on that dimension. The DDM cabinet always exists for any set of dimensions, but it cannot always "beat" all alternative cabinets, and the probability that it is preferred to all others declines as the number of dimensions and parties rises. Whether the DDM cabinet is staffed by one (strong) party[6] or by a coalition, it is expected to govern—even as a minority—as long as it is majority-preferred to all alternative cabinets. Hence, the limitations inherent in cabinet structures can yield minority one-party and coalition governments. To borrow language from Shepsle's (1979) landmark work, in the Laver-Shepsle model—and in all institution-focused research—structure can induce an equilibrium when, in an institution-free world, chaos would reign.

To appreciate the contrast between these predictions and those generated by the institution-free school, recall the contrast in assumptions about the nature of policy space. Institution-free theory assumes a continuous policy space, in which all policy positions are feasible (if not desired) options. A party at the core dominates all other points, given the absence of alternative majorities backing alternative positions in this continuous policy space. Institution-focused theory assumes a partitioned policy space, in which only a subset of policy positions is feasible and in which institutions define the feasible and infeasible positions. The role of institutions is to divide up the policy space and select out the policy positions that are capable of being implemented, in other words. In the Laver-Shepsle model, a portfolio allocation held by a strong party dominates all other portfolio allocations, given the absence of alternative majorities backing alternative cabinets in the feasible subset of policy space. A DDM cabinet is likely to dominate all other portfolio allocations if dimensions and parties are few in number.

Like institution-free theory, this institution-focused model fares well in identifying incumbents. Strong parties do tend to govern, although less often in Denmark and Germany than in the ten other parliamentary democracies that Laver and Shepsle studied (1996, ch. 8). Across all twelve democracies, parties that form part of majority-preferred DDMs are more likely to govern than are other parties (ibid., ch. 9). Moreover, simulations for the twelve democracies and for hypothetical party systems indicate that governments based on majority-preferred DDMs are relatively long-lived and, in particular, are more robust than governments based on strong parties, since just which party qualifies as a strong party can rather easily change (ibid., ch. 10).

Yet, further consideration of the findings on duration uncovers a problem for the Laver-Shepsle model. Since postwar Italy lacks a majority-preferred DDM and lacks a strong party, Laver and Shepsle expect "many 'cabinet cycles' [in Italy]. . . . [For] every cabinet . . . there is some majority-preferred alternative cabinet that will not be vetoed. In such circumstances our model, by implication, predicts that government formation would be chaotic, as any cabinet that might form can be beaten by some other" (personal communication, June 1994). This reasoning accounts for the short duration of Italian governments but does not illuminate the constant presence of the Christian Democrats in power. Amid cycles and chaos, how can the DC keep entering office over and over again? And why do government programs in Italy correspond more closely to the DC's policies than to any other party's policies, as reported earlier (Mastropaolo and Slater 1992)?[7]

THEORY-ORIENTED EMPIRICAL RESEARCH

A large body of research on coalition composition and duration incorporates ideas from the game-theoretic literature but does not use formal deductive methodology (e.g., Franklin and Mackie 1983; Lijphart 1984; Powell 1982; Sanders and Herman 1977; Taylor and Herman 1971; Warwick 1979). One prominent contributor is Dodd (1974, 1976), who shows that minimal winning coalitions tend to be more long-lived than either minority or surplus governments. Dodd argues that cleavage conflict shapes the *a priori* willingness to bargain among parties and that party system fractionalization and instability cause information uncertainty. Conflict and fractionalization thus account for both the size and the duration of cabinets. Whereas Dodd (1976, 49) dwells on the challenges meeting minority cabinets, which survive "at the mercy of a hostile parliament," Strøm (1990b, 69) underscores the costs of coalitions, which "typically involve policy compromises as well as projected electoral misfortunes." Strøm contends that minority cabinets tend to result where policy benefits from governing are low (where strong parliamentary committees give opposition parties the opportunity to influence policy) and, above all, where electoral costs are high (where elections are competitive and decisive, so that incumbency carries a penalty and bargaining power hinges on electoral verdicts). Strøm (1985) finds that, although minority governments have shorter tenures than do majority governments, the best predictor of duration is the salience of elections.

Close inspection of evidence on governments again reveals anomalies. Dodd so concentrates on surplus coalitions in Italy that he neglects to explain why minority governments are quite common there. Nor does he clarify why Dutch governments have longer lives than Italian governments do, which contradicts his logic (data in, e.g., Dodd 1976, 168; cf. discussion in Grofman 1989; Schofield 1987). Strøm (1990b, 151) expects minorities to govern with "intermediate frequency" in Italy, since electoral costs and policy benefits from governing there are low. As he documents, however (and as Table 2.1 suggests), the percentage of minority cabinets in Italy stands "well above the mean" for the fifteen countries he examines (ibid., 132). Why? Strøm cites electoral costs, even though they are relatively low (ibid., 171). Just how Italian politicians weigh the costs of coalition in bargaining over governments remains unresolved.

Other analysts emphasize that governments are subjected to a stream of random shocks throughout their terms in office. Adherents of this "events" approach, arguing against the school represented by Dodd and Strøm, object that "structural attributes do not determine the timing of the event that marks the government's dissolution" (Browne, Frendreis, and Gleiber 1988, 931; cf. Browne, Frendreis, and Gleiber 1986; Casstevens 1989; Cioffi-Revilla 1984; Ozinga, Casstevens, and Casstevens 1989; Robertson 1983). In a synthesis of the events and attributes approaches, King et al. (1990) demonstrate that, even allowing for the force of random events, some types of government—such as those in fractionalized and polarized party systems (e.g., Finland or Italy) and those with minority status—are likely to end more quickly than others (for a critique, see Warwick and Easton 1992). This finding leads King and colleagues (1990, 869) to urge the development of micropolitical theories of cabinet dissolution.

I conclude from their call that it is not very fruitful to ask whether a past government was pushed (by an unforeseeable terminal event) or jumped (at a time fixed when the government formed). The compelling questions are:

How did political actors reason about a fall? How did they face—or exploit or create—the possibility of a fall? What made it more or less likely for politicians to act as they did? Those questions underpin this book.

The Puzzle Reevaluated

A sketch this brief cannot do justice to the immense body of research on coalitions. It suffices nonetheless to establish the interest and significance of the questions just posed. The survey of predictions and evidence also indirectly points to several guidelines for dealing with the questions.

Each of the four major schools in the field has difficulty in handling some aspect of the outcomes in coalitional behavior found in Italy. In other words, the conjunction of short duration and low alternation upsets expectations from all schools. In office-driven theory, officeholders have incentives to prolong, not truncate, governments' lives. Institution-free versions of policy-driven theory explain constancy in party control of government but do not illuminate quick cabinet collapses under permanent incumbents. A prominent institution-focused model encounters the opposite problem. It accounts for short duration but not a perpetual governing party in a setting such as the Italian one. Theory-oriented empirical research does not clarify the frequency with which the DC has headed minority governments in Italy—a frequency that restricts alternation, since most of Italy's minority executives have contained the DC alone.

In one way or another, each problem named involves the costs and benefits of assembling and dismantling coalitions. Office-driven incumbents attach a price to relinquishing office and so should do all they can to avert government falls. If they accept falls, confident that they will rise up as officeholders again, then their assurance is in itself perplexing: How can they bounce back from breakups at no cost, given that, in office-driven theory, opposition parties strive to seize power and will reject any ally not needed for a majority? The institution-free, policy-driven school identifies no mechanism that could cause differences in government duration between two systems when each system is dominated by a core party able to extract maximum policy benefits from governing. Where a focus on institutions generates the expectation of ever-changing cabinets, it is incomprehensible instead how one party could recur in all ruling portfolio allocations—and incur limited policy losses as an incumbent. In theory-oriented empirical research, low electoral costs should be associated with few, not many, minority governments.

Hence, any study of anomalous combinations of short duration and low alternation would do well to probe the costs of coalition. Three questions to guide the study have already been framed: How do politicians reason about government falls? How do they face, exploit, or create the possibility of falls? What makes it more or less likely for them to act as they do? A fourth question encompasses the others and aims straight at the puzzle here: What conditions make it likely that incumbents will provoke cabinet collapses, anticipating—and experiencing—few sacrifices in the process?

Additional guidelines regard the assumptions to be adopted in exploring the puzzle. As Laver and Shepsle (1994, 1996, 1999) observe, spatial theories of voting, when tested against data from parliamentary democracies, take on the assumption that executive coalitions issue spontaneously from the preferences of legislative parties. Likewise, applications of minimal winning theory entail assumptions about voting rules. To elaborate: Counting coalitions as minimal winning when they control exactly half of a legislature's seats amounts to assuming that the government has an advantage in the event of a tie. But in the Swedish parliament, for instance, ties are decided by drawing lots (Bergman 1995). Similarly, counting coalitions as minimal winning when they control "half-plus-one" of the seats entails the assumption that abstentions and absences do not count in favor of a government. Abstentions instead do benefit a government in Sweden since 1975, for plurality support suffices on investiture, provided that an absolute majority does not vote against the candidate for prime minister (Bergman 1995). In Italy, the rules make clear that absences at investiture favor a government, but disputes have occurred over how to treat abstentions (Manzella 1991, 216–18). Investiture aside, rules that require a two-thirds majority for the approval of (some) legislation also cast doubt on the "half-plus-one" criterion for identifying minimal winning coalitions.[8]

Beyond these examples, the general lesson is that as soon as any ostensibly institution-free theory is applied to any institutional arena, it picks up implicit institutional assumptions. All the same, institution-free theories have the advantage of highlighting that institutions do not fall from heaven and are not eternal. Politicians invent, amend, and transform rules. Thus, institutions cannot be assumed away if any empirical examination is undertaken. Yet neither should institutions be viewed as completely rigid (cf. Mershon 1994).

This chapter has also suggested that when hypotheses are checked against empirical evidence, black and white assumptions about politicians' motivations shade into gray. Exponents of policy-driven theory, when confronted with data on the infrequency of minimal connected winning coalitions that are not also minimal winning, conclude that office ambitions must be at play (Laver and Schofield 1990, 101). The frequency of minority governments forces recognition of policy motivations. Politicians who seek office or policy cannot afford to ignore votes, which, even if not valued intrinsically, open avenues to office or policy influence. Three types of goals for politicians, then, should be acknowledged (cf. Strøm 1990a).

So far, the puzzle of short-lived governments that are composed of permanent incumbents has not been resolved and has instead been heightened. Chapter 3, heeding the guidelines developed here, proposes an explanation that accommodates the coexistence of instability and stability.

3 Explaining Variations in the Costs of Coalition

Coalition theories of all sorts assume that expected costs push politicians away from some behaviors and expected benefits pull them toward others. In the institution-focused perspective, institutions operate on and through actors' evaluations of incentives and disincentives. According to the institution-free school, actors' evaluations of costs and benefits spring directly from their motivations. If actors prize office, they equate sharing office with relinquishing benefits. If actors are driven by policy, they steer away from policy compromise. If they hunt votes, they try to avoid actions in coalition that will penalize them at election time. The notion of costs is always implicit but is typically underdeveloped in coalition studies, for the mechanisms that might generate variations in costs are not often specified and modeled.

The argument I advance draws from, and revises, existing studies of coalitions. It addresses what reduces the costs of coalition, and it shows how cabinets can undergo constant change and yet remain much the same.

An Outline of the Explanation

The essence of my argument is that political actors do not just see prices attached to coalition bargaining: They attempt to set those prices. I assume that actors pursue gains, that they project beyond the short term, and that, if they anticipate losses, they do what they can to cut their losses. Actors will not always avoid what they identify as a costly course of action but will at times follow that course and try to lower its costs. I assume that actors face uncertainty and deal with imperfect information. Hence, although they aim for advantage, outcomes can fall short of their intentions. I further assume that all actors care to some extent about office, policy, and votes (Strøm 1990a). The relative priority given these objectives varies, but no political actor is utterly unmoved by the prospect of holding office, just as none is completely oblivious to policy or electoral concerns.

The game of bargaining over governments is also a game of maneuvering around or modifying the costs that coalitions entail. Political actors incur costs when they *build a coalition*. They must award ministerial portfolios to other parties, as stressed in office-driven theory. They must compromise on policy with other parties in order to come up with the government's program, as spatial theory highlights for parties outside the core. Partners in a new cabinet look ahead to the electoral benefits or burdens that governing will bring (Strøm 1990b). As Leiserson (1968) and Axelrod (1970) reason, potential allies spend time and effort in negotiating to overcome differences.

Similarly, it is costly to *sustain a coalition*. As allies govern, they divide the spoils of office, uphold old policy agreements and strike new ones, make decisions that do not please all voters, and bargain among themselves. Governing parties meet costs when *a coalition breaks apart*. At least until a new coalition emerges, the ex-partners may be threatened with removal from office, are handicapped in their efforts to influence policy, and are open to accusations of ineffectiveness or irresponsibility, which could cost them votes. Maneuvers to destroy a coalition, unless unilateral from start to finish, carry bargaining costs as well. Thus, actors engaged in a coalition risk or incur *office, policy, electoral,* and *bargaining* costs at distinct stages in the coalition's history.[1]

Political actors do not simply encounter prices but attempt to manage them. When building a coalition, actors can increase the number of portfolios; they can limit public information about policy compromises so as to ease agreement inside the coalition; and they can delegitimize opponents (cf. Sartori 1976) so as to escape voters' blame. To diminish bargaining costs, actors can devise rules to guide bargaining. Once installed, a coalition is sustained at relatively low cost if allies expand spoils and emphasize special-interest legislation. Along similar lines, actors can take steps to curtail risks when a coalition breaks up. Throughout the history of a coalition, actors can lower its costs by choosing to manipulate various levers, such as office benefits, information, reputation, and rules.

Is this sort of choice equally open and viable in all political settings? I think not. Building on existing themes in the literature, I argue that the sizes and positions of *parties in policy space*, the distribution of *voters' preferences in policy space*, and *political institutions* (in particular, electoral laws, legislative rules, and links between the executive and the legislature) affect how costly it is to break, make, and maintain coalitions and affect which cost-reduction strategies actors are likely to see as available and potentially successful.[2] As Figure 3.1 shows, spatial and institutional conditions are hypothesized to influence costs directly. For example, when a government falls, a party occupying the core of policy space faces a relatively low risk

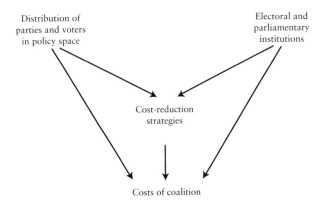

FIGURE 3.1. Influences on the Costs of Coalition

of not regaining office. The anonymity afforded legislators by a secret ballot means that they can sabotage a government with little fear of losing office, antagonizing voters, or complicating bargaining. With a decentralized,
specialized committee system in parliament, ex-allies can shape policy even
after they end a coalition. A party's electoral penalties for toppling a cabinet can be small if its electorate is dominated by subcultural voters, who
vote not on the basis of policy outcomes but in testimony to their enduring
identity (as Catholics, for instance).

Spatial and institutional conditions are also hypothesized to influence
costs indirectly, by structuring the opportunities actors have to try to lower
costs. To illustrate: Office benefits are more easily increased if a core party
controls government for some length of time and if preference voting directs
politicians' attention to the utility of attracting personal followings through
the distribution of spoils.[3] An effort to delegitimate opponents is more feasible if policy space is polarized (that is, great distances separate parties).

Another aspect of political settings conducive to cost-reduction maneuvers needs to be considered. If actors operate under uncertainty, as I assume,
then cost-reduction strategies themselves pose risks. A strategy is not assured of success, and it may arouse conflict with other actors. Thus, actors
are most likely to experiment with a cost-reduction strategy, first adopting
or later altering it, if some change in spatial or institutional conditions
brings them to recalculate the costs of coalition.[4]

As noted in Chapter 1, this argument has two related and distinct parts.
Factors often assumed to be exogenous to the process of coalition formation
and dissolution—electoral and parliamentary institutions and the configuration of parties and voters in policy space—determine variations in the
costs of coalition. So, too, do the deliberate choices of parties—choices that

are endogenous to coalition politics. The causal arrows drawn in Figure 3.1 highlight the posited combination of environmental and strategic sources of variations in costs, of direct and indirect effects of spatial and institutional conditions.

A Closer Look at the Explanation

The central hypotheses now outlined, four elements of the logic warrant special notice. The first concerns what might be deemed the problem of endogeneity. As Figure 3.1 displays, I argue that institutional and spatial conditions constrain politicians. On the other hand, as just observed, I contend that institutions are subject to some degree of manipulation. That is, politicians are constrained but also push against institutional constraints. This assertion leads naturally to the questions: Which institutions are they most likely to modify? Which institutions are most usefully viewed as exogenously fixed and which instead as in the power of the actors to change? Of the three sets of rules emphasized here, links between the executive and the legislature (in particular, the vote of investiture) arguably have the deepest constitutional import and, at the other extreme, parliamentary rules of procedure (such as use of the secret ballot) tend not to have constitutional import. Many democracies impose supramajoritarian decision rules on constitutional changes and require only pluralities for changes in parliamentary procedure (Herman 1976, 270–79, 415–31).

Just as I assert that politicians are constrained by institutions but can also modify them, I believe that, especially in the long run, politicians are capable of influencing voters' preferences (e.g., Przeworski and Sprague 1986) and of moving their own parties in policy space (Panebianco 1988, chs. 13–14). In other words, in the long run, both sets of independent variables in my argument are to some extent dependent on politicians' behavior. This problem is common in political science, of course. In Chapters 4 through 8, I consider institutional redesign as a cost-reduction strategy. Chapter 9 discusses ways of assessing long-run change.

Second, it should be stressed that, in this argument, actors incur costs. My argument responds to a puzzle about system-wide outcomes: the combination of governmental instability and stability, of short duration and restricted turnover. I do not depict those outcomes as penalties inflicted on an entire system. In some frameworks, to be sure, short cabinet duration is conceptualized as costly for the political system as a whole (e.g., Linz 1978b). Here, instead, short duration is understood as a consequence of low costs (and hence of spatial and institutional conditions). If parties expect a breakup to carry low costs, they may try to hasten a government's demise.

If they expect a breakup to yield benefits, they are even more likely to engineer a fall.[5] A party's exclusion from office after it has contributed to a fall (a party-specific datum that enters into the system-wide alternation rate) provides one indicator of the policy costs of cabinet dissolution. I take up this and other measures later in this chapter.

To insist that actors incur costs leads to the third point. Like most analysts of coalition, I think it useful to treat parties as unitary actors. Of course, parties are complex organizations, and some institutions (such as the secret ballot and preference voting) invite indiscipline. I focus on parties, however, because much of the available data pertains to parties and, above all, because parties tend to join and leave coalitions as blocs (cf. Laver and Schofield 1990). Chapters 4 through 8 operate on the assumption that parties have aims, strategies, expectations—in brief, that parties are actors as portrayed above. In Chapter 9, I relax the unitary actor assumption and study factions.[6]

Finally, it is important to underscore that my interest in costs by no means precludes attention to benefits. In general, to envision costs is to acknowledge the possibility of benefits; the sequel to a choice can be negative or positive, damaging or advantageous, or also, on balance, neutral. More specifically, as a colleague of mine once remarked, governing is not simply a dirty job and some poor soul has got to do it. Executive power holds out the prospect of benefits: offices beyond legislative seats, the capacity to shape public policy, greater esteem in the electorate's eyes. But that is not all, and there's the rub. Parties run risks when they create coalitions and also (as is often noted) when they quit coalitions. I explore as problematic—as an empirical question freighted with theoretical import—just what the balance of costs and benefits in coalition politics might be. I expect benefits and costs to vary systematically across political settings and to reflect in part the purposive behavior of politicians.[7]

Procedures and Measures in Empirical Analysis

Before applying and evaluating this explanation about the costs of coalition, a number of issues of research design and methods deserve discussion. The first involves my two-pronged approach. I undertake broad cross-national comparisons and an in-depth study of Italy. A multicountry comparison has the obvious advantage of providing substantial variation in configurations of parties and voters in policy space. Chapters 6 through 8 examine four unipolar party systems (Ireland, Norway, Sweden, and pre-1973 Denmark), one bipolar system (Germany), and six multipolar systems—two with strong core parties (Italy and the Netherlands) and four without (Belgium, Finland, Fourth Republic France, and post-1973 Denmark).[8] These nations also present a wide range of electoral and parliamentary institutions, as shown below. Moreover, they evince differing patterns of cabinet duration and alternation in office, as seen in Figure 1.2. All the same, cross-national empirical research on coalitions necessarily relies on fairly large leaps in inference about the causal mechanisms linking one aggregate indicator to another.

Detailed inspection of Italy in Chapters 4 and 5 redresses this problem. Intensive study of one country allows the analyst to move closer to decision-making processes, to sift more finely through varied sources of evidence, and to pursue traces of politicians' reasoning and calculations in ways not possible when the field of observation spans many national settings. Since Italy exhibits significant variation in spatial and institutional conditions over time, it offers an apt site for testing the explanation formulated here. In addition, because the Italian record poses a stiff challenge to coalition theories—and because scientific understanding advances by assimilating anomalies into a general framework—the empirical analysis of coalition politics in this case holds special theoretical promise. Yet it is worth repeating that Italy is extreme but not unique. Several other countries feature short-lived cabinets and limited alternation. I posit that some of the spatial and institutional conditions present in Italy also appear in those cases (and are rare or absent in still other cases, such as Ireland); and some strategies employed in Italy should appear in those cases as well. Chapters 6 through 8 present cross-national findings that support these hypotheses.

Second, beyond giving the rationale for my intensive investigation of Italy, I should specify the criteria I use in selecting countries for comparison. My argument deals with the politics of coalition in parliamentary democracies. Put differently, its domain excludes democracies that do not have parliamentary systems (such the French Fifth Republic, Switzerland, and the United States) and parliamentary democracies that in peacetime have had nothing but single-party governments (Canada, New Zealand until 1996, and the United Kingdom). Nonetheless, as part of an effort to increase the observable implications of the theory, Chapter 9 assesses hypotheses suggested by it against evidence from the United States.

Within the domain of the argument as originally framed, Chapters 6 through 8 compare parliamentary democracies that have seen rule by at least one coalition government. As already indicated, the database I have constructed for those chapters covers Belgium, Denmark, Finland, Fourth Republic France, Germany, Ireland, Italy, the Netherlands, Norway, and Sweden. For this subgroup of coalitional systems, data are available on such key variables as parties' policy positions. These countries, too, assure wide variation on spatial and institutional conditions. The latter criterion is crucial, for the "efficiency [of estimates of causal effects] is greatest when we have evidence from a larger range of values of the explanatory variables" (King, Keohane, and Verba 1994, 99). With regard to data availability, consider the seven studies whose coverage is summarized in Appendix B. Taken together, they provide data on government composition, parties' locations in policy space, and voters' behavior since the end of World War II (Franklin, Mackie, and Valen 1992; Laver and Budge 1992; Laver and Hunt 1992; Laver and Schofield 1990; Laver and Shepsle 1994; Strøm 1990b; Woldendorp, Keman, and Budge 1993). These sources are recent, heavily cited, and thus quite useful in illustrating current knowledge about coalition politics. As Appendix B suggests, my database embraces all "data-rich" countries. I am thus able to check my judgment calls against those made for other data sets, adopt other scholars' measures of policy space, and refer to others' findings in interpreting my own. Although coalition politics is somewhat less thoroughly documented for Finland and Fourth Republic France than for the most studied nations, I include them so as to increase the number of multipolar party systems in the database. For each of the ten countries, the database runs from the first post–World War II election to January 1, 1993.

   Third, to evaluate my hypotheses, I must measure when governments begin and end, a task that is not as straightforward as it might seem. Analysts use different criteria to demarcate a government's life, as reflected in different reports of average government duration. For instance, German government duration from 1949 to 1987 averaged 37 months according to Laver and Schofield (1990, 152) and only 20 months according to Woldendorp, Keman, and Budge (1993, 53). In the data set compiled by Strøm (1985, 1990b), Italian governments lasted 10 months on average between 1946 and 1987, whereas Laver and Schofield (1990, 152) measure average government duration in Italy as 13 months over the same span. (Either way, Italy has the most short-lived governments of any extant parliamentary democracy.) I count a new government with each change of party composition, parliamentary election, change of prime minister, and accepted resignation of the cabinet. All analysts of coalition politics use the first criterion. Nearly all follow the second, for elections are very likely to alter the seat distribution in parliament, and both office-driven and policy-driven predictions depend on seat distribution. I agree with Strøm (1990b, 58) that the third and fourth criteria are justified since "such occasions . . . present an opportunity for renegotiation of government and legislative coalitions."[9] The results of applying these criteria are detailed in Appendix C, which lists governments for all ten countries in this database.[10] The sources consulted for information on governments, and on all other items in the database, are described in Appendix D.

Closely related to the task of isolating governments is that of isolating governing parties. In my judgment, parties qualify as governing parties when they contribute representatives to the government in the form of ministers.[11] When a party officially disavows membership in a government and asserts that its leaders present in a cabinet do not act as party representatives, it is not a governing party. For a few governments, this criterion differentiates my data set from others. For example, Strøm (1990b) and Woldendorp, Keman, and Budge (1993) code the Popular Republican Movement (MRP) as a component party of the French government launched by Pierre Mendès-France in June 1954. Yet on June 18–19, 1954, the MRP decided not to participate in the Mendès-France government. On June 19, two MRP leaders accepted portfolios in the cabinet named by Mendès-France and "explained that they did so in a personal capacity and not as members of the party." On June 23, the MRP expelled the two leaders (*Keesing's Contemporary Archives* 1954, 13630–632, quoted at 13632). I thus do not count the MRP as a member party of the Mendès-France government.

In government or out, a group that repeatedly constitutes a single parliamentary group amounts to a single party. To elaborate: I define a party as a group of politicians that contests elections under a distinctive label or declares that it intends to do so (cf. Sartori 1976). Electoral teams and parliamentary groups often but not always coincide. Where two electoral labels repeatedly form a single parliamentary group (the case of the German Christian Democratic Union/Christian Social Union) I treat the parliamentary group as a party. This rule of thumb is commonly used among analysts of coalition (e.g., Laver and Schofield 1990; Lijphart 1984). Electoral teams and parliamentary groups were highly fluid and internally divided in Fourth Republic France. For France, I count as a party whatever entity declared that it was an electoral team, regardless of the degree of internal division it displayed.[12]

Finally, a test of the argument offered here plainly entails measuring the costs (and benefits) of coalition. To tap office costs, I count the number of ministers and junior ministers per party in a cabinet; I figure the percentage share of all ministerial and junior ministerial posts each party controls; and I compute the ratio between that share and the party's share of the seats in the lower house that are held by a government. These counts are all made at the time of a government's formation, which is operationalized as within one month of its official inauguration. I code ministers or junior ministers from parties that disavow participation as independents.

I measure electoral costs and benefits as changes in parties' shares of the vote between pairs of consecutive elections to the lower house of parliament. Policy payoffs are indexed in two ways: by participation in government, which gives parties special instruments of influence on policy, and by

the distance between party platforms and declarations of government policy, which is estimated using data on party and government positions in
Laver and Budge (1992). To calculate the office, electoral, and policy costs
of coalition breakups, I code information on which parties were (and were
not) responsible for cabinet collapses. For this information, I rely primarily
on *Keesing's Contemporary Archives*, a source often used in coalition studies (e.g., Budge and Keman 1990; Dodd 1976; Strøm 1990b).[13] Bargaining
costs are captured by the time elapsed between the fall of one government
and the rise of its successor.

Further details on these measures appear in the analysis carried out in
Chapters 4 through 8. Indeed, a good way to drive home the logic underlying this research design and set of measures is to sketch out how the next
five chapters proceed.

A Preview of the Empirical Analysis

Part II scrutinizes coalition politics in Italy. In Chapter 4, I examine
the Italian historical record for qualitative evidence of behavior that could
reasonably be interpreted as attempts at reducing the costs of coalition. For
example, I observe that in Italy written guidelines for portfolio distribution
were developed in summer 1968. From the timing and the content of the
guidelines, as well as declarations made by the guidelines' authors, I infer
that the rules were invented in a deliberate attempt to cut bargaining costs
in building coalitions.

In Chapter 5, I measure the costs of Italian coalitions as outlined earlier,
and, finding low costs, I look for quantitative evidence of the strategic manipulation of costs and benefits. For instance, in Italy the number of ministerial portfolios rises steadily with the number of allies in a coalition. This
fact and other data on offices presented in Chapter 5 lead me to identify the
addition of new portfolios as an intentional effort to lower the office costs
of building coalitions. I compare costs and strategies across parties and
across time in order to assess the impact of variations in spatial and institutional conditions. The logic behind the comparisons works as follows: If
spatial conditions matter, then different parties (a core party, say, as opposed to a party that never holds core status) should incur different costs
and should diverge in their pursuit of cost-reduction strategies. If spatial or
institutional conditions change over time, then the costs and strategies characteristic of different parties should also undergo some shift.

Part III reproduces, for nine additional countries, the quantitative analysis performed earlier for Italy. Chapter 6 lays the basis for the cross-national
study by discussing variations in spatial and institutional conditions.

Chapter 7 weighs the influence of those factors on the costs of building and sustaining coalitions. Chapter 8 investigates the costs of breaking coalitions. Given my central hypotheses, I expect to find systematic, consistent distinctions in the record of costs incurred and strategies implemented across different kinds of party systems. Distinctions should also appear across countries with contrasting electoral and parliamentary institutions. At least some similarities in costs and strategies, on the other hand, should emerge across countries that resemble each other in spatial terms (such as Italy and the Netherlands, where strong core parties dominate multipolar party systems). Whatever differences in outcomes separate spatially similar countries should become comprehensible by taking institutions into account.

So designed, the empirical analysis in Parts II and III mounts a vigorous attack on what some readers might view as the "small-N problem." Readers worried about this problem would object that the universe of countries to which the book's argument might apply is limited. They would see justification in extending their criticism to the field as a whole: In this perspective, virtually all coalition analysts who undertake empirical tests confront a small N.

One way of responding to these concerns is to assert the fundamental importance of the subject of study. "It is a simple fact of political life that coalition lies at the very heart of European politics," as Laver and Schofield (1990, 13) remark. In this rebuttal, governmental coalitions in parliamentary democracies demand scholarly attention, regardless of the (small) number of country cases available. I would not have spent years studying coalitions if I thought they were trivial. Nevertheless, my rebuttal moves beyond the one just described.

The existence and severity of a small-N problem hinge on how cases are understood. The problem would be intractable indeed if an entire country were conceptualized as a case. But that is not my design here. Chapters 4 through 8 organize comparisons across sets of governments, across parties, and across time into numerous observable implications of my hypotheses. Moreover, Chapter 9 redefines the phenomena relevant to the theory so as to acquire still more observations (cf. King, Keohane, and Verba 1994, ch. 6). Chapter 9 formulates additional hypotheses to be tested, in essence asking the question: If the reasoning is correct, what else may be affected by spatial and institutional conditions (besides the costs of coalition as originally measured)? Answering this question involves, among other things, switching the level of analysis from parties to party factions.

The first step in carrying out these plans for empirical analysis is to turn to Italy, the recurring anomaly in coalition studies. The in-depth study begins with an effort to uncover and appraise evidence that Italian politicians have deliberately maneuvered to lower the various costs of coalition.

Part TWO

4 *The Pursuit of Cost-Reduction Strategies*

Italy displays ephemeral governments but permanent incumbents. The pattern is personified in Giulio Andreotti, a Christian Democrat who held posts in thirty-six governments between 1947 and 1992, including seven turns as prime minister. How can cabinets fall at such low cost and with so little impact on alternation in office?

The argument advanced in Chapter 3 indicates the following answer. The array of political parties, the nature of voters' loyalties, and the electoral and parliamentary institutions found in Italy lower the costs associated with breaking and building coalitions and favor strategies that further lower those costs. Italy's coalitions are not easily sustained, since breakups cause little damage. Because this logic is put into practice, instability accompanies stability in Italian government.

My test of these claims about Italy proceeds in two steps. In this chapter, I look for evidence of behavior that could plausibly be construed as politicians' deliberate efforts to limit the costs of coalition. Chapter 5 investigates whether spatial and institutional conditions do in fact influence costs and cost-reduction strategies in Italy.

I expect to discover that Italian politicians have actually handled such instruments as information and office benefits in attempts to curb the costs of coalition. In what follows, I review the evidence from the historical record. It fulfills this expectation.

Expansion of Offices

The number of posts in Italian governments has increased since 1946. As Figure 4.1 shows, declines have occasionally interrupted the overall rise, but the total of cabinet members has never returned to the level characteristic of the late 1940s. The number of undersecretaries, as junior or deputy ministers are called in Italy, has grown at an especially rapid rate. The early

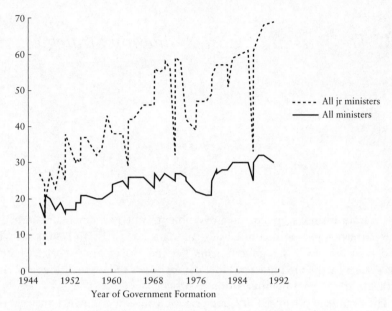

FIGURE 4.1. Ministers and Undersecretaries in Italian Governments, 1946–92

1960s and the early 1980s saw the start of marked upturns in both senior and junior ministerial slots. Thus, whereas the coalition installed after Italy's first postwar elections in 1946 contained nineteen ministers and twenty-seven undersecretaries, the government whose tenure ended with the 1992 elections was made up of thirty ministers and sixty-nine undersecretaries.

As can easily be imagined, a larger number of offices has meant a more complex division of labor within Italian cabinets. Several Italian ministries are devoted to rather narrow specializations (such as the Merchant Marine), and the bailiwicks of some departments overlap. In the most salient instance of overlap, since 1947 Italian governments have featured a Ministry of the Treasury *and* a Ministry of Finance *and* a Ministry of the Budget.[1] Ministers without portfolio, allocated such jurisdictions as Civil Defense or Relations with Parliament, appear in almost all governments.[2]

To illustrate this fragmentation of responsibility, Table 4.1 (see p. 36) compares four governments, two from Italy and two from Finland. The first column for each government identifies the jurisdictions assigned to ministers, and the second identifies the number of junior ministers per minister.[3] As the table exhibits, in Italy the ministerial-level organization of the Christian Democratic (DC)–only cabinet formed by Giuseppe Pella in August 1953 was more streamlined than that of the five-party coalition assembled by

Giulio Andreotti in July 1989. In addition, Pella named substantially fewer undersecretaries than did Andreotti. Differences between Italy and Finland clearly overshadow the differences within Italy, however. Both the two-party coalition under Urho Kekkonen, initiated in July 1953, and the four-party coalition under Harri Holkeri, launched in April 1987 and still in office when Andreotti VI assumed power, were relatively simple in structure. Several Finnish departments, such as the Ministry of Transport and Public Works, exercised authority in a broad area covered by multiple departments in Italy. Several Finnish cabinet members under Holkeri, such as the Minister of Finance who also served as junior minister at Justice, performed "double duty." Like all but two of Finland's postwar governments, the Kekkonen and Holkeri coalitions lacked ministers without portfolio. Like all Finnish premiers, Kekkonen and Holkeri managed with few junior ministers.

Explaining cross-national differences is the task of Part III. For now, consider how an increase of offices such as that observed in Italy would affect the costs of coalition. New departments can concentrate energies and resources on newly important policy areas, so that at least some parties (in particular, those staffing the new posts) might be able to pull policy closer to their preferences than they otherwise would (cf. Laver and Shepsle 1994, 1996). Some parties, that is, might be able to defray some of the policy costs of constructing and maintaining coalitions. Evidence consistent with this notion can be culled from analyses of Italian public administration and public policy. In 1947, for example, Premier Alcide De Gasperi of the DC spearheaded the founding of the Budget Ministry in an effort to restrict spending, defend the *lira*, and impose deflationary policies on the Treasury and Finance Ministries. The new direction in economic policy quickly became known as the "Einaudi line," after the first Budget Minister appointed (Cassese 1983, 212–14; 1985, 296–97; De Cecco 1989; Harper 1986, ch. 9). In 1956, the DC championed the creation of the Ministry of State Holdings as a way to strengthen the party's control over the public sector. In accordance with the strategy, one Christian Democrat or another supervised that ministry in all of the twenty-seven Italian cabinets ruling between 1956 and 1980 (Bottiglieri 1984, 288–98; Cassese 1983, 227–29; 1985, 212–14; Montalenti 1978).

The available evidence also suggests, however, that the proliferation of offices has contributed to inefficacy and incoherence in Italian public policy. With multiple ministers working in one policy area, at best "*the* policy of the government in that area has been the result of long consultations between the Ministers (and also the parties and the ministerial bureaucracies) responsible for that area. In the worst case, . . . there has been more than one government policy in that area" (Cotta 1988, 131, emphasis in original). Scholars routinely cite the complexity of the cabinet structure as one factor (along with others, including the frequency of many-party coalitions)

TABLE 4.1.
Cabinet Structure in Italy and Finland: Examples from 1953 and 1989

| | ITALY | | | | FINLAND | | | |
| | PELLA | | ANDREOTTI VI | | KEKKONEN IV | | HOLKERI I | |
Policy Jurisdictions	Senior	Junior	Senior	Junior	Senior	Junior	Senior	Junior
Prime Minister	M	4	M	1	M		M	1
Vice Premier			M				M	
FOREIGN AND SECURITY POLICY								
Foreign Affairs	M[a]	2	M	4	M		M[b]	1[c]
Defense	M	2	M	4	M		M	
Civil Defense			m					
INTERNAL ORDER/STATE INSTITUTIONS								
Justice	M	1	M	3	M		M	[d]
Interior	M	1	M	4	M		M	
Public Administration	m		m					
Regions/Reforms			m					
Relations with Parliament			m					
ECONOMICS								
Budget	M[a]	1	M	2				
Finance	M	2	M	5	M	1	M	1
Treasury	M	4	M	5				
Industry	M	3	M	4	M		M	[d]
Agriculture	M	2	M	3	M		M	[d]
Labor	M	2	M	3			M	
Foreign Trade	M	1	M	2	[e]		[e]	
European Community Policy			m					
State Holdings			M	1				
South	m		m	2				
SOCIAL AND CULTURAL POLICY								
Education	M	2	M	4	M		M	1
Health			M	3			[e]	
Culture			M	2				
Tourism			M	2				
Science/Research			M	2				
Social Affairs			m		M	1	M	1[c]
Urban Areas			m					

TABLE 4.1. (*Continued*)

| | ITALY | | | | FINLAND | | | |
| | PELLA | | ANDREOTTI VI | | KEKKONEN IV | | HOLKERI I | |
Policy Jurisdictions	Senior	Junior	Senior	Junior	Senior	Junior	Senior	Junior
			INFRASTRUCTURE					
Public Works	M	1	M	3	e			
Transportation	M	1	M	3	M	1	M	
Posts/Communi-								
cations	M	1	M	3			e	
Merchant Marine	M	1	M	2				
Environment			M	1			M	

SOURCE: Petracca 1980, 146–47; *Corriere della Sera*, July 23 and 26, 1989; data from the Office of the Prime Minister and the Library of Parliament, Finland.

NOTE: Entries identify ministers present (M, minister with portfolio; m, minister without portfolio) and the number of junior ministers per minister. For Finland, second ministers are counted as junior ministers (see Note 3).

a Prime Minister held this portfolio.

b Vice Premier held this portfolio.

c Another junior minister here headed another department as a full minister.

d The only junior minister here headed another department as a full minister.

e Jurisdiction named under another department (e.g., Ministry of Social Affairs and Health).

engendering a policy-making process that is lengthy, laborious, muddled, reactive rather than proactive, and blocked or even immobile (e.g., Cassese 1980, 1985; Cerase 1990; Guarnieri 1989; Pasquino 1995a, 1995b; for a less-negative view, see Criscitiello 1994). Coining a telling phrase, Cheli (1978) asserts that "multidirectional disconnected government" (*governo a direzione plurima dissociata*) prevailed in Italy by the mid-1950s.

What, then, might have motivated the continued upward trend in cabinet posts in Italy? Recall that, to the degree that offices are flexible rather than fixed, surplus coalitions need not exact sacrifices of office rewards, as Chapter 2 discussed. An increase in portfolios, in other words, can offset the office costs of building coalitions (cf. Riker 1962). A paper trail of politicians' calculations—in the form of two dozen memoranda written by key participants in coalition bargaining—suggests that Italian parties have firmly grasped this principle. In these notes (published in Venditti 1981), two Christian Democrats drew up alternative cabinet scenarios over the course of the 1970s. Especially illuminating are two memoranda from 1970 (Venditti 1981, appendix B, exhibits 3 and 4), prepared during the interregnum between the resignation of one government (Rumor II) and the rise of another (Rumor III). The authors depicted two potential outcomes for negotiations over the new executive, and in each case based the totals of ministers and undersecretaries on the dimensions of recent cabinets, to which they referred by name. Thus, in their reasoning, the past put a floor under bargaining demands.

Moreover, the memoranda reveal the utility of lifting the ceiling on cabinet posts. The authors forecasted the number of slots that the DC might fill in a four-party surplus coalition as opposed to a one-party minority cabinet. They projected, for the former scenario, thirty-two DC undersecretaries out of a total of fifty-six, and, for the latter, a total of forty-six undersecretaries, all supplied by the DC. The DC's share of undersecretaries in the four-party scenario loosely corresponded to the DC's weight in the coalition's parliamentary delegation.[4] If that share had been sliced out of a total of forty-six offices, rather than fifty-six, the DC would have had six fewer undersecretaries in the coalition; but the memorandum-writers did not record this possibility. They apparently trusted that the DC would be able to lower the price it paid to enter the coalition by elevating the total of undersecretaries to fifty-six. As it turned out, the DC obtained thirty-three of fifty-six undersecretaryships in the four-party coalition (Rumor III) inaugurated in March 1970.

Italian politicians have enlarged spoils outside the cabinet as well. Beginning in the late 1940s, the Christian Democrats expanded and occupied the already sizable, already politicized state bureaucracy and public sector inherited from fascism (Bottiglieri 1984; Di Palma 1979; Donolo 1980; Ginsborg 1989, ch. 5; Tarrow 1990). Although the DC dominated access and appointments in the civil service and public agencies, some positions went to its coalition partners, such as the presidency of the Social Security Institute (held by a Social Democrat from 1949 to 1965) and the presidency of the Disability Insurance Institute (held by a Liberal from 1949 to 1964). As DC secretary from 1954 to 1959, Amintore Fanfani contributed powerfully to entrenching the party in the state. The public sector developed further after the Socialists joined government in the early 1960s. By the early 1980s, state corporations controlled more than three-fourths of all banking institutions, made half of all fixed investments, and employed more than one-fourth of the industrial labor force in Italy (Hellman 1992b, 399).

All the same, what really distinguishes the state and para-state sector in Italy is neither its size nor its rate of growth since World War II, but instead the extent to which it has been penetrated by political parties, Christian Democracy above all. Abundant cross-national data on public spending and public employment bear out the first part of this affirmation, on size and growth (e.g., Cassese 1983, ch. 13; OECD 1990, 1993; Schott 1984, ch. 3). Analogous indices cannot be devised to tap the degree of partisan appropriation of the state.[5] Absent comparative quantitative data, qualitative evidence can be adduced to corroborate the claim that in Italy the DC and the state have undergone "a formidable level of fusion" (Ginsborg 1989, 204). First, and most simply, a wide range of social scientists subscribe to this idea and view Italy as unusual in this respect (e.g., Cassese 1988; Dente and Regonini 1987; Hine 1993; La Palombara 1987; Mair 1994; Mény 1993; Morlino 1994; Pasquino 1987b). Cross-national research on party government furnishes a second set of relevant scholarly judgments (Castles and Wildenmann 1986; Katz 1986b, 1987; Pasquino 1987a). Among eight countries studied, only Italy illustrates "the danger . . . that the bureaucracy will be so thoroughly colonized by the party in power that it will lose its expert qualifications. Administration becomes infected with partisan favoritism, and efficiency is sacrificed as the state service is transformed into a machine for creating and distributing patronage" (Katz 1987, 16; cf. Vassallo 1994).[6]

Measures available for Italy suggest that the patronage machine is well oiled indeed. First, between 1973 and 1990, about 250,000 Italians entered the civil service via the regular recruitment procedure of competitive examinations, while about 350,000 bypassed the examinations but still became civil servants (Cassese 1993, 325).[7] Italy's foremost authority on public administration treats this datum as a sign of widespread patronage and concludes that "the principal problem faced by the [Italian] public sector is recruitment not based on tasks and merit" (ibid., 327). Second, party representatives are easily discerned and counted at the commanding heights of the Italian state and para-state administration (see, e.g., Bonaccorsi 1979; Cazzola 1976, 1979; Lanza 1979; Spanò 1979; numerous periodical sources cited in Leonardi and Wertman 1989, ch. 8). Thus, for instance, Cazzola (1985, 203) reports that in the mid-1970s the Italian Socialist Party (PSI) boasted "10 per cent of the members of the boards of directors and 5 per cent of the presidents among special credit institutions; 14 per cent of the board members and 7.5 per cent of the presidents among social security agencies; roughly 20 per cent of the vice presidencies among savings banks; 15 per cent of the board members and 7 per cent of the presidents among agricultural agencies" and so forth. As of 1983, the giant IRI (Institute for Industrial Reconstruction) state holding company had a DC president and a Republican vice president; a Socialist served as president of the ENI (State Hydrocarbons Agency) and a Social Democrat, as president of EFIM (Manufacturing Industry Financing Agency) (ibid., 204). From the mid-1980s until 1993, Channel One of the state television corporation (RAI-TV, *Radio Televisione Italiana*) was controlled by the DC, the smaller Channel Two by the Socialists, and the smallest Channel Three by the Communists (the Democratic Party of the Left by 1993) (Marletti 1988; Mazzoleni 1994; Gundle 1995).

Under the DC and its allies in government, the public administration amounted to party territory, mined thoroughly and systematically for partisan advantage. Italy's governing parties equated the state apparatus with party assets and shared the wealth in rough proportion to party size. What lay beneath, and shored up, governing power was the *sottogoverno* (literally, subgovernment), a term invented around 1950 (Beccaria 1988, 211) that denotes, simultaneously, both the parties' practice of patronage and the agencies exploited for patronage. By 1968 (ibid., 210), the proportional division of spoils acquired the label of *lottizzazione* (allotment). A joke current in the mid-1960s mocked the results: "Today at the RAI they hired twelve people: five Christian Democrats, three Socialists, two Social Democrats, one Republican, and one who is competent" (quoted in Venditti 1981, 18).

With the enlargement of *sottogoverno* and its colonization by party followers, Italy's governing parties have had at their disposal means for shaping policy, mediating interests, and rewarding clienteles that can survive the fall of a cabinet. This strategy has worked comparatively well in Italy in part because the potential for alternation in government is limited, which in part, in turn, is an intended consequence of politicians' choices.

Delegitimization of Opponents

From the late 1940s until roughly 1990, parties at or near centrist positions defined the Italian Communist Party (PCI) and the neo-Fascist Italian Social Movement (Movimento Sociale Italiano, MSI) as inadmissible allies, outside the circle of legitimate contenders for cabinet posts.[8] The centrist parties publicized this rejection and ideological justifications for it. For instance, in campaign posters issued by the DC in 1948, mothers snatched children out of the jaws of Communist wolves, and a huge Stalin stomped on the monument to Italy's unknown soldier (Ginsborg 1989, 155). Even in the 1987 elections, a DC slogan maintained that "when the DC is stronger the PCI counts for less." In 1987, as well, DC campaign literature announced that "the authoritarian, bureaucratic, centralized governing culture is not acceptable for Italy, and Italians have never accepted it from 1947 to today" (both published as supplement to *Il Popolo*, May 23, 1987).

As these examples suggest, the PCI was often treated as more dangerous than the MSI. The PCI was linked to the West's enemy in the Cold War. It long qualified as Italy's second-biggest party, bested only by the DC; the neo-Fascists, in contrast, usually polled 5 or 6 percent of the national vote.[9] The PCI's formidable organizational network and the loyalty of its followers made some wags refer to it as "Italy's second church." Thus, although an eminent Catholic jurist spoke of a *conventio ad excludendum* operating against "one or more parties" in Italy (Elia 1973, 333), the chief object of the agreement was exclusion of the Communists. For decades, "the core of Italy's unwritten constitution [was] the ineligibility of the PCI for government" (Donovan 1988, 127).

To understand this ineligibility, consider the conditions under which the PCI briefly controlled, and then relinquished, cabinet ministries (Harper 1986; Mershon 1994; Pasquino 1986, 1987a, 1988; Vassallo 1994). From April 1944 until May 1947, Italian governments reflected the interparty co-operation characteristic of the anti-Fascist Resistance. In particular, coalitions incorporated the Christian Democrats, Communists, and Socialists, the three parties that dominated the Resistance and that drew the most votes in the June 1946 elections to the Constituent Assembly.[10] The DC's leader, De Gasperi, became Prime Minister in December 1945 with the Left's support. Nonetheless, he regarded the alliance with the Left as "necessary but not desirable," advantageous but "forced" and "unnatural" (Ginsborg 1989, 61, 100). Hence, when Pope Pius XII pressed him to oust the PCI and PSI from government in late 1946, De Gasperi replied that such a move could not be made, for church–state relations were not yet regulated and the peace treaty was not yet signed (Ginsborg 1989, 133–36; Orfei 1976, 73–75).

The extraordinary fluidity of domestic and international politics persuaded De Gasperi and other DC leaders of the utility of national unity coalitions. Other governing arrangements became feasible as domestic settlements were reached and Cold War alignments emerged. In January 1947, De Gasperi proposed and took a trip to the United States, where policy makers agreed with him on the urgency of combating the Left. Also in January, the Socialists split; what had been the Socialists' anti-Communist right wing would soon adopt the name of Social Democratic Party. In February 1947, Italy and its former enemies concluded a treaty. The Truman Doctrine was announced in mid-March, expressing and amplifying international tensions. Less than two weeks later, the Italian Constituent Assembly approved the Lateran Pacts, originally negotiated between the Vatican and Mussolini in 1929. With church–state relations resolved, De Gasperi expected the Constituent Assembly to enact the constitution even if the government excluded the Left. De Gasperi resigned on May 13, 1947, and returned to office without the Left on May 31. After resigning, De Gasperi still hoped for a large coalition and attempted to enlist the Social Democrats (Partito Socialista Democratico Italiano, PSDI),[11] Republicans (Partito Repubblicano Italiano, PRI), and Liberals (Partito Liberale Italiano, PLI). Although he failed, his one-party cabinet included two Liberals and one Republican as individuals rather than as representatives of their parties. The PLI, PRI, and PSDI officially entered government in December 1947 and, as discussed later in this chapter, would repeatedly ally themselves with the DC over the next forty-five years.

To judge from the declared ideological grounds for delegitimating opponents, Italy's centrist parties saw broad, continuing collaboration as essential in a recently established regime that featured deep social divisions and what they perceived as antisystem parties on the left and right. Their shared evaluations of threat and uncertainty shaped a preference for long-term governing alliances greater than minimal winning size (for a similar argument applied cross-nationally, see Budge and Keman 1990, chs. 2, 3). Self-proclaimed prosystem parties joined in coalitions to make governments credible as defenses against extremes and to enforce their definitions of the PCI and MSI as antisystem. The DC and the parties close to it thus regularly added up to a "majority founded on the exclusion of the two poles" of the left–right spectrum (Farneti 1983, 65).

Nonideological benefits have flowed from delegitimation of opponents. Since the "pariah" parties have together commanded 30 to 40 percent of the seats in the Chamber of Deputies, governments have fallen without risking full alternation in power (cf. Sartori 1976; Levite and Tarrow 1983; Pempel 1990; Strøm, Budge, and Laver 1994). Delegitimation has also helped to shield incumbent parties from electoral punishment. For instance, a 1968 survey of the mass public showed that 55 percent of the respondents would never vote for the PCI under any circumstances, while 32 percent refused to vote for the MSI (Sani 1975, 478). In 1985, 39 percent of the citizens sampled rejected the idea of voting for the PCI, and 61 percent spurned the MSI. Among Italians locating themselves at the center of the left–right spectrum, those figures rose to 58 percent and 67 percent, respectively (Mannheimer and Sani 1987, 108–13). Data such as these testify to the "growing legitimation" of the Communists at the mass level (ibid., 110), and yet also indicate that, even in the 1980s, substantial numbers of Italian voters repudiated the PCI and the MSI as electoral options. Although it is possible to identify individual-level traits that are correlated with voters' hostility toward the PCI and the MSI (including left–right self-placement, as just noted), that hostility should also be interpreted as a response to, and product of, the appeals and behavior of the centrist parties (cf. Przeworski and Sprague 1986). The delegitimation of opponents has electoral effects. So, too, does the recurrence of large alliances, to which I now turn.

Expansion of Coalitions

Italian politicians have typically sought surplus coalitions. Christian Democracy always governed with other parties between 1948 and 1953, the only time it held a majority in the Chamber of Deputies.[12] Italy's few minimal winning coalitions have received external support on their votes of investiture. All but four minority governments have been buttressed by external parliamentary support, and all but one have formed after multiple attempts. Minorities have governed as temporary conveniences during phases of exceptional discord among the numerous usual allies (Pasquino 1977, 296–65; Zuckerman 1979, 152–53).

What good are oversized governments? Surplus status has guarded legislation against wayward parliamentarians from the governing majority who have voted against government bills behind the mask of the secret ballot.[13] Less dramatic but still advantageous, surplus status has served as a buffer against truant parliamentarians failing to attend committee meetings or floor votes. Many-party coalitions have cut risks not only inside but also outside parliament, for they have spread the blame for ineffective or unpopular policies. Studies of electoral behavior in Italy and other democracies find that "increasing the number of parties in government weakens the economically inspired, anti-government vote," a result attributed to the "diffusion of government responsibility" that large coalitions permit (Lewis-Beck 1986, 341, 342; cf. Lewis-Beck 1988; Bellucci 1984). In addition, to echo a theme raised earlier, the inclusion of most or all self-declared prosystem parties in Italy's coalitions has highlighted their distance from the parties they have viewed as antisystem.

True, oversized coalitions carry potential costs. Yet, as suggested earlier and documented in Chapter 5, growth in the number of cabinet portfolios can absorb the office costs of erecting large coalitions. Moreover, politicians can contain bargaining costs by devising and amending informal rules about membership in government and by standardizing bargaining procedures. The next three sections discuss these strategies.

Reliance on Rules: Coalition Formulae

The repeated inclusion of certain parties in surplus coalitions and the repeated exclusion of other parties have added up to the following patterns in government composition in Italy.

Under *centrism* (1947 to 1963), the Christian Democrats allied with the Social Democrats (PSDI), Republicans (PRI), and Liberals (PLI).

In *center–left* coalitions (1963 to 1976), the Socialists replaced the Liberals in governing with the DC, PSDI, and PRI.

Under *national solidarity* (1976 to 1979), the Communists joined other parties in supporting minority DC governments through parliamentary accords.

And in *five-party* coalitions (1979 to the 1992 elections), both the Socialists and the Liberals governed with the DC, PSDI, and PRI.

Italians use the term "formulae" to refer to these coalition designs. These prescriptions for governing alliances have helped to delimit the phases in postwar Italian politics, and their names have become catchwords in Italian political discourse. Table 4.2 portrays how much these alliance designs have been replicated, and when.

The formulae are not simply regularities in outcomes. They are also constraints on the process of coalition formation. The formulae represent socially shared knowledge among politicians, sets of expectations about which choices are likely and which are legitimate, about what costs and benefits will accrue from opting for one alternative or another. Through the formulae, centrist politicians have put limits on their own behavior (Mershon 1994).

These informal rules lower the costs of making and breaking coalitions. The formulae prescribe customary governing partners and proscribe unacceptable contenders for governing power and thus narrow the range of unsettled issues in coalition formation. The formulae also codify and perpetuate expectations that politicians who undo one cabinet will be able to enter negotiations for the next cabinet and try to improve on portfolio assignments or policy influence. The formulae have reduced the risks of breaking apart a particular cabinet and raised hopes about bargaining over a new one. The stability of coalition formulae has fostered cabinet instability.[14]

Revision of Rules

Incumbents have altered formal and informal rules in hopes of counteracting electoral losses. A change in formal rules designed to buttress the centrist coalition was tried and failed. The centrist parties suffered sizable losses in the local elections of 1951 and 1952, and they expected setbacks in the parliamentary elections scheduled for 1953. Not long before the 1953 elections, the Christian Democrats secured the passage of a new electoral law that would have given almost two-thirds of the seats in the Chamber of Deputies to an alliance of parties that received one vote more than half of all votes cast.[15] Premier De Gasperi planned the majoritarian electoral law as the cornerstone of a "protected democracy," required to battle the "still very strong enemy alignment" in domestic and international politics (De Gasperi as quoted in Ginsborg 1989, 191–92; cf. Bottiglieri 1984). The law was bitterly opposed by the PCI and PSI, who labeled it the "swindle law." It also produced fissures within the centrist coalition, as dissenting—and prominent—politicians left the PLI, PRI, and PSDI.

The law never took effect, for the 1953 elections awarded only 49.2 percent of the popular vote to the centrist alliance and the DC lost the parlia-

TABLE 4.2.
Italian Governments, 1946–96

Government	Date Formed	Date Resigned	Parties in Cabinet	Seats in Chamber (%)	Type
De Gasperi II	7/46	1/47	DC + PCI + PSI[a] + PRI	81	S
De Gasperi III	2/47	5/47	DC + PCI + PSI + DL[b]	77	S
De Gasperi IV	5/47	12/47	DC	37	MIN
De Gasperi V	12/47	5/48	DC + PSDI[a] + PRI + PLI	58	S
De Gasperi VI	5/48	10/49	DC + PSDI + PRI + PLI	64	S
De Gasperi VII	11/49	1/50	DC + PRI + PLI	58	S
De Gasperi VIII	1/50	4/51	DC + PSDI + PRI	60	S
De Gasperi IX	4/51	7/51	DC + PRI	55	S
De Gasperi X	7/51	6/53	DC + PRI	55	S
De Gasperi XI	7/53	7/53	DC	45	MIN
Pella	8/53	1/54	DC	45	MIN
Fanfani I	1/54	1/54	DC	45	MIN
Scelba	2/54	6/55	DC + PSDI + PLI	50	MW[c]
Segni I	7/55	5/57	DC + PSDI + PLI	50	MW[c]
Zoli	5/57	6/58	DC	45	MIN
Fanfani II	7/58	1/59	DC + PSDI	49	MIN
Segni II	2/59	2/60	DC	46	MIN
Tambroni	3/60	7/60	DC	46	MIN
Fanfani III	7/60	2/62	DC	46	MIN
Fanfani IV	2/62	5/63	DC + PSDI + PRI	51	MW
Leone I	6/63	11/63	DC	41	MIN
Moro I	12/63	6/64	DC + PSI + PSDI + PRI	61	S
Moro II	7/64	1/66	DC + PSI + PSDI + PRI	61	S
Moro III	2/66	6/68	DC + PSI + PSDI + PRI	61	S
Leone II	6/68	11/68	DC	42	MIN
Rumor I	12/68	7/69	DC + PSI-PSDI + PRI	58	S
Rumor II	8/69	2/70	DC	42	MIN
Rumor III	3/70	7/70	DC + PSI + PSDI + PRI	58	S
Colombo I	8/70	3/71	DC + PSI + PSDI + PRI	58	S
Colombo II	3/71	1/72	DC + PSI + PSDI	57	S
Andreotti I	2/72	2/72	DC	42	MIN
Andreotti II	6/72	6/73	DC + PSDI + PLI	50	MW[c]
Rumor IV	7/73	3/74	DC + PSI + PSDI + PRI	59	S
Rumor V	3/74	10/74	DC + PSI + PSDI	57	S
Moro IV	11/74	1/76	DC + PRI	45	MIN
Moro V	2/76	4/76	DC	42	MIN

(*Continued on next page*)

TABLE 4.2. (*Continued*)

Government	Date Formed	Date Resigned	Parties in Cabinet	Seats in Chamber(%)	Type
Andreotti III	7/76	1/78	DC	42	MIN
Andreotti IV	3/78	1/79	DC	42	MIN
Andreotti V	3/79	3/79	DC + PSDI + PRI	46	MIN
Cossiga I	8/79	3/80	DC + PSDI + PLI	46	MIN
Cossiga II	4/80	9/80	DC + PSI + PRI	54	S
Forlani	10/80	5/81	DC + PSI + PSDI + PRI	57	S
Spadolini I	6/81	8/82	PRI + DC + PSI + PSDI + PLI	58	S
Spadolini II	8/82	11/82	PRI + DC + PSI + PSDI + PLI	58	S
Fanfani V	12/82	4/83	DC + PSI + PSDI + PLI	56	S
Craxi I	8/83	6/86	PSI + DC + PSDI + PRI + PLI	58	S
Craxi II	8/86	3/87	PSI + DC + PSDI + PRI + PLI	58	S
Fanfani VI	4/87	4/87	DC	37	MIN
Goria	7/87	3/88	DC + PSI + PSDI + PRI + PLI	60	S
De Mita	4/88	5/89	DC + PSI + PSDI + PRI + PLI	60	S
Andreotti VI	7/89	3/91	DC + PSI + PSDI + PRI + PLI	60	S
Andreotti VII	4/91	4/92	DC + PSI + PSDI + PLI	56	S
Amato I	6/92	4/93	PSI + DC + PSDI + PLI	53	MW
Ciampi	4/93	1/94	DC + PSI + PSDI + PLI	53	MW
Berlusconi	5/94	12/94	FI [+ CCD[d]] + League + AN	58	MW[d]
Dini	1/95	1/96	Non-partisan		

SOURCES: Farneti 1983, 36–39; Petracca 1980; Pollio Salimbeni 1989; Strøm 1990b, 140–41; *Corriere della Sera*, various issues.

NOTE: S, surplus coalition (total = 28); MW, minimal winning coalition (total = 7); MIN, minority government (total = 20). Party abbreviations are defined in the text and in Appendix A.

[a] This table always designates the Socialists as the PSI, even though the party had a different name before 1947 (when the Social Democrats exited) and from 1966 to 1969 (when the Socialists and Social Democrats reunited). Similarly, the table always refers to the Social Democrats as the PSDI.

[b] The Democratic Labor Party (DL) won just one Assembly seat in 1946 and did not survive the 1948 elections.

[c] Exactly half of seats controlled by coalition.

[d] The Christian Democratic Center (CCD) allied with Forza Italia (FI) on the PR ballot in the 1994 elections, but then constituted a separate parliamentary group. If parliamentary parties are counted as the units comprising the Berlusconi coalition, it has surplus status.

mentary majority it had won in 1948. The law was rescinded soon after. Hence, the majoritarian law not only failed to diminish the costs of setting up and sustaining governments, but also exacted a substantial price. The DC's allies in centrism had new leverage, for the DC now needed their support to pass votes of investiture and approve legislation.

Faced with weaknesses in the centrist coalition, the Christian Democrats experimented with adjustments to the coalition formula. One government (Segni I, installed in 1955) drew parliamentary support from the Monarchists, and three others (Pella in 1953, Zoli in 1957, and Segni II in 1959) accepted support from both the Monarchists and the neo-Fascist MSI. These experiments in cooperation with the extreme right climaxed and ended in 1960, when riots in northern cities greeted the DC-only government under Fernando Tambroni, which survived on the MSI's votes alone (Ignazi 1994b, ch. 2).

An "opening to the left" proved to be a more durable answer to centrism's losses. It became an admissible option for growing segments of the DC after the PSI renounced unity of action with the PCI in 1956. The PSI's return to government was intended to isolate the Communist Party and win the government greater working-class support. Patiently engineered by Aldo Moro, Fanfani's successor as DC secretary, the center–left coalition was inaugurated in 1963 with American consent and despite the PSI's decline in the 1963 elections (Ginsborg 1989, ch. 8; Tamburrano 1971).

Codification of Bargaining Procedures

In summer 1968, a prominent Christian Democrat and his aide began to develop systematic guidelines for bargaining over new governments. The basic principle inspiring the guidelines was that shares of ministries should follow the relative strengths of factions within the DC and of parties allied with the DC. This principle conformed to what had already been established as common practice in 1953, due to the failure of the majoritarian electoral law (Dogan 1984, 170). But the standard procedure was extended and routinized immediately after the 1968 elections. In a series of memoranda, DC cabinet member Adolfo Sarti and his aide, Massimiliano Cencelli, calculated factional strength on the DC National Council down to hundredths of percentages and updated measurements between DC Congresses, taking into account such changes as splits in factions and the appointment of new regional-level secretaries (Venditti 1981, app. 1); they dealt with qualitative differences among cabinet posts, identifying four tiers from top (such ministries as Foreign Affairs, Interior, and Treasury) to bottom (Tourism and Scientific Research) (ibid., 112–13); they weighed the post of prime minister as equal to two ministerial portfolios, and one ministerial portfolio was equal to three undersecretaries (Dogan 1984, 169–72). Although Sarti and Cencelli consistently computed that fewer posts would go to the DC in coalition scenarios as opposed to one-party scenarios, the first explicit comparison of parties' strengths among their published memoranda appears in 1973 (Venditti 1981, attachment 13).

Why were these guidelines written when they were? Recall the makeup of center–left coalitions. The inclusion of the Socialists complicated coalition bargaining. The PSI had a larger share of votes and parliamentary seats than did the DC's other partners, and so was better equipped to advance bargaining demands. Consequently, government crises averaged thirty-six days during the 1963–68 legislature, up from twenty-three days during the 1958–63 legislature.[16] The 1968 parliamentary elections gave slight gains to the DC and losses to the reunited PSI-PSDI, and ushered in "the crisis . . . of the center-left, . . . accepted by all because no other possible [coalition] was seen" (Venditti 1981, 16). Immediately after the 1968 elections, Sarti and Cencelli began to codify bargaining procedures, and Sarti told journalists about "the Cencelli manual," the name by which the guidelines have since been known (ibid., 11–12).

This codification of procedures saved on bargaining costs. Premiers-designate have adhered to the Cencelli manual in efforts to make governments easier to erect and then uphold. The habitual governing parties have found it convenient to bolster their claims for office by citing the guidelines. The Cencelli manual has structured coalition negotiations so frequently and so thoroughly in Italy since 1968 that one politician has quipped that the manual amounts to "the true Constitution of the Republic" (a former president of the Liberal Party, quoted in Venditti 1981, 50). One journalist has tracked use of the Cencelli manual for all government formations between 1968 and summer 1981 (Venditti 1981). According to Cazzola (1985, 202), the manual lies "at the base of all [coalition] bargaining" in Italy.[17]

Restriction of Information

Italian governments are typically installed and terminated with important information left hazy or hidden from public view. Consider the process of investiture. Italy's constitution stipulates that a government takes office when the prime minister and cabinet swear loyalty to the Republic before the president (article 93). Within ten days of its inauguration, a new government must present its program to Parliament and submit to a vote of confidence in both the Chamber of Deputies and the Senate (article 94). Since questions of confidence require a roll-call vote (article 94.2), investiture entails a public assumption of responsibility on the part of all parliamentarians, who must go on record as endorsing the government, opposing it, abstaining in judgment, or not attending the vote. Not only is the identity of the executive transparent, but so also is the legislative majority it commands.

What remains opaque is governmental policy. Most programs announced at investiture are "grandiose enough to impress public opinion and ambiguous enough to be accepted by every [party] delegation" in the government (Marradi 1982, 65). Such documents provide poor guidance as to how the government will act during its tenure. As Baldassarre (1985, 331) observes, "almost never has the approval of a governmental program effectively determined the boundaries of action and priorities in implementation of the government's political course." Granted, a pioneering research team has content-analyzed government programs in eleven parliamentary democracies, including Italy, in order to locate the policy positions of governing coalitions (Laver and Budge 1992). Yet even that team concedes that in Italy programs are "rather rhetorical" and "coalitions usually succeed in putting into effect only a small part of the program" (Mastropaolo and Slater 1992, 319).[18]

Vague programs make policy concessions more palatable and bargaining less contentious when constructing coalitions. By wrapping policy packages in high-sounding, nonbinding, ambiguous language, the members of incoming governments can reach agreements and defer the resolution of disagreements more easily than would otherwise be the case. This strategy is especially attractive given the complex division of labor within Italian cabinets, discussed earlier.

Italian politicians also communicate limited information about the circumstances surrounding the finish of governments. Table 4.3 summarizes the reasons why Italian cabinets have resigned.[19] Between 1946 and 1992, no government was ever forced to resign by the Italian Parliament's approval of a motion of no confidence. Why? According to Balboni (1988, 49), "the [same] allies have historically always been obliged to govern together: . . . [I]t would not be advisable to accentuate contrasts necessarily destined to find some settlement." In other words—in words familiar in the game-theoretic literature—the absence of approved motions of no confidence reflects the ability of Italian politicians to exercise rational foresight. Cabinet leaders have looked ahead to disaster in the offing and have resigned in advance, before any majority could vote in favor of a motion of no confidence. Cabinet leaders have saved face and guarded power, according to this logic, by foreseeing, and forestalling, an adverse outcome in the vote on a motion of censure.

The story does not stop here. Few motions of no confidence have come before the Italian legislature. The Parliament rejected seven no-confidence motions between 1948 and 1990; an eighth motion of no confidence, introduced in 1988, never arrived at a vote and did not trigger the fall of the government, which instead broke apart due to internal disputes over nuclear energy policy (Manzella 1991, 307; on the 1988 motion, Catanzaro and

TABLE 4.3.
Causes of Cabinet Resignations in Italy, 1946–92

Cause of Resignation	Percentage of Cabinets	Number of Governments
Motion of no confidence, vote held	0	0
Motion of no confidence tabled, no vote	0	0
Motion of confidence tabled, no vote	1.9	1
Bill with confidence attached, vote held	1.9	1
Vote of investiture held, investiture denied	9.6	5
Agreement to enlarge cabinet	11.5	6
Policy disagreement, no vote in Parliament	46.2	24
Policy disagreement, vote held in Parliament	13.5	7
Party schism/merger	7.7	4
Election, regularly scheduled	7.7	4
TOTAL	100.0	52

SOURCE: Coding of information in *Keesing's Contemporary Archives.*

Nanetti 1989, 13–14; *Keesing's Contemporary Archives* 1988, 35986–87).
Hence, between 1946 and 1992 no Italian cabinet resigned because it anticipated that a motion of no confidence would succeed.

Only one executive (Cossiga I, in 1980) resigned because it anticipated
that a motion of confidence it had scheduled would fail. And only one
(Moro II, 1966) resigned because it met defeat on a piece of legislation
whose passage it had made a matter of confidence. The issues at stake when
Cossiga I and Moro II relinquished power—the role of the PCI and church–
state relations, respectively—are fundamental to postwar Italian politics.[20]
The fact remains that of the forty-seven cabinets that survived investiture
from 1946 to 1992, only two ended because a vote measuring and broad-
casting the Parliament's lack of confidence in the executive seemed imminent or occurred.

Thus, Italian governments, having gained the confidence of Parliament,
very rarely collapse due to a manifest loss of that confidence. Five minority
cabinets could not obtain the legislature's confidence in the first place, and
failed at investiture. All but one of these were DC-only governments. All
signalled political transitions, as disagreements among Italy's centrist parties eroded and undid the legislative majorities usually undergirding minority executives.[21]

In a reversal of the image just described, six minority cabinets from 1946
to 1992 were overthrown amicably, because of agreements among Italy's

centrist parties. All were DC-only governments that surrendered power after party leadership organs concurred on the need to invite one or more allies into a coalition anchored by the DC. Their successors won at investiture, as legislative majorities ratified the understandings reached earlier outside Parliament.

The demise of Italian governments can most commonly be traced to policy disagreements that emerge after investiture and do not engage the confidence of Parliament. Indeed, as Table 4.3 exhibits, fully 46.2 percent of the governments formed between 1946 and 1992 fell due to disagreements that were not expressed in a legislative division. For example, in February 1960, the National Council of the Liberal Party (PLI) voted to withdraw parliamentary support from the government, which it criticized as "slipping more and more to the left" (PLI resolution as quoted in *Keesing's* 1960, 17350). Three days later, Premier Antonio Segni exercised rational foresight and resigned, thereby averting a clash in the parliamentary arena. Some legal experts (Balboni 1988, 48–49; Manzella 1991, 306–308) go so far as to say that such preemptive resignations run counter to the constitution, which asserts that "each chamber grants or revokes confidence by means of a motion stating the justification (*mozione motivata*)" (article 94). Claims about constitutionality could be, and have been, debated. However the debates are decided, the point is that preemptive resignations allow the antigovernmental contingent *not* to stand up, be heard, and be counted in the legislature. Equally important, policy disagreements culminating in parliamentary confrontations over specific pieces of legislation terminated only 13.5 percent of the cabinets from 1946 to 1992. Even those confrontations did not guarantee full exposure of alignments in Parliament, since on four of those seven occasions voting proceeded by secret ballot.

The balance of parliamentary forces is subject to visible change at election time, of course. Yet only four Italian cabinets between 1946 and 1992 (7.7 percent) left office because regularly scheduled elections were at hand.[22] Changes in the units undertaking electoral competition, all of them party schisms or mergers within the Socialist/Social Democratic family, prompted the resignation of another four governments.

The overall message of Table 4.3 is that once the hurdle of investiture is surmounted, few Italian cabinets fall because parliamentary majorities hostile to them have come into full public view. Premiers are most often deprived of power because the leaders of one or more centrist parties have signalled their intention to withdraw from the current governing majority. Party leaders occasionally signal their readiness to cooperate in a new coalition or orchestrate the defeat of a government-sponsored bill on a secret ballot. Coded rhetoric and covert action serve to limit the embarrassment, loss of votes and bargaining power, and tension in negotiations over subsequent coalitions that might ensue from clear parliamentary confrontations. Such a restriction of information is particularly advantageous when the same parties assume that they are obliged to govern and their largest opponents, forbidden to govern.

Not only as cabinets founder have Italy's ruling parties deemed it prudent to refrain from accentuating contrasts in the parliamentary arena. They have attempted to mute legislative conflicts throughout their terms of office, which I now discuss.

Special-Interest Legislation

A central theme in studies of the Italian Parliament is that its legislation is both voluminous and trivial (cross-national data in Di Palma 1977, 41–42, 48, 69; cf. Baldassarre 1985; Cotta 1995; Della Sala 1987; Guarnieri 1989; Motta 1985; Nocifero and Valdini 1992). As Di Palma (1977, 83) documents, "the overwhelming majority of legislation . . . devote[s] itself to the distribution of narrow benefits." For example, 37 percent of the legislative proposals in a 1963–72 random sample addressed career and financial benefits, regulations, or legal questions for the civil service (*ibid.*, 85–86). Bills like these are tagged *leggine* (literally, little laws).

Along with the frequent passage of *leggine*, two other aspects of parliamentary behavior should be noted: the size of the majorities backing enacted bills, and the kinds of bills not enacted. Most laws have been approved by large majorities, which include Communists (Di Palma 1977, 54–64; data on 1988–92 majorities in Nocifero and Valdini 1992, 36–64). Moreover, legislation submitted by both government and opposition has tended to avoid or finesse controversial issues. Analyses of two random samples of legislative projects attest to this tendency (1948–68 and 1963–72 data in Di Palma 1977, 82–92). So does the fact that, as of 1992, the Italian Parliament had not enacted the measures needed for compliance with twenty-one judgments of the European Court of Justice; Italy accounted for almost one-fourth of such cases of noncompliance in the entire European Union (Gallagher, Laver, and Mair 1995, 104).

Delays in implementing the 1948 constitution and in repealing Fascist legislation provide further evidence of the avoidance of open parliamentary conflict. The Constitutional Court and the Superior Council of the Judiciary were not created until 1955 and 1958, respectively (Guarnieri 1992). Only in 1970 did Parliament pass the enabling legislation for the referendum and establish the twenty regional governments defined in the constitution (Gourevitch 1980, ch. 9; Putnam et al. 1993, ch. 2). Efforts to revise Fascist-era family legislation began in 1966 and produced a new family code signed into law in 1975 (Ginsborg 1989, 499; Hellman 1987, 50–53). In 1974, a ministerial committee started working on reform of the criminal code, which dated from 1930; Parliament enacted a new code of criminal procedure only in 1988 (Colombo 1990).

By focusing on special-interest legislation, parliamentarians have located common ground for policy compromise, facilitated bargaining, and so cut the price of maintaining governments. The costs of dismantling governments have also decreased, since politicians have reason to hope that they can avert electoral punishment by servicing targeted constituencies. In other senses, too, as Cotta (1995, 87) remarks, "It is not by chance that *leggine* have prevailed. . . . On more controversial measures, the veto powers within both the [governing] majority and the opposition have in general easily blocked or delayed the parliamentary process." Vetoes have led to the partial implementation of vague government programs. The slow implementation of the constitution has reflected a veto as well: the DC's "unwillingness . . . to share power with the opposition or to tolerate potentially crippling restraints on its power to govern Italy" (Zariski 1993, 298).

Conclusions

The evidence marshaled here indicates that Italian politicians have attempted to lower the costs of coalition by a variety of means. Chapter 5 assesses the other component of the argument for Italy: whether spatial and institutional conditions have aided politicians in their efforts.

Before taking up that task, I should take this opportunity to emphasize and elaborate three points already raised. Remember that Chapter 3 discussed, among other things, the possibilities and uncertainties surrounding cost-reduction strategies, the view of institutions as dependent and independent variables, and the advantages of scrutinizing coalition politics in Italy. I am now equipped to develop those points further.

The general notion of "strategy" suggests both possibility and uncertainty, both flexibility and constraint, both achievement and imperfection. To envision political actors as "strategic" is to endorse the idea that what happens in politics arises from choice and chance. The role of chance cannot be denied. Neither can the role of creative choice. In the specific framework here, parties have nontrivial choices. As I have repeatedly stressed, parties do not just see prices in coalition politics, but also try to set prices. They do not just reach out for whatever benefits are at hand, but also grapple with the problem of redefining the costs and benefits of coalition. Uncertainty exists all the same. Parties and other political actors are not omnipotent in the real world, and they are not assumed to be in this framework. In the real world and in this framework, choices have consequences, some of which are unintended or unwelcome or both. The fate of Italy's majoritarian electoral law in 1953 illustrates that events after a choice do not always match the plans and hopes preceding it. Moves to reduce the costs of coalition can fail.

The approval and the repeal of the so-called swindle law illustrate, in addition, that political institutions are both objects of, and constraints on, actors' choices. In 1952, the leaders of Christian Democracy knew that relatively proportional electoral rules, such as those used in Italy in 1946 and 1948, rarely manufacture a parliamentary majority for a party winning an electoral plurality. In 1948, the DC had managed to gain a majority in the Chamber of Deputies (53.1 percent of the seats) with 48.5 percent of the popular vote. That sort of luck was unlikely to recur, especially in light of the DC's decline in the local elections of 1951 and 1952. The DC thus spearheaded the rewriting of the electoral rules. The Christian Democrats fashioned new rules because they recognized how the old rules constrained them.

At the same time that the centrist parties were choosing new rules, they anticipated institutional constraints. They tailored the seat bonus in the new electoral law to a size that they hoped would guarantee that jurists they put forward as nominees to the Constitutional Court would obtain parliamentary approval (Floridia 1995, 12). According to enabling legislation approved in early 1953, each of the five members of the court selected by Parliament had to muster a 60 percent majority (Bonini 1996, 98).[23] According to the new electoral law, a majority electoral bloc would receive 64.4 percent of the seats in the lower house. In this instance and in the argument advanced in this book, institutions appear as both independent and dependent variables.

The final point to underscore is the special leverage afforded by subjecting Italy to in-depth study. As Laver and Schofield (1990, 102) note, many empirical evaluations of coalition theories "are based merely on predictive success." In other words, many tests count the observed frequency of expected outcomes without seeking to discern whether it is the causal mechanisms posited in theory that generate the outcomes. Such a research design leaves open the possibility that the predictions hold true for the "wrong reasons." I want to exclude that possibility and to establish that the right reasons apply. This chapter's close scrutiny of Italy has allowed the operation of one set of causal mechanisms—politicians' deliberate pursuit of cost-reduction strategies—to be investigated, not simply inferred. What underlies the combination of governmental instability and stability such as that found in Italy? I have now amassed evidence supporting the idea that politicians' strategic behavior has contributed to those outcomes. It is particularly important to locate and track the causal mechanisms at work in Italy since the Italian outcomes pose such vexing questions for coalition theories. The next step is to explore how the configuration of policy space and political institutions in Italy have affected the costs of making and breaking coalitions.

5 Costs and Outcomes in Italian Coalition Politics

Chapter 4 narrated events consistent with two central elements of the logic underpinning this book. If spatial and institutional conditions influence the costs of coalition and cost-reduction strategies, then parties should differ in costs and strategies. In addition, if spatial and institutional conditions shift over time, then costs and strategies should exhibit some change. In keeping with these hypotheses, it was Italy's core party that engineered the revision of both the electoral laws and the formulae for the composition of governments. The politicians who codified procedures in coalition bargaining also came from Christian Democracy. And the Italian Socialists' entry into government, followed by a re-ranking of winners and losers in the 1968 elections, prompted the drafting of the Cencelli manual.

In this chapter, I appraise my hypotheses against quantitative evidence on the costs of coalition in Italy. Comparisons across parties reveal that the Christian Democratic Party (DC), which dominated the Italian policy space from 1946 to 1992, incurred low costs in coalition politics. For instance, the DC relinquished relatively few offices to build coalitions as opposed to one-party cabinets. Comparisons across time also permit an assessment of the argument. With the 1976 elections, the Socialists (PSI) became the essential member party of any DC-based coalition able to constitute a majority while excluding the Communists (PCI). As expected, the costs of coalition between 1976 and 1992 differed from those between 1946 and 1976.

Most of the data inspected in this chapter cover the years 1946–92, but events since 1992 provide crucial evidence on intertemporal variations. The 1992 elections marked vast change in spatial and institutional conditions in Italy, as shown in the conclusion to this chapter. Costs and outcomes in Italian coalition politics were transformed.

The chapter first outlines the context for electoral competition and examines the electoral fortunes of governing parties in Italy. I then consider legislative rules and ties between the executive and the legislature. That discussion lays the basis, in turn, for an investigation of the office, policy, and bargaining costs attached to Italy's governing coalitions.

The Electoral Arena:
Voters, Parties, and Electoral Rules

Religion and class have powerfully shaped vote choices in postwar Italy (e.g., Barnes 1974, 1977, 1984; Galli and Prandi 1970; Sani 1977; Spreafico and La Palombara 1963). Hence, a six-nation comparison finds that "only in Italy do changing social cleavages [religion and class] have more of an effect than changing economic evaluations" on the probability of voting for incumbents (Lewis-Beck 1988, 157; cf. Bellucci 1984, 1985; Lewis-Beck 1986; but see Bellucci 1991). Such limits on rational policy voting have informed a well-known typology of Italian electoral behavior (Parisi and Pasquino 1979), which distinguishes a vote of opinion, motivated by a broad interest in policy; a vote of belonging, affirming an enduring allegiance to either the Catholic or the Communist subculture; and a vote of exchange, awarded in return for patronage goods. Mannheimer and Sani (1987, 93) use a 1985 survey to estimate that subcultural voters constituted 60 percent of the DC electorate and 67 percent of the PCI electorate. Other data suggest that exchange voters formed sizable proportions of the DC and Social Democratic (PSDI) electorates, that opinion voters predominated in the Liberal (PLI) and Republican (PRI) electorates, and that the PSI, especially after the early 1960s, drew opinion and exchange voters (e.g., Caciagli 1988; Cazzola 1985; De Mucci 1990; Katz 1985). It is accepted wisdom that socioeconomic change has recently eroded the subcultural vote and augmented the opinion vote in Italy.

Content analyses of party manifestos show two leading dimensions of party competition in Italy: a socioeconomic left–right dimension and a technocracy–social harmony dimension (Mastropaolo and Slater 1987). The first dimension involves such issues as agrarian reform, nationalization, and the role of organized labor; the second subsumes the confrontation between Catholic and secular values. The location and strength of parties in this policy space established the DC as a core party from 1946 through 1992 (Laver and Schofield 1990; Schofield 1993). The 1976 elections made the PSI pivotal,[1] for it became the essential ally in any DC-based coalition capable of commanding a majority while excluding the PCI (Pasquino 1981). The DC's sizable losses in the 1992 elections ended its status as a core party (Schofield 1993). As a result of the 1992 elections, too, the PSI ceased to be pivotal.[2]

From 1946 until 1993, elections to the Italian Parliament were held under a relatively pure version of party-list proportional representation (PR) rules (e.g., Farneti 1983, 84–92; Manzella 1991, ch. 2; Wertman 1977). As Table 5.1 illustrates, those electoral laws helped to fragment opposition parties and safeguard the parliamentary delegations of the DC's small governing al-

TABLE 5.1.
Italian Electoral Results, 1946–92:
Votes and Seats Won in Elections to the Chamber of Deputies

Party	YEAR OF ELECTION											
	1946	1948	1953	1958	1963	1968	1972	1976	1979	1983	1987	1992
VOTES (PERCENTAGE SHARE OF VALID VOTES)												
Greens	—	—	—	—	—	—	—	—	—	—	2.5	2.8
DP	—	—	—	—	—	—	—	1.5	0.8	1.5	1.7	—
PDUP	—	—	—	—	—	—	0.7	w/DP	1.4	w/PCI	—	—
PSIUP	—	—	—	—	—	4.4	1.9	—	—	—	—	—
PRad	—	—	—	—	—	—	—	1.1	3.5	2.2	2.6	—
RC	—	—	—	—	—	—	—	—	—	—	—	5.6
PCI[a]	18.9	[b]	22.6	22.7	25.3	26.9	27.2	34.4	30.4	29.9	26.6	16.1
PSI	20.7	31.0[b]	12.7	14.2	13.8	[c]	9.6	9.6	9.8	11.4	14.3	13.6
PSDI	—	7.1	4.5	4.6	6.1	14.5[c]	5.1	3.4	3.8	4.1	2.9	2.7
PRI	4.4	2.5	1.6	1.4	1.4	2.0	2.9	3.1	3.0	5.1	3.7	4.4
DC	35.1	48.5	40.1	42.3	38.3	39.1	38.7	38.7	38.3	32.9	34.3	29.7
PLI	6.8	3.8	3.0	3.5	7.0	5.8	3.9	1.3	1.9	2.9	2.1	2.8
League	—	—	—	—	—	—	—	—	—	—	1.3	8.7
PNM	2.8	2.8	6.9	4.8	1.7	1.3	[d]	[d]	—	—	—	—
MSI	—	2.0	5.8	4.8	5.1	4.5	8.7[d]	6.1[d]	5.3	6.8	5.9	5.4
Other	11.3	2.3	2.8	1.7	1.3	1.5	1.3	0.8	1.8	3.2	2.1	8.2

lies. Accordingly, the number of parties represented in the Chamber of Deputies after any given election ranged from nine to sixteen.[3] Note also that Italy's PR rules assigned a small bonus of seats to parties with large electorates, as the DC explicitly acknowledged in the early 1950s. By the same token, they did little to magnify the parliamentary impact of a loss at the polls. For example, the DC's share of the popular vote dropped from 42.3 percent in 1958 to 38.3 percent in 1963. The DC's share of Chamber seats declined only slightly more, from 45.8 percent in 1958 to 41.3 percent in 1963.

The system of preference voting in effect from 1946 until 1991 enabled Italian voters to influence which candidates on a party list gained election to the Chamber of Deputies. Voters had the option of marking the names or numbers of up to three or four candidates (depending on district size) from the party list they endorsed. Seats in a district were distributed *across* parties in proportion to each party's list vote. The order in which candidates *within* each party earned seats was determined by the preference votes can-

TABLE 5.1. *(Continued)*

Italian Electoral Results, 1946–92:
Votes and Seats Won in Elections to the Chamber of Deputies

YEAR OF ELECTION

Party	1946	1948	1953	1958	1963	1968	1972	1976	1979	1983	1987	1992
					SEATS (NUMBER)							
Greens	—	—	—	—	—	—	—	—	—	—	13	16
DP	—	—	—	—	—	—	—	6	0	7	8	—
PDUP	—	—	—	—	—	—	0	w/DP	6	w/PCI	—	—
PSIUP	—	—	—	—	—	23	0	—	—	—	—	—
PRad	—	—	—	—	—	—	—	4	18	11	13	—
RC	—	—	—	—	—	—	—	—	—	—	—	35
PCI[a]	104	[b]	143	140	166	177	179	227	201	198	177	107
PSI	115	183[b]	75	84	87	[c]	61	57	62	73	94	92
PSDI	—	33	19	22	33	91[c]	29	15	21	23	17	16
PRI	23	9	5	6	6	9	15	14	15	29	21	27
DC	207	305	263	273	260	266	266	263	261	225	234	206
PLI	41	19	13	17	39	31	20	5	9	16	11	17
League	—	—	—	—	—	—	—	—	—	—	1	55
PNM	16	14	40	25	8	6	[d]	[d]	—	—	—	—
MSI	—	6	29	24	27	24	56[d]	35[d]	31	42	35	34
Other	50	5	3	5	4	3	4	4	6	6	6	25
TOTAL	556	574	590	596	630	630	630	630	630	630	630	630

SOURCES: Farneti 1983, 36–39; Rhodes 1988, 187; Sani 1994, 41.

NOTE: Dashes indicate that the party did not contest the election in question. Party abbreviations are defined in the text and in Appendix A.

[a] Democratic Party of the Left in 1992.

[b] Joint slate of Communists and Socialists.

[c] Reunified Socialists and Social Democrats.

[d] Joint slate of Monarchists and Italian Social Movement.

didates secured (for details, see Katz 1985, 1986a; Wertman 1977). Under these rules, Chamber elections not only pitted party against party, but also induced candidates of the same party to run against each other, for preference votes. Such intraparty competition has been at least as fierce as interparty competition during election campaigns, as one manual for political candidates cautions (Pustetto 1991, 35–36, 79–81). The provision for multiple preference votes, further, made prudent some degree of cooperation

among at least a few of a party's candidates within a district, as part of the
drive for preference votes. In the run-up to the 1987 parliamentary elections, for instance, newspaper advertisements and campaign ephemera
abounded in which voters within a district were advised to cast their preference votes for one set or another of three or four DC politicians (Mershon
campaign archives, University of Virginia, 1987). Hence, it is often claimed
that preference voting has encouraged factionalism in Italian parties (Katz
1986a; Zuckerman 1979). Amid growing criticism of these effects, a 1991
referendum reduced to one the number of preference votes that any voter
could cast (McCarthy 1992).[4]

The Electoral Costs of Building
and Sustaining Coalitions

In the aggregate, as Strøm (1990b, 124, 181–82) documents, Italy's
governing parties have suffered smaller average electoral losses than have
governing parties in many other democracies. Like Strøm, I measure electoral costs as mean shifts in vote shares between pairs of consecutive elections to the lower house of parliament. To explore how spatial and institutional conditions influenced the electoral fortunes of incumbents in Italy
between 1948 and 1992, Table 5.2 disaggregates the analysis by party and
distinguishes between a party's presence in office on election eve and its role
in all governments formed from one election to the next.[5]

Electoral payoffs for all governing parties in Italy have depended on the
segmentation of the electorate and the configuration of parties in policy
space. An incumbent party for five decades, Christian Democracy scored
slight electoral gains when it governed alone on election eve (an increase of
0.8 percent of the vote, on average, as listed in the first column of Table
5.2). The DC also lost the least votes (a mere 0.1 percent, on average) when
it governed with allies for most of the time between elections. This two-part
finding supports the notion that exchange voters respond strongly to spoils
delivered by a single governing party and that multiparty governments blur
responsibility and spread blame. A third item deserves notice, however: the
losses that the DC posted in coalition from 1976 to 1992. The DC became
more vulnerable with the erosion of the subcultural vote, the rise in opinion voting, the more intense interparty competition for spoils growing out
of the PSI's pivotal position, and the less favorable conditions for the ideological delegitimation of opponents.

As Table 5.2 displays, the DC's habitual allies—with one exception—received more votes when they held opposition, rather than governing, status
immediately before elections. The Social Democratic exception reflects its

TABLE 5.2.
Electoral Gain or Loss, by Party and Party Status in Government, 1948–92

	DC	PSI	PSDI	PRI	PLI
Status immediately before election					
One-party government	+0.80(n = 4)	NA	NA	NA	NA
Coalition government	−1.23(n = 7)	−0.93(n = 3)	+0.04(n = 6)	−0.46(n = 5)	−0.43(n = 3)
Opposition	NA	−0.61(n = 8)	−0.92(n = 5)	+0.38(n = 6)	−0.34(n = 8)
Dominant status between elections					
One-party government	−2.20(n = 2)	NA	NA	NA	NA
Coalition government	−0.11(n = 9)	−0.08(n = 5)	−0.79(n = 8)	+0.22(n = 5)	+0.35(n = 4)
Opposition	NA	−1.34(n = 6)	+0.95(n = 2)	−0.18(n = 6)	−0.77(n = 7)
Coalition government 1976–92	−2.87(n = 3)	+1.27(n = 3)	−0.37(n = 3)	+0.47(n = 3)	+0.30(n = 3)

SOURCE: Calculations based on government status data reported in Table 4.2, and electoral data in Table 5.1.

NOTE: Entries are mean changes in parties' percentage point share of the vote between pairs of consecutive elections to the Chamber of Deputies. Numbers of applicable interelectoral periods are in parentheses. The baseline year is 1946 for all parties except the PSDI, which first contested elections in 1948. Dominant status is coded as whatever status (in one-party government, in coalition government, in opposition) was most frequent between two successive elections. NA, Not applicable. Party abbreviations are defined in the text and in Appendix A.

pool of exchange voters (cf. Strøm 1990b, 172). The Republican Party ben-efited more from preelectoral opposition than did the Liberal Party, for its more centrist position allowed the PRI to attract more opinion voters dis-satisfied with government policy (Mannheimer and Sani 1987, 168).

The costs of coalition on election eve tended to be offset by advantages accruing from longer-term governing roles. That is, the PSI, PRI, and PLI performed better when they shared governing power for most of the span since the previous election than when they joined the opposition. The left-most and rightmost governing parties, the PSI and PLI, suffered more from interelectoral opposition than did the PSDI and PRI and spent more time in opposition. The PSDI operated in opposition even less than did the PRI; and when the PSDI's dominant interelectoral status was opposition, it cam-paigned on its prospective role in coalitions (Galli and Prandi 1970, 39–42; Leonardi 1981, 178–79). From 1976 to 1992, all but one of the DC's allies reaped electoral benefits from participation in coalitions. The gains were greatest for the Socialist Party, whose rightward moves captured opinion voters and whose pivotal contributions to DC-based majorities helped it to tap and deliver spoils. Overall, then, the parties prescribed as the DC's al-lies under coalition formulae usually won electoral credit for brief exits from coalition and banked on reentering government, looking for addi-tional credit.

The patterns arrayed in Table 5.2 do not only suggest that spatial condi-tions influence the electoral costs of coalition. They also comport with the idea that parties' purposive behavior can curb electoral losses. The repeated negotiation of multiparty governments appears to have shielded Italy's in-cumbents from punishment at the polls. So, too, have the delegitimation of major opposition parties and the passage of abundant special-interest legis-lation. Electoral institutions have molded the strategies that Italian politi-cians have pursued. The quest for preference votes, for instance, has given parliamentarians incentives to cater to special interests. I now turn to the in-centives and constraints created by parliamentary institutions and consider how those institutions have affected the office costs of coalition.

Parliamentary Institutions

According to a noted constitutional lawyer, "No modern parliament [other than the Italian] raises so many negative conditions for a govern-ment" (Andrea Manzella, quoted in Spotts and Wieser 1986, 111). One neg-ative condition is the vote of investiture, which must be held in both houses of Parliament, as Chapter 4 observed. Governments that survive the votes of investiture meet other obstacles. No rule has ever assigned the government direct responsibility for setting the legislative calendar. Until 1971, there were no ceilings on the number of bills that private members could propose in either the Chamber of Deputies or the Senate; and until 1981, there were very few limits on obstructionism (Baldassarre 1985). Governments can attempt to compel parliamentary majorities to emerge through the provision for executive decrees, which expire unless enacted by Parliament within sixty days of their issue.

The Italian Parliament has standing, specialized committees whose powers to take final action on legislation make them "miniparliaments" (Hellman 1992b, 373). The committees have handled the bulk of Italian legislation—about 63 percent of the legislative proposals in a 1963–72 sample and 54 percent of enacted laws from 1987 to 1992 (Di Palma 1977, 201; Nocifero and Valdini 1992, 11). Both within and outside committees, governing parties have typically sought to avert upsets by including the major opposition parties in the preparation of legislative proposals. This practice has furnished a defense against the secret ballot, which was required on final votes in the Chamber of Deputies until 1988, and has given shelter to governing parties' parliamentarians who have voted against government bills.

The Office Costs of Building Coalitions

Table 5.3 measures the office price that Christian Democracy paid when it governed with coalition partners. Part A of the table reports the mean percentage shares of portfolios held by the DC in different types of governments. In one-party governments, the DC occasionally awarded a few cabinet posts to independent experts. In coalitions, the DC sacrificed this near monopoly on cabinet slots. The DC relinquished a greater percentage of offices when the coalition embraced the medium-sized PSI and still more in the 1976–92 coalitions when the PSI made a pivotal contribution to the governing majority.

Part B of the table establishes that the division of portfolios between the DC and its allies illustrates a well-known finding from cross-national portfolio studies: The largest party in a coalition obtains a share of senior cabinet posts that is somewhat smaller than that party's share of the parliamentary seats controlled by the government (Browne and Franklin 1973; Budge and Keman 1990, ch. 4; Laver and Schofield 1990, ch. 6; Schofield and Laver 1985). The disadvantage that the DC met was only slightly less pronounced for shares of undersecretary posts. Intervals of one-party government thus compensated the DC for disproportionate shares of portfolios surrendered to allies at other times (cf. Marradi 1982).[6]

Part C of Table 5.3 shows average numbers of offices. In these terms, the

TABLE 5.3.

Office Payoffs (Ministers and Undersecretaries) by Type of Government, 1946–92

Office Payoffs	One-Party Governments (n = 16)	All Coalitions (n = 36)	Coalitions Including PSI (n = 22)	1976–92 Coalitions Including PSI (n = 11)
A. Mean percentage share of all Ministers[a]				
DC	94.4	61.0	55.3	52.1
Non-DC[b]	5.6	39.0	44.7	47.9
Mean total number of ministers	22	25	27	29
Mean percentage share of all undersecretaries[a]				
DC	99.1	64.2	55.3	54.2
Non-DC[b]	0.9	35.8	44.7	45.8
Mean total number of undersecretaries	36	47	53	60
B. Mean ratios[c] of cabinet post shares to government seat shares[d] for DC				
Ministers	.94	.82	.83	.78
Undersecretaries	.99	.85	.83	.81
C. Mean number of posts held by DC				
Ministers	20	15	15	15
Undersecretaries	36	29	29	33

SOURCE: Calculations based on portfolio data in Petracca 1980 and *Corriere della Sera*, various issues, and seat data in Table 5.1.

[a] Entries are mean percentage shares for all governments of the type listed at the head of each column.

[b] Includes non-party experts and politicians from parties other than the DC.

[c] Entries are mean ratios for all governments of the type listed at the head of each column.

[d] Government seat share is defined as a party's percentage share of the seats in the Chamber that are controlled by all governing parties.

DC spent less to construct coalitions than might be expected—and much less than office-driven theory would predict. On average, it cost Italy's core party *nothing* in number of cabinet slots to include the PSI in a coalition, even when the PSI was pivotal. Indeed, DC undersecretaries were *more* numerous in coalitions containing a pivotal PSI than in other types of coalitions.

As Figure 5.1 reveals, portfolio inflation was the cost-management strategy that produced these outcomes. Offices, especially undersecretary-ships, were like balloons, inflated when needs arose. The number of allies changed, but the number of Christian Democrats in government remained remarkably stable.

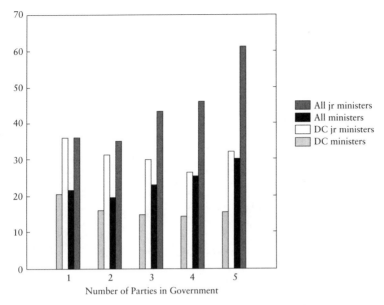

FIGURE 5.1. Office Payoffs, by Number of Parties in Italian Government, 1946–92 (Means)

The distinction between ministers and undersecretaries is worth weighing. As coalitions expanded from two parties to three, four, and then five parties, the number of ministers was pumped up steadily, the number of undersecretaries rather unevenly. The largest boosts in undersecretaries separated two- from three-party coalitions and four- from five-party coalitions. Why? None of Italy's two-party coalitions included the PSI, and all five-party coalitions governed when the PSI was pivotal. The competition for office between the DC and the PSI led to mutual accommodation and thus drove portfolio inflation.

As Figure 5.2 plots, the steepest increases in ministerial and undersecretary posts occurred when the PSI reentered government after a sojourn in the opposition (the early 1960s, when center–left coalitions were prepared and implemented, and the early 1980s, when five-party coalitions were instituted). Those hikes enabled the DC to protect or even add to its portfolios. Why have undersecretaryships been more elastic balloons than senior cabinet posts? Undersecretaries are arguably less visible to voters and imply a less permanent, more flexible, commitment of resources.[7] Moreover, in a long-standing "informal division of ministerial labour, [an undersecretary] is left free to distribute the patronage of the ministry in his constituency" (Allum 1973, 90). The secret ballot made it "necessary . . . to satisfy the

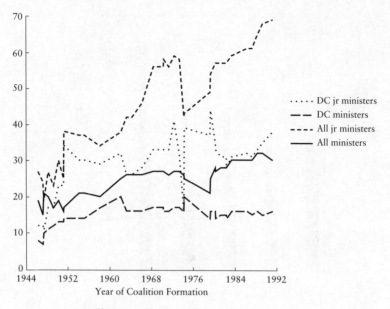

FIGURE 5.2. Office Payoffs in Italian Coalitions, 1946–92

greatest possible number of deputies," and coalition builders used under-secretary posts as a convenient currency with which to gratify deputies and buy loyalty (Dogan 1984, 164; cf. Venditti 1981). Since parliamentary rules require that members of government—both ministers and undersecre-taries—step down from parliamentary committees (Nocifero and Valdini 1992, 70), an increase in cabinet posts has the advantage of enlarging ac-cess to committee positions for parliamentarians without cabinet respon-sibilities. Members of multiple committees, as indicated earlier, are well equipped to pipe narrow benefits to clienteles.

Before exploring the impact of legislative rules on policy costs, I should confront a question posed by this manipulation of office rewards: Is the ag-gregate value of the cabinet more aptly viewed as fixed or variable? If politi-cians regard the value of the cabinet as fixed (so that creating new posts di-lutes the worth of old ones), then they should express their counts of offices in percentage terms. If they see the value as variable, then their counts should in some way convey increases in cabinet value with new portfolios. Published notes from coalition bargaining—those discussed in Chapter 4—show that Italian politicians focus on *both* cabinet shares and the value added by new posts. Especially revealing is a memorandum from the early 1970s (Venditti 1981, appendix A, exhibit 8). Its multiple columns report, for scenarios involving totals of thirty-three, forty-eight, fifty-one, and fifty-

seven posts, the number of undersecretaryships that hypothetical governments would have owed each DC faction if the allotment of offices had mir-
rored the shares of seats held by factions on the DC National Council. With
forty-eight DC undersecretaries, one faction would have been able to add to
its undersecretaries (the faction headed by Paolo Emilio Taviani, which
would have obtained five, as opposed to two in Rumor III of 1970) without
subtracting posts from several factions overrepresented in Rumor III. This
example suggests that the use of two yardsticks is not so much inconsistent
as expedient: The authors of the memorandum were major figures in the
Taviani faction.[8]

The Policy Costs of Building Coalitions

It stands to reason that the more the program of a coalition government departs from the most-preferred policies of one of its constituent parties, the greater the policy sacrifice the coalition has imposed on that party.
Accordingly, to assess the policy costs and benefits of assembling coalitions
in Italy, I estimate the distance between party ideals and government an-
nouncements of policy. I locate party positions by turning to content analyses of parties' policy declarations at election time. The same scheme used to
code parties' election manifestos has also guided the content analysis of authoritative policy documents issued by governments just before or just after
their inauguration (Laver and Budge 1992, reanalyzing and extending data
in Budge, Robertson, and Hearl 1987).[9] In such analyses, for instance, the
themes sounded by Christian Democracy in its 1948 electoral campaign
earned a score of +10 on a left–right scale ranging from –100 (extreme left)
to +100 (extreme right). The official program of the first executive installed
after the April 1948 elections, a DC-PSDI-PRI-PLI coalition headed by
Alcide De Gasperi, ranked a +4 on the same 200-point left–right scale. The
disparity between DC policy and government policy in this case amounted
to 6 points (Mastropaolo and Slater 1992, 320).

De Gasperi's 1948 coalition was not unusual. Table 5.4 lists the mean absolute distance between party and government positions in Italy, for all governing parties and all cabinets for which left–right scalings of policy pronouncements are available.[10] Between 1948 and 1983, one-party cabinets
framed programs that, on average, lay 10 points away from the DC's left–
right preferences. The mean difference between coalition policies and DC
proclivities was smaller: 6.2 points. The contrast in means is statistically significant, according to the two-sample separate variances t test.

Ordinarily, then, the Christian Democrats made fewer policy concessions
to seal agreements on coalitions as opposed to one-party cabinets. This result

TABLE 5.4.

Mean Absolute Distance on Left–Right Spectrum Between Party and Government Positions, by Party and Party Status in Government, 1948–83

	DC	PSI	PSDI	PRI	PLI
One-party government	10.0 ($n = 14$)	NA	NA	NA	NA
Coalition government	6.2 ($n = 24$)*	15.2 ($n = 13$)	9.9 ($n = 21$)	10.8 ($n = 18$)	5.4 ($n = 8$)
Opposition	NA	13.5 ($n = 25$)	14.1 ($n = 17$)	10.5 ($n = 20$)	14.2 ($n = 30$)**

SOURCE: Calculations based on measures of party and government positions in Mastropaolo and Slater 1992 and on government status data in Table 4.2.

NOTE: Entries are mean absolute distances on a 200 point left–right scale between party positions and government positions, for each party listed. For the DC, t tests compare the means of two groups of governments including the DC: one-party cabinets and coalitions. For parties other than the DC, t tests compare the means for governments including, and those excluding, the party in question. Numbers of applicable governments are in parentheses. NA, Not applicable. Party abbreviations are defined in the text and in Appendix A.

* $p < .05$. ** $p < .01$ (separate variances t tests).

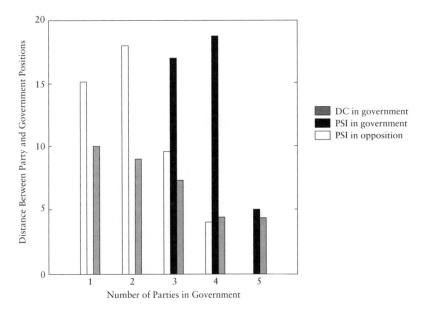

FIGURE 5.3. Distance on Left–Right Spectrum Between Party and Government Positions, by Party and Number of Parties in Italian Government, 1948–83 (Means)

might seem surprising. Recall, however, that Italian executives must marshal a legislative majority at investiture in order to survive. Recall, too, that the DC won a majority of Chamber seats only once, in 1948. Under those constraints, when the DC prepared to rule alone, it crafted programs deviating from its ideals and designed to appeal to potential supporters. The DC could not be certain of the benevolence of habitual allies temporarily excluded from power, and thus treated policy promises as a substitute for the office goods it otherwise would have shared. On the other hand, the DC could expect that coalition partners would very likely endorse their own incumbency, and so pulled coalition programs relatively close to DC predilections. Indeed, as Figure 5.3 depicts, the distance between government programs and DC preferences narrowed, on average, as the number of governing parties rose from one to two, three, and then four. Those differences in means do not attain statistical significance. The fact remains that, for Italy's core party, adding allies did *not* mean acquiescing to higher policy costs.

Investigation of the distance between coalition programs and junior partners' preferences yields further evidence of the DC's dominance of the policy-making process. Compare the bottom two rows of Table 5.4. "Save for the Liberals, and to a [much] lesser extent for the Social Democrats, government participation seems to make little difference to [the] policy payoffs" accruing to the DC's allies, as the original analysts of these policy measures observe (Mastropaolo and Slater 1992, 326). Between 1948 and 1983, the PLI proved to be the only party among the DC's allies that derived significant policy benefits from incumbency, and the PLI was also the one that least often joined governing coalitions.

Even when the PSI held pivotal status, the Christian Democrats preserved their influence on coalition programs. Figure 5.3 illustrates that the policies announced by five-party coalitions came rather close to Socialist ideals. As stressed above, all five-party coalitions ruled when the PSI was pivotal. What is more, the pivotal PSI shaped policy in and out of government. When all available governments are included in the analysis, regardless of party composition, the distance between government programs and PSI proclivities averages 16.8 points on the left–right spectrum between 1948 and 1976, and only 5.1 points between 1976 and 1983. This difference in means is statistically significant.[11] And this difference is just what spatial theories of voting would predict: Since the "pivotal role . . . is exercised *in the legislature*, not the executive . . . , *it does not matter whether or not the pivotal party is in government*. Even if it is in opposition, the fate of the government remains in its hands" (Laver and Schofield 1990, 88, emphasis in original). In spite of the sway of the PSI, the mean disparity between government programs and DC priorities was 7.8 points between 1976 and 1983, virtually the same as it was between 1948 and 1976 (7.5 points). To judge from the content of party manifestos and government documents, the pivotal PSI secured policy benefits at no cost to the DC. These data are consistent with, and attest to, the DC's long-standing position at the core of the Italian policy space.

It bears repeating that these data are based on statements of intention, not records of achievement. Chapter 4 showed that Italian governments, at investiture, have couched their statements of intention in ambiguous and high-flown language. Moreover, as Marradi (1982, 60) notes, "the DC is aware that it can accede to many of its partners' requests in the program drafting stage, since it retains an almost absolute control upon which policy measures to take, which to block, and which to subvert." Hence, it is worthwhile to consider alternative evidence on the policy payoffs received by governing parties in Italy.

Relevant evidence can be gathered from two groups of sources: quantitative analyses of variations in public spending and taxation (e.g., Boix 1997; Budge and Keman 1990, ch. 5; Cameron 1978; Hicks and Swank 1992) and qualitative case studies of policy making (e.g., Bottiglieri 1984; Dente 1990; Lange and Regini 1987; Regini and Regonini 1981; Salvati 1980, 1985). In the first group, an authoritative fifteen-nation comparison finds that "parties of the left do spend a little more than parties of the right," although "the difference [in spending levels] . . . emerges only for majority governments whose party composition remains unchanged over a number of years" (Blais, Blake, and Dion 1993, 40, covering the 1960–87 period). A revised analysis of annual changes in spending amends the result: Both minority and majority governments of the left increase spending a little more than governments of the right. Again, continuity in office counts, since "that small impact means a big difference over the long haul" (Blais, Blake, and Dion 1996, 517, covering 1962–91 and eighteen nations). Focusing specifically on Italy, another research team concludes that "changes in [the DC's] coalition partners produced little discernible effect on patterns in public finances" (Gallagher, Laver, and Mair 1995, 351, drawing on Klingemann, Hofferbert, and Budge 1994).[12] Given inertia in expenditures, the DC's longevity in power, and frequent shifts within the constellation of junior allies, it is not surprising that those shifts left largely intact the DC's influence on the financial resources deployed and raised by the state.

Qualitative studies send a similar message about the DC's imprint on government policy. To be sure, there are spectacular exceptions to the rule that enacted policies were aligned with DC preferences. The passage of divorce legislation in 1970 and the failure of the effort to repeal it in 1974 come immediately to mind (Kogan 1981, chs. 5, 7). Moreover, scholars concur that turning points in Italian policy initiatives have coincided with changes in coalition formulae. In particular, it is accepted wisdom that the reforms proposed by the center–left coalitions stood out as "the most ambitious . . . of the postwar period" (Pasquino 1995a, 72; Tarrow 1990). Even more important, however, much of the blueprint for policy created by the center–left was not implemented; the DC promised more reforms to the Socialists than it delivered (see, among many others, Ferrera 1989; Pasquino 1987b; Salvati 1981). And inaction and delay testified to the DC's influence just as much as action did. For instance, one common interpretation of Italy's huge public deficits from the 1970s through the early 1990s is that the DC protected its constituencies and successfully resisted any attempt to combat tax evasion and introduce an effective system of taxation (Dente 1991; Salvati 1985). Not by chance, the Italian record figured prominently in research that reached the judgment that "the weightiest political consequence of long-term dominance lies in the ability of the dominant party to shape, over time, the nation's nexus of public policies, its rules of political conflict, and the benefits and burdens imposed on different socioeconomic sectors of the society" (Pempel 1990, 334).

In sum, Christian Democracy dominated but did not dictate government policy. When the DC anchored coalitions instead of ruling alone, it sacrificed little on policy, relinquished few offices, and curbed electoral losses. To what extent did the DC and its allies manage to defray the costs of breaking coalitions? In order to detect the impact of spatial and institutional conditions on those costs, I again disaggregate by party and track trends over time. I also identify which parties were responsible for cabinet collapses.[13]

The Electoral Costs of Destroying Governments

As before, I measure electoral costs as mean shifts in shares of the vote between pairs of consecutive elections. My concern now is to ascertain how a party fares at the polls after it has contributed to the fall of most of the governments formed in the span between two elections. Of course, factors other than a party's role in provoking or preventing cabinet dissolutions—such as levels of inflation and unemployment—can bring voters to penalize or reward incumbent parties (e.g., Eulau and Lewis-Beck 1985; Lewis-Beck 1988; Powell and Whitten 1993). I simply wish to observe whether parties that have caused cabinet failures encounter electoral punishment.

Until 1992, the Christian Democrats and Socialists benefited electorally from knocking down governments. Yet, as Table 5.5 shows, distinctions separated the DC and PSI in this regard.[14] The DC gained at the polls when it helped to upset most of the cabinets between two successive elections (advancing 0.3 percent, on average), whereas the PSI contained its electoral losses when it toppled governments (slipping only 0.03 percent, on average). From 1976 to 1992, when the PSI held pivotal status, it won votes despite, or due to, its responsibility for terminating every government launched after 1974. The DC, in contrast, suffered for its role in government falls after 1976.

The electoral payoffs for demolishing governments, like those for erecting governments, have reflected the segmentation of the electorate and the array of parties in policy space. For decades, the DC undid governments with impunity, since loyal subcultural voters long dominated the DC electorate, and exchange voters long expected a continuing flow of spoils from the large, centrally located DC.[15] Cabinet dissolutions cost the DC votes after 1976 because, as noted earlier, subcultural voting waned, opinion voting increased, the pivotal PSI put up stiffer competition for spoils, and ideological justifications for delegitimating opponents had less force.

After 1976, furthermore, responsibility for breakups became more of an electoral liability for the PSDI and PRI and more of an electoral advantage for the PSI. Some voters seem to have defected in response to perceived disruptions of policy (opinion voters prevalent within the PRI electorate), others in response to potential complications in patronage (the PSDI's exchange voters). Still other voters rewarded the pivotal PSI for its capacity to

TABLE 5.5.
Electoral Gain or Loss, by Party and Responsibility for Government Collapse, 1948–92

Dominant Role in Collapses Between Elections	DC	PSI	PSDI	PRI	PLI
Responsible	+0.30(n = 10)	-0.03(n = 8)	-0.50(n = 4)	-0.10(n = 4)	-0.80(n = 1)
Not responsible	-8.40(n = 1)	-1.73(n = 3)	-0.40(n = 7)	+0.06(n = 7)	-0.32(n = 10)
Responsible 1976–92	-2.25(n = 4)	+1.00(n = 4)	-1.10(n = 1)	-0.75(n = 2)	-0.80(n = 1)

SOURCE: Calculations based on coding of information in *Keesing's Contemporary Archives* and electoral data in Table 5.1.

NOTE: Entries are mean changes in parties' percentage share of the vote between pairs of consecutive elections to the Chamber of Deputies. Numbers of applicable interelectoral periods are in parentheses. The baseline year is 1946 for all parties except the PSDI, which first contested elections in 1948. Dominant role is coded as whatever role (responsible or not responsible for collapse) was most frequent between two successive elections. Party abbreviations are defined in the text and in Appendix A.

influence policy and tap spoils, a capacity exhibited and exploited in government falls (cf. Mannheimer and Sani 1987, 167–82). The rightmost PLI was exposed to relatively severe electoral punishment for dismantling cabinets, which helps to explain why it risked such punishment rarely.

On the whole, though, these differences across parties were small. No party courted electoral disaster when it extinguished a government.

The Office Costs of Destroying Governments

As typically measured, the office price of ending governments is negligible in Italy. As Table 5.6 displays, the ratio of the DC's share of cabinet ministers to its share of the government's parliamentary delegation averaged 0.83 when the DC had contributed to the demise of the preceding cabinet. This figure diverged hardly at all from the mean weighted share of ministerial posts (0.89) that the DC acquired when the party had done nothing to undermine the previous executive.

More broadly, all five governing parties received a weighted share of senior cabinet posts that stayed roughly steady, on average, whether or not they had overthrown the preceding government. The same statement holds true for weighted shares of undersecretary posts. Not a single pair of ratios in the top two rows of Table 5.6 evinces a statistically significant difference.

This finding runs counter to conventional assumptions about the office costs of breakups. It becomes even more striking when average numbers are considered. The total of cabinet posts varied little according to whether or not the PSDI, PRI, or PLI had pulled down the prior government. But a government's ministers and undersecretaries, on average, were significantly *more* numerous after the Socialists had sabotaged, as compared to sustained, its predecessor. With the PSI's percentage of offices unaltered and the number of all offices up, more Socialists filled cabinet slots. Office *benefits* went to the PSI after it had eliminated a government, above all when the PSI was pivotal. Along similar lines, but only from 1976 to 1992, a constant share and a significantly larger total of offices meant that more Christian Democrats attained cabinet positions after the DC had toppled a government. In this sense, too, the competition between the DC and PSI drove portfolio inflation.

The Policy Costs of Destroying Governments

One basic assumption widespread in the study of political parties—so widespread, indeed, that it can easily go unremarked—is that member-

TABLE 5.6.
Office Payoffs, by Party and Responsibility for Government Collapse, 1946–92

| | Was Party Responsible for Collapse at Time t − 1? | | | | | | | | | |
| | DC | | PSI | | PSDI | | PRI | | PLI | |
Offices at t	No	Yes	No	Yes	No	Yes	No	Yes	No	Yes
RATIOS OF CABINET POST SHARES TO GOVERNMENT SEAT SHARES[a] (MEANS)										
Party ministers	0.89	0.83	1.30	1.23	1.84	1.84	3.00	2.25	2.09	2.12
Party undersecretaries	0.91	0.89	1.39	1.34	1.70	1.53	1.85	1.55	2.16	1.85
Number of cabinets	21	30	3	18	21	8	17	8	12	4
NUMBER OF POSTS (MEANS)										
All ministers	23	24	21	25**	24	23	23	25	24	24
All undersecretaries	42	45	35	49**	44	44	41	48	44	44
Number of cabinets	21	30	20	31	33	18	35	16	43	8
NUMBER OF POSTS 1976–92 (MEANS)										
All ministers	26	30*	NA	27	27	30	28	26	27	28
All undersecretaries	53	62*	NA	56	55	61	55	56	55	59
Number of cabinets	5	11	0	16	14	2	11	5	11	3

SOURCE: Calculations based on portfolio data in Petracca 1980; *Corriere della Sera*, various issues; and seat data in Table 5.1 and coding of information in *Keesing's Contemporary Archives*.

NOTE: Means are computed, party by party, for two groups of cabinets: those whose predecessor was a cabinet the party helped to topple and those whose predecessor fell for reasons other than the party's withdrawal of support. The t tests compare the means of the two groups (i.e., for each party, entries in the *yes* and *no* columns). Party abbreviations are defined in the text and in Appendix A.

[a] Government seat share is defined as a party's share of the Chamber seats controlled by all governing parties.

*p < .05; **p < .001 (separate variances t tests).

ship in government offers parties special opportunities to influence policy (cf. Strøm 1990b, 42–44). Table 5.7 examines policy benefits at risk by designating the governing status of parties that have been behind government falls. It shows the policy payoffs by reporting how often parties that bring about one government's demise participate in the next government and/or produce a change in incumbent parties.[16] Table 5.7 illustrates the DC's unerring ability to regain office after an exit. Yet three similarities across Italian governing parties are noteworthy. First, they have tended to overturn cabinets only when assigned long-term governing roles in a coalition formula. This pattern applied even to the leftmost PSI, excluded from the centrist formula, and the rightmost PLI, excluded from center–left coalitions. As argued, the security and stability of coalition formulae freed the component parties to destabilize cabinets. Second, parties responsible for cabinet collapses rather often ruled in successor governments, especially after 1976, when the PSI was pivotal.[17] Finally, parties responsible for breakups more often than not triggered a change in government composition. By this criterion, the policy consequences of rupturing coalitions or one-party cabinets, before or after the PSI became pivotal, are roughly alike.

From 1976 to 1992, the PSI decided governments' fates with astonishing frequency. At the same time, the contest between the DC and the pivotal PSI altered the ties between the executive and the legislature. Cabinets met increased difficulties in relying on parliamentary majorities. As one sign of those difficulties, the first Italian government with a Socialist premier—Craxi I, a surplus coalition—saw defectors reduce its support to a minority fully 163 times during its tenure in office from August 1983 to June 1986 (Di Scala 1988, 224). As a result of such challenges, executive decrees became much more common after 1976 (Della Sala 1987, 39; Motta 1985, 265; Nocifero and Valdini 1992, 19). These changes generated reactions in turn. Legislation in August 1988 limited the conditions under which executive decrees could be issued, and in October 1988 the Chamber of Deputies radically circumscribed use of the secret ballot (Barrera 1989). The Italian Parliament approved additional institutional reforms in the 1990s, as discussed later.

To what degree did a party's moves to upset one government impair its ability to shape the policies promoted by the next government?[18] To address this question, Table 5.8 analyzes the scores featured in Table 5.4, which are derived from the coding of party manifestos and government programs and are bounded by values of −100 (extreme left) and +100 (extreme right). Table 5.8 reveals that the disparity between government programs and DC ideals averaged 7.8 points when the DC had overthrown the previous executive. That number is statistically indistinguishable from the corresponding mean (7.3 points) when the failure of the preceding cabinet could not be attributed to the DC's conduct.

TABLE 5.7.

Party Status in Government and Coalition Formula, and Government Composition,
at and After Government Collapses, by Party Responsible for Government Collapse, 1946–92

	Party Responsible for Collapse at Time $t-1$					
	DC	PSI	PSDI	PRI	PLI
	ALL COLLAPSES 1946–92					
Status in government at $t-1$ (%)					
In government	100.0	62.5	66.7	25.0	25.0
Out of government	0	37.5	33.3	75.0	75.0
Status in coalition formula at $t-1$ (%)					
In coalition formula	100.0	84.4	100.0	87.5	87.5
Out of coalition formula	0	15.6	0	12.5	12.5
Status in government at t (%)					
In government	100.0	59.4	50.0	50.0	50.0
Out of government	0	40.6	50.0	50.0	50.0
Government composition at t (%)					
Parties change after fall	58.1	68.8	72.2	56.3	50.0
Parties same as before fall	41.9	31.2	27.8	43.8	50.0
Number of collapses	31	32	18	16	8

(Continued on next page)

TABLE 5.7. (*Continued*)

	Party Responsible for Collapse at Time *t* – 1				
	DC	PSI	PSDI	PRI	PLI
COALITION COLLAPSES 1946–92					
Status in government at t (%)					
In government	100.0	68.2	45.5	55.6	66.7
Out of government	0	31.8	54.5	44.4	33.3
Government composition at t (%)					
Parties change after fall	50.0	68.2	72.7	66.7	66.7
Parties same as before fall	50.0	31.8	27.3	33.3	33.3
Number of coalition collapses	18	22	11	9	3
ALL COLLAPSES 1976–92					
Status in government at t (%)					
In government	100.0	75.0	100.0	80.0	100.0
Out of government	0	25.0	0	20.0	0
Government composition at t (%)					
Parties change after fall	54.5	62.5	50.0	60.0	66.7
Parties same as before fall	45.5	37.5	50.0	40.0	33.3
Number of collapses 1976–92	11	16	2	5	3

SOURCE: Calculations based on coding of information in *Keesing's Contemporary Archives* and government status data in Table 4.2.

NOTE: Entries are the percentage of cases in which a party (or government) had the designated status. A *coalition formula* refers to a relatively durable coalition design (e.g., the centrist formula, composed of the DC, PSDI, PRI, and PLI, lasted from 1947 to 1963); a party included in a formula need not serve in *every* cabinet ruling under the formula (e.g., the PLI served in five of the seventeen cabinets formed under centrism, as Table 4.2 details). Parties are coded as included in coalition formulae during the following periods: DC 1946–92; PSI 1946–47, 1963–76, 1979–92; PSDI 1947–76, 1979–92; PRI 1947–76, 1979–92; PLI 1947–63, 1979–92. Party abbreviations are defined in the text and in Appendix A.

TABLE 5.8.

Mean Absolute Distance on Left–Right Spectrum Between Party and Government Positions, by Party, Party Status in Government, and Responsibility for Government Collapse, 1948–83

			Was Party Responsible for Collapse at Time $t - 1$?							
	DC		PSI		PSDI		PRI		PLI	
Status in Government at t	*No*	*Yes*	*No*	*Yes*	*No*	*Yes*	*No*	*Yes*	*No*	*Yes*
In government	7.3	7.8	18.5	14.5	10.7	7.8	13.5	5.3	5.8	4.0
Out of government	NA	NA	15.4	11.0	17.9	8.7	11.5	8.7	11.5	31.8*
Number of cabinets	15	23	16	22	25	13	25	13	33	6

SOURCE: Calculations based on measures of party and government positions in Mastropaolo and Slater 1992, government status data in Table 4-2, and coding of information in *Keesing's Contemporary Archives.*

NOTE: Means are computed for two groups of cabinets: those whose predecessor was a cabinet the party helped to topple and those whose predecessor fell for reasons other than the party's withdrawal of support. The *t* tests compare the means of the two groups (i.e., for each party, entries in the *yes* and *no* columns.) NA, Not applicable. Party abbreviations are defined in the text and in Appendix A.

*p=.05 (separate variances *t* test).

For parties other than the DC, the table controls for membership in, and exclusion from, incoming governments. In all instances but one, the mean discrepancy between party and government positions was slightly smaller when the party had toppled, rather than tolerated, the outgoing government. The exception involves the rightmost of the DC's junior partners. After the Liberals had ruined one cabinet and stayed out of the next, the new premier announced policies that, on average, lay relatively far away from the PLI's preferences. Between 1948 and 1983, the PLI was the only party among the DC's habitual allies to suffer significant and adverse policy consequences from hastening government falls. This finding is the mirror image of one cited earlier: The PLI, alone among the DC's allies, derived significant policy benefits from incumbency.

Again, Italian governments at investiture have been obliged to muster the support of a parliamentary majority. From 1946 to 1992, in election after election, the same party won the largest share of Chamber and Senate seats. The same parties remained inside the circle of legitimate contenders for cabinet posts, and the same parties (with two partial exceptions) recurred in successive parliamentary majorities. (The PSI opposed the inauguration of centrist governments, and the PLI, of center–left governments.) The authors of government programs had cause to care more about which parties played continuing roles in making governments than about which party moved to break one government or another. This discussion leads naturally to the next topic: negotiations over new governments.

The Costs of Bargaining over Coalitions

Time is the obvious surrogate for the cost of bargaining a government into being. Of course, politicians do not devote every minute to bargaining during the interregnum between governments. Nonetheless, it is reasonable to presume that a prime minister who enters office ten weeks after the resignation of his or her predecessor has expended more energy in negotiations than has a prime minister whose installation occurs only ten days after the fall of the preceding government.[19] Coalition analysts and country specialists routinely point to long interregna as signs of bargaining complexity (e.g., King et al., 1990; Laver and Schofield 1990; on Italy, Pridham 1988, ch. 6; on the Netherlands, Gladdish 1991; on Belgium, Timmermans 1994). Thus, the measure for bargaining costs I adopt—save for one class of exceptions—is the number of days separating the demise of a government and the rise of its successor. I make the exceptions when parliamentary elections intervene: For governments launched after an election, I count the time from election day to the announcement of a cabinet. This decision rule reflects the assumption that parties dedicate themselves to campaigning during election campaigns, and that they wait until the electorate has rendered its verdict and redistributed parliamentary seats before commencing negotiations over a new government.[20]

As indexed by time, the bargaining costs of launching Italian governments are high. Between 1946 and 1992, on average, Italian politicians spent twenty-nine days in negotiating over new governments, substantially longer than politicians in most other parliamentary democracies (for detailed cross-national comparisons, see Chapter 7; see Strøm 1990b, 144, 67 for similar findings in a fifteen-nation study). Despite the invention of devices to simplify bargaining, government crises in Italy have become more protracted during the postwar period. To be more specific, between the 1946 and 1976 elections, the average crisis lasted twenty-five days; the mean crisis duration was thirty-eight days between 1976 and 1992, when the DC faced a pivotal PSI (calculated from data in *Keesing's Contemporary Archives*). This difference in means is statistically significant.[21]

Table 5.9 draws more finely grained comparisons, across time and across types of governments. Between 1947 and 1963, when the centrist formula applied, coalitions were on average constituted more quickly than one-party cabinets. The same held true when the center–left and five-party formulae were followed (1963–76 and 1979–92, respectively). Between 1976 and 1979, when the PCI belonged to the legislative coalitions backing minority executives, both one-party and multiparty governments on average took over six weeks to emerge. With the exception of national solidarity, then, the formulae seem to have facilitated agreement on coalitions. The relatively long gestation of one-party cabinets squares with the idea, stressed in Chapter 4, that they served as second-best solutions to government crises, which were accepted after protocoalitions had disintegrated. That long gestation sheds further light on the motivations for the DC's policy concessions on one-party cabinets, treated earlier.

An indirect measure of the bargaining cost of toppling a government is the number of days required to erect its replacement. (No reliable data are available on time expended in coordinating moves to destroy governments.[22] Absent that direct measure, I turn to the leading value of crisis duration, and I omit cases before parliamentary elections on the assumption that the crises that ensue are dominated and defined by the electoral results.) Between 1947 and 1963, falls of one-party cabinets ushered in crises lasting 15 days on average, and falls of coalitions, crises lasting 11.4 days. Under the center–left formula, too, between 1963 and 1976, DC-only executives were terminated at slightly greater cost than were coalitions. It is possible to compare one-party and multiparty governments across, but not within, three other periods. In 1946 and 1947, before any coalition formula

TABLE 5.9.

Duration of Government Crises, by Period and Type of Government, 1946–92

	1946–47	1947–63	1963–76	1976–79	1979–92	1946–92
Days before formation of government g						
One-party cabinet	NA	20.0($n = 8$)	38.0($n = 5$)	46.5($n = 2$)	45.0($n = 1$)	30.5($n = 16$)
Coalition	32.0($n = 2$)	15.4($n = 10$)	29.5($n = 11$)	48.0($n = 1$)	35.4($n = 12$)	28.2($n = 36$)
Days between fall of government g and formation of government $g + 1$						
One-party cabinet	NA	15.0($n = 7$)	33.3($n = 3$)	51.0($n = 2$)	NA	25.6($n = 12$)
Coalition	20.5($n = 2$)	11.4($n = 7$)	28.5($n = 10$)	NA	32.5($n = 10$)	25.2($n = 29$)

SOURCE: Calculations based on government data in Table 4.2 and information on government crises in *Keesing's Contemporary Archives*, various issues.

NOTE: Entries in the first part of the table are the mean number of days between the fall of one government (or, when elections intervene, between election day) and the rise of another government. Entries in the second part of the table are means of the leading values of crisis duration; government falls leading to parliamentary elections are omitted. Numbers of applicable cabinets are in parentheses. NA, Not applicable.

had solidified, the resignation of DC-PSI-PCI governments opened crises of roughly three weeks. More time was needed to identify the successors to ruptured coalitions when the five-party formula was the rule (1979–92), and much more time was consumed in replacing failed one-party cabinets between 1976 and 1979. On the whole, Italian parties have *not* paid a uniformly higher price to negotiate the sequels to coalitions as opposed to one-party governments.

From 1946 to 1992, the interregna between Italian governments stretched to four years and forty-four days in all. Time invested in bargaining should also be evaluated for what it returns. In Italy, the office costs of building cabinets, even surplus coalitions, were low. The acquisition of governing allies brought policy closer to, not further away from, the DC's ideals. The recurrence of coalitions helped to limit the electoral costs of incumbency. Some parties under some conditions achieved office benefits from undoing governments. By the light of party platforms and government programs, a party's betrayal of a government did little damage to its influence over policy. Most voters appeared to be "indulgent [and] . . . rapidly forgetful" about cabinet collapses (a former deputy quoted in *Corriere della Sera*, June 28, 1986).

In such a system, as Andreotti summarized in a noted saying, "power wears out those without it" (*il potere logora chi non ce l'ha*), and power reinforces the powerful. To judge from events since the 1992 elections, that Italy no longer exists. The roots of the transformation lie in the two classes of exogenous explanatory factors highlighted here, which in turn have affected the possibilities for endogenous management of the costs of coalition. I now take up evidence bearing out this claim.

Coalition Politics in Italy Since 1992

The April 1992 parliamentary elections marked a profound shift in spatial and institutional conditions in Italy. The Lombard/Northern League and the Rete (anti-Mafia Network) recast the dimensions of party competition and campaigned against patronage and corruption. The DC's support dipped below 30 percent, which meant that the DC no longer qualified as a core party (Schofield 1993). The 1992 elections were the first national elections held after the secret ballot was restricted in Parliament, the single preference vote introduced, and the PCI transformed into the Democratic Party of the Left (Partito Democratico della Sinistra, PDS). According to my argument, some change in the costs of coalition and cost-reduction strategies should have ensued.[23]

The first postelection coalition joined the same four parties that governed on election eve. But the allies were led by Italy's second Socialist premier, their coalition had minimal winning size, and they divided among them a total of sixty portfolios. The preelection coalition contained ninety-nine portfolios overall. The second postelection government was headed by Italy's first non-party premier, Carlo Azeglio Ciampi, who almost succeeded in allying with the PDS, Greens, and PRI; last-minute disagreements left him with a four-party minimal winning coalition, a new edition of its predecessor that allocated an unprecedented share of portfolios (twelve out of sixty-two) to non-party experts.[24] In August 1993, pressured by referendum results and Ciampi's exhortations, Parliament passed new electoral laws, which combine plurality and proportional rules for Chamber and Senate elections and impose a threshold of 4 percent for representation in the Chamber.

Held under the new laws, the March 1994 elections produced even more sweeping change: the end of fifty years of uninterrupted DC incumbency. Public outrage at widespread corruption inflicted devastating losses on the Popular Party (Partito Popolare Italiano [PPI], as the DC renamed itself in January 1994) and the PSI. Undone by corruption, the PLI and PSDI did not even contest the elections.[25] In May 1994, media magnate Silvio Berlusconi became premier. His government embraced Forza Italia ("Go Italy!"), the movement he founded in early 1994; the Northern League; the National Alliance, the renamed MSI; and the Centrist Union (Unione di Centro, UDC) and the Christian Democratic Center (Centro Cristiano Democratico, CCD, a right-wing splinter from the DC), which were Forza Italia's electoral allies in some constituencies. The coalition contained sixty-four portfolios and by one standard had minimal winning size.[26] Berlusconi resigned in December 1994 when the Northern League withdrew.[27]

In January 1995, economist Lamberto Dini became Italy's second non-party premier, guiding a cabinet made up of fifty-five ministers and undersecretaries. For the first time in postwar Italy, not a single member of Parliament was included in the executive. The Dini government passed its votes of investiture thanks to support from the PDS, and endured until January 1996, a termination date "agreed [on] at the time of its establishment" (Ignazi 1997, 421). After Dini resigned and another non-party formateur failed to launch a new government, early elections were called.

The April 1996 parliamentary elections accelerated the pace of change in Italian politics.[28] As Table 5.10 confirms, the units entering electoral competition in 1996 differed radically from those that dominated campaigns between 1946 and 1992. Whereas the 1994 elections featured four alliances, two alliances were opposed in 1996: the Olive Tree (Ulivo), which arched from the center to the left (and to the extreme left, if the electoral cooperation of Communist Refoundation [Rifondazione Comunista, RC] is considered, even though the RC stopped short of official membership in the al-

TABLE 5.10.
Italian Electoral Results, 1994 and 1996:
Votes and Seats Won in Elections to the Chamber of Deputies

	1994		1996	
	Percentage of Votes[a]	*Number of Seats*[b]	*Percentage of Votes*[a]	*Number of Seats*[b]
Communist Refoundation	6.0	39	8.6	35[c]
Network	1.9	6	—	—
Greens	2.7	11	2.3	*16*
PDS	20.4	109	21.1	*171*
Socialists	2.2	14	—	—
Democratic Alliance	1.2	18	—	—
	(Total seats for Progressives = 213)			
Segni Pact	4.6	13	—	—
PPI	11.1	33	with Prodi	
For Prodi (PPI, SVP, PRI, UD)	—	—	6.8	75
Dini List	—	—	4.3	26
	(Total seats for Pact for Italy = 46)		(Total seats for Olive Tree = 323[c])	
Northern League	8.4	117	10.1	59
Pannella List	3.5	0	1.9	0
Forza Italia	21.0	99	21.0	123
CCD-CDU	with Forza Italia		5.8	30
National Alliance	13.5	109	15.7	93
	(Total seats for Freedom Pole and Good Government Pole = 366[d])		(Total seats for Freedom Pole = 246)	
Others	3.6	5	2.4	2

SOURCE: *Corriere della Sera*, April 23, 1996; D'Alimonte and Bartolini 1995, 320; Ignazi 1997, 417–418.

NOTE: The subdivisions in the table reflect electoral alliances. The 1994 elections featured four alliances: Progressives (Network, Greens, RC, PDS, Socialists, Democratic Alliance, Socialist Renewal, Social-Christians); Pact for Italy (PPI, Segni Pact); Freedom Pole (FI, League, UDC, CCD); and Good Government Pole (FI, AN, UDC, CCD). The 1996 elections saw two alliances: Olive Tree (Greens, PDS, PPI, SVP, PRI, UD, Dini List) and Freedom Pole (FI, AN, CCD-CDU). Party abbreviations are defined in the text and in Appendix A.

[a] Votes on PR ballot.

[b] Seat totals show seats won on both PR and plurality ballots, as allocated at election time.

[c] The Communist Refoundation (RC) cooperated electorally with the Olive Tree alliance but did not join the Olive Tree. Without support from the RC, the Olive Tree controlled 288 Chamber seats (italicized in the rightmost column).

[d] The 366 seats won by the Freedom Pole and Good Government Pole in 1994 included a total of 41 seats earned by such minor allies of the Forza Italia as the CCD and UDC.

liance); and the Freedom Pole on the center–right and right, which joined Forza Italia, former right-wing Christian Democrats, and the National Alliance. The Northern League, running alone, garnered more votes than expected and indirectly contributed to the Olive Tree's success in capturing seats in single-member districts (D'Alimonte and Bartolini 1997; Donovan 1996; Ignazi 1997). Analysts of the election not only commented on the salience of regionalism but also, as noted earlier, debated the existence of "old–new" and "ideological–pragmatic" dimensions in Italian politics. Thus, it is highly unlikely that the largest party in 1996, the PDS, inhabited the core of the policy space.

In May 1996, the Catholic economist who founded the Olive Tree, Romano Prodi, constructed a coalition that enjoyed a majority in the Senate but not in the Chamber of Deputies, as Table 5.10 indicates. The Prodi government passed its vote of investiture thanks to support from the RC. Equally important, the party that held the vice premiership and that supplied the largest number of ministers and junior ministers in the Prodi cabinet was the PDS. The executive when installed comprised twenty-one ministers and forty-eight undersecretaries, five and sixteen of whom, respectively, were non-parliamentarians (Camera dei Deputati 1998a; Donovan 1996; Ignazi 1997).

Prodi remained in office almost two-and-a-half years. Reflecting the balance of power in the Chamber of Deputies, "the most sensitive political problem for the Prodi government [throughout its tenure] lay in the relationship between the Ulivo coalition and Rifondazione Comunista. . . . On almost every crucial socioeconomic issue, Rifondazione underlined its peculiar standing and forced the government to bargain with it" (Ignazi 1997, 423). In the end, the RC forced the government to resign: In October 1998, after RC leaders expressed open opposition to the budget, Prodi was defeated in the Chamber on a motion of confidence; Rifondazione split on the decision (Camera dei Deputati 1999b). For the first time in postwar Italy, a government fell because it scheduled a motion of confidence and failed on the vote. In late October 1998, Massimo D'Alema of the PDS assembled a coalition including the Olive Tree parties and the chunk of the RC (quickly constituted as a separate party) that had voted in favor of Prodi. Italy's first cabinet headed by an ex-Communist was composed of twenty-seven ministers and fifty-six undersecretaries, ten and fifteen of whom, respectively, were non-parliamentarians (Camera dei Deputati 1998b).[29]

It used to be cheap to create and destroy Italian coalitions. That era seems to be over. Italian institutions and, even more dramatically, the Italian policy space have been redrawn. Cabinet builders now exercise limited flexibility in manipulating offices to cement their legislative majority (cf. della Cananea 1996). Politicians now have reason to fear that a coalition breakup will cost them loss of office, reduced policy influence, or punishment at the polls. From Berlusconi to Prodi and D'Alema (and back to Berlusconi in 2001), alternation in office is now a fact, not a threat.

The relatively long duration of the Prodi government looks puzzling against the backdrop of spatial theories of coalition. As already stressed, Italian governments under the DC were anomalous in light of spatial theory, in that the DC qualified as a core party from 1946 to 1992; and in theory the presence of a core party should have meant stable governments—not the combination of stability and instability found in Italy. In a neat reversal of the paradox, Italian governments are longer-lived now that there is no core party. This book's argument about the costs of coalition accommodates the long-standing paradox and its recent reversal.

Conclusions

One assumption common among Americans and Europeans is the idea that the composition of governments, and changes in government, should respond in some way to electoral outcomes. In democracies, after all, what citizens want is supposed to influence what politicians do. Beyond that, we tend to believe that effective government presumes some degree of continuity in office, and yet also that alternation in government is natural and naturally democratic, given the "social dynamics and political openness" characteristic of advanced industrial democracies (Pempel 1990, 6). It is precisely in this light that the evolution of the research program of spatial theories of voting—and, more broadly, theories of coalition—is so striking. Social choice is no lasting choice at all: Voting under simple majority rule in multidimensional policy space generates one majority after another, in an endless cycle of voting. Convinced by the results of the "chaos theorems" and related work, "political theorists . . . now generally accept that the will of the people is a will-o'-the-wisp" (McLean and Urken 1995, 7). Once predictions of chaos became part of the canon, the question pressed: "Why so much stability?" (Tullock 1981).[30] Political scientists now generally accept the answer that institutions imbue political decision making with whatever stability we see.

This chapter has shown that in Italy institutions and the arrangement of policy space have structured parties' choices and, operating through those choices, have produced instability alongside stability. Under the conditions prevailing in Italy until 1992, politicians managed to maneuver around the costs of building and breaking coalitions. The will of the Italian people was not ephemeral cabinets and permanent incumbents. Italy is well known for that combination, nonetheless.

The next task in this inquiry is to expand the scope to additional countries. What is the record of the costs of coalition in parliamentary democracies other than Italy? What effects have spatial and institutional conditions had on costs and cost-reduction strategies in other systems? Part III takes up those questions.

Part Three

CROSS-NATIONAL COMPARISONS

6 *The Bases for Comparison*

VARIATIONS IN INSTITUTIONS AND POLICY SPACE

The chapters in Part III compare costs and strategies across parties, across time, and across countries in order to weigh the impact of spatial and institutional conditions on the costs of coalition. The expectations underlying the comparisons across parties and across time should be unmistakable after the single-country focus of Part II. Parties advantaged to different degrees by their location in policy space should diverge in the costs they incur and in the cost-reduction strategies they pursue. Changes over time in spatial or institutional conditions should produce changes in the costs and strategies characteristic of different parties. Consider cross-national comparisons. Costs incurred and strategies implemented should vary across different kinds of party systems—for example, those with and without strong core parties. Distinctions should also emerge across countries with contrasting electoral and parliamentary institutions.

Given this logic, a natural first step in the empirical investigation is to sketch the political institutions and configurations of policy space in the ten nations under study. If the two classes of exogenous explanatory variables were to manifest no or negligible variation across these countries, then Chapters 7 and 8 would afford no additional leverage on the problem of stability *cum* instability. Thanks to the research design, substantial variations do appear.

Electoral Institutions

Whereas Ireland uses a single transferable vote (STV) version of proportional representation (PR), the other nine countries feature some form of party-list PR. Beyond this basic categorization, the electoral systems differ in the degree of proportionality attained and the role of personalized voting. As Table 6.1 displays, proportionality in translations of vote shares into seat shares reaches moderate levels in Belgium, Fourth Republic France, Ireland,

TABLE 6.1.
Electoral Institutions in Ten Parliamentary Democracies, 1945–93

Country	Proportionality[a]	Preference Voting[b]	Dates of Major Changes	Impact of Change on Proportionality
Belgium	Moderate	1	None	—
Denmark	Very high	2	1953[e]	Less proportional
			1964[e]	More proportional
Finland	High	3	None	—
France IV	Moderate	1	1951[c]	Less proportional
Germany	High	Not used	1953[d,e,f]	More proportional
			1956[d]	More proportional
			1985[c]	More proportional
Ireland	Moderate	2	None	—
Italy	High	3	1948[c]	Less proportional
			1956[c,e]	More proportional
			1991[g]	Neutral
			1993[c,d,e]	Less proportional
Netherlands	Very high	1	1956[d,e,f]	More proportional
Norway	Moderate	1	1953[c]	More proportional
			1989[d,e]	More proportional
Sweden	Very high	1	1949[c]	More proportional
			1970[d,e,f]	More proportional

SOURCES: Katz 1986a, 91, 94, 98; Lijphart 1994, 54–55, 160–62 and passim; Nohlen 1984, 219–21; country-specific sources on electoral reforms as listed in Note 1.

[a] Values on the least-squares index of *dis*proportionality (Lijphart 1994) are coded as follows: under 2 = very high proportionality; from 2 to 3 = high proportionality; from 3 to 6 = moderate. In countries with major changes in rules, the value coded is that for rules in longest use.

[b] This index of preference voting combines cross-national rankings on the minimum number of voters needed to modify the party-defined order of candidates (Katz 1986a, 94) and the percentage of intraparty defeats attributable to the preference vote (ibid., 98). A value of 3 on the index identifies the highest impact on candidates' election/defeat, and a value of 1, the lowest impact.

[c] Change in method of allocating seats (includes use of supplementary seats).

[d] 20 percent or greater change in district size.

[e] 20 percent or greater change in national legal threshold (or adoption of such threshold).

[f] 20 percent or greater change in size of lower house.

[g] Preference voting restricted.

and Norway, high levels in Finland, Italy, and Germany, and very high levels in Denmark, the Netherlands, and Sweden. These differences in proportionality depend on such arrangements as district size, method of seat allocation, and use of supplementary seats, as a distinguished tradition in political science has demonstrated (e.g., Grofman and Lijphart 1986; Lijphart 1984, 1994; Rae 1967). All of the list PR systems except Germany include some provision for intraparty preference voting (Katz 1986a, 88–91). Under STV, to the extent that a party puts up more candidates than it can elect, "voters determine which particular candidates will be elected by determining the order in which they reach the quota" (ibid., 91). As exhibited in Table 6.1, preference voting has a weak impact on candidates' election (or defeat) in Belgium, Fourth Republic France, the Netherlands, Norway, and Sweden, and a stronger impact in Denmark, Finland, Ireland, and Italy. Indeed, amid mounting criticism that preference voting induced factionalism, a 1991 referendum restricted preference voting in Italy, as Chapter 5 discussed. Table 6.1 registers this change and the dates of other major electoral reforms. Most of the revisions enacted have moved toward greater proportionality (Lijphart 1994, 54–55).[1]

Another important difference across these systems involves the possibility of cross-party voting. In Fourth Republic France, Germany, and Ireland, voters have been able to cast ballots for candidates of more than one party. In France, the 1951 electoral reforms not only altered formulae for seat allocation, as noted in Table 6.1, but also introduced *panachage*, which allows voters to delete candidates from their most preferred party's list and add candidates from other parties' lists. Since 1953, German voters have expressed two votes, one for a candidate in a single-member district and the other for a nationwide party list. The candidate backed on the first vote does not have to belong to the party chosen on the second. Under STV, Irish voters rank candidates in the order they prefer, regardless of the candidates' party affiliations. Electoral institutions in the other countries studied close off such opportunities for cross-party voting.

Parliamentary Institutions

Parliamentary rules and links between the executive and the legislature evince substantial variation across these nations as well. According to a constitutional lawyer who has twice headed the premier's office in Italy, "no government is weaker in parliament than the Italian" (quoted in Spotts and Wieser 1986, 111). Taken together, three rules summarized in Table 6.2 bear out this judgment for the countries examined here. In particular, governments are obliged to pass votes of investiture in Belgium, Germany, the

TABLE 6.2.

Parliamentary Institutions in Ten Democracies

Country	Vote of Investiture	Government Control over Agenda[a]	Secret Ballot	Committee Strength[b]
Belgium	Yes	4	Possible	4
Denmark	No	3	No	3[c]
Finland	No	3	Possible	3
France IV	Yes	1	No	4
Germany	Yes[d]	4	No	5
Ireland	Yes	7	No	1
Italy	Yes	2	Required[e]	4
Netherlands	No	1	No	2
Norway	No	4	Possible	5
Sweden	No[f]	3	No	4

SOURCES: Döring 1995, 225; Herman 1976, 405–11, 468–73, 477, 487–89, 495; Larsson 1994, 170–71; Strøm 1990b, 73, 79; Strøm, Budge, and Laver 1994, 322.

[a] Index shows increasing control over plenary agenda. Döring's (1995) scoring of control of the plenary agenda is based on information and evaluations gathered from country specialists. I reverse this coding of agenda control, so that "the Government alone determines the plenary agenda" is given a value of 7, and "the Chamber itself determines the agenda," a value of 1. For Fourth Republic France (which is not included in Döring's data set), I follow Döring's criteria in coding information from MacRae 1967, 57–61, 67–70; Williams 1966, 226–32.

[b] Index shows increasing strength (with the strongest committee systems assigned a score of 5). Strøm's (1990b) index of committee strength combines data on the number of standing committees, their special- ization, their correspondence to ministerial departments, restrictions on committee membership, and allo- cation of committee chairs.

[c] Since 1972, score of 4. I follow Strøm's (1990b) criteria in coding information from Damgaard 1992 and Mattson and Strøm 1995.

[d] Under the constructive vote of no confidence, a vote expressing no confidence in the sitting government must simultaneously identify and install a replacement government.

[e] Chamber final votes until 1988.

[f] Since 1975, yes.

French Fourth Republic, Ireland, Italy, and (since 1975) Sweden. Govern- ment control of the parliament's plenary agenda is most tenuous in the French Fourth Republic, Italy, and the Netherlands (Döring 1995; MacRae 1967; Williams 1966). Only in the Italian Chamber (until 1988) are secret ballots required on final votes. Out of these ten democracies, only Italy lands on the side of legislative assertiveness for all three rules.

Two additional sets of parliamentary institutions deserve mention: com- mittees and supramajoritarian rules. Among these countries, as Table 6.2 re- ports, the parliamentary committee system is least developed in Ireland and most developed and decentralized in Germany and Norway. A strong com-

mittee structure such as that found in Norway and Italy affords the opposition influence over policy, as Chapter 2 observed, and thus favors minority government (Strøm 1990b). Supramajoritarian rules instead give politicians incentives to seek surplus coalitions. Such rules are used often in
Finland, where since 1919 a two-thirds majority has been required for approval of the budget, bills affecting taxation for over one year, price freezes,
and incomes policies (Arter 1987, 43). From 1919 to 1992, furthermore,
one-third of Finnish members of Parliament could postpone most kinds of
legislation for one to two years (Anckar 1992, 161–62; Nousiainen 1994,
97–98). Supramajoritarian rules have also constrained decision making in
Belgium, where constitutional amendments need a two-thirds majority.
Since the early 1960s, conflicts between the French and Flemish communi-
ties have prompted debates—and some settlements—on constitutional revision. Since 1970, bills on ethnocultural or linguistic policy must be passed
both by a two-thirds majority overall and by a majority within each linguistic group (Covell 1982; Fitzmaurice 1983, 50–53; Herman 1976, 415–
31). These rules do much to explain the frequent appearance of surplus
coalitions in Belgium after the late 1960s.[2]

It should also be noted that directly elected presidents are found in
Finland and Ireland. Finnish presidents are more powerful than their Irish
counterparts but less powerful than presidents in the French Fifth Republic
(Arter 1987; Lijphart 1984). Most analysts agree that Finland is at bottom
a parliamentary system, unlike the Fifth Republic (e.g., Anckar 1992).

Parties and Voters in Policy Space

Analysts disagree on how to characterize party systems and locate
parties in policy space (e.g., Budge, Robertson, and Hearl 1987; Laver and
Hunt 1992; Sartori 1976; cf. Epstein and Mershon 1996). I do not attempt to
resolve the controversies here. Rather, I adopt categories and measures that
facilitate intertemporal comparisons and that have seen fairly broad application. More specifically, in the multicountry study as in Chapter 5, my de-
pictions of dimensions of party competition and party policies are based on
content analyses of parties' election manifestos (Laver and Budge 1992, reanalyzing and extending data in Budge, Robertson, and Hearl 1987).[3]

I follow Schofield in classifying Belgium, Finland, Italy, the Netherlands,
and post-1973 Denmark as "multipolar" party systems, Germany as a
"bipolar" system, and Ireland, Norway, Sweden, and pre-1973 Denmark as
"unipolar" systems (Laver and Schofield 1990; Schofield 1987, 1993).[4] As
the labels suggest, parties in multipolar systems face competitors in several
directions, whereas a single party attracts and orients competition in a

unipolar system. A small party can tip the balance of power between two relatively large parties in a bipolar system. Although Schofield does not treat the French Fourth Republic, it seems reasonable to regard that system as multipolar (Pétry 1987, 1992a, 1992b). All of these classifications depend on the number of dimensions in policy space, the effective number of parties,[5] and the sizes and positions of parties. A closer look at the party systems illustrates the commonalities within each type and the distinctions across types.

Multipolar systems have a relatively high effective number of parties and are often two-dimensional. Where the effective number of parties is quite high, as in Finland, multipolar competition can occur along one dimension. As already stressed, in Italy the Christian Democrats (DC) qualified as a core party from 1946 to 1992, and the Socialists (PSI) were pivotal from 1976 to 1992. Table 6.3 also indicates that in the Netherlands the Catholic People's Party (KVP) or its heir, the Christian Democratic Appeal (CDA, which joined the KVP and two Protestant parties in the 1977 elections), has occupied the core of the policy space for most of the postwar period. The Center Party (KP, called the Agrarian Union before 1965) has usually been the median party in Finland. Belgian elections have less often established the Christian Socials (PSC/CVP) as a core party (in 1950, 1961, and again from 1968 to 1981). This record and linguistic divisions make the PSC/CVP a weak core party. Since the "earthquake" election of 1973, the Danish Social Democrats (SD) have held core status only in 1979 (Schou and Hearl 1992, 170–72). In Fourth Republic France, the Radicals (RAD) typically stood at the median on the left–right dimension but inhabited the two-dimensional core only in 1946 (Pétry 1992a, 1992b, personal communication 1997).[6]

In Germany, unlike the other countries here, two large parties contend against each other and a smaller third party decides the outcome of that competition. The median party in this bipolar system has often been the small Free Democrats (FDP). Whenever the FDP has not controlled the median, the Christian Democrats (CDU/CSU) have (Klingemann and Volkens 1992, 198).

Degrees of left-wing dominance differentiate unipolar systems. The Swedish Social Democrats (SAP) contained the median legislator from 1944 to 1952, again in 1958, and then from 1964 to 1988 (Strøm and Bergman 1992, 123). In Norway, the Labor Party (DNA) was located at the median from 1945 to 1961 and again in 1973 and 1977. Otherwise, a center–right party has taken the median position (Strøm and Leipart 1993, 879). The Danish SD, a median party from 1960 to 1968, has encountered even more serious competition to its right than has Norwegian Labor. Its losses and the gains of new rivals in 1973 transformed the Danish party system (Schou and Hearl 1992, 170–72). The Irish two-dimensional system has lacked a core

TABLE 6.3.

Dimensions of Party Competition, Number of Parties,
and Presence of Core Party in Ten Parliamentary Democracies

Country	Number of Dimensions	Effective Number of Parties	Median/Core Party
Belgium	2	4.5	Weak PSC/CVP core
Denmark pre-1973	1	3.8	SD median 1960s
Denmark post-1973	2	5.7	SD core only once
Finland	1	5.2	KP median
France IV	2	4.9	RAD left–right median
Germany	1	2.8	FDP median
Ireland	2	2.7	No core
Italy	2	3.4	DC strong core
Netherlands	2	4.6	KVP/CDA strong core
Norway	1	3.2	DNA median 1945–61
Sweden	1	3.2	SAP median

SOURCES: Laver and Schofield 1990, 113, 136, 148, 159, passim; Lijphart 1984, 122; Schofield 1993, 22-31. See also Notes 3 and 4.

NOTE: For France, the table shows the mean effective number of parties for the 1946–58 period. Otherwise, the effective number of parties is averaged over the 1945–87 period. As discussed in Chapter 2, median and core parties have the capacity to transform minorities into majorities. In unidimensional policy space, the median is equivalent to the core. Party abbreviations are defined in the text and in Appendix A.

party; thus Fianna Fáil one-party governments have alternated with Fine Gael-Labour coalitions (but see Laver 1992a; Mair 1987, ch. 4).

The property of voters' preferences of greatest interest here is the extent to which a national electorate is segmented or subdivided into blocs, with each bloc steadfastly backing "its" party and securely insulated from the appeals of rival parties. Parties that can draw on such reservoirs of support should meet relatively low electoral costs of coalition. A salient theme in studies of postwar Belgian, Dutch, and Italian electoral politics is that religious and class identities have indeed segmented the electorate and anchored particular sets of voters to particular parties (e.g., Daalder 1966; Hill 1974; Galli and Prandi 1970; Lijphart 1968). As discussed in Chapter 5, specialists on Italian electoral behavior investigate the subcultural vote and concur that socioeconomic change has recently eroded the subcultural vote and expanded the opinion vote. The same measures tapping subcultural belonging have not been used outside Italy.[7] Yet scholars agree that in the Netherlands the Catholic, Protestant, Socialist, and Liberal "pillars," which stood firm in the 1950s, "have now largely crumbled" under the impact of secularization, economic growth, and mass education (Daalder 1987, 223; cf. Irwin and Dittrich 1984). In Belgium, the Catholic, Socialist, and Liberal pillars have also weakened, and linguistic conflicts came to the fore by the early 1960s (Covell 1981; Dewachter 1987; Mabille 1992; Mughan 1992). Whereas the German electorate during the Weimar Republic contained institutionalized Catholic and Socialist "camps," in postwar Germany the two major parties have sought—and, especially by the 1970s, acquired—relatively broad constituencies (Baker, Dalton, and Hildebrandt 1981; Dalton 1984, 1988; Lepsius 1978; Urwin 1974). In Fourth Republic France, "religious and class differences seemed to . . . serve as persistent bases of political division" among voters, despite periodic surges of support for protest parties (MacRae 1967, 259; cf. Williams 1966).[8]

Religious subcultures are absent in Protestant Scandinavia. Class identities long fastened Finnish industrial workers to the Social Democrats and Communists, and farmers to the Agrarians. In the 1950s, industrial and rural working-class Norwegians voted solidly for the Labor Party, whereas middle-class voters supported center–right parties. Class loyalties similarly aligned the Danish and Swedish electorates. By the 1970s, however, the class lines that had once partitioned Scandinavian electorates began to blur (Arter 1987, ch. 2; Borre 1984; Pedersen 1987; on differences within Scandinavia, see Sainsbury 1990).

In Ireland, too, social cleavages segment the electorate less sharply today than in the past. Electoral politics in Ireland has traditionally been viewed as a candidate-focused "politics without social bases" (Whyte 1974). Although a vigorous debate has recently developed to challenge that characterization (Laver 1992a; Mair 1987, 1992; Marsh 1992), scholars concur that Ireland joins the prevailing European trend "toward the fragmentation and 'particularization' of political preferences" (Gallagher, Laver, and Mair 1995, 226).

Conclusions

Given that variations in political institutions and configurations of policy space do appear across these ten countries, this question now commands attention: Do the variations just outlined determine variations in the costs of coalition? Chapter 7 examines the office, policy, electoral, and bargaining costs of setting up government coalitions. Chapter 8 investigates the price that parties have paid for rupturing coalitions. I take the findings on Italy presented in Part II as a reference point throughout the analysis that follows.

7 *The Costs of Building Coalitions*

To say that this chapter and the next carry out cross-national comparisons is, in a way, misleading. To be sure, the data set under scrutiny covers ten countries from the end of World War II to January 1, 1993. And various sections of Chapters 7 and 8 organize comparisons by country. For instance, the study of office costs starts with the Netherlands, where the party system is much like the Italian, and proceeds to Finland, which admits of slightly greater variation in the conditions for party competition.

Even so, I do not treat entire countries as units of analysis here. In the following pages, I assess evidence on 291 governments and fifty-nine governing parties (with such parties defined as those ruling for at least half of the span between two consecutive elections). I am interested in attributes of governments (including programs espoused and days taken to form) and attributes of parties (cabinet offices held, policies championed at election time, electoral gains or losses). With data on those attributes, I estimate the costs of coalition that parties incur, and I am able to evaluate the explanation advanced earlier for variations in costs.

This chapter first investigates the office price of putting together coalition governments. It then turns to other kinds of risks and rewards in coalition politics. The ten-country analysis, as noted earlier, appraises the exogenous component of the book's central argument more thoroughly than the endogenous component. The exogenous forces posited as influences on the costs of coalition are, of course, those discussed in Chapter 6: the array of parties and voters in policy space, electoral laws, parliamentary rules, and links between the executive and the legislature. Although the ten-country analysis does not afford the close-up, detailed view of strategic behavior enjoyed in the study of Italy, inferences about parties' efforts to limit costs may be drawn, and some evidence of such efforts does appear.

The Office Costs of Building Coalitions

Chapter 5 confirmed that spatial and institutional conditions have influenced the office costs of erecting Italian coalitions. Do analogous effects appear in the Netherlands, the country that most nearly resembles Italy in spatial terms? To address this question, Figure 7.1, like Figure 5.1, displays average numbers of officeholders in the core party and in the entire government for coalitions joining different numbers of allies.[1] Figure 7.1 cannot fully duplicate the comparisons in Figure 5.1, for the Dutch Christian Democrats (KVP/CDA) have never governed alone, unlike the Italian Christian Democrats (DC). Figure 7.1 does show that as coalitions have stretched from two to five parties, governmental offices overall have tended to rise, and the number of KVP/CDA ministers and junior ministers has declined only slightly.

Yet glances at the vertical scales of Figures 5.1 and 7.1 are enough to establish that Dutch portfolio inflation is a pale copy of the Italian phenomenon. Dutch five-party coalitions average fewer than fifteen junior ministers, whereas the relevant number for Italy is more than fifty. Why? Since Dutch governments do not confront votes of investiture, and since secret ballots are the exception rather than the rule in the Dutch Parliament, the builders of Dutch cabinets lack the incentives of their Italian counterparts to use office as "glue" to bind assertive parliamentarians to governments. Disincentives operate as well. Additions of cabinet posts can trigger resignations in Dutch parliamentary parties, for in the Netherlands (and Norway) ministers cannot hold seats in Parliament; the same is true for Dutch junior ministers since 1948 (Andeweg and Bakema 1994, 66; Gladdish 1991, 59; Strøm 1994, 43). Finally, unlike the Italian DC, the KVP/CDA lost its core status a few times—while retaining office—before the early 1990s.

The Finnish Agrarian/Center Party (KP) briefly lost core status in the early postwar period, unlike the Italian DC and the Dutch KVP/CDA.[2] Moreover, the KP has not achieved the uninterrupted incumbency that sets apart the DC and the KVP/CDA. Although "green–red" coalitions dominated by the KP and Social Democrats (SSDP) have been rather common, the SSDP has occasionally governed without the KP (even in 1972, when the KP was the median party [Laver and Schofield 1990, 117]). Seven nonpartisan cabinets have formed, which in part testifies to the prerogatives of the Finnish president (Arter 1987).

Given these contrasts between Italy and the Netherlands, on the one hand, and Finland, on the other, some differences in outcomes should emerge. And they do. Figure 7.2 (see pg. 102) depicts only those governments containing the KP.[3] It reveals that the number of ministers and junior

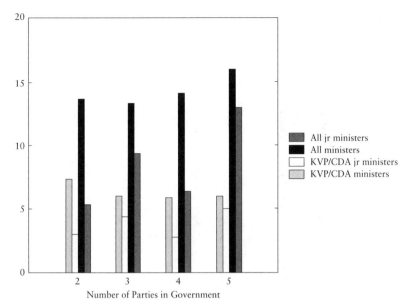

FIGURE 7.1. Office Payoffs, by Number of Parties in Dutch Government
(Means)

ministers has remained roughly the same, on average, across the KP's one-
party governments and coalitions—even coalitions spanning five parties.
The Center Party pays an obvious office price for assembling coalitions. All
the same, it responds to institutional incentives to coalesce: The Finnish
Parliament follows supramajoritarian rules. Those rules also raise obstacles
to manipulating offices, for in Finland "a change in law is required to establish a new ministry" (Nousianinen 1994, 89). In Italy, too, as already discussed, new ministries demand new legislation; and, as Table 4.1 illustrated,
Italian parliamentarians have supplied laws for a half-dozen new ministries
over the postwar period. Table 4.1 also indicated that in Finland fewer new
ministries have been founded—a result that can now be attributed in part
to the Finnish supramajoritarian rules. But those rules do not tell the whole
story: Once more, the KP's early loss of core status, its sojourns in the opposition, and the role of the presidency have worked against portfolio inflation in Finland. Hence, ministers without portfolio—which bypass the
need for legislation—are extremely rare. A grand total of three ministers
without portfolio were appointed in the forty-one Finnish governments
from 1946 to 1992. The grander total for the fifty-two Italian governments
from 1946 to 1992 was 218.

The logic of comparison so far has been to limit spatial variations and

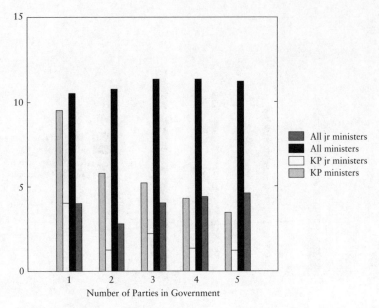

FIGURE 7.2. Office Payoffs, by Number of Parties in Finnish Government (Means)

then extend them slightly (by juxtaposing Italy and the Netherlands and then moving to Finland), while at the same time searching for signs that institutions help to account for differences in outcomes. Consider now Norway and Ireland, which introduce greater spatial variations. The comparisons just executed for Finland—of the KP's one-party governments and coalitions—cannot be duplicated for Norway, for the Labor Party (DNA) has always governed alone. In Ireland, Fianna Fáil (FF) maintained a commitment to one-party government until 1989, so that only two FF-based coalitions are available for study. (The FF initiated its third coalition in mid-January 1993.) Labor was Norway's median party from 1945 to 1961 and in 1973 and 1977, as observed earlier. If the Irish party system were unidimensional, FF would generally qualify as the median party on the left–right spectrum; but Irish politics is probably best characterized as two dimensional (Laver and Schofield 1990; Schofield 1987, 1993).

Despite the spatial differences, the Labor and FF one-party governments charted in Figures 7.3 and 7.4 look rather similar. Furthermore, for both Norway and Ireland, fluctuations in the totals of ministerial and junior ministerial posts have not prevented parties from relinquishing offices as governments have embraced additional allies. In particular, even though the Center Party (SP) was Norway's median party in 1981 and 1985, both the

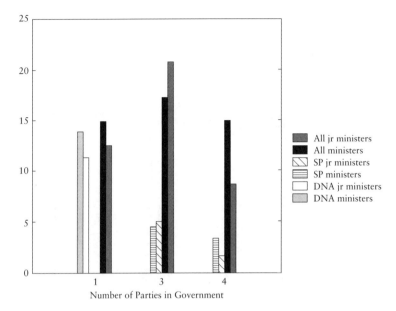

FIGURE 7.3. Office Payoffs, by Number of Parties in Norwegian
Government (Means)

smallish SP and in Ireland the bigger Fine Gael (FG) have paid an office
price when they have governed with more parties rather than fewer. The
similarities should not be overstressed: When the SP governed as a median
party, it received weighted shares of cabinet posts (the well-known measures
reported for Italy in Table 5.3) that were relatively high—relative to the SP's
weighted shares at other times and relative to the Fine Gael. Nonetheless,
similarities do exist. They may be explained by institutional constraints. In
Norway, as stated earlier, ministerial office is incompatible with membership in Parliament. The 1937 Irish constitution specifies that the number of
ministers should range from seven to fifteen (Farrell 1994, 73).

    Given the reasoning here and given the evidence on the first five coun-
tries, the guiding hypotheses for the last five countries may be cast as follows. If spatial conditions influence the office costs of building coalitions,
then patterns in Sweden and, to a lesser degree, Denmark should resemble
those just discerned for Norway. Germany should look distinctive in some
fashion, and France and Belgium should approximate Finland. (Again, as
remarked in Chapter 6, Sweden, pre-1973 Denmark, and Norway are
unipolar systems with more or less dominant Social Democrats. Germany is
the only bipolar system in this group. France and Belgium, like Finland, are
multipolar systems without strong core parties.) If institutions shape office

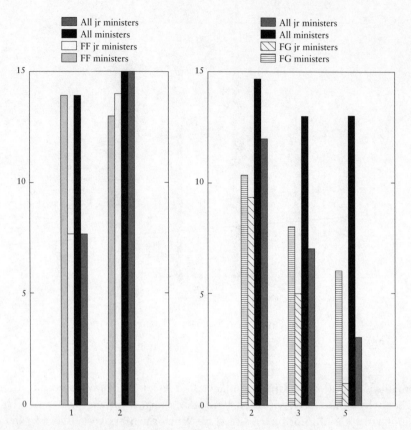

FIGURE 7.4. Office Payoffs, by Number of Parties in Irish Government (Means)

costs, then differences between, say, France and Belgium should be traceable to differences in rules.

These expectations are all upheld. Suffice it to note, without reproducing graphs for every country, that in Sweden and Denmark, as in Norway, one-party governments have featured only slightly fewer cabinet posts than have coalitions. Coalitions have imposed a greater office sacrifice on the Danish Social Democrats (SD) than on the Swedish, which is consistent with the Danish SD's inability to maintain control of the median and, after 1973, the two-dimensional core.[4] In Germany, the Free Democratic Party has received unusually high weighted shares of cabinet posts when it has occupied the median. The Radicals in Fourth Republic France, like the Center Party in Finland, sacrificed offices in larger as opposed to smaller coalitions.

As Figure 7.5 shows, however, the Belgian Christian Socials (PSC-CVP)

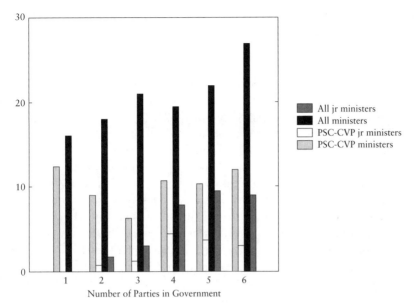

FIGURE 7.5. Office Payoffs, by Number of Parties in Belgian Government (Means)

have demonstrated a capacity to guard—and even enhance—their office benefits in large coalitions. Although Belgian portfolio inflation does not approach Italian proportions, it outstrips the Dutch. (Check the vertical axes once more.) These outcomes might well seem surprising.

To understand the outcomes, first consider the strategic opportunities. The Belgian Christian Socials, like the Finnish Center Party and unlike the Italian and Dutch Christian Democrats, lost core status in the early postwar period and were excluded from a few governments (three formed in 1946 and one in 1954). In 1968, the two linguistically distinct Christian Social wings became two separate parties, the French PSC and Flemish CVP.[5] From 1968 to 1999, those two parties always governed together. From 1958 to 1999, indeed, the Christian Socials always governed. Their strategic position to manipulate office resources, then, may be judged as weaker than that of the Italian DC or Dutch KVP/CDA, but at least as strong as that of the Finnish KP or French Radicals.

Beyond these opportunities, what incentives have the Christian Socials had to increase cabinet posts? The dominant party in a multipolar system, again, faces rivals in multiple directions. The Belgian Christian Socials have met—and joined—resurgent linguistic competition since roughly 1960. Ethnic disputes have severely strained governing alliances, and have at times ruptured them. In 1962, for instance, French-speaking parliamentarians from the governing Christian Social and Socialist parties voted against government legislation redefining the border between French- and Flemish-language zones. In 1963, Flemish parliamentarians from the Christian Socials rejected the government's proposals on language policy (*Keesing's Contemporary Archives* 1963, 19601; De Ridder and Fraga 1986). Episodes such as these presaged the party split of 1968.

The effect of ethnic disputes on offices is visible in Figure 7.6, which plots trends over time as Figure 5.2 did. It discloses two turning points, the early 1960s (when junior ministers were invented and ministers added) and the early 1980s (when ministerial ranks were thinned). In the early 1960s, the informal rule developed that ministerial posts should be divided equally among French and Flemish speakers. This rule was enshrined in the constitution in 1970. So, too, the constitutional reforms of 1970 recognized the role of junior ministers (Covell 1981; Frognier 1988; Hearl 1992; Molitor 1988). Recall, as well, that the two-thirds rule for constitutional amendments was extended to ethnocultural and linguistic legislation in 1970, and that such legislation since 1970 also requires a majority within each linguistic group. These hurdles have proven more difficult to surmount than investiture: Regionalization, which the 1970 reforms left unresolved, was approved only in 1980; the regions acquired additional powers in 1988 and again in July 1993, when Belgium became a federal state (Covell 1981, 1982; De Ridder and Fraga 1986; Deruette 1994; Downs 1996; Hooghe 1991). Since the advent of regionalization, offices once attached to the national government have been transferred to subnational levels. (For example, in 1979 seven of the twenty-five ministers in Maartens I held either community or regional responsibilities, whereas in June 1993 fifteen ministers served in the national government and a total of thirty ministers served in the various regional and community governments [data furnished by the Institut Belge d'Information et de Documentation].) With regionalization enacted, moreover, the many-party surplus coalitions characteristic of the 1970s have all but disappeared. All but one of Belgium's five- and six-party coalitions governed between 1970 and 1980.

The builders of Belgian coalitions have used office to guarantee restive linguistic representatives a voice in policy making and to tie those representatives to the governing majority. What is more, they have institutionalized this use of office. Linguistic conflicts have led to mutual accommodation among Belgian elites and have thus driven both portfolio inflation (in the short run) and institutional change (in the short and longer run).

To recapitulate: Given Italy's spatial and institutional conditions, Italian politicians have been able and willing to manipulate offices so as to offset the office costs of building coalitions. An echo of this pattern appears in the

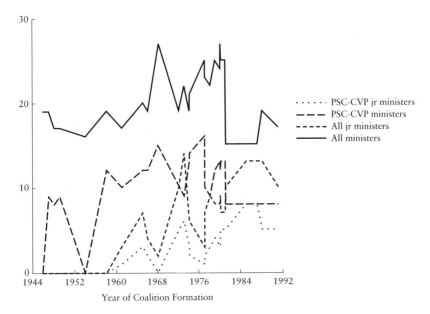

FIGURE 7.6. Office Payoffs in Belgian Coalitions, 1946–92

Netherlands, where the party system roughly resembles the Italian. That the echo is faint becomes comprehensible when institutions and finer spatial distinctions are taken into account. Beyond those two fairly similar countries, as differences in party systems become more pronounced—as attention shifts to Finland and then to Norway and Ireland, for example—more pronounced differences in outcomes emerge. Variations in institutions also contribute to variations in the office costs incurred in the construction of governments. The single party system that might seem to upset the argument actually serves to underscore it. Christian Democrats are somewhat less advantaged in Belgium as opposed to the Netherlands or Italy, but have neutralized office costs nevertheless. The Belgian maneuvers do not match the Italian. That they surpass the Dutch reflects the impact of institutions—and inducements from party competition to redesign institutions.

The Belgian experience also illustrates the problems with two hypotheses that might appear to provide plausible alternatives to the reasoning here. The first might be labeled the "administrative needs" explanation for variations in ministerial ranks, and the second, the "bureaucratic accretion" explanation. First, analysts routinely contend that the post–World War II expansion of the role of the state has propelled cabinet growth (e.g., on Norway, Eriksen 1988, 184). In Belgium, however, the scope of state activity (measured as the percentage of gross domestic product represented by current state expenditures, calculated annually) expanded at a roughly constant rate from 1970 to 1981 and then contracted gradually thereafter (OECD 2000), at the same time that numbers of officeholders in governing coalitions fluctuated conspicuously, as Figure 7.6 (and, less directly, Figure 7.5) displayed. More broadly, among these countries, the scope of state activity in 1991 is weakly correlated with numbers of ministers and junior ministers in 1991.[6] Of course, administrative needs have something to do with cabinet bailiwicks; ministers with responsibilities for health policy were relatively rare in Europe in 1945 and are abundant today. Even so, what underlies the kinds of variations seen in Figures 7.5 and 7.6 is not an administrative logic but a political one—a deliberate and successful effort to absorb the office costs of building coalitions.

According to the second hypothesis, turf battles within and among complex bureaucracies slowly and inexorably push up the numbers of cabinet offices. The correlation between time (date of government formation) and numbers of ministers is weak in Belgium, Fourth Republic France, Germany, and the Netherlands and strong in the other six countries here.[7] What attenuates the correlation in Belgium is the occurrence of discontinuities and reversals: the proliferation of junior ministers after 1960 and the contraction in ministerial posts after 1980. (Chapter 5 gave another example of reversal, in Italy after 1992.) This hypothesis, like the first, is not completely off the mark. What happens at t-1 often predicts t rather well. But not always, and not only, is this mechanism at work. Again, the evidence in Figures 7.5 and 7.6 attests to attempts to manage the office costs of building coalitions.

The Policy Costs of Building Coalitions

Are parties that are able to contain the office costs of assembling coalitions also able to limit policy costs, so that the policies they prefer are embraced and espoused by the entire government? Perhaps all aspiring incumbents are forced to compromise their positions to some degree, yielding to allies (or even opponents) in order to govern. Yet, if the argument here holds true, then the programmatic concessions required to seal governing alliances should differ across parties. In particular, the extent to which parties deviate from their ideal policies when constructing coalitions should depend on configurations of policy space and on institutional constraints and incentives.

To evaluate these expectations, I again turn to measures based on content analyses of parties' election manifestos and of the policy documents issued by newly launched governments (Laver and Budge 1992, reanalyzing

and extending data in Budge, Robertson, and Hearl 1987). Thus, it is possible to observe the disparity between, for instance, the position of the
Social Democrats in the 1960 Danish elections and the position of the Social
Democratic–Radical Liberal (SD-RV) coalition that formed immediately
after those elections. The left-wing proposals in the SD's 1960 campaign
earned a ranking of –31 on a left–right scale bounded by –100 (extreme left)
and +100 (extreme right). When Prime Minister Viggo Kampmann presented his SD-RV cabinet to the newly elected Folketing in 1960, he outlined
a more centrist program (rated at –18 on the 200-point left–right scale). On
this occasion, then, the disparity between SD policy and government policy
came to 13 points (Schou and Hearl 1992, 157).

Table 7.1 reports scores summarizing such observations over relatively
long spans of time. The table shows, to cite Denmark once more, that from
1945 to 1971—as long as the Danish party system was unipolar—the average distance between Social Democratic positions and government positions was 11.6 points on the 200-point spectrum. Beyond this example,
Table 7.1 lists the mean distance on the left–right dimension between party
policy and government policy, for all major parties and for all governments
for which left–right scalings of policy pronouncements are available. The
table's first column focuses on parties that have typically been located at the
core in their party systems. Since no data on governments' policy positions
are available for Finland, the table excludes that country altogether; data
for Ireland are confined to two coalitions in 1981–82.[8]

Do core parties dictate government policy, as spatial theories of voting
predict? In none of the systems examined in Table 7.1 have the core party's
stances coincided perfectly with government programs. Still, no core party
has done substantially worse than its competitors in pulling government policy toward party positions. Among all the parties arrayed in the table's first
column, the Italian and Dutch Christian Democrats and the German Free
Democrats have been the most successful at inscribing their left–right preferences in government policy. The post-1973 Danish Social Democrats, the
Belgian Christian Socials, and the Swedish Social Democrats instead stand
out for the discrepancy between their left–right preferences and governmental declarations. These contrasts cannot be traced to the parties'
longevity at the core, for the German FDP spent the 1950s out of the core,
unlike the Italian DC and the Dutch KVP/CDA; and the Belgian PSC/CVP
and the Swedish SAP have inhabited the core more often than has the Danish
SD (Hearl 1992; Klingemann and Volkens 1992; Schou and Hearl 1992;
Strøm and Bergman 1992). More generally, among all the parties exhibited
in Table 7.1, the mean distance between party policy and government policy
is only weakly correlated with the party's time at the core (the number of
governments formed when the party occupied the core, as a percentage of all

TABLE 7.1.
Mean Absolute Distance on Left–Right Spectrum Between Party and Government Positions, by Party and Party System

	Most frequent core party	Other parties[a]			
Belgium	PSC/CVP	PSB/BSP	Liberals	VU	FDF
1946–81 (n = 28)	19.1	32.8	16.0	18.6	18.8
Denmark	SD	RV	V	KF	
1945–71 (n = 11)	11.6	8.4	18.4	30.7	
1973–82 (n = 7)	18.7	18.1	16.7	18.6	
France IV	RAD	SFIO	MRP	RI	GAUL
1946–58 (n = 26)	16.2	26.7	13.3	26.0	38.5
Germany	FDP	SPD	CDU/CSU		
1949–87 (n = 15)	8.5	22.9	8.9		
Ireland	FF	Labour	FG		
1981–82 (n = 2)	10.5	3.5	20.5		
Italy	DC	PSI	PSDI	PRI	PLI
1948–83 (n = 38)	7.6	14.1	11.8	10.6	12.3
Netherlands	KVP/CDA	PvdA	ARP	CHU	VVD
1946–81 (n = 11)	10.4	28.9	13.6	13.6	14.2
Norway	DNA	V	SP	KRF	H
1949–89 (n = 20)	17.3	14.0	16.1	19.4	20.3
Sweden	SAP	CP	FP	M	
1945–88 (n = 22)	22.4	18.3	18.1	45.7	

SOURCES: Calculations based on measures of party and government positions in Hearl 1992; Klingemann and Volkens 1992; Laver 1992b; Mastropaolo and Slater 1992; Pétry 1992a; Schou and Hearl 1992; Strøm and Bergmann 1992; Strøm and Leipart 1992; Tops and Dittrich 1992.

NOTE: Entries are mean absolute distances on a 200-point left-right scale between party positions and government positions, for each party listed. Finland is omitted because of missing data. Numbers of applicable governments are in parentheses. Party abbreviations are defined in the text and in Appendix A.

[a] Ordered left to right.

governments for which data on policy positions are available).[9] Hence, core parties sway but do not dictate public policy. The strength of their influence is not a simple function of the length of their time at the core.

The imprint that parties leave on government policy is a function of participation in government. The research team headed by Budge and Laver has established that "parties in government (with only idiosyncratic exceptions) are consistently closer to the government program than parties out of government" (Budge and Laver 1992, 411). The reanalysis of data in Table 7.2 details this pattern. Parties tend to realize policy benefits when they shoulder cabinet responsibilities. Exceptions to the tendency, such as the People's Union (VU) and the Francophone Democratic Front (FDF) in Belgium, reveal more than idiosyncrasies about coalition politics.

The exceptions are discussed in a moment. For now, note that previous studies have not settled whether policy benefits differ between one-party governments and coalition governments. To be sure, most parties most of the time have alternated between opposition and multiparty government. And, as just implied, the most common conclusion from comparisons of a party's records in opposition and coalition is that the party enhances its policy influence by joining coalitions. Only a few parties—all with long-standing core status—have repeatedly ruled alone and repeatedly cemented coalitions as well. In particular, seventy-nine of the eighty-seven single-party cabinets in this data set have been constituted by one of the parties displayed in the first column of Table 7.1.

Figure 7.7 tracks left–right policy payoffs for those parties, comparing the executives they have staffed alone and their coalitions encompassing different numbers of allies. More precisely, the figure summarizes the results from analyses of variance, conducted separately for each country, in the mean distances between the core party's policy and governmental policy across governments with different numbers of parties. The figure omits Finland and also Ireland, since the Irish data pertain to two FG–Labour coalitions. It can depict only one-party cabinets for Norway, for Norwegian Labor has never shared office with allies.[10]

Norwegian Labor aside, three groups of parties appear in Figure 7.7. First, a few long-standing core parties have discovered that coalitions diminish the policy benefits of governing. For the Danish Social Democrats before 1973 and the Swedish Social Democrats, acquiring allies entails accepting priorities and plans that depart from the party's own: As governing partners increase, so, too, does the mean distance on the left–right spectrum between government programs and the core party's ideals. Only for pre-1973 Denmark, though, do the contrasts in means attain statistical significance at the .05 level. This datum squares with the weakness of the Danish SD as a core party, already stressed.

TABLE 7.2.

Mean Absolute Distance on Left–Right Spectrum Between Party and
Government Positions, by Party, Party Status in Government, and Party System

	Parties[a]				
Belgium, 1946–81	PSB/BSP	PSC/CVP	Liberals	VU	FDF
Government	30.3(n = 17)	17.9(n = 24)	13.8(n = 11)	46.5(n = 2)	41.3(n = 3)
Opposition	36.7(n = 11)	26.8(n = 4)	17.4(n = 17)	14.9(n = 15)	12.1(n = 10)
Denmark, 1945–71	SD	RV	V	KF	
Government	9.8(n = 8)	4.0(n = 3)	12.0(n = 3)	22.0(n = 2)	
Opposition	16.7(n = 3)	10.0(n = 8)	20.8(n = 8)	32.7(n = 9)	
Denmark, 1973–82					
Government	18.8(n = 5)	NA	17.0(n = 3)	28.0(n = 1)	
Opposition	18.5(n = 2)	18.1(n = 7)	16.5(n = 4)	17.0(n = 6)	
France IV, 1946–58	SFIO	RAD	MRP	RI	GAUL
Government	25.5(n = 17)	15.5(n = 24)	10.8(n = 21)	23.2(n = 20)	44.4(n = 9)
Opposition	28.9(n = 9)	24.5(n = 2)	24.0(n = 5)	35.3(n = 6)	29.5(n = 6)
Germany, 1949–87	SPD	FDP	CDU/CSU		
Government	15.8(n = 6)	9.1(n = 13)	9.7(n = 10)		
Opposition	27.6(n = 9)*	4.5(n = 2)*	7.2(n = 5)		
Ireland, 1981–82	Labour	FF	FG		
Government	3.5(n = 2)	NA	20.5(n = 2)		
Opposition	NA	10.5(n = 2)	NA		

TABLE 7.2. (*Continued*)

Parties[a]

	PSI	PSDI	PRI	DC	PLI
Italy, 1948–83					
Government	15.2(n = 13)	9.9(n = 21)	10.8(n = 18)	7.6(n = 38)	5.4(n = 8)
Opposition	13.5(n = 25)	14.1(n = 17)	10.5(n = 20)	NA	14.2(n = 30)**
	PvdA	KVP/CDA	ARP	CHU	VVD
Netherlands, 1946–81					
Government	23.5(n = 6)	10.4(n = 11)	13.3(n = 6)	15.0(n = 6)	11.5(n = 6)
Opposition	35.4(n = 5)*	NA	14.5(n = 2)	9.5(n = 2)	17.4(n = 5)
	DNA	V	SP	KRF	H
Norway, 1949–89					
Government	14.2(n = 12)	12.8(n = 4)	8.4(n = 7)	10.3(n = 7)	11.9(n = 7)
Opposition	21.9(n = 8)	14.3(n = 16)	20.2(n = 13)	24.3(n = 13)*	24.8(n = 13)*
	SAP	CP	FP	M	
Sweden, 1945–88					
Government	23.9(n = 18)	19.0(n = 6)	14.3(n = 4)	14.5(n = 2)	
Opposition	15.8(n = 4)	17.9(n = 16)	19.0(n = 18)	48.8(n = 20)***	

SOURCES: Calculations based on government composition data in Appendix C and on measures of party and government positions from works cited in Table 7.1.

NOTE: Entries are mean absolute distances on a 200-point left-right scale between party and government positions, for each party listed. Finland is omitted because of missing data. Numbers of applicable governments are in parentheses. Most frequent core parties are in italics. For each party, t tests compare the means for governments including, and those excluding, the party in question. NA, Not applicable. Party abbreviations are defined in the text and in Appendix A.

[a] Ordered left to right.

* $p < .05$. ** $p < .01$. *** $p < .005$ (separate variances t tests).

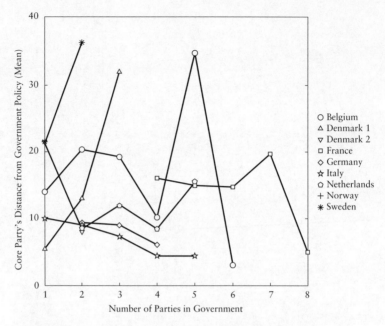

FIGURE 7.7. Distance on Left–Right Spectrum Between Party and Government Positions, by Core Party and Number of Parties in Government (Means)

Second, for the Belgian Christian Socials, the Dutch Christian Democrats, and the French Radicals, the policy costs of coalition vary with the number of allies engaged. The Christian Socials' five-party coalitions exact a policy sacrifice relative to their one-party cabinets and, above all, their four- and six-party coalitions. The KVP/CDA pays a greater policy price to build five-party coalitions as opposed to two- and four-party coalitions. The Radicals conceded remarkably little on policy in order to launch France's single eight-party coalition; but the government whose declarations the Radicals so successfully molded lasted less than three weeks, failed in the face of the Algerian coup, and ushered in the transition to the Fifth Republic. In this group, only the differences for the Belgian PSC/CVP approach statistical significance ($p \approx .08$).

What makes Belgium special, once again, is the prominence of linguistic conflicts and the accompanying pressures for constitutional revision. In Belgium, only five-party coalitions have incorporated one or more of the so-called "community" parties, founded expressly to defend linguistic-regional interests: the People's Union (VU), the Francophone Democratic Front (FDF), and the Walloon Rally (RW). Each time that a coalition included community representatives, it seems, the governing parties agreed to disagree on left–right, socioeconomic issues in order to concentrate on forging agreement on constitutional reform. This story is not only suggested in Figure 7.7 (and Table 7.2, with regard to the VU and FDF). It is also told in historical narratives of constitutional change in Belgium (Covell 1981, 1982; De Ridder and Fraga 1986; Hooghe 1991; Lemaître 1982; Mabille 1992). According to the narratives, too, the presence of community parties in the government was intended—by all participants—to raise the probability that proposed constitutional amendments would win the approval of a two-thirds majority in each house of Parliament.[11]

Consider now the third group of parties featured in Figure 7.7. When the post-1973 Danish Social Democrats, the German Free Democrats, and the Italian Christian Democrats take on coalition partners, they see a tighter fit, not a looser one, between their party's platform and the cabinet's inaugural address. As the number of governing parties rises, the mean distance between government programs and the core party's ideals declines. These findings hang on just one coalition for the Danish SD, however, and just two coalitions with more than two parties for the German FDP. The means plotted for Italy involve a total of twenty-four coalitions. Thus, only the Italian DC has repeatedly extracted advantages in policy terms with the addition of governing allies. (Although the differences in means in the five-way analysis of variance for Italy do not attain statistical significance, the two-way t-test for Italy does reveal significant differences, as noted in Chapter 5.) Figure 7.7 illustrates that the policy benefits of coalition charted in Figure 5.3 are unique to the DC.

The data in Tables 7.1 and 7.2 and Figure 7.7 point to similarities—and distinctions—among the Italian and Dutch Christian Democrats and the German Free Democrats. When policy distances are examined without regard to cabinet composition (in Table 7.1), all three parties look quite successful at aligning government policy with their left–right ideals. Once a party's roles as an incumbent and in opposition are designated (in Table 7.2), it is clear that the German FDP puts its strongest stamp on public policy from the ranks of the opposition. Identifying variations in the number of governing parties (in Figure 7.7) highlights the unmatched capacity of the Italian DC to score policy benefits in coalition.

Spatial conditions make sense of the similarities and distinctions. As already emphasized, the Italian DC and the Dutch KVP/CDA qualify as strong core parties in multipolar party systems. The DC, unlike its Dutch analog, held core status continuously between 1946 and 1992. The FDP has usually occupied the median in the bipolar German party system. In such a system, a small party tips the balance of power between two large parties.

On the whole, the extent to which parties compromise their own priorities in coalition reflects their location, and leverage, in policy space. At the same time, almost all parties realize some policy benefit when they move from the opposition into government. Evidence of institutional effects on policy payoffs—in particular, the need for a two-thirds majority to approve constitutional reform—appears in Belgium. The office and policy goods that parties obtain in coalition are the product of interparty bargaining over new governments, to which I now turn.

The Bargaining Costs of Building Coalitions

I measure bargaining costs as the number of days separating the demise of a government and the rise of its successor, except when elections intervene. For governments launched after parliamentary elections, as Chapter 5 explained, I count the time from election day to the announcement of a cabinet.

The average government in this data set took more than three weeks to form. One-party majority governments have been constituted much more quickly, on average, than have surplus coalitions: in seven days, as opposed to thirty-two. Between those extremes, eighteen days of negotiations have prepared the inauguration of the average minority government, and twenty-nine days, the average minimal winning coalition. Minority one-party cabinets closely resemble minority coalitions. On average, eighteen days have readied the former, and seventeen days, the latter. Those minimal winning coalitions connecting adjacent parties on the left–right spectrum have taken shape after a mean of thirty-three days, which upsets Axelrod's (1970) argument that policy compatibilities streamline bargaining. Contrary to Leiserson's (1968) expectations, those minimal winning coalitions containing the smallest possible number of parties have emerged on average after thirty-seven days.[12] To judge from the aggregate evidence on crisis duration, then, the deals required to consummate majority coalitions and even minimal winning coalitions have carried a relatively high price—relative both to one-party majority governments (which elections rarely make possible) and to minority governments.

The bargaining costs entailed in erecting governments also differ substantially across countries. Table 7.3 portrays both within-nation and cross-national variations. The array of means illustrates, among other things, the extraordinarily long gestation of Dutch minimal winning and surplus coalitions. The table also hints, and analyses of variance confirm, that the cross-national differences in bargaining costs are even more pronounced than are the differences in means across cabinet types.[13] The bargaining costs of building governments are relatively low in Denmark, both before and after

TABLE 7.3.
Days Spent in Government Formation, by Type of Government and Party System

	ONE-PARTY GOVERNMENTS		COALITION GOVERNMENTS			All Governments
	Majority	Minority	Minority	MWC	Surplus	
Belgium	4.7(n = 3)	24.5(n = 2)	24.0(n = 2)	27.7(n = 15)	48.8(n = 12)	32.7
Denmark 1[a]	NA	8.6(n = 9)	2.8(n = 4)	7.3(n = 3)	NA	6.9
Denmark 2[a]	NA	17.0(n = 5)	10.2(n = 6)	NA	NA	13.3
Finland	NA	33.5(n = 4)	6.4(n = 7)	24.3(n = 3)	35.8(n = 20)	26.8*[b]
France	NA	32.0(n = 1)	15.9(n = 10)	8.0(n = 3)	10.2(n = 16)	12.6
Germany	0.0(n = 1)	0.0(n = 2)	NA	30.4(n = 15)	19.5(n = 4)	24.3*
Ireland	12.0(n = 5)	15.0(n = 4)	16.5(n = 2)	13.6(n = 7)	NA	13.8
Italy	NA	30.5(n = 16)	49.5(n = 4)	21.0(n = 4)	26.2(n = 28)	28.9**
Netherlands	NA	NA	24.7(n = 3)	84.3(n = 8)	73.2(n = 9)	70.4
Norway	8.0(n = 6)	13.6(n = 10)	16.5(n = 4)	14.7(n = 3)	NA	12.8
Sweden	2.5(n = 4)	10.2(n = 13)	18.0(n = 2)	9.0(n = 5)	NA	9.3
ALL	6.9(n = 19)	18.1(n = 66)	16.6(n = 44)	29.3(n = 66)	33.0(n = 89)	27.6[b]

SOURCES: Calculations based on government data in Appendix C and information on government crises in *Keesing's Contemporary Archives*, various issues.

NOTE: Entries are the mean number of days between the fall of one government (or, when elections intervene, between election day) and the rise of another government. Analyses of variance assess differences in means across different types of government within each country. Numbers of applicable cabinets are in parentheses. NA, Not applicable; MWC, minimal winning coalition.

[a] Denmark 1 = pre-1973 Denmark; Denmark 2 = post-1973.

[b] Computed including Finland's nonpartisan governments (mean days = 22.7, n = 7), which do not appear in other columns. The average for Finland's partisan governments is 28.5.

* p < .10. ** p < .05.

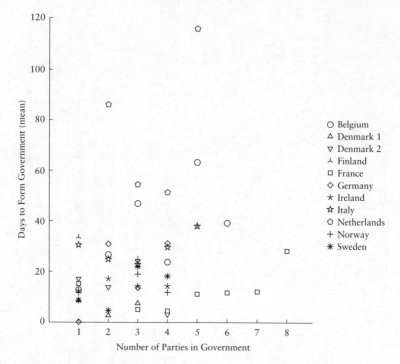

FIGURE 7.8. Days to Form Government, by Number of Parties in Government (Means)

the fateful elections of 1973, and in France, Ireland, Norway, and Sweden. Bargaining costs are higher, on average, in Belgium, Finland, Germany, and Italy. The Netherlands is in a league of its own.

Leaving aside the majority criterion in Leiserson's logic, one might suppose that the more parties earn a place at the cabinet table, the more protracted bargaining becomes. As incumbents multiply, so, too, would the complexity of their interactions. This notion, though intuitively appealing, is put to rest by Figure 7.8. As the plot of means establishes, there is no linear relationship between the number of governing parties and the time needed to agree on the installation of a government. Moreover, cross-national distinctions overshadow differences across governments composed of different numbers of parties.[14] The average three- or four-party coalition takes no more time to patch together than the average two-party coalition. Seven-party coalitions are about as rapidly negotiated as the average one-party government. (Granted, this last comparison hangs on France, which is home to all of the seven-party coalitions in the data set.)

Both Table 7.3 and Figure 7.8 suggest a contrast between unipolar sys-

tems, all of which evince low bargaining costs, and other types of party systems, where such costs are often but not always higher. If the argument proposed in this book is correct, then variations in bargaining costs should be
comprehensible in terms of spatial and institutional attributes. More specifically, since a unipolar party system and a small effective number of parliamentary parties are ingredients of a simple, straightforward competitive environment, they should be associated with rapid settlements on new
governments. Perhaps the simplicity of a bipolar system promotes swift
agreement as well. Since parliamentary elections are very likely to register
some (even if small) change in parties' sizes and positions in policy space,
they should lead to lengthy negotiations. Since an investiture requirement
gives legislators the opportunity to reject bargaining outcomes—and gives
would-be executives an incentive to work to avert rejection—such rules
should prolong bargaining. It is also possible that a strong legislative committee structure would encourage parties to draw out bargaining, reasoning
that if intransigence prompted their exclusion from government, they could
nonetheless influence policy in committee.

To evaluate the impact of spatial conditions on time spent in bargaining,
I estimate the following model:

$$B_g = a + b_1 U_g + b_2 BI_g + b_3 N_g + b_4 E_g + e_g \qquad (7.1)$$

where B_g is the number of days of bargaining that has prepared government
g, U_g is a dummy variable coded 1 when government g forms in a unipolar
party system and 0 otherwise, BI_g is a dummy variable coded 1 when government g forms in a bipolar party system, N_g is an index of the number and
size of parliamentary parties when government g forms,[15] and E_g is a
dummy coded 1 when government g takes office immediately after a parliamentary election. All 291 governments in this data set enter into the analysis. A second set of models probes institutional effects on crisis bargaining:

$$B_g = a + b_1 U_g + b_2 BI_g + b_3 N_g + b_4 E_g + b_5 I_g + b_6 CS_g + e_g \qquad (7.2)$$

where I_g is a dummy coded 1 when government g faces an investiture
requirement and CS_g is the index of committee strength discussed in
Chapter 6.

Table 7.4 records the coefficients, t statistics, and adjusted R^2 values that
these computations yield.[16] The leftmost column shows that, in the first
model, the most powerful predictors of length of bargaining are the type of
party system and the timing of government formation relative to elections.
The standard error of the estimate (SEE) is extremely high, however.
Scrutiny of the residuals reveals three spectacular outliers, all from the
Netherlands: the surplus coalition launched by Joop den Uyl in May 1973,

TABLE 7.4.

Days Spent in Government Formation: Findings from Three Classes of Models

DEPENDENT VARIABLE: DAYS SPENT IN GOVERNMENT FORMATION

Independent Variables	Model 7.1	7.1A	7.1B	7.2	7.2A	7.2B	7.3	7.3A
Unipolar system	−26.44† (−7.22)	−22.50† (−7.76)	−22.14† (−8.93)	−27.18† (−7.25)	−23.19† (−9.20)	−22.82† (−8.80)	−19.73† (−6.15)	−19.48† (−7.43)
Bipolar system	−10.47* (−1.78)	−6.68 (−1.44)	—	−4.08 (−0.65)	−5.30 (−1.19)	−7.86* (−1.85)	−8.51 (−1.58)	−6.98* (−1.69)
Postelection timing	25.88† (9.14)	21.82† (9.70)	21.41† (9.55)	24.39† (8.52)	20.40† (9.43)	21.93† (9.70)	22.58† (8.44)	20.67† (9.36)
Effective number of parties	0.02 (0.02)	0.37 (0.39)	—	0.02 (0.01)	—	—	—	—
Investiture	—	—	—	−2.25 (−0.76)	—	0.94 (0.40)	4.77 (1.63)	4.51* (1.87)
Committee strength	—	—	—	−3.68** (−2.53)	−1.50 (−1.29)	—	0.83 (0.55)	—

TABLE 7.4. (*Continued*)

Independent Variables	Model	7.1	7.1A	7.1B	7.2	7.2A	7.2B	7.3	7.3A
					DEPENDENT VARIABLE: DAYS SPENT IN GOVERNMENT FORMATION				
Netherlands		—	—	—	—	—	—	41.32[†]	21.39[†]
								(6.70)	(4.41)
Constant		20.58[***]	18.11[†]	19.22[†]	35.64[†]	25.39[†]	19.23[†]	11.58[*]	15.47[†]
		(3.44)	(3.83)	(12.61)	(4.36)	(5.56)	(8.73)	(1.77)	(6.74)
Number		291	288[a]	288[a]	291	288[a]	288[a]	291	288[a]
Adjusted R^2		.29	.32	.32	.30	.33	.32	.40	.37
SEE		23.25	18.30	18.34	23.04	18.25	18.30	22.41	17.73

NOTE: Entries are unstandardized regression coefficients with *t* statistics in parentheses. Dashes indicate that the designated variable did not enter the regression analysis. SEE, standard error of the estimate.

[a] Three Dutch outliers omitted.

* $p = .07.$ ** $p < .05.$ *** $p < .01.$ † $p < .001.$

the minimal winning coalition headed by Andreas van Agt in December 1977, and the minimal winning coalition forged by Ruud Lubbers in November 1989. (All three governments assumed office immediately after elections and while the KVP/CDA lacked core status.)

With the three outliers removed, as the second column of Table 7.4 conveys, the SEE declines and the predictive power of the model increases. The gestation of governments in unipolar party systems is about twenty-two days shorter than that of governments in bipolar and multipolar systems, holding other variables constant. Conversely, executives initiated after parties have contested parliamentary elections take about twenty-two days longer to form than do other governments. (Cabinets in the German bipolar system are also relatively quickly constituted, but that coefficient lacks statistical significance.) The third column discloses that the dummies for a unipolar party system and postelection timing together account for 32 percent of the variance in the length of negotiations over new governments.

Consider now the addition of variables tapping institutional features. The fourth column of Table 7.4 reports on all 291 governments and provides a benchmark for the findings in the next two columns. It appears that the legislative committee system has a greater impact on bargaining costs than does investiture. Contrary to expectations, the stronger committees are, the briefer government crises become; the coefficient for investiture also has the wrong sign. Dropping the three Dutch outliers, however, deprives the coefficient for committees of statistical significance, as the fifth column exhibits. And without the three outliers, the coefficient for investiture switches sign, as portrayed in the sixth column. Recall that unusually weak committees operate in the Dutch legislature, that Dutch executives do not confront investiture, and that exceptionally high bargaining costs put the Netherlands in a league of its own.

To control for country effects, I estimate a third set of models:

$$B_g = a + b_1 U_g + b_2 BI_g + b_3 E_g + b_4 I_g + b_5 CS_g + b_6 NE_g + e_g \qquad (7.3)$$

where NE_g is a dummy coded 1 when government g rules in the Netherlands. The rightmost column of Table 7.4 shows a powerful country effect indeed: Even without the three most extreme cases, the estimation indicates that twenty-one more days are needed in the Netherlands than elsewhere to conclude settlements on executives. Isolating the "Dutch delay" leaves intact the influence on crisis duration exercised by unipolar competition, postelection timing, and investiture. Furthermore, the coefficient for a bipolar system approaches conventional levels of statistical significance in both the sixth and the last columns. Put differently, when controls are in place for postelection timing, investiture, and the Netherlands, the simplicity of Germany's bipolar system appears to reduce bargaining costs.

Together, the five dummies included in the reduced form of model 7.3 (labeled model 7.3A in Table 7.4) explain 37 percent of the variance in crisis duration.

Even for model 7.3A, though, the SEE is high, which raises questions about additional country effects. Multiple reestimations of the model, performed with a different country variable each time, demonstrate that the dummies for post-1973 Denmark, Fourth Republic France, and Italy have a statistically significant impact on the length of bargaining. Even accounting for type of party system, postelection timing, investiture, and the "Dutch delay," negotiations over new cabinets are more protracted in Italy, and less so in France and post-1973 Denmark, than would be expected. Only for Denmark does the magnitude of the country coefficient resemble that of the Dutch coefficient; parties in the Danish multipolar system spend twenty-three fewer days in bargaining over cabinets than do parties elsewhere.[17] The unusual frequency of early elections in Denmark helps to make sense of this pattern. Eight of the nine parliamentary elections held in Denmark between 1973 and 1993 were called ahead of the mandated four-year schedule; and, as Chapter 8 discusses, early elections in some ways function as an alternative to extended crisis negotiations.

But how can the findings for the Netherlands be interpreted? Some experts emphasize that Dutch party leaders hammer out written agreements on policy for protocoalitions, which must be ratified by the party organizations involved before a coalition can take office (Kopecký and Nijzink 1995, 2). In this reasoning, the need for party approval of policy documents gives would-be executives an incentive to try to avert rejection and thus drags out crisis bargaining, much as investiture does (Nijzink, personal communication, April 1995). Sounding another theme, Gladdish (1991, 135) dwells on "the two major assumptions [widespread in the Netherlands] . . . that elections are unlikely to effect radical changes in major party strengths, and . . . that new cabinets will continue to be built around the center. These understandings enable prolonged negotiations to be undertaken without any anxiety about the continuity of governmental and parliamentary business." Finally, it is claimed that "a long interregnum is the price that is paid for cabinet stability" in the Netherlands (Andeweg and Irwin 1993, 114; cf. Maas 1986).

Each of these arguments has trouble when cross-national comparisons are pursued. In keeping with an informal rule in place since roughly 1960, "representative party bodies" must approve the written policy agreements produced by Belgian protocoalitions (Hearl 1992, 250). The two assumptions cited for the Netherlands are also common in Italy. Yet, crisis duration in Belgium and (to a lesser degree) Italy can be accommodated within a model comprised of spatial and institutional factors, as just indicated. Last, outside of the Netherlands long interregna do not "buy" cabinet stability.

The experience of Belgian, Finnish, and Italian governments illustrates this point. More broadly, a landmark fifteen-nation study has established that crisis duration is unrelated to cabinet duration, once controls for postelection timing are included (King et al. 1990). The same study concludes instead that attributes of party systems—fractionalization and polarization, which are components of "complex party systems and hence complex bargaining environments"—do much to determine government duration, as noted in Chapter 2 (King et al. 1990, 869).

The determinants of crisis duration differ from those of government duration. In the Netherlands, the effective number of parties and thus fractionalization are relatively high, whereas polarization (as indexed by electoral support for extremist parties) is low.[18] Accordingly, executives are longer-lived in the Netherlands than in Belgium, Finland, France, and Italy. The negotiations that have prepared Dutch cabinets are extremely time-consuming, nevertheless. The logic that I have developed leads me to stress commonalities between the party systems of Italy and the Netherlands. In both multipolar systems, a strong core party faces competitors in several directions. (In the other multipolar systems, again, the Belgian Christian Socials and Finnish Centrists are somewhat less advantaged as core parties, and the French Radicals and post-1973 Danish Social Democrats have inhabited the core still less often.) In both Italy and the Netherlands, the core party manifests an unusual ability to mold government policy. In Italy, and less so in the Netherlands, the core party neutralizes the office costs of coalition. Bargaining costs are high in both systems, and highest in the Netherlands, where the KVP/CDA lost core status a few times before the early 1990s.

It seems reasonable to interpret time expended in crisis negotiations as the price that Dutch parties have paid to secure relatively low policy and office costs of erecting coalitions, given spatial conditions in the Netherlands that resemble, but do not equal, those in Italy. In line with this interpretation, the three most protracted crises in the Netherlands occurred when the KVP/CDA lacked core status. Does evidence of the import of the spatial similarities—and distinctions—between Italy and the Netherlands also emerge in the analysis of electoral costs?

The Electoral Costs of Building
and Sustaining Coalitions

Chapter 5 documented that the electoral rewards and penalties for Italy's governing parties have depended on the segmentation of the electorate and the configuration of parties in policy space. Do the same factors shape the electoral price of incumbency in other party systems? Table 7.5 furnishes an overview of electoral results in the ten countries studied here since the end of World War II. The data it reports pertain to parties that have governed for most of the span between two successive elections.[19] The table's leftmost column spotlights the party that has most often occupied the core in each party system. The first row for each system in the table exhibits the mean change in vote share that parties have registered after spending most of the interelectoral period in government. The second row for each system shows the chance of a loss—that is, out of all electoral campaigns that a party has waged as an incumbent, the percentage of contests in which the party has suffered some decline in votes.

To appreciate what the numbers in the table convey, consider the records of the Swedish Social Democrats (SAP) and the French Christian Democrats (MRP, Popular Republican Movement). The long-governing SAP slipped from 47.8 percent of the vote in 1960 to 47.3 percent in 1964 (a loss of 0.5 percent), rebounded with 50.1 percent of the vote in 1968 (a gain of 2.8 percent), and then fell to 45.3 percent in 1970 (a loss of 4.8 percent). Over these three interelectoral periods, the SAP's mean change in vote share was −0.83 percent, and its chance of a loss was 67 percent. The SAP's "electoral scorecard" from 1960 to 1970 approximates its average performance as an incumbent between 1948 and 1994: As listed in Table 7.5, over all twelve interelectoral periods that the SAP spent as a governing party from 1948 to 1994, the SAP lost 0.9 percent of the popular vote on average and ran a 75 percent risk of slumping at the polls. This average shift is small, but in 1976, a loss of 0.9 percent sufficed to deprive the SAP of national office for the first time since 1936.

In the French Fourth Republic, the MRP met stiffer electoral penalties for governing, yet assumed a role in all but five of the regime's thirty cabinets. The MRP's share of the vote rose from 24.9 percent in 1945 to 28.1 percent in June 1946, slid to 26.3 percent in November 1946, dived to 12.5 percent in 1951, and in 1956 dipped further, to 11.1 percent. Over all four interelectoral periods in the history of the Fourth Republic, then, the mean change in the MRP's vote share was −3.45 percent and its chance of a loss was 75 percent. Hence, by one indicator of the long-term electoral performance of governing parties, the odds of a loss, the SAP and MRP look identical. By another measure, the mean change in the vote, the two parties present noteworthy contrasts. What drives such differences in electoral records over the long run?

Closer inspection of Table 7.5 reveals, first, the electoral resiliency of long-standing core parties. In Italy and the Netherlands (again, the two multipolar systems with strong core parties), incumbent Christian Democrats stand a fair chance of being exposed to electoral punishment, but the

TABLE 7.5.

Electoral Gain or Loss and Chance of an Electoral Loss for Governing Parties, by Party and Party System

	Most Frequent Core Party	Other Parties[a]			
Belgium, 1946–91	PSC/CVP	PSB/BSP	Liberals	VU	FDF
Mean Δ in vote share	–1.7(n = 14)	–2.5(n = 8)	–0.7(n = 8)	–2.6(n = 2)	–0.1(n = 1)
Chance of a loss	57%	100%	63%	100%	100%
Denmark, 1945–71	SD	RV	V	KF	
Mean Δ in vote share	–1.3(n = 6)	–1.1(n = 3)	+0.8(n = 4)	–1.6(n = 3)	
Chance of a loss	83%	100%	25%	100%	
Denmark, 1971–90					
Mean Δ in vote share	–2.2(n = 4)	–2.1(n = 1)	+3.1(n = 5)	+0.4(n = 4)	
Chance of a loss	50%	100%	20%	75%	
Finland, 1945–91	KP	SKDL	SSDP	LKP	SFP
Mean Δ in vote share	–0.3(n = 11)	–3.2(n = 4)	–0.6(n = 11)	+0.04(n = 5)	–0.2(n = 11)
Chance of a loss	67%	80%	64%	60%	82%
France IV, 1945–56	RAD bloc	SFIO	MRP	CONS bloc	GAUL
Mean Δ in vote share	+1.4(n = 2)	–3.1(n = 3)	–3.5(n = 4)	+1.3(n = 2)	–17.8(n = 1)
Chance of a loss	50%	100%	75%	0%	100%
Germany, 1949–94	FDP	SPD	CDU/CSU		
Mean Δ in vote share	–0.6(n = 10)	–0.2(n = 5)	+1.0(n = 8)		
Chance of a loss	60%	40%	63%		

TABLE 7.5. (*Continued*)

	Most Frequent Core Party	Other Parties[a]			
Ireland, 1948–92	FF	Labour	FG		
Mean Δ in vote share	−1.9(n = 9)	−1.2(n = 5)	−3.1(n = 5)		
Chance of a loss	67%	83%	60%		
Italy, 1946–92	DC	PSI	PSDI	PRI	PLI
Mean Δ in vote share	−0.5(n = 11)	−0.1(n = 5)	−0.8(n = 8)	+0.2(n = 5)	+0.4(n = 4)
Chance of a loss	55%	60%	63%	40%	25%
Netherlands, 1946–89	KVP/CDA	PvdA	ARP	CHU	VVD
Mean Δ in vote share	−0.7(n = 13)	+1.3(n = 6)	−0.4(n = 6)	−0.7(n = 6)	−0.9(n = 7)
Chance of a loss	54%	33%	67%	80%	71%
Norway, 1945–93	DNA	V	SP	KRF	H
Mean Δ in vote share	+0.02(n = 9)	−4.0(n = 2)	−0.1(n = 3)	+1.2(n = 3)	−1.4(n = 2)
Chance of a loss	44%	100%	67%	33%	100%
Sweden, 1948–94	SAP	CP	FP	M	
Mean Δ in vote share	−0.9(n = 12)	−1.5(n = 5)	−2.4(n = 3)	+2.8(n = 3)	
Chance of a loss	75%	80%	100%	0%	

SOURCES: Calculations based on electoral data in Mackie and Rose 1991, with corrections in Lijphart 1994 and updates from *Keesing's Contemporary Archives*, and government composition data contained in Appendix C.

NOTE: This table records a party's electoral performance only when it qualifies as an incumbent, that is, when the party has governed for more than half of an interelectoral period. For each system, entries in the first row are mean values in incumbent parties' percentage share of the vote between pairs of consecutive elections to the lower house of the legislature; entries in the second row show the percentage of interelectoral periods that the party as an incumbent scored electoral losses. For each party, the baseline for computing changes in vote shares is the first postwar election that the party or bloc contested. Numbers of applicable interelectoral periods are in parentheses. Party abbreviations are defined in the text and in Appendix A.

[a] Ordered left to right.

effects of those losses are likely to "wash out"—to be balanced, sooner or later, by gains. The change in vote share for the DC and KVP/CDA is, on average, small. Roughly the same can be said for the Finnish KP, the Swedish and Norwegian Social Democrats, and the German Free Democrats, which have all inhabited the median position in their party systems for relatively long stretches. For parties with less time at the core—the Belgian Christian Socials, the French Radical bloc, the Danish Social Democrats, and Fianna Fáil in Ireland—the odds of a downturn when campaigning from incumbency are not wildly different (they do not drop below 40 percent or exceed 85 percent); but the electoral swings do not even out. On average, losses prevail, save for the French Radical bloc. The Radical exception hinges on two elections and disregards fragmentation after electoral gains.[20]

Consider now the electoral fortunes of still less advantaged parties, those that have rarely or never occupied the core. In the Italian and Dutch multipolar systems, movements in vote shares have, on average, been relatively limited for the governing allies of the DC and KVP/CDA. In Finland and Germany, the same applies to the KP's and FDP's partners in government, with the striking exception of the Finnish Communists (SKDL). Instead, in Sweden and Norway, several non–Social Democratic incumbents have witnessed, on average, relatively pronounced dips or surges in support. In systems with weaker core parties (once more, Belgium, France, Denmark, and Ireland), quite a few governing parties run a high risk of lagging at the polls, and the electoral swings, once more, do not even out.

The comparisons just made may be summarized as follows: For stronger core parties, the electoral costs of incumbency are low. For weaker core parties, cabinet responsibilities bring greater electoral shifts on average. In multipolar and bipolar systems with strong or fairly strong core parties, all or almost all incumbents are sheltered from electoral boom and bust. Such protection is lacking if the core party is weak—or if the system is unipolar. One interpretation of this last finding would be that working-class identities impart electoral solidity to governing Social Democrats at the single, left pole of the Swedish and Norwegian systems; they do not prevent nonworker voters from deserting or flocking to governing center–right parties.

There is reason to pause before embracing this interpretation. Multiple interpretations are compatible with the data presented in Table 7.5. Center-right incumbents in Sweden and Norway might be vulnerable to electoral swings above all because they have governed in recent decades, when class loyalties are on the wane. Beyond Scandinavia: Are French and Irish incumbents vulnerable because core parties are weak in those systems, because those national electorates are not sharply segmented, or because electoral laws (*panachage* in 1951 and 1956 for France, single transferable vote for Ireland) permit cross-party voting? Are non-core incumbents in Italy and the Netherlands spared electoral upheaval because core parties are strong, because electorates are segmented, or because many-party coalitions blur responsibility? On the basis of Table 7.5 alone, it is impossible to isolate and appraise the influences that institutions, spatial configurations of voters and parties, and party strategies exert on the electoral costs of governing.

To disentangle cause and effect, I estimate the following model, which includes measures tapping electoral laws, spatial conditions, and party strategies:

$$V_i = a + b_1PL_i + b_2(C_iU_i) + b_3(C_iM_i) + b_4SG_i + b_5GP_i + e_i \qquad (7.4)$$

where V_i is the mean shift in vote share that party i has encountered after spending most of the interelectoral period in government, PL_i is a dummy variable for the kind of laws under which party i has contested elections (coded 0 for laws that close off opportunities for cross-party voting, 1 for laws that open them),[21] C_i is a dummy for the strength of the party that has most often occupied the core in party i's system (coded 0 for weaker core parties, 1 for stronger), U_i is a dummy coded 1 where party i competes in a unipolar system, M_i is a dummy coded 1 where party i competes in a multipolar system, SG_i is the degree of segmentation in the national electorate confronting party i,[22] and GP_i is the mean number of parties in all governments that party i has joined. The interactive terms C_iU_i and C_iM_i allow for a test of the hypothesis that the impact of a core party on mean vote shifts depends on the type of party system. I also estimate the analogous model for mean values of vote shifts without regard to their direction, up or down:

$$\pm V_i = a + b_1PL_i + b_2(C_iU_i) + b_3(C_iM_i) + b_4SG_i + b_5GP_i + e_i \qquad (7.5)$$

where $\pm V_i$ is the absolute value of the mean vote shift that party i has seen after incumbency. Any party that has governed for the better part of at least one interelectoral period enters into these analyses, so that I examine sixty-three cases overall. (I treat a party governing in Denmark's unipolar system and its multipolar system as constituting two cases, as I did for Tables 7.1, 7.2, and 7.5.)

I expect the results produced by the second model to differ from those yielded by the first. In particular, the spatial measures should prove to be satisfactory as predictors not of mean vote shifts, but of *absolute values* of mean vote shifts. For instance, the more firmly the national electorate is subdivided into blocs, the closer to zero a party's mean vote shift should be. The less segmented the electorate, the higher the gains—and losses—should be. Thus, segmentation should predict the mean vote shift rather poorly. Rules admitting cross-party voting could induce swings up or down, and so electoral laws, like spatial conditions, should predict absolute values of mean vote shifts relatively well and should predict the mean shift poorly.

Table 7.6 reports the coefficients, t statistics, and adjusted R^2 values resulting from these computations. The leftmost column shows that, in the full version of the first model, the number of governing parties is the single best predictor—indeed, as the t value indicates, the only good predictor—of the mean shift in an incumbent party's vote share. Contrary to expectations, however, as parties take on more and more allies in government, their mean vote shifts are likely to become more negative. Scrutiny of the residuals demonstrates that two outliers drive this result: the French Gaullist bloc, whose vote share plummeted from 21.8 percent in 1951 to 4 percent in 1956, the only election it contested as an incumbent in the Fourth Republic; and the Irish Clann na Poblachta (literally, Children of the Republic), whose share plunged from 13.2 percent in 1948 to 4.1 percent in 1951, the only election it contested as an incumbent. (On the CP, which waged its last electoral campaign in 1961, see Mair 1987, ch. 1.) The Gaullists governed in six-party coalitions, on average, and the Clann na Poblachta, in five-party coalitions. With those two cases omitted, the model fails miserably. Both the full model (7.4A, in the second column) and a reduced form (7.4B, third column) evince zero predictive capacity.

To explore the roots of this failure, it is useful to observe the success of the second model. When all sixty-three cases are analyzed, the number of governing parties is the only good predictor of the absolute value of an incumbent party's mean vote shift. Again, though, the two outliers from France and Ireland distort the findings. With the outliers removed, two significant influences on mean electoral gains/losses emerge: the number of governing parties and the interactive term for a strong core party in a multipolar system. (Compare the fourth and fifth columns of the table, labeled 7.5 and 7.5A.) These two factors alone account for 17 percent of the variance in the absolute value of an incumbent's mean vote shift, a finding reported in the rightmost column. As the coefficients reveal, the configuration of policy space has a greater impact on mean vote losses/gains than does the mean number of allies in a party's governments. Governing parties in multipolar systems with a strong or fairly strong core party display a mean shift in vote gains/losses that is 0.81 percent lower than parties in other systems. When the mean number of allies increases by one, the absolute value of the mean vote shift rises by about 0.4 percent of the total vote. What pushes incumbents' mean vote shifts toward zero, then, is the structure of party competition, not pure party-list electoral rules and not high segmentation in the electorate. Increases in governing allies push mean vote shifts away from zero.

Away from zero, but up or down? To judge from what Table 7.6 says

TABLE 7.6.
The Electoral Consequences of Incumbency: Findings from Two Classes of Models

DEPENDENT VARIABLES

Independent Variables	Model	MEAN SHIFT IN VOTE SHARE			ABSOLUTE VALUE OF MEAN SHIFT		
		7.4	7.4A	7.4B	7.5	7.5A	7.5B
Personalized electoral laws		-0.89 (-0.94)	0.30 (0.52)	—	0.92 (1.18)	-0.16 (-0.44)	—
Strength of core × unipolar		-0.01 (-0.01)	-0.03 (-0.04)	—	0.25 (0.27)	0.25 (0.57)	—
Strength of core × multipolar		0.77 (0.83)	0.56 (0.99)	0.30 (0.68)	-1.08 (-1.38)	-0.87** (-2.43)	-0.81*** (-2.91)
Segmentation		0.24 (0.42)	-0.23 (-0.65)	—	-0.35 (-0.72)	0.07 (0.32)	—
Mean number of governing parties		-1.02*** (-3.05)	-0.22 (-1.00)	-0.27 (-1.41)	1.12† (4.02)	0.39*** (2.80)	0.39*** (3.18)

(Continued on next page)

TABLE 7.6. (*Continued*)

			DEPENDENT VARIABLES				
		MEAN SHIFT IN VOTE SHARE			ABSOLUTE VALUE OF MEAN SHIFT		
Independent Variables	*Model*	7.4	7.4A	7.4B	7.5	7.5A	7.5B
Constant		1.74	-0.04	-0.13	-1.36	0.30	0.41
		(1.29)	(-0.05)	(-0.20)	(-1.21)	(0.57)	(0.98)
Number		63	61[a]	61[a]	63	61[a]	61[a]
Adjusted R^2		.12	.00	.01	.24	.14	.17
SEE		2.62	1.58	1.55	2.18	1.00	0.98

NOTE: Entries are unstandardized regression coefficients with *t* statistics in parentheses. Dashes indicate that the designated variable did not enter the regression analysis. SEE, standard error of the estimate.

[a] French Gaullists and Irish CP omitted.

* $p = .07$. ** $p < .05$. *** $p < .01$. † $p < .001$.

about the first model, that question has no answer. Figure 7.9A and B gives different answers for different types of parties and thus explains why the first model fails and the second, for absolute values, performs reasonably well. Figure 7.9A illustrates that, among parties that have most often occupied the core in their systems, the mean vote shift moves up (after a bump down) as allies increase. Among the non-core incumbents depicted in Figure 7.9B, as allies increase, a (rough) downward trend in the mean vote share appears.[23] The stronger core parties in multipolar systems (with tags for Italy, the Netherlands, and Finland in Figure 7.9A) tend to govern with several allies and have mean vote shifts near zero. The tags in Figure 7.9B show that most non-core incumbents in Italy, the Netherlands, and Finland are also characterized by numerous governing partners and restricted mean vote shifts.

To take stock of the results so far: Parties' competitive environments and alliance strategies help to determine the electoral price of incumbency. Governing parties in multipolar systems with a strong or fairly strong core party pay very little, on average, for shouldering cabinet responsibilities. The number of governing allies that parties choose also shapes their electoral fortunes, but the impact differs across core and non-core incumbents. Larger coalitions translate into electoral protection for the parties that have most often qualified as the core in their systems. But larger coalitions expose non-core incumbents to greater electoral punishment, on average. Taken together, these findings imply that one conclusion from Chapters 4 and 5—that building many-party coalitions limits electoral risks for virtually all incumbent parties—applies only to multipolar systems with strong cores (Italy and the Netherlands) or fairly strong cores (Finland). Finally, electoral laws and segmentation in the electorate exert relatively weak influences on electoral costs. Two hypotheses must be rejected in light of the evidence here: that rules admitting cross-party voting amplify incumbents' mean vote shifts; and that high segmentation dampens those shifts.

Other hypotheses about electoral laws and segmentation could and should be tested, however. The additional propositions regard within-nation variations over time and are suggested by research on aggregate electoral volatility (or the net change between successive elections in vote shares won by all parties, members of government and opposition alike). Several analysts have emphasized that revisions of electoral laws are "associated with higher mean levels of electoral volatility" (Bartolini and Mair 1990, 152; cf. D'Alimonte and Bartolini 1995; Pedersen 1983). Some contend, further, that the waning of class and religious loyalties since the early 1970s has led to higher electoral volatility in a number of European countries (Dalton, Beck, and Flanagan 1984; Pedersen 1979; for a recent overview of evidence, see Gallagher, Laver, and Mair 1995). It could be supposed, based on these

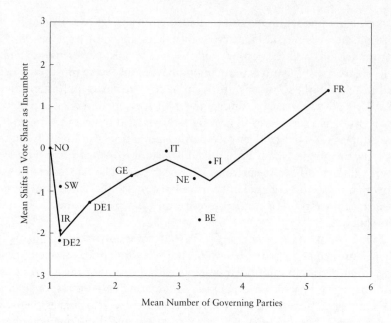

FIGURE 7.9A. Vote Shifts for Core Party as Incumbent, by Mean Number of Governing Parties.

studies, that governing parties undergo relatively substantial fluctuations in support when elections are held under new rules. Moreover, governing parties might be expected to have seen more sizable electoral swings in the past two decades than in the early postwar period.

Evidence from most of the countries marches with the first hypothesis. Figure 7.10 (see pg. 136) compares the mean shift in incumbents' vote shares, averaging the absolute values of those shifts across all governing parties, in two types of elections: those held immediately after the introduction of new electoral laws and those held under unaltered rules. (Since Belgium, Finland, and Ireland did not modify electoral laws between 1945 and 1993, they are not considered here. For dates of electoral reforms, refer to Table 6.1.)[24] Only in Denmark do governing parties experience narrower, rather than broader, vote swings in elections carried out under new rules. In Denmark, new laws were used in the elections of September 1953 and 1964, whereas the "earthquake election" of 1973 ushered in a phase of electoral instability (Borre 1984, 1992; Nannestad 1989; Pedersen 1987). Hence, the Danish exception reflects the timing of electoral reforms and points to the next hypothesis.

Figure 7.11 (see pg. 137) charts mean vote shifts, averaging the absolute values of those shifts across all governing parties, for two periods: the mid-

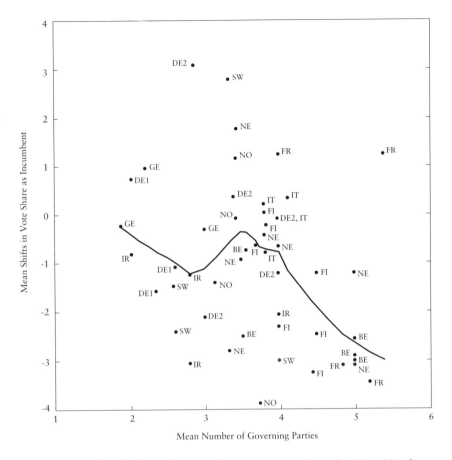

FIGURE 7.9B. Vote Shift for Non-Core Parties as Incumbents, by Mean Number of Governing Parties.

1940s to the early 1970s and the early 1970s to the early 1990s.[25] (Since the French Fourth Republic gave way to a new regime in 1958, it is excluded here. The data in Figure 7.10 and Table 7.5 document that French governing parties were subjected to sizable electoral swings.) In Denmark and Finland and, even more dramatically, in the Netherlands, Norway, and Sweden, swings in incumbents' mean vote shares are magnified in the past two decades. In contrast, governing parties in Belgium and Germany have recently become more insulated from electoral fluctuations. With mean vote losses/gains averaged across all incumbents, Ireland and Italy display virtually no variation between periods. Yet a central message of the earlier discussion is that different governing parties within the same country may

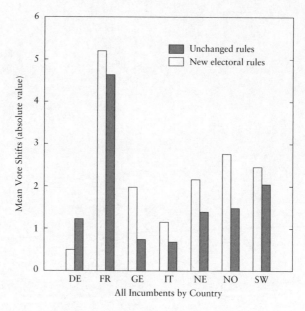

FIGURE 7.10. Vote Shifts for Incumbent Parties, by
Country and Type of Election (Means of Absolute
Values)

meet different electoral fates. For example, notwithstanding the overall
Dutch datum, movements in vote shares for the Dutch Christian Democrats
(KVP/CDA) have become more limited, on average, in recent decades.[26]
Thus, just as "there has been no pervasive trend toward increased electoral
volatility in Western Europe" (Gallagher, Laver, and Mair 1995, 234), there
has been no uniform tendency for governing parties in recent decades to
witness larger declines or surges at the polls.[27]

Across these countries, in sum, the keys to understanding a party's average performance as an incumbent in elections over the postwar period (or,
for France, elections throughout the Fourth Republic) are supplied by that
party's competitive environment and by the number of partners it has had
in government. When postwar elections are sorted into two groups, with
each country examined separately, it appears that redesigned electoral laws
expose governing parties to greater fluctuations in the vote. The fading of
class and religious loyalties (as indexed by time) has produced much less
consistent effects.[28]

These judgments in hand, it should be stressed that the determinants of
the long-run electoral price that parties pay for governing need not be identical to the determinants of voters' decisions in the short run. To be sure,

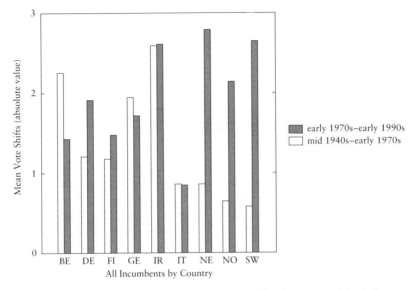

FIGURE 7.11. Vote Shifts for Incumbent Parties, by Country and Period (Means of Absolute Values)

trends over the long haul are composed of short-term ups and downs. And whatever the temporal perspective, it is clear that positions in government tend to cost parties votes when the parties do not occupy the core of policy space. As two analysts of short-run electoral change have observed, "Most incumbents lose votes in most elections" (Powell and Whitten 1993, 410). In this sample, the average governing party in the average election shed about 1.4 percent of the vote (about 1 percent of the vote, not counting the spectacular tumbles of the French Gaullists and the Irish Clann na Poblachta). Similarly, an eighteen-nation study reports that the average governing party sustained an average loss of 1 percent over the 1948–79 period (Rose and Mackie 1983).

Yet, in at least one important respect, the long-run story told here differs from the short-run story recounted by other researchers. Rates of unemployment, inflation, and growth have been absent from this account. A vast literature has instead established that incumbents' management of the economy drives short-term changes in voters' intentions and choices (e.g., Anderson 1995; Eulau and Lewis-Beck 1985; Lewis-Beck 1986, 1988; Leyden et al. 1995; Norpoth, Lewis-Beck, and Lafay 1991; Powell and Whitten 1993). Simply put, the economy matters in the short run. Institutions matter, too, as a subset of this literature has underscored. In particular, institutional arrangements (including multiparty coalitions) that blur responsibility for policy outcomes diminish the impact of economics on voters' choices (Anderson 1995; Lewis-Beck 1986, 1988; Powell and Whitten 1993).

In light of the research on economics and elections, it is useful to redefine the dependent variable of interest as the gain or loss in vote share that a party has experienced in each election.[29] I disaggregate the analysis of vote shifts by estimating the equation:

$$\Delta V_{it} = a + b_1 PL_{it} + b_2 NL_{it} + b_3 CP_i + b_4(C_i U_i) +$$
$$b_5(C_i M_i) + b_6 SG_i + b_7 P73_{it} + b_8 GP_{it} + b_9 IN_{it} +$$
$$b_{10} VS_{it-1} + b_{11} \Delta V_{it-1} + e_{it} \qquad (7.6)$$

where ΔV_{it} is the shift in vote share that party i encounters in election t (as compared to election $t–1$), PL_{it} is a dummy variable coded 1 when party i contests election t under laws permitting cross-party voting, NL_{it} is a dummy variable coded 1 when party i contests election t under new electoral laws, CP_i is a dummy variable coded 1 when party i is the party that has most often occupied the core in its party system, $P73_{it}$ is a dummy variable coded 1 when party i contests election t after January 1973, GP_{it} is the mean number of parties in all governments that party i has joined between election $t–1$ and t, IN_{it} is a dummy variable coded 1 when party i campaigns in election t having held incumbent status for most of the span since the previous election, VS_{it-1} is the vote share that party i received in the previous election, and ΔV_{it-1} is party i's shift in vote share in election $t–1$ (as compared to $t–2$). The interactive terms and the measure of segmentation are those in models 7.4 and 7.5.

The tenth and eleventh variables in the model call for special comment. Serious challenges are involved in conducting regressions on data that pool cross-sectional and time-series variation (Maddala 1971; Sayrs 1989; Stimson 1985). This party-per-election data set contains information on fifty-nine parties across ten countries competing in 136 elections, for a total of 624 observations. Since the greatest number of elections analyzed in any one country (Denmark) is nineteen, cross-sectional data dominate the time-series data.[30] Given this design, either of two procedures is appropriate: The model could include a group of dummy variables denoting the temporal sequence of the election in each country (Stimson 1985, 929), or it could incorporate previous vote shares and previous vote swings (as in Powell and Whitten 1993). For the sake of comparability with the landmark Powell and Whitten analysis, I pursue the latter strategy.[31]

Table 7.7 summarizes the results of the computations. The first column suggests that the previous vote share and previous vote swing are the only good predictors of the current shift in vote share. When two prominent outliers are removed, the coefficient for incumbent status acquires more

TABLE 7.7.

Disaggregating the Analysis of the Electoral Consequences of Incumbency

Independent Variables	Model	DEPENDENT VARIABLE: SHIFT IN VOTE SHARE				
		7.6	7.6A	7.6B	7.6Cᵃ	7.6Cᵇ
Laws permitting cross-party vote		0.23 (0.52)	0.60 (1.41)	0.58* (1.57)	—	—
New electoral laws		-0.07 (-0.15)	0.08 (0.17)	—	—	—
Long-standing core party		0.47 (1.11)	0.74** (1.79)	0.72** (1.73)	4.30** (1.80)	0.69* (1.63)
Strength of core × unipolar		0.05 (0.11)	0.14 (0.33)	—	—	—
Strength of core × multipolar		-0.03 (-0.08)	-0.14 (-0.40)	—	—	—
Segmentation		0.10 (0.46)	0.12 (0.58)	—	—	—
Since 1973		-0.20 (-0.72)	—	—	—	—
Mean N governing parties		-0.09 (-0.52)	0.15 (0.82)	0.14 (0.84)	—	—

(Continued on next page)

TABLE 7.7. (Continued)

Independent Variables	Model	DEPENDENT VARIABLE: SHIFT IN VOTE SHARE				
		7.6	7.6A	7.6B	7.6C[a]	7.6C[b]
Incumbent status		-0.88	-1.61***	-1.61†	0.34	-1.26‡
		(-1.34)	(-2.50)	(-2.54)	(0.56)	(-4.23)
Previous vote share		-0.03***	-0.04†	-0.03†	-0.17†	-0.03***
		(-2.54)	(-2.75)	(-2.62)	(-2.74)	(-2.44)
Previous shift in vote share		-0.17‡	-0.12†	-0.12†	-0.31†	-0.10***
		(-4.14)	(-2.88)	(-2.86)	(-3.42)	(-2.35)
Constant		0.70	0.68	0.71†	0.49	0.82†
		(1.31)	(1.33)	(2.84)	(0.82)	(3.17)
Number		560	558[c]	558[c]	49	509[c]
Adjusted R^2		.07	.07	.07	.37	.07
SEE		3.16	3.04	3.08	1.87	3.11

NOTE: Entries are unstandardized regression coefficients with t statistics in parentheses. Dashes indicate that the designated variable did not enter the regression analysis. SEE, standard error of the estimate.

[a] Italian cases only.

[b] Italian cases omitted.

[c] Two French outliers omitted.

* $p = .10$. ** $p = .07$. *** $p < .05$. † $p < .01$. ‡ $p < .001$.

weight, as the second column exhibits; and the coefficient for the dummy identifying long-standing core parties approaches conventional levels of statistical significance.[32] Incumbency costs parties votes at election time, but the party that most often inhabits the core of its system is somewhat shielded from electoral punishment. Although the SEE is dampened slightly with the deletion of the outliers, the predictive capacity of the model is still rather poor. Paring down the model to several key independent variables, as in the third column, alters neither the SEE nor the R^2. Distinguishing between Italy and other countries highlights the electoral stability of Italian governing parties (above all the DC) and the electoral losses suffered by incumbents in other systems, as the fourth and fifth columns convey.[33] The R^2 for the estimation excluding Italy remains low.

The addition of economic variables would presumably boost the proportion of the variance explained. My preliminary analysis of data on unemployment rates, changes in gross domestic product, and inflation (for Germany, Ireland, Italy, the Netherlands, and Sweden from the mid-1960s to the early 1990s) supports that notion.[34] The excursion into the realm of economics and elections persuades me of four other things. First, the degree of improvement in explanatory power achieved by the addition of economic indicators is likely to vary across countries. Second, the countries evincing relatively small improvements are likely to include Italy and the Netherlands, while relatively large improvements can be expected for Ireland. Third, it is worth investigating whether such contrasts reflect differences in the configuration of policy space as much as differences in the extent to which institutions clarify (or cloud) responsibility for policy making. Finally, that investigation lies beyond the scope of this book. All the same, the third point leads naturally to this chapter's conclusions.

Conclusions

One recurring theme in this analysis of electoral costs is that the structure of party competition protects some parties from, and exposes others to, electoral punishment for incumbency. Core parties with many governing allies in multipolar systems benefit electorally from incumbency— both from visibility and from diluted responsibility in a crowded field. When the analysis is disaggregated, it appears that long-standing core parties in all types of party systems are sheltered from vote losses. For two-dimensional systems, this latter finding is consistent with spatial theory— and, indeed, verges on the tautological in spatial theory. To elaborate: In a two-dimensional system, only the largest party can qualify as the core. It will remain a core party only if it stays large—if it avoids electoral disaster.

Core parties are expected to govern. Hence, long-standing core parties in two-dimensional systems, by definition, meet low electoral costs of incumbency. In a unidimensional system, on the other hand, a party of any size can occupy the median position. It can remain at the median and continue to govern even if it pays a high electoral price for incumbency. It is not obvious—not given by definition within spatial theory—that the ruling Swedish Social Democrats, for instance, should on average sacrifice little at the polls. Why does incumbency cost the Swedish SAP so little, in fact? The explanation is absent from spatial theory. Since spatial theories of coalition do not model party-voter interactions (but see Austen-Smith and Banks 1988; Laver 1997; Schofield 1993), they are silent on the causal mechanism(s) generating the electoral resiliency of long-standing core parties in one- and two-dimensional systems.

Neither does extant theoretical work on coalitions have anything to say about the strategic opportunities open to parties that inhabit the core of policy space for long stretches of time. The Dutch and Italian Christian Democrats, strong core parties in multipolar systems, have been able to offset the office costs of building coalitions. The Belgian Christian Socials, though somewhat less advantaged than their counterparts in Italy and the Netherlands, have also neutralized office costs, responding to incentives to cement governing majorities with office rewards. Strong core parties in multipolar and bipolar systems have displayed an unusual capacity to align government policy with their left–right preferences. In the multipolar systems, especially the Dutch, these accomplishments have carried the expense of protracted government crises.

But the point is that, under certain spatial and institutional conditions, some parties are able to maneuver around the electoral, office, and policy costs of creating coalitions. Can similar statements be made about the costs of rupturing coalitions?

8 *The Costs of Breaking Coalitions*

Chance ends some governments. Prime Minister Hans Hedtoft of Denmark died in office in January 1955, for example, and was succeeded by fellow Social Democrat, Hans Christian Hansen, who in turn died in office in February 1960. The electoral calendar terminates other executives. In the Netherlands, the four-party coalition led by Jan de Quay of the Christian Democrats, installed in May 1959 in the wake of parliamentary elections, lasted until May 1963, when elections again took place, in accordance with the four-year Dutch schedule.

Still other governments collapse as a result of deliberate party choice. Chapters 4 and 5 cite numerous such instances in Italy. Parties outside Italy, of course, decide to truncate governments. And it is a fact of political life in all parliamentary democracies that "unlike voting in cabinet meetings, . . . the threat to bring down a government can be enacted only once" (Laver and Schofield 1990, 171). To appreciate this point, consider the Fine Gael–Labour coalition headed by Garret Fitzgerald in Ireland between December 1982 and January 1987.

While the power of the Fine Gael ministers over their own destiny was built into the structure of cabinet decision making by virtue of Fine Gael's position as a majority party in cabinet, the bargaining power of Labour ministers could only be exercised on the basis of adventures in brinkmanship. . . . The only real power that the Labour ministers had over their Fine Gael colleagues derived from the threat to withdraw from the cabinet and bring down the government, a course of action that they finally did take in January 1987 in protest at further proposed cutbacks in health spending. (Laver and Schofield 1990, 171)

What consequences do parties meet when they make good on the threat to quit government? Notwithstanding the substantial achievements to date in theoretical and empirical research on coalition formation and dissolution, the answers to that question are not yet clear. The task of this chapter is to furnish such answers and to demonstrate that the empirical evidence adduced supports the overall argument of the book. Differences across parties and across countries in the costs of breaking coalitions should depend on variations in institutional arrangements and configurations of policy space.

Much of the quantitative analysis in this chapter replicates that conducted for Italy in Chapter 5. More specifically, the pages that follow contain ten-country analogs to Tables 5.6 and 5.8 on office and policy costs, respectively. The analysis here also corresponds to that in Chapter 7. This chapter features an analog to Table 7.4 on bargaining costs. Beyond that, however, I present some simple models—and a few very powerful ones—in which the dependent variable is an attribute of a party each time it participates in government.

The first step in this investigation is to establish how often governments come to an end due to party choice. I next assess the office costs of breaking coalitions.

How Governments End: The Role of Party Choice

Table 8.1 reports, country by country, the percentage of cabinet resignations that can be attributed to the decisions of one party or another. (As noted earlier, I relied primarily on *Keesing's Contemporary Archives* when coding information about which parties were, and were not, responsible for cabinet collapses.)[1] As the first column of the table shows, party choices have prompted the demise of over 80 percent of the governments in Belgium, Fourth Republic France, and Italy—all systems where governments are short-lived. At the other extreme stand Norway and Sweden, where one or more parties hold responsibility for under 40 percent of cabinet resignations and where average government duration is relatively long. Although mean duration reaches its maximum in Ireland in this data set, party choices have finished over 70 percent of Irish governments.[2]

The second column of Table 8.1 isolates the party responsible for the largest number of resignations in each country. It illustrates, among other things, that Christian Democrats have moved to terminate most executives in Belgium and the Netherlands. Not only junior allies but also dominant parties rupture coalitions. And Fianna Fáil has brought half of Irish governments to a premature end, which, as discussed below, reflects the frequency with which FF one-party majority governments have exercised the prerogative to call early elections.

These broad-brush comparisons provide the introduction to the more finely grained evaluation of the consequences of government falls, to which I now turn.

TABLE 8.1.
Frequency of Party Responsibility for Government Collapse,
by Country and Party

	Percentage of Cabinet Resignations for Which One or More Parties Responsible	Party Behind Most Falls (% Falls)
Belgium *(n = 33)*	81.8	PSC/CVP (66.7)
Denmark *(n = 26)*	69.2[a]	RV (40.7)
Finland *(n = 40)*	57.5[a]	SSDP (37.5)
France IV *(n = 30)*	83.3	PCF (66.7)
Germany *(n = 22)*	45.5	FDP (36.4)
Ireland *(n = 18)*	72.2	FF (50.0)
Italy *(n = 52)*	92.3	PSI (61.5)
Netherlands *(n = 20)*	45.0	KVP/CDA (30.0)
Norway *(n = 23)*	39.1	DNA, KRF, H, SP (17.4)
Sweden *(n = 24)*	25.0	CP (20.8)

SOURCES: Coding of information in *Keesing's Contemporary Archives* and other sources named in Appendix D.

NOTE: Parties counted are those that qualify as a governing party (in government for more than half of at least one interelectoral period). Party abbreviations are defined in the text and in Appendix A.

[a] Percentages are computed on a total that does not include one government for which data are missing.

The Office Costs of Breaking Coalitions

In Italy, spatial conditions have a clear impact on the office costs of destroying governments: As Chapter 5 detailed, the Italian Christian Democrats (DC) and Socialists (PSI) have reaped office benefits from breakups. What effects can be discerned in the other party systems under examination here? Table 8.2 lists for the eleven systems the same sorts of measures that appear in Table 5.6: weighted shares, and total numbers, of cabinet posts. For economy of presentation, Table 8.2 focuses on the ministerial level only.[3] The table shows that, on average, for almost all parties, weighted shares dipped slightly and—in contrast to the experience of the Italian DC and PSI—total offices stayed roughly constant after the party had contributed to a government's fall. Outside Italy, then, almost all parties suffered a small penalty in office terms for having upset a cabinet. These statements hold true even for the Dutch Christian Democrats (KVP/CDA) and the Finnish Center Party (KP), for those core parties have faced the institutional disincentives and obstacles to adding offices that were identified in Chapter 7.

TABLE 8.2.

Ministerial Office Payoffs, by Party, Responsibility for Government Collapse, and Party System

BELGIUM

Ministerial Offices at t	PSB/BSP No	PSC/CVP No	LIBERALS No	No	No
	Yes	Yes	Yes	Yes	Yes

Ministerial Offices at t	PSB/BSP		PSC/CVP		LIBERALS	
	No	Yes	No	Yes	No	Yes
Weighted party share (means)[a]	0.95	0.99	0.98	1.00	1.42	1.62
Number of cabinets joined	13	7	10	20	10	4
All ministers (means)	20	19	19	20	19	21
Number of cabinets	19	14	11	22	25	8

DENMARK, 1945–72

Ministerial Offices at t	SD		RV		V		KF	
	No	Yes	No	Yes	No	Yes	No	Yes
Weighted party share (means)	0.93	0.89	1.94	1.69	0.96	1.00	1.05	0.97
Number of cabinets joined	8	3	2	2	1	2	1	2
All ministers (means)	16	17	16	17	17	15	17	15
Number of cabinets	10	4	9	5	11	3	11	3

DENMARK, 1973–93

Ministerial Offices at t	SD		RV		V		KF	
	No	Yes	No	Yes	No	Yes	No	Yes
Weighted party share (means)	0.94	0.96	NA	1.60	1.13	1.28	0.76	0.92
Number of cabinets joined	2	3	0	1	5	2	2	3
All ministers (means)	19	19	18	20	19	20	18	20
Number of cabinets	5	6	5	6	6	5	6	5

Was Party Responsible for Collapse at Time t – 1?

TABLE 8.2. (*Continued*)

Was Party Responsible for Collapse at Time $t-1$?

FINLAND

Ministerial Offices at t	SKDL		SSDP		KP		LKP		SFP	
	No	Yes	No	Yes	No	Yes	No	Yes	No	Yes
Weighted party share (means)	0.81	0.61	0.90	0.94	0.96	0.91	1.79	NA	1.26	NA
Number of cabinets joined	5	2	16	5	20	8	16	0	23	0
All ministers (means)	11	12	12	11	12	11	11	11	11	11
Number of cabinets	30	9	24	15	27	12	36	3	36	3

FRANCE IV

Ministerial Offices at t	SFIO		RAD		MRP		RI		GAUL BLOC	
	No	Yes	No	Yes	No	Yes	No	Yes	No	Yes
Weighted party share (means)	1.08	0.91	1.27	1.16	0.79	0.88	1.16	0.88*	0.80	0.92
Number of cabinets joined	11	8	16	11	18	6	14	8	2	7
All ministers (means)	19	20	20	18	19	19	20	18	18	19
Number of cabinets	20	14	18	11	22	7	17	12	10	16

GERMANY

Ministerial Offices at t	SPD		FDP		CDU/CSU	
	No	Yes	No	Yes	No	Yes
Weighted party share (mean)	0.91	0.92	1.30	1.40	0.93	0.94
Number of cabinets joined	5	2	11	4	13	2
All ministers (means)	19	18	19	18	19	17
Number of cabinets	17	4	13	8	18	3

(*Continued on next page*)

TABLE 8.2. (Continued)

	Was Party Responsible for Collapse at Time t − 1?					
Ministerial Offices at t	No	Yes	No	Yes	No	Yes
IRELAND	LABOUR		FF		FG	
Weighted party share (means)	1.20	1.42	0.99	0.99	0.91	0.89
Number of cabinets joined	1	3	6	7	1	3
All ministers (means)	14	15*	14	14	14	15*
Number of cabinets	12	5	8	9	12	5

	No	Yes	No	Yes	No	Yes	No	Yes	No	Yes
ITALY	PSI		PSDI		PRI		DC		PLI	
Weighted party share (means)	1.30	1.23	1.84	1.84	3.00	2.25	0.89	0.83	2.09	2.12
Number of cabinets joined	3	18	21	8	17	8	21	30	12	4
All ministers (means)	21	25**	24	23	23	25	23	24	24	24
Number of cabinets	20	31	33	18	35	16	21	30	43	8

	No	Yes	No	Yes	No	Yes	No	Yes	No	Yes
NETHERLANDS	PVDA		KVP/CDA		ARP		CHU		VVD	
Weighted party share (means)	0.95	0.88	0.94	0.91	1.23	1.38	1.05	1.18	1.04	0.63
Number of cabinets joined	6	1	13	6	9	2	9	1	9	1
All ministers (means)	14	13	14	14	14	13	15	12	15	13
Number of cabinets	16	3	13	6	16	3	16	3	14	5

TABLE 8.2. (*Continued*)

Was Party Responsible for Collapse at Time *t* – 1?

NORWAY

Ministerial Offices at t	DNA		V		SP		KRF		H	
	No	*Yes*	*No*	*Yes*	*No*	*Yes*	*No*	*Yes*	*No*	*Yes*
Weighted party share (means)	*1.00*	*1.00*	1.08	1.06	1.03	1.31*	1.09	1.11	0.98	0.85
Number of cabinets joined	*10*	*4*	3	1	4	3	4	3	4	3
All ministers (means)	*16*	*14**	16	15	15	18	15	17	15	17
Number of cabinets	*18*	*4*	20	2	18	4	18	4	18	4

SWEDEN

Ministerial Offices at t	SAP		CP		FP		M	
	No	*Yes*	*No*	*Yes*	*No*	*Yes*	*No*	*Yes*
Weighted party share (means)	*0.93*	*0.95*	1.18	1.04	1.12	1.00	0.95	NA
Number of cabinets joined	*15*	*1*	4	2	2	2	2	0
All ministers (means)	*18*	*17*	18	17	18	19	18	19
Number of cabinets	*21*	*2*	18	5	19	4	19	4

SOURCES: Calculations based on portfolio data and seat data in sources described in Appendix D, coding of information in *Keesing's Contemporary Archives*, and other sources named in Appendix D.

NOTE: For each country and each party listed, the top row of entries reports mean ratios of ministerial post shares to government seat shares. The third row reports means of total ministerial posts. Means are computed, party by party, for two groups of cabinets: those whose predecessor was a cabinet the party helped to topple and those whose predecessor fell for reasons other than the party's withdrawal of support. The *t* tests compare the means of the two groups (i.e., for each party, entries in the *yes* and *no* columns). Parties are ordered left to right, and most frequent core parties are in italics. NA, not applicable.

[a] Weighted party share of ministerial offices = a party's share of ministerial offices weighted by its share of lower house seats controlled by all governing parties, averaged across all governments in which the party served.

*p < .05. ** p < .01 (separate variances *t* tests).

Only six of the differences within pairs arrayed in Table 8.2 attain statistical significance. Two of those differences involve a loss of offices. The Independent Republicans (RI) in Fourth Republic France and the Labor Party in Norway (DNA) paid a significant price in office terms when they knocked down governments. Close scrutiny reveals that the substantive significance of three of the other findings is limited. The office benefits extracted from government falls by the Fine Gael and Labour in Ireland are more apparent than real, given a small N. It is also impossible to disentangle multiple effects on the Norwegian Center Party's weighted share of ministers due to a paucity of cases.[4] Hence, the only parties to have repeatedly registered office benefits from toppling cabinets are located in Italy.

The "small-N problem" is standard in empirical analyses of coalition politics. Nonetheless, there is a straightforward way to increase the number of observations—redefine the units of analysis as parties within government. Such a strategy has been followed in several studies of portfolio allocation (Browne and Franklin 1973; Browne and Frendreis 1980; Schofield and Laver 1985). The unequivocal conclusion of this research is that a party's share of ministerial portfolios in an executive coalition (Y) marches very closely with the share of seats that the party contributes to the government's legislative coalition (X). In particular, Browne and Franklin (1973, 460) showed that, for 324 parties in 114 coalitions in thirteen parliamentary democracies,

$$Y = -0.01 + 1.07 \, X \, (R^2 = 0.86)$$

Perfect proportionality, of course, would be represented by the equation $Y = a + bX$, where $a = 0$ and $b = 1$. (The perfectly proportional relationship is often termed the Gamson hypothesis after William Gamson's [1961] seminal work.) For 700 parties in 197 coalitions in the ten parliamentary democracies in my data set,[5] regressing a party's share of ministries with its government seat share yields the result

$$Y = 0.06 + 0.76 \, X \, (R^2 = 0.89)$$

This relationship, like the one uncovered by Browne and colleagues, is nothing short of spectacular.[6]

As before, it is wise to consider not only shares but also numbers of offices. Browne and Frendreis (1980, 765) established that, for 394 parties in 132 coalitions in thirteen parliamentary democracies, the number of ministerial posts that a party acquires in coalition (O) is almost identical to the number of portfolios that a party would be predicted to receive $(G,$ often dubbed the Gamson prediction) if the rule of proportionality-to-party-size were followed as closely as possible in the subdivision of cabinet offices:

$$O = 0.97 + 0.83 \ G \ (R^2 = 0.93)$$

Similarly, for the 700 parties in the 197 coalitions here,

$$O = 1.12 + 0.77 \ G \ (R^2 = 0.90)$$

The explanatory power of the Gamson prediction is remarkable indeed.[7] The evidence is persuasive that, on the whole, a norm of proportionality operates in portfolio allocation, whether the relationship is between X and Y or between G and O.

The question now is: Does the relationship hold regardless of a party's role in provoking cabinet dissolutions? To address this issue, I estimate two equations,

$$Y_{ig} = a + b_1 X_{ig} + b_2 RF_{ig-1} + e_{ig} \tag{8.1}$$

and

$$O_{ig} = a + b_1 G_{ig} + b_2 RF_{ig-1} + e_{it}, \tag{8.2}$$

where RF_{ig-1} is a dummy variable coded 1 when party i has helped to dismantle the immediate predecessor to government g. I perform the regression for shares (y) and numbers (o) of junior ministerial offices as well. (Note that these data do not capture instances where a party responsible for the fall of government $g-1$ is excluded from government g; such instances are explored later.

Tables 8.3 and 8.4 summarize the results of the computations.[8] In Table 8.3, the first and fourth columns divulge that a party's responsibility for the fall of one government has no influence at all on the share of senior and junior offices it obtains in the next: The coefficient (b_2) for the lagged responsibility variable is zero. The first and fourth columns in Table 8.4 instead register positive and significant effects: Parties helping to upset governments appear to enhance, not damage, their capacity to staff posts in successor coalitions. To investigate what underpins the result, I reestimate the models, excluding all Italian cases. As the second and fifth columns of Tables 8.3 and 8.4 exhibit, with Italy omitted, the coefficient b_2 is uniformly small and insignificant. On the other hand, in analyses confined to Italy, which the third and sixth columns portray, parties realize significant office benefits from rupturing executives.

Can other country effects be detected? Save for two exceptions, other single-country regressions produce findings similar to those listed in the second and fifth columns of Tables 8.3 and 8.4. The first exception emerges in Finland: Responsibility for the fall of the outgoing government significantly diminishes Finnish parties' shares of junior ministers in the incoming coali-

TABLE 8.3.

Government Seat Share and Responsibility for Fall of Preceding Government
as Determinants of a Party's Share of Coalition Offices

	SHARE OF MINISTERS			SHARE OF JUNIOR MINISTERS		
Independent Variables	All ten countries	All but Italy	Italy only	All ten countries	All but Italy	Italy only
Government seat share	0.76†	0.78†	0.71†	0.88†	0.94†	0.78†
	(74.40)	(61.04)	(46.74)	(34.91)	(25.50)	(49.12)
Responsibility for fall of preceding government	0.01	0.00	0.02*	−0.00	−0.01	0.02**
	(0.97)	(0.39)	(1.90)	(−0.21)	(−0.80)	(2.36)
Constant	0.06†	0.05†	0.07†	0.03***	0.01	0.05†
	(15.66)	(11.49)	(10.82)	(2.86)	(0.55)	(7.67)
Number	669	541	128	540	412	128
Adjusted R^2	.89	.87	.95	.70	.61	.96
SEE	0.06	0.06	0.05	0.13	0.14	0.05

SOURCES: Calculations based on government composition and portfolio data summarized in Appendix C, coding of information in *Keesing's Contemporary Archives*, and other sources named in Appendix D.

NOTE: Entries are unstandardized regression coefficients; *t* statistics are in parentheses. Government seat share is defined as a party's percentage share of the seats in the lower house of the legislature that are controlled by all governing parties. SEE, standard error of the estimate.

* $p = .07$. ** $p < .05$. *** $p < .01$. † $p < .001$.

TABLE 8.4.
Gamson Prediction and Responsibility for Fall of Preceding Government as Determinants of a Party's Number of Coalition Offices

Independent Variables	NUMBER OF MINISTERS			NUMBER OF JUNIOR MINISTERS		
	All ten countries	All but Italy	Italy only	All ten countries	All but Italy	Italy only
Gamson prediction	0.76†	0.79†	0.70†	0.86†	0.95†	0.76†
	(77.56)	(60.31)	(45.35)	(92.38)	(70.15)	(43.08)
Responsibility for fall of preceding government	0.24**	0.09	0.73***	0.52***	−0.03	1.86***
	(2.51)	(0.85)	(3.13)	(2.93)	(−0.28)	(3.55)
Constant	1.08†	0.88†	1.75†	0.55†	0.04	2.56†
	(15.03)	(10.54)	(10.44)	(5.20)	(0.57)	(6.96)
Number	669	541	128	540	412	128
Adjusted R^2	.90	.87	.95	.95	.92	.95
SEE	1.18	1.11	1.25	1.88	0.91	2.77

SOURCES: Calculations based on government composition and portfolio data summarized in Appendix C, coding of information in *Keesing's Contemporary Archives*, and other sources named in Appendix D.

NOTE: Entries are unstandardized regression coefficients; t statistics are in parentheses. Gamson prediction is defined as the number of portfolios that a party would receive if the rule of proportionality-to-party-size were followed as closely as possible in the subdivision of government portfolios. SEE, standard error of the estimate.

$* p = .07.$ $** p < .05.$ $*** p < .01.$ $† p < .001.$

tion. Second, in Sweden, responsibility for overthrowing the executive gives a small but significant boost to parties' shares and numbers of ministers. A look at the residuals reveals an important outlier, however; and once the outlier is removed, the coefficient b_2 declines and loses statistical significance.[9]

Thus, by the light of disaggregated analyses, too, it is only in Italy that parties have repeatedly generated office benefits from toppling cabinets. Chapter 7 showed that although the Belgian and Dutch Christian Democrats have offset the office costs of constructing coalitions, their achievements have not matched those of the Italian DC. It is now clear that Belgian and Dutch parties have not managed to extract additional office goods, beyond their usual proportional assignment, in the wake of government falls.

The goal of comparative inquiry is to replace country labels with variable names (Przeworski and Teune 1970). The variables of interest here are properties of policy space and institutions. The distinctive mix of spatial and institutional conditions in Italy—Christian Democracy's long-standing dominance of the Italian party system, the competition between the DC and the pivotal PSI from 1976 to 1992, the investiture requirement, the use of the secret ballot, the role of patronage in the quest for preference votes—has enabled Italian parties to expand the number of offices when erecting coalitions and after undoing governments.

The Policy Costs of Breaking Coalitions

Operating on the common assumption that membership in the executive affords parties special opportunities to influence policy, Table 8.5 approaches the policy consequences of breaking up cabinets in much the same way that Table 5.7 did. To be more specific, Table 8.5, like Table 5.7, captures policy payoffs by tracking how often parties that bring about one government's demise prompt a change in incumbent parties and participate in the next government. Like Table 5.7, also, this table covers only those parties that have ruled for over half of at least one interelectoral period. As the top row for each party system displays, almost all parties have tended to provoke a change in the partisan composition of government after having hastened the resignation of a cabinet.

More striking variations across parties are depicted in the second row for each system, where inclusion in the executive is examined. Seven parties have never attained power after having terminated a government: the Volksunie (VU) and the Francophone Democratic Front (FDF) in Belgium; the Communists (PCF) in France; the Liberals (LKP), Conservatives (KK), and Swedish People's Party (SFP) in Finland; and the Conservatives (M) in Sweden. The first three parties just cited are routinely categorized as "anti-

TABLE 8.5.

Government Composition and Party Status in Government After Government Collapses, by Party Responsible for Government Collapse, and Party System

Government at t	*Party Responsible for Collapse at Time t − 1*					
BELGIUM	PSB/BSP	PSC/CVP	LIBERALS	VU	FDF	
Governing parties change (%)	64.3	59.1	100.0	100.0	100.0	
Party in government (%)	50.0	90.9	50.0	0.0	0.0	
Number of collapses	14	22	8	3	3	
DENMARK, 1945–72	SD	RV	V	KF		
Governing parties change (%)	75.0	80.0	100.0	100.0		
Party in government (%)	75.0	40.0	66.7	66.7		
Number of collapses	4	5	3	3		
DENMARK, 1973–93	SD	RV	V	KF		
Governing parties change (%)	83.3	56.7	60.0	40.0		
Party in government (%)	50.0	16.7	40.0	60.0		
Number of collapses	6	6	5	5		
FINLAND	SKDL	SSDP	KP	LKP	SFP	KK
Governing parties change (%)	78.8	86.7	83.3	100.0	100.0	100.0
Party in government (%)	22.2	33.3	66.7	0	0	0
Number of collapses	9	15	12	3	3	4

(Continued on next page)

TABLE 8.5. (Continued)

Party Responsible for Collapse at Time t − 1

Government at t						
FRANCE IV	PCF	SFIO	RAD	MRP	RI	GAUL
Governing parties change (%)	80.0	71.4	72.7	85.7	83.3	75.0
Party in government (%)	0.0	57.1	100.0	85.7	66.7	43.8
Number of collapses	20	14	11	7	12	16
GERMANY	SPD	FDP	CDU/CSU			
Governing parties change (%)	50.5	62.5	33.3			
Party in government (%)	50.0	50.0	66.7			
Number of collapses	4	8	3			
IRELAND	LABOUR	FF	FG			
Governing parties change (%)	100.0	75.0	100.0			
Party in government (%)	75.0	75.0	75.0			
Number of collapses	6	9	6			
ITALY	PSI	PSDI	PRI	DC	PLI	
Governing parties change (%)	68.8	72.2	56.3	58.1	50.0	
Party in government (%)	59.4	50.0	50.0	100.0	50.0	
Number of collapses	32	18	16	31	8	

TABLE 8.5. (*Continued*)

Government at t	Party Responsible for Collapse at Time t − 1				
NETHERLANDS	PVDA	*KVP/CDA*	ARP	CHU	VVD
Governing parties change (%)	100.0	83.3	100.0	100.0	80.0
Party in government (%)	33.3	*100.0*	66.7	33.3	20.0
Number of collapses	3	6	3	3	5
NORWAY	*DNA*	v	SP	KRF	H
Governing parties change (%)	50.0	100.0	100.0	100.0	100.0
Party in government (%)	*100.0*	50.0	75.0	75.0	75.0
Number of collapses	4	2	4	4	4
SWEDEN	*SAP*	CP	FP	M	
Governing parties change (%)	100.0	60.0	50.0	50.0	
Party in government (%)	*50.0*	40.0	50.0	0.0	
Number of collapses	2	5	4	4	

SOURCE: Calculations based on coding of information in *Keesing's Contemporary Archives* and other sources and government composition data in Appendix C.

NOTE: Entries are the percentage of cases in which a party (or government) had the designated status. Entries need not sum to 100. Parties are ordered left to right, and most frequent core parties are in italics. Party abbreviations are defined in the text and in Appendix A.

system" parties.[10] The latter three, though not antisystem, anchor the right end of the left–right dimension. At the other extreme, five parties have always or almost always ruled after having truncated a government: the Christian Socials (PSC/CVP) in Belgium; the Radicals (RAD) in France; the Christian Democrats in Italy and the Netherlands (DC and KVP/CDA); and Labor (DNA) in Norway. The Finnish Center Party (KP) would join this group if nonpartisan cabinets were disregarded. Each of the six, as already stressed, is the party most often inhabiting the core of the policy space in which it competes. Spatial conditions, then, affect the consequences of cabinet dissolutions.

As in the treatment of Italy in Chapter 5, it is useful to ask: To what degree did a party's moves to upset one government impair its ability to shape the policies promoted by the next? Table 8.6 relies on the now-familiar scores derived from the content analyses of party manifestos and government programs (Budge, Robertson, and Hearl 1987; Laver and Budge 1992). According to these measures, most parties made small and insignificant policy sacrifices, on average, after having overturned an executive. One exception, noted in Chapter 5, is the rightmost of the habitual incumbents in Italy, the Liberal Party. The other two exceptions are the Socialists and Liberals in Belgium. For those parties, the divergence between party and government policies narrowed when they served in the successor to a cabinet whose failure they had precipitated. These findings, however, depend largely on the record of governments installed when linguistic–regional conflicts and constitutional reform, rather than left–right, socioeconomic issues, dominated the political agenda. And as one expert on Belgium comments, "the most crucial negotiations [on the Constitution have] take[n] place during the formation of a government" (Covell 1982, 468); the settlements thus reached have been incorporated into the nascent government's program and ratified at investiture (Covell 1981, 1982).

It is fruitful to disaggregate the analysis of policy payoffs, much as I did for the office costs of breaking coalitions. Controlling for several potential influences on the disparity between party and government policy, I estimate the following model:

$$P_{ig} = a + b_1 CP_{ig} + b_2(C_i U_i) + b_3(C_i M_i) + b_4 GP_{ig} +$$
$$b_5 RF_{ig-1} + e_{ig} \tag{8.3}$$

where P_{ig} is the absolute value of the distance on the left–right spectrum between the preferences of party i and the priorities of government g (as measured through the coding of party manifestos and government programs),[11] CP_{ig} is a dummy variable coded 1 when party i occupies the core of the policy space at the time that government g is formed, C_i is a dummy

TABLE 8.6.

Mean Absolute Distance on Left–Right Spectrum Between Party and Government Positions, by Party, Party Status in Government, Responsibility for Government Collapse, and Party System

Status in Government at t	Was Party Responsible for Collapse at Time t − 1?									
	No	Yes	No	Yes	No	Yes	No	Yes	No	Yes
BELGIUM, 1946–81	PSB/BSP		PSC/CVP		LIBERALS		VU		FDF	
In government	38.2	19.3*	15.1	19.3	17.8	6.8**	46.5	NA	41.3	NA
Out of government	27.2	44.7	17.9	64.0	15.1	25.3	14.5	17.5	13.9	8.0
Number of cabinets	15	12	9	18	19	8	15	2	10	3
DENMARK, 1945–71	SD		RV		V		KF			
In government	5.3	8.3	NA	4.0	NA	10.0	NA	22.0		
Out of government	1.0	27.0	8.0	12.5	19.7	NA	37.1	NA		
Number of cabinets	5	4	5	4	7	2	7	2		
DENMARK, 1973–82	SD		RV		V		KF			
In government	28.5	12.3	NA	NA	27.0	12.0	NA	28.0		
Out of government	18.5	NA	17.0	18.6	3.0	21.0	15.8	19.5		
Number of cabinets	4	3	2	5	2	6	4	2		

(Continued on next page)

TABLE 8.6. (Continued)

Was Party Responsible for Collapse at Time t − 1?

FRANCE IV, 1946–58

Status in Government at t	SFIO		RAD		MRP		RI		GAUL BLOC	
	No	Yes	No	Yes	No	Yes	No	Yes	No	Yes
In government	22.1	29.3	13.7	17.5	11.8	9.7	22.6	20.3	39.5	45.9
Out of government	30.5	27.6	24.5	NA	28.3	7.0	49.3	29.3	33.0	28.8
Number of cabinets	13	13	15	11	19	7	14	12	3	12

GERMANY, 1949–87

Status in Government at t	SPD		FDP		CDU/CSU	
	No	Yes	No	Yes	No	Yes
In government	18.3	11.0	7.2	14.7	11.4	4.5
Out of government	26.8	34.5	4.0	5.0	6.3	11.0
Number of cabinets	10	4	10	4	11	3

ITALY, 1948–83

Status in Government at t	PSI		PSDI		PRI		DC		PLI	
	No	Yes	No	Yes	No	Yes	No	Yes	No	Yes
In government	18.5	14.5	10.7	7.8	13.5	5.3	7.3	7.8	5.8	4.0
Out of government	15.4	11.0	17.9	8.7	11.5	8.7	NA	NA	11.5	31.8**
Number of cabinets	16	22	25	13	25	13	15	23	33	6

NETHERLANDS, 1946–81

Status in Government at t	PVDA		KVP/CDA		ARP		CHU		VVD	
	No	Yes	No	Yes	No	Yes	No	Yes	No	Yes
In government	22.3	22.0	11.6	7.5	13.8	11.0	15.0	NA	11.5	NA
Out of government	35.4	NA	NA	NA	18.0	NA	NA	7.0	19.7	19.0
Number of cabinets	9	1	8	2	6	1	6	1	9	1

TABLE 8.6. (*Continued*)

Was Party Responsible for Collapse at Time *t* − 1?

Status in Government at t	*DNA* No	*DNA* Yes	V No	V Yes	SP No	SP Yes	KRF No	KRF Yes	H No	H Yes
NORWAY, 1949–89										
In government	10.0	26.7	11.7	16.0	2.3	16.0	5.5	16.7	13.0	10.3
Out of government	21.9	NA	15.1	3.0	20.2	NA	25.1	15.0	24.2	33.0
Number of cabinets	12	3	15	2	17	3	16	4	16	4

Status in Government at t	*SAP* No	*SAP* Yes	CP No	CP Yes	*FP* No	*FP* Yes	M No	M Yes
SWEDEN, 1945–88								
In government	22.4	65.0	13.3	30.5	12.5	16.0	14.5	NA
Out of government	10.7	31.0	16.1	11.0	17.1	28.0	52.8	24.0
Number of cabinets	19	2	17	4	18	3	18	3

SOURCE: Calculations based on government composition data in Appendix C; measures of party and government positions from works cited in Table 7.1; and coding of information in *Keesing's Contemporary Archives* and other sources named in Appendix D.

NOTE: Parties are ordered left to right, with typical median party italicized. Entries are mean absolute distances on a 200-point left–right scale between party positions and government positions, for each party listed. On each row means are computed, party by party, for two groups of cabinets: those whose predecessor was a cabinet the party helped to topple and those whose predecessor fell for reasons other than the party's withdrawal of support. The *t* tests compare the means of the two groups (i.e., for each party, entries in the *yes* and *no* columns). This table omits Finland and Ireland due to missing data. NA, Not applicable. Party abbreviations are defined in the text and in Appendix A.

* *p* < .07 (separate variances *t* test). ** *p* < .05.

for the strength of the party that has most often inhabited the core in party i's system (coded 0 for weaker core parties, 1 for stronger), U_i is a dummy coded 1 where party i competes in a unipolar system, M_i is a dummy coded 1 where party i competes in a multipolar system, GP_{i_g} is the number of parties in government g that party i has joined, and $RF_{i_{g-1}}$ is a dummy variable coded 1 when party i has helped to dismantle the immediate predecessor to government g. The interactive terms C_iU_i and C_iM_i allow for a test of the hypothesis that a party's ability to mold public policy depends on the structure of the party system. (Again, note that these data do not comprehend instances where a party responsible for the fall of government $g-1$ is excluded from government g; Tables 8.5 and 8.6 appraise such instances.)

Table 8.7 reports the coefficients, t statistics, and adjusted R^2 values yielded by the computations. As the first column exhibits, parties ruling in multipolar systems with a strong core party have pulled government policy relatively close to their ideals, other things being equal. The addition of a coalition ally has pushed public policy away from an incumbent party's preferences. A high standard error of the estimate (SEE) accompanies a low R^2 in this model, however. Inspection of the residuals identifies four prominent outliers.[12] Omitting the outliers dampens the SEE slightly but leaves the R^2 unchanged, which the second column of Table 8.7 records. Regardless of the treatment of outliers, a party's core status and its responsibility for the fall of an outgoing cabinet have had little effect on the divergence between the party's priorities and those of an incoming executive.

To probe the apparent (and absent) relationships, I reestimate the models, first deleting all Italian cases and then dwelling on Italy alone. (The latter analysis must drop the interactive terms since they take on a single value for Italy.) A comparison of the third, fourth, and fifth columns of Table 8.7 underscores the Italian Christian Democrats' unusual capacity to shape government policy, which was documented in Chapter 7. Again, too, when Italian parties have acquired a new coalition ally, the disparity between party and government policy has narrowed, rather than widened. In none of the computations conducted does a party's choice to terminate one cabinet exercise an influence on the distance between its agenda and that of the successor in which it serves.

According to the evidence collected from party manifestos and government programs, a party suffers no real damage in policy terms if it manages to enter the successor to an executive it has ended. This message is sent by Table 8.6 and (more concisely) by Table 8.7. The catch is contained in the word *if*. As detailed in Table 8.5, most parties have not entered all successors to the executives they have ended; only long-standing core parties have managed this feat. And perhaps the firmest conclusion of the relevant research to date, which Chapter 7 echoed, is that the policies espoused by op-

TABLE 8.7.

Core Status, Structure of Policy Space, Number of Governing Parties,
and Responsibility for Fall of Preceding Government as Determinants
of the Distance Between Party and Government Positions

	DEPENDENT VARIABLE: POLICY DISTANCE				
Independent Variables	All ten countries	All ten countries	All but Italy	All but Italy	Italy only
Party at core	−1.31	−1.35	−0.58	−0.63	−5.08**
	(−0.86)	(−0.95)	(−0.33)	(−0.36)	(−2.39)
Strength of core × unipolar	−1.01	−1.50	−1.10	—	—
	(−0.50)	(−0.78)	(−0.53)		
Strength of core × multipolar	−7.68†	−7.20†	−4.79*	—	—
	(−5.23)	(−5.22)	(−1.94)		
Number of governing parties	0.84*	0.73*	1.00**	1.06**	−1.69**
	(1.96)	(1.82)	(2.19)	(2.50)	(−2.03)
Responsibility for fall of preceding government	−0.34	−0.96	−0.55	0.15	−0.35
	(−0.26)	(−0.78)	(−0.36)	(0.10)	(−0.19)
Constant	15.92†	16.07†	14.59†	13.42†	17.17†
	(7.31)	(7.86)	(6.28)	(6.63)	(5.13)
Number	450	446[a]	348[a]	348[a]	98
Adjusted R^2	.08	.08	.02	.01	.04
SEE	13.32	12.49	13.29	13.32	8.80

SOURCES: Calculations based on government composition data in Appendix C; measures of party and government positions from works cited in Table 7.1; and coding of information in *Keesing's Contemporary Archives* and other sources named in Appendix D.

NOTE: Entries are unstandardized regression coefficients; *t* statistics are in parentheses. Finnish parties are omitted due to missing data. SEE, standard error of the estimate.

[a] Four outliers (2 from France, 1 from Belgium, 1 from Sweden) excluded.

* $p \approx .07$. ** $p < .05$. *** $p < .01$. † $p < .001$.

position parties consistently lie further away from government programs than do the policies advocated by incumbent parties. (This fact helps to explain the low R^2 values listed in Table 8.7.) Spatial conditions thus matter for the policy consequences of cabinet falls.

The Bargaining Costs of Breaking Coalitions

Chapter 7 demonstrated that variations in the bargaining costs of constructing coalitions depend on variations in parliamentary institutions and spatial conditions. In particular, an investiture requirement lengthens bargaining over new governments, as does the redefinition of parties' sizes and positions at election time. The simplicity of interparty competition in unipolar and bipolar party systems shortens negotiations. Even accounting for these effects, government crises in the Netherlands are unusually protracted.

Those findings provide the benchmark for the investigation that follows. To weigh the impact on bargaining exerted by party choices to hasten cabinet falls, I add a dummy variable to a model introduced in Chapter 7, estimating the equation

$$B_g = a + b_1 U_g + b_2 BI_g + b_3 E_g + b_4 I_g + b_5 CS_g + b_6 NE_g +$$
$$b_7 RF_{g-1} + e_g \tag{8.4}$$

where B_g is the number of days of bargaining that has prepared government g, U_g is a dummy variable coded 1 when government g forms in a unipolar party system, BI_g is a dummy coded 1 when government g forms in a bipolar system, E_g is a dummy coded 1 when government g takes office immediately after a parliamentary election, I_g is a dummy coded 1 when government g faces an investiture requirement, CS_g is the index of committee strength, NE_g is a dummy coded 1 when government g rules in the Netherlands, and RF_{g-1} is a dummy coded 1 when one or more parties were responsible for the fall of the immediate predecessor to government g.[13]

The first two columns of Table 8.8 display the results of these computations. The third column reproduces the analogous results from Chapter 7, for ease of comparison, and the fourth trains attention on the 276 cases for which data are available on party responsibility for predecessors' falls. The findings in the first two columns parallel those in the third and fourth columns, with one obvious exception: Holding other factors constant, eight fewer days are needed to negotiate the replacements for executives that have resigned due to party choice. By this light, party moves to dismantle cabinets save time that would otherwise be spent in crisis bargaining.

TABLE 8.8.

Effect of Party Responsibility for Government Falls on
Days Spent in Government Formation

Independent Variables	Model	DEPENDENT VARIABLE: DAYS SPENT IN GOVERNMENT FORMATION				
		8.4	8.4A	7.3A	7.3B	8.4B
Unipolar system		−20.51†	−20.92†	−19.48†	−19.38†	−19.93†
		(−6.09)	(−7.72)	(−7.43)	(−7.18)	(−7.10)
Bipolar system		−10.08*	−9.97**	−6.98*	−7.35*	−9.03**
		(−1.81)	(−2.30)	(−1.69)	(−1.74)	(−2.12)
Postelection timing		21.76†	18.23†	20.67†	21.16†	—
		(7.24)	(7.45)	(9.36)	(9.29)	
Investiture		6.27**	6.59***	4.51*	5.35**	6.81***
		(2.06)	(2.67)	(1.87)	(2.17)	(2.76)
Committee strength		0.77	—	—	—	—
		(0.49)				
Netherlands		42.39†	20.65†	21.39†	22.35†	21.51†
		(6.63)	(4.16)	(4.41)	(4.46)	(4.32)
Any party behind fall of $g-1$		−4.12	−8.02***	—	—	−9.20***
		(−1.27)	(−3.00)			(−2.90)
Timing after regularly scheduled election		—	—	—	—	15.36†
						(4.35)
Timing after early election forced by defeat		—	—	—	—	21.54†
						(7.13)
Timing after strategic early election		—	—	—	—	13.43**
						(2.43)
Constant		14.51*	21.40†	15.47†	14.87†	22.00†
		(1.94)	(6.73)	(6.74)	(6.32)	(6.22)
Number		279	276[a]	288[a]	276[b]	276[b]
Adjusted R^2		.41	.39	.37	.37	.39
SEE		21.51	17.55	17.73	17.81	17.50

NOTE: Entries are unstandardized regression coefficients; t statistics are in parentheses. Dashes indicate that the designated variable did not enter the regression analysis. SEE, standard error of the estimate.

[a] Three Dutch outliers omitted.

[b] Three Dutch outliers omitted, as well as cases with missing data on the lagged responsibility variable.

* $p \approx .07$. ** $p < .05$. *** $p < .01$. † $p < .001$.

There are several ways to explore what underlies this pattern, which might seem surprising. One way is to perform multiple reestimations of model 8.4A, deleting a different country each time and checking for any changes in the coefficient for RF_{g-1}. Another is to re-run the model, adding a different country dummy variable each time. The first set of reestimations reveals that, whatever the nation removed, the variable identifying party actions behind cabinet falls retains a negative sign, statistical significance, and a magnitude similar to that registered in the second column of Table 8.8. According to an informal rule recognized in Fourth Republic France and the Netherlands, "*Qui casse, paie*" (Maas 1986, 223; MacRae 1967, 69); that is, a party that breaks a coalition must pay for the damage by spearheading the first attempt to make a new cabinet. Yet even where that rule is not in force, it seems, the detection of the agent ending a government reduces uncertainty, communicates information, and so defines and directs the ensuing negotiations over a new government.

Second, the dummies for post-1973 Denmark, Finland, Fourth Republic France, and Italy have a statistically significant influence on the duration of crisis bargaining. Even considering the impact of type of party system, post-election timing, investiture, the "Dutch delay," and responsibility for predecessors' falls, cabinet crises consume more time than would be expected in Finland and Italy, and less time than would be expected in post-1973 Denmark and France. As in the analysis of bargaining costs in Chapter 7, only the Danish coefficient resembles the Dutch in magnitude.[14]

Not only are Danish crises unusually brief, but also Danish parliamentary elections are extremely frequent. The first column of Table 8.9 reports early elections as a percentage of all elections held between 1945 and 1992 in the ten countries studied here. (I operationalize early elections as those occurring more than four months before the date mandated constitutionally, which is indicated in the second column; I exclude from the count any elections entailed in the process of constitutional revision.) As Table 8.9 illustrates, early elections are most common in Ireland and Denmark. In contrast, they are absent altogether in Norway, where the Constitution prohibits premature dissolution of the legislature (Strøm and Leipart 1993). Given this record, as the third column shows, only 2.5 and 2.2 years have separated elections in Denmark's unipolar system (1945–72) and multipolar system (1973–92), respectively; the corresponding figure is 4 years for Norway. The two rightmost columns of Table 8.9 distinguish between two types of early elections: those called at the discretion of the government in the hope of electoral advantage and those forced on the government by a defeat that seemed imminent or occurred (on this distinction, see Grofman and Van Roozendaal 1994; Lupia and Strøm 1995; Smith 1996).[15]

Executives in Denmark, Fourth Republic France, and Ireland plainly

TABLE 8.9.

Frequency of Early Elections, Maximum and Average Intervals Between
Elections, and Elections Timed for Advantage, by Party System

	Early as Percentage of All Elections 1945–92	Maximum Number of Years Between Elections	Average Number of Years Between Elections	EARLY ELECTIONS AS PERCENTAGE OF ALL ELECTIONS	
				Timed for Advantage	Forced by Defeat
Belgium (n = 16)	62.5	4	2.9	0.0	100.0
Denmark 1 (n = 11)	72.7	4	2.5	27.3	72.7
Denmark 2 (n = 9)	88.9	4	2.2	11.1	88.9
Finland (n = 13)	38.5	4	3.7	0.0	100.0
France IV (n = 4)	50.0	5	3.0	25.0	75.0
Germany (n = 12)	25.0	4	3.7	8.3	91.7
Ireland (n = 15)	100.0	5	3.0	46.7	53.3
Italy (n = 12)	41.7	5	3.9	0.0	100.0
Netherlands (n = 14)	35.7	4	3.4	0.0	100.0
Norway (n = 12)	0.0	4[a]	4.0	0.0	100.0
Sweden (n = 15)	6.7	3[b]	3.0	0.0	100.0

SOURCES: Gallagher, Laver, and Mair 1995, 30; *Keesing's Contemporary Archives*; Mackie and Rose 1991; Pétry 1992a; Williams 1966; subsidiary sources named in Appendix D.

NOTE: In parentheses is the total number of parliamentary elections held between 1945 and 1992.

[a] Early elections impossible.

[b] Before 1970, four years.

stand out for their propensity to schedule early elections in maneuvers for advantage. One team of scholars has gauged it relatively easy to call early elections in Denmark and Ireland (Strøm, Budge, and Laver 1994, 322). In the French Fourth Republic, an outgoing government could dissolve the National Assembly only under very restrictive conditions; and constitutional provisions in force until late 1954 led many French politicians to deem early dissolution impossible (Williams 1966, 250–51).[16] Nonetheless, in December 1955 the restrictive conditions were fulfilled and, "in a surprise to the Assembly," the cabinet headed by Edgar Faure (Radical Party) called early elections (MacRae 1967, 132).[17]

Do the different kinds of elections differ in their influence on crisis bargaining? The rightmost column of Table 8.8 summarizes the results from another variant of model 8.4, in which three dummy variables take the place of E_g: the first is coded 1 when government *g* is launched immediately after a regularly scheduled election; the second is coded 1 when government *g* is launched after an early election dictated by defeat; and the last, when *g* is launched after an early election timed for advantage.[18] Note that, once more, the coefficient for the variable identifying party actions behind cabinet falls has a negative sign, statistical significance, and a magnitude similar to that in the second column: *Qui casse* pares down the duration of crisis negotiations. Equally interesting, strategic early elections do less to prolong bargaining than do regularly scheduled elections and, especially, early elections imposed by adversity. When Denmark is removed from the analysis, however, the coefficient for strategic early elections rises substantially; no such change emerges when any of the other countries are deleted. In Denmark alone, strategically timed early elections abbreviate negotiations over new cabinets.

Parliamentary elections not only affect bargaining costs. They also afford voters the opportunity to punish—or reward—parties that have terminated governments. I now turn to the electoral performance of parties responsible for rupturing executives.

The Electoral Costs of Breaking Coalitions

Again, the findings from Chapter 7 provide the benchmark for the analysis. Chapter 7 showed that the aggregate electoral cost of incumbency (that is, a party's electoral performance averaged over all elections in which it has competed as an incumbent) reflects a party's competitive environment and its alliance strategies. Disaggregating the treatment of electoral costs underscored the electoral price that parties outside Italy have paid for incumbency.

I analyze the electoral costs of breaking governments by reestimating versions of model 7.6, incorporating a new variable and comparing the determinants of short-term vote swings up or down with the determinants of absolute values of vote shifts:

$$\Delta V_{it} = a + b_1 PL_{it} + b_2 CP_i + b_3 GP_{it} + b_4 IN_{it} + b_5 VS_{it-1} +$$
$$b_6 \Delta V_{it-1} + b_7 RF_{it} + e_{it} \qquad (8.5)$$

and

$$\pm \Delta V_{it} = a + b_1 PL_{it} + b_2 CP_i + b_3 GP_{it} + b_4 IN_{it} + b_5 VS_{it-1} +$$
$$b_6 \Delta V_{it-1} + b_7 RF_{it} + e_{it} \qquad (8.6)$$

where $\pm \Delta V_{it}$ is the absolute value of the vote shift that party *i* sees in election *t* (as compared to election *t–1*) and RF_{it} is a dummy variable coded 1 when party *i* has been responsible for the fall of most governments serving between election *t-1* and *t*.

Table 8.10 is devoted to the results of the computations. Inspection of the residuals for the estimations reported in the first and fifth columns of the table reveals two salient outliers, which are omitted from the other estimations. (The outliers here, as in Chapter 7, are the French Popular Republican Movement in 1951 and the French Gaullists in 1956.) In the second column, it is once more evident that incumbents shed votes and that core parties are sheltered from electoral punishment. As before, too, the previous vote share and previous vote swing help to account for the current vote gain or loss. The new finding is that parties responsible for the end of governments appear to suffer limited and insignificant electoral consequences. Implementing a now-familiar procedure, the third column excludes Italy from the analysis, and the fourth focuses on Italy alone. As exhibited, in Italy parties that trigger the fall of a cabinet tend to increase, not decrease, their vote share.

The series of analogous computations for the absolute values of vote shifts yields largely similar results, with three exceptions. In the rightmost column on Italy, unlike the fourth, the coefficient for RF_{it} is negative and attains conventional levels of statistical significance. By this light, choices to terminate executives enhance the electoral security of Italian parties. Running separate single-country regressions yields small, nonsignificant coefficients for the responsibility dummy in eight of the other nine countries. In a second exception, the French parties look something like the Italian, once the outliers are omitted: In France as in Italy, a party's moves to truncate governments exert a positive, nonsignificant influence on vote shifts and a significant influence on absolute values of vote swings; but in France the effect on absolute values is positive, not negative. French parties, even more than the Italian, benefited electorally from engineering cabinet falls. The last, least interesting, exception involves the sign of the coefficients for the variables recording previous electoral performance. Naturally, the bigger the party, the more votes it can lose or gain.

In Fourth Republic France, given the restrictive conditions for dissolving the National Assembly, it was widely believed that "parties did not have to concern themselves with the possibility of losing votes if they brought down the government" (Pétry 1992a, 385). Italian parties apparently acted on the same belief. The common assumption was correct.

Electoral security, unlike hope, does not spring eternal. The Fourth Republic collapsed in 1958, and the rewriting of electoral laws in the Fifth Republic, along with the new rules about the presidency, dramatically reshaped the French party system (e.g., Pierce 1995). Electoral support for the Italian Christian Democrats dipped in 1992 after electoral reforms were in-

TABLE 8.10.

Effect of Party Responsibility for Government Falls on the Electoral Consequences of Incumbency

| | DEPENDENT VARIABLES | | | | | | | |
| | SHIFT IN VOTE SHARE | | | | ABSOLUTE VALUE OF SHIFT | | | |
Independent Variables	All Ten Countries	All Ten Countries	All but Italy	Italy Only	All Ten Countries	All Ten Countries	All but Italy	Italy Only
Electoral laws	0.22 (0.57)	0.60 (1.62)	0.56 (1.46)	—	0.32 (1.21)	0.05 (0.21)	0.01 (0.03)	—
Long-standing core party	0.49 (1.14)	0.74* (1.77)	0.82* (1.90)	4.00* (1.77)	0.18 (0.61)	0.03 (0.12)	0.07 (0.23)	-4.80*** (-2.85)
Mean number of governing parties	-0.07 (-0.39)	0.15 (0.90)	0.18 (1.01)	-0.30 (-0.71)	0.12 (1.05)	-0.05 (-0.42)	-0.10 (-0.83)	0.72** (2.30)
Incumbent status	-0.94 (-1.46)	-1.63** (-2.57)	-1.85*** (-2.77)	1.40 (0.76)	-0.64 (-1.45)	-0.15 (-0.35)	-0.04 (-0.08)	-2.71* (-1.99)
Previous vote share	-0.03** (-2.42)	-0.03** (-2.55)	-0.03** (-2.20)	-0.19*** (-2.94)	0.04† (4.28)	0.04† (4.62)	0.04† (3.89)	0.23† (4.65)
Previous shift in vote share	-0.16† (-4.07)	-0.11*** (-2.80)	-0.09** (-2.14)	-0.29*** (-3.02)	—	—	—	—

TABLE 8.10. (Continued)

	DEPENDENT VARIABLES							
	SHIFT IN VOTE SHARE				ABSOLUTE VALUE OF SHIFT			
Independent Variables	All Ten Countries	All Ten Countries	All but Italy	Italy Only	All Ten Countries	All Ten Countries	All but Italy	Italy Only
Absolute value of previous shift	—	—	—	—	0.22† (5.48)	0.15† (3.79)	0.15*** (3.46)	0.02 (0.23)
Responsibility for falls	-0.18 (-0.57)	-0.16 (-0.54)	-0.21 (-0.61)	0.70 (1.13)	-0.07 (-0.33)	-0.03 (-0.15)	0.12 (0.51)	-1.21** (-2.54)
Constant	0.77*** (2.94)	0.73*** (2.87)	0.76*** (2.78)	0.43 (0.70)	1.14† (6.03)	1.32† (7.27)	1.40† (7.21)	0.21 (0.46)
Number	558	556a	507a	49	558	556a	507a	49
Adjusted R^2	.08	.07	.06	.37	.13	.11	.09	.42
SEE	3.15	3.04	3.11	1.88	2.17	2.06	2.10	1.41

NOTE: Entries are unstandardized regression coefficients; t statistics are in parentheses. Dashes indicate that the designated variable did not enter the regression analysis. SEE, standard error of the estimate.

a Two French outliers omitted.

* $p = .07.$ ** $p < .05.$ *** $p < .01.$ † $p < .001.$

troduced and the Communists changed themselves into the Democratic Party of the Left. Those events, in turn, furthered the unveiling of corruption, as Chapter 5 discussed; and then in 1994, after additional electoral reforms, the renamed DC suffered a precipitous decline and the entire party system was redrawn. In the Netherlands, too, the long-standing core party encountered severe electoral damage in 1994, following the gradual, long-standing erosion of religious practice and of the impact of the religious cleavage on vote choice (Andeweg and Irwin 1993, 99, 98; Keman 1995; van der Eijk and Niemöller 1992, 263–83). Yet in the Netherlands, the major parties today are still those that governed in the past.

Conclusions

The costs of breaking coalitions and the costs of making coalitions are not the same. It is only in Italy that parties have registered office and electoral benefits from ousting executives. The costs of toppling governments are higher in the Netherlands than in Italy, which helps to explain why Dutch cabinets last longer, on average, than Italian ones. Such costs were relatively low in Fourth Republic France, even though the costs of erecting coalitions were fairly substantial. The brevity of the regime, along with its short-lived governments, is comprehensible in this light.

The findings and the argument here both build on, and move beyond, extant research on coalitions. Attributes of party systems—fractionalization and polarization, which are components of "complex party systems and hence complex bargaining environments"—are associated with short cabinet duration (King et al. 1990, 869). But the attributes do not *explain* short duration, in the sense that they do not identify the causal mechanisms generating government falls. The landmark study just cited concludes that "cabinets in such [complex] systems appear to be especially sensitive to the impact of random events. . . . In less fractionalized and less polarized systems larger—and less frequent—random shocks may be needed to produce the same disturbing effects" (ibid., 869).

I would reframe the point. It is not so much that governments in some systems are especially vulnerable to shock. Parties in some systems exploit and realize the possibility of cabinet dissolutions, because they expect benefits or at least no losses to ensue. Parties' expectations reflect their readings of institutional constraints and their understandings of their own and other parties' locations and leverage in policy space. Chance at times ends governments. So do choices made by parties, as structured by institutional and spatial conditions.

9 Conclusions

Most political scientists care about democracy, given the normative biases that bring most of us to enter the profession. Voting, elections, and representative government go to the heart of what democracy is and means. Not surprisingly, many political scientists have written about party competition for votes in elections and party competition for control of government. Indeed, as one scholar has recently observed, "government formation provides one of the most heavily theorized and [thoroughly] . . . tested fields in political science" (Downs 1998, 38)

This chapter recapitulates the themes and findings of the chapters that precede it, as conclusions typically do. In laying out the summary, I revisit the broad correlation between cabinet duration and alternation in office that was first depicted in Figure 1.2.

I also seek to drive home the contribution of the book as a whole. The second part of the chapter addresses further implications of the argument, moving beyond the data set compiled for Chapters 4 through 8. I next develop what might be called the methodological and epistemological "lessons" of the book. These lessons involve, among other things, the importance of focusing on anomalies and of rethinking the connection between theoretical and empirical work on coalitions. Finally, I consider trade-offs in the study of coalition politics and discuss the place of this research within contemporary political science.

Recapitulation

In postwar Italy until 1992, transitory cabinets were staffed by permanent incumbents. The instability of Italian executives occasioned concern among U.S. policy makers, stern commentary in newspapers on both sides of the Atlantic, and none-too-subtle jokes. The stability in Italian government often escaped notice. I train attention on that stability—on the perpetual incumbency of one political party and the limited degree to which parties alternated between government and opposition in Italy. And I probe how stability was tied to instability in Italian government.

This recapitulation examines what tackling the Italian puzzle tells us about stability, instability, and the costs and benefits of coalition. It also suggests how this research sheds new light on Italian politics and on the study of political parties.

STABILITY, INSTABILITY, AND PAYOFFS IN COALITION POLITICS

As Part I of the book demonstrates, the conjunction of short cabinet duration and restricted turnover poses a puzzle of general interest in the study of coalition politics. What explains the combination of instability and stability? How can governments break up at such low cost and with so little effect on alternation? For all its richness, the existing literature on coalitions offers no ready answer to these questions. Each of the four major schools of research has difficulty in handling some aspect of the outcomes in coalitional behavior found in Italy. At the same time, salient themes and shared emphases in the field point to the ingredients of an analytical framework capable of accommodating the puzzle. Those ingredients, in shorthand form, may be identified as purposive action, costs and benefits, and constraints and opportunities. The central hypotheses made from those ingredients are that the costs and benefits of building and breaking coalitions vary in systematic ways, that the variations arise in part from political parties' deliberate efforts to redefine payoffs in coalition politics, and that they also reflect the constraints and opportunities created by the institutions of parliamentary democracy and the configuration of parties and voters in policy space.

Part II organizes comparisons within Italy—across parties, across sets of governments, and across time—into numerous observable implications of the hypotheses advanced in Part I. The Christian Democratic Party (DC), advantaged by its size and position in policy space, championed the rewriting of Italy's electoral laws in the early 1950s and spearheaded adjustments in coalition formulae in the late 1940s, the early 1960s, and the late 1970s. It is reasonable to interpret these and other choices made by the DC as attempts to limit the costs of assembling and dismantling coalitions. On the whole, the attempts succeeded (even though the majoritarian electoral rules were quickly abandoned). For instance, when the DC anchored coalitions instead of ruling alone, it curbed electoral losses, sacrificed little on policy, and surrendered few offices. Pursuit of the strategy used to manage office costs—progressive increases in total cabinet posts with the addition of allies—was not only made possible by the DC's long-standing dominance of the Italian party system. It also made sense in light of Italy's parliamentary institutions. The vote of investiture and the provision for the secret ballot gave incentives to Italian coalition builders to apply office as "glue" that would bind assertive parliamentarians to governments. And since members of the executive in Italy are required to step down from parliamentary committees, an increase in cabinet posts enlarged access to committee positions for backbenchers.

Part III of the book explores the applicability of the argument outside Italy. The cross-national comparisons show that distinctions appear in the record of costs incurred and strategies implemented across different kinds of party systems. Distinctions also emerge across countries with contrasting electoral and parliamentary institutions. There are some similarities in costs and strategies across such countries as Italy and the Netherlands, which are rooted in similarities in the arrangement of policy space.

For example, consider the bargaining costs of erecting coalitions. An investiture requirement prolongs the negotiations over new cabinets, as does the redefinition of parties' sizes and positions through elections. The simplicity of interparty competition in unipolar and bipolar party systems shortens the bargaining process. Even accounting for all these effects, government crises in the Netherlands are unusually time consuming. True, bargaining costs are higher than average in both Italy and the Netherlands, both multipolar systems, but they are highest in the Netherlands. It seems reasonable to interpret time expended in crisis negotiations as the price that Dutch parties have paid to secure relatively low policy and office costs of constructing coalitions, given spatial conditions in the Netherlands that resemble, but do not equal, those in Italy: The Dutch Christian Democrats, unlike their Italian counterparts, lost their core status a few times before the early 1990s.

It is worthwhile to take stock of other types of payoffs, beyond the example of bargaining costs. Core parties in Italy, Belgium, and the Netherlands have been able to neutralize the *office* costs of building coalitions. In other party systems, core parties have forfeited offices when adding allies in coalition. The Dutch maneuvers in inflating portfolios do not match the Italian record, a difference that reflects the Dutch Christian Democrats' occasional loss of core status before the early 1990s, the presence of institutional disincentives to increasing offices in the Netherlands (the rule that cabinet members must resign their seats in Parliament), and the absence of institutional incentives that Italian coalition leaders instead do confront (the vote of investiture). No other core party in the ten systems studied here, not even the Belgian Christian Socials, has boasted a strategic position rivaling that of the Italian or Dutch Christian Democrats. Accordingly, the Belgian efforts to augment posts in coalition pale beside the Italian. That they surpass the Dutch may be ascribed in part to the fact that the Belgian Christian Socials have encountered, and joined, resurgent linguistic competition; that is, the architects of Belgian coalitions have used office to guarantee restive linguistic representatives a voice in policy making and to tie those representatives to the governing majority. Institutional factors—the vote of investiture and the need to muster a two-thirds legislative majority to pass constitutional reforms and linguistic legislation—have also encouraged the strategic use of office in Belgium.

Among the core parties under examination, only the Italian DC has managed to derive office benefits from toppling governments. As I have repeatedly stressed, the Italian DC inhabited the core of the policy space continuously from 1946 to 1992, an advantage that no other party in this study enjoyed—not even the Dutch Christian Democrats, although they did qualify as a core party for relatively long stretches of time. In Italy, the investiture requirement, the provision for the secret ballot, and the role of patronage in the search for preference votes all operated to persuade politicians of the utility of expanding offices after overturning governments and when assembling coalitions.

Observe now the *policy* payoffs of launching coalitions. The Italian Christian Democrats and the German Free Democrats (FDP) have succeeded in aligning the government's program more closely with their own preferences when they have acquired a new coalition ally. This finding hinges on only a few cases for the German FDP, however, since the FDP has never ruled alone and has almost always joined two-party coalitions. The Italian DC had a unique capacity, then, to score policy benefits in coalition. For the French Radicals and the Dutch Christian Democrats, the distance between party ideals and governmental plans evinced inconsistent, insignificant variations across coalitions with different numbers of partners. The sizable concessions made by the Belgian Christian Socials on socioeconomic policies in five-party coalitions reflected the priority given to linguistic issues and the need for a two-thirds majority to approve constitutional reform. The fact that the policy sacrifices imposed on Social Democrats in coalition were more conspicuous in Denmark than in Sweden comports with the relative weakness of the Danish SD as a core party.

In line with these findings, in Chapter 8 the regression analysis of the policy consequences of rupturing coalitions controls for the type of party, the type of party system, and the number of governing parties. The analysis reveals that a party faces no real penalty in policy terms if it manages to enter the successor to an executive it has overthrown. The word *if* is important, because most parties have not entered all successors to the executives they have overthrown; only long-standing core parties have performed this feat.

Spatial conditions thus matter for the policy costs of building and breaking coalitions.

Consider once more the costs of *bargaining* over governments. For six of the countries studied, including Italy, the time expended in putting together coalitions does not differ substantially, on average, from the time expended in negotiating one-party governments. The extraordinarily long gestation of Dutch coalitions puts the Netherlands in a class by itself. Even with the "Dutch delay," variations in the length of negotiations over new governments can be explained by the provision for investiture, postelection timing, and the type of party system. The same factors do much to account for the bargaining costs of dissolving cabinets. In addition, relatively little time is needed to negotiate the replacements for executives that have collapsed as a result of party choice. It seems, then, that the detection of an agent terminating a government lowers uncertainty, conveys information, and guides the ensuing bargaining over a new government. Cabinet crises consume more time in Italy and Finland, and less time in France and Denmark, than would be predicted by the model incorporating as independent variables the role of investiture, postelection timing, the type of party system, the "Dutch delay," and party responsibility for predecessors' falls.

According to conventional wisdom and widely known research (e.g., Powell and Whitten 1993; Rose and Mackie 1983), positions in government impose *electoral* burdens on parties. This study has identified exceptions to the rule: Italian incumbents—above all the Italian Christian Democrats—fare relatively well at the polls. It is also noteworthy that in Italy and France parties benefited electorally from engineering government falls. Recall, finally, that long-standing core parties in all types of party systems are protected from vote losses.

The overall message of the empirical analyses in this book is that only in Italy do parties repeatedly extract benefits from building and breaking coalitions. Party benefits from triggering cabinet falls were evident in Fourth Republic France, whereas the costs of creating coalitions were fairly substantial there, which helps to illuminate the collapse of the regime. In Finland and Belgium, also multipolar systems, some costs of building coalitions are offset or negligible, but neither office nor electoral benefits to rupturing executives appear. Understandably, governments in Finland and Belgium are somewhat longer-lived than those in France and Italy.

The overall inference is that exogenous factors (electoral and parliamentary institutions and attributes of party systems) and endogenous factors (parties' choices, as structured by institutional and spatial conditions) account for the otherwise puzzling combination of governmental stability and instability. Granted, the ten-country analysis addresses exogenous forces more fully, whereas for Italy I appraise both the endogenous and exogenous components of the book's central argument. Yet, Chapters 7 and 8 do uncover some evidence of parties' strategic behavior, and it is reasonable to interpret from quantitative findings that parties outside of Italy, under certain conditions, have also deliberately attempted to limit sacrifices in coalition. The cross-national differences introduced in Figure 1.2 can be explained in light of the costs of coalition and parties' efforts to maneuver around costs, which in turn are understandable in light of spatial and institutional conditions.

Note that the discussion here and throughout the book does not include one logical possibility: the combination of brief duration and high alternation. The closest real-world approximation to this scenario is Second Republic Spain, where a two-year sequence of left-wing governments (dubbed the *bienio rojo*, the "red two years") was replaced by a two-year sequence of right-wing governments (the *bienio negro*), which was then succeeded by several left-wing governments. Multiple coalitions ruled within each phase, so that executives in the Second Republic lasted less than three and a half months, on average (Linz 1978b, 172). Hence, cabinets in Second Republic Spain were even more short-lived than those in Fourth Republic France and 1946–92 Italy (where mean duration was about five months and ten months, respectively). Given changes in the party composition of coalitions, the alternation rate in the Spanish Second Republic can be estimated at 22 percent.[1] This figure is slightly below the rate found in Belgium, Finland, and the Netherlands, somewhat higher than that in Fourth Republic France (18 percent), and triple the alternation rate in 1946–92 Italy (7 percent). Therefore, in Spain between 1931 and 1936, executives fell with exceptional frequency and saw fairly pronounced swings in partisan makeup. One recurring theme in the literature on the Second Republic is that cabinet instability, coupled with abrupt alternation between and within *bienios*, contributed powerfully to the collapse of the regime and the onset of the Spanish Civil War (Gunther, Sani, and Shabad 1978, ch. 2; Linz 1978a, 1978b; Varela Díaz 1978). Thus, the logical possibility left unexamined in this book appears to be unworkable in practice.

RETHINKING ITALIAN POLITICS

This research not only answers otherwise vexing questions about the instability and stability of governmental coalitions. It also enriches the understanding of Italian politics in at least four ways. First, it recasts our thinking about the polarization of the Italian party system. Giovanni Sartori (1966, 1976) has made a powerful and influential argument that the party system in Italy (and in Weimar Germany, Second Republic Spain, Fourth Republic France, and Finland) may be classified as a case of "polarized pluralism," in which a large number of parties compete and great distances separate parties. Many other analysts have emphasized the strength of extreme right and extreme left parties in Italy (e.g., Di Palma 1977; Farneti 1983; Powell 1982). And, as noted several times above, polarization has been found to be associated with short cabinet duration (King et al. 1990). Sartori was and is distinctive in isolating a dynamic of party competition that, he claims, is induced by polarization. In Sartori's words (1976, 132, 136, 137, 139), the "distinctive features" and "systemic properties" of polarized pluralism include "the presence of relevant anti-system parties" on left and right, "centrifugal drives [and] . . . congenital ideological patterning" in party competition, and "peripheral turnover" in government.

My reasoning owes a clear debt to Sartori's work. Much more than Sartori and other Italianists, however, I tie my research to the game-theoretic literature on parties and coalitions, and I use it to grapple with the well-known but poorly comprehended juxtaposition of instability and stability in Italian national government. Put differently, I am interested in short cabinet duration along with limited turnover. Much more than Sartori and other Italianists, I probe how the context for electoral competition and also parliamentary institutions affect how governing parties are willing and able to manipulate office benefits, information, reputation, and rules in the search for strategic advantage.[2] Put differently, my argument goes beyond the notion that Italian governments "could afford to be short-lived because neither of the two anti-system oppositions could present itself as the nucleus of a credible alternative government and create the conditions for meaningful alternation" (Gianfranco Pasquino, personal communication, August 1999). That notion, though helpful, does not suffice to explain the perplexing conjunction of instability and stability in Italian politics.

The second, related point has to do with the DC's longevity as an incumbent in Italy. All scholarly monographs and textbooks on postwar Italian politics must deal in some way with the DC's amazing grip on national governing power. An eminent team of political scientists has studied the presence of one-party dominance in Israel, Italy, Japan, and Sweden and its absence in Britain, Germany, and other parliamentary democracies (Pempel 1990). Despite the strengths of these works, they do little to get close to the decision-making processes entailed in government formation and dissolution, and they thus overlook the ways that the DC incurred— and engineered—such low costs of coalition. The DC's role as the "*mamma eterna*" of Italian government (to echo one memorable sobriquet [Tarrow 1990]) cannot be apprehended without recognizing the party's ability to maneuver around the costs of coalition.

Third, this research illuminates recent developments in Italian politics. I stress the profound changes in the Italian party system and the consequent changes in Italian coalitions since the 1992 elections. Nonetheless, I also see continuities. Since 1992, the term *Second Republic* has often been bandied about in Italian political debate, but it is very much open to question (cf. Sabetti 2000, 242). Renumbering republics usually involves switching constitutions (the obvious comparison is France in 1958), and that has not yet occurred in Italy. The Italian electoral laws were rewritten in 1993, but the institutional scaffolding of the First Republic is largely in place: The 1948 constitution is still in force, and Italy still has two co-equal houses of Parliament, an indirectly elected president, a rather weak prime minister, judicial review, and so forth. There is substantial continuity in institutional scaffolding alongside remarkable change in partisan actors.[3]

Fourth, this research contributes to a reassessment of the connection between expertise on Italy (or on any other country) and scientific progress in comparative politics. I now elaborate on that point.

ANALYZING PARTIES AS STRATEGIC ACTORS

Robert Putnam's acclaimed research on "making democracy work" in the twenty Italian regions (Putnam et al. 1993) has persuaded many political scientists that fundamental lessons in comparative politics can be learned from Italy. The frequency with which the words "social capital" appear in conference papers, journal articles, and even newspaper items testifies to the influence of Putnam's ideas. (In essence, "social capital" is the stock of mutual trust, networks of interaction, and norms of reciprocity that exists among citizens and, Putnam argues, promotes good government.) The term has gained even wider currency since the publication of Putnam's much-cited article—and most recently, book—on declining social capital in the United States (1995, 2000). Putnam has transformed our understanding of how ordinary citizens' habits, beliefs, traditions, associations, and actions shape the effectiveness of institutions of democratic governance.

I do not aspire to Putnam's fame, but I do hope to help reorient our thinking about party competition for control of government. In my view, research on government formation and dissolution needs to be much more attentive to the possibilities for, impact of, and limits on political parties' strategic behavior. This insistence on analyzing parties as strategic actors has led one reader of my work to affirm that, at the same time that it explores the costs of coalition, it distills "a set of organizing principles for the much broader literature on government formation" (Michael Laver, personal communication, October 1999). As contended in Chapter 8, it is less than fruitful to assert that the structural characteristics of some party systems make executives especially vulnerable to shock, for such an assertion leaves unidentified the causal mechanisms generating government falls. To repeat: Parties in some systems exploit and realize the possibility of cabinet dissolutions, because they expect benefits or at least no losses to ensue. Parties' expectations reflect their readings of institutional constraints and understandings of their own and other parties' locations and leverage in policy space.

In my judgment, I have been able to forge a novel set of organizing principles for a well-tilled field in comparative politics because of—not despite—my expertise in the politics of postwar Italy. It takes an Italianist to appreciate the "fine Italian hand" in coalition politics. It takes a comparativist with a focus on Italy to expose and elaborate the relevance of lessons from Italy for the study of other parliamentary democracies. And it takes a comparativist with an interest in game-theoretic forms of rational choice research to isolate and analyze the puzzle at the heart of this book.

Implications

It has become something of a ritual for political scientists to close their written work with a call for more research. The ritual has a reason: We want to convey the import of what we have done, the questions that our findings raise for areas of study other than our own, and the range of uses to which the analytical tools we have fashioned might be put. Rather than simply inviting other scholars to adhere to an agenda that I propose, I sketch here three examples of how my argument can be extended to guide further research (cf. King, Keohane, and Verba 1994). First, I show how the level of analysis can be switched from parties to party factions. Second, I investigate the differential implementation of cost-reduction strategies—in particular, the way that the rate of increase in cabinet posts might vary across different types of offices. Third, I weigh the long-run consequences of short-run decisions to offset the costs of coalition.

VARIATIONS IN OFFICE COSTS
ACROSS PARTY FACTIONS

If my argument about parties is right, then variations in the costs of coalition borne by party factions should also be comprehensible in light of spatial and institutional conditions. For instance, within a party, some factions should find it cheaper than others to construct coalition governments, and which factions pay least should depend on the array of all factions in policy space.

In related research (Mershon 1998, 2001, n.d.), I evaluate this hypothesis for Italy's core party. Leaving aside the details,[4] the bottom line is that the evidence available for the 1963–79 period lends additional support to my argument. The Christian Democratic factions that sacrificed the fewest offices to build coalitions were those at or near the left–right median in the party. Moreover, the 1964 move from majoritarian rules to proportional representation in internal DC elections yielded changes in the office costs of coalition incurred by DC factions. Overall, cabinet portfolios were awarded in proportion to faction size. Variations in the degree of proportionality testify to the impact of institutional changes (the 1976 introduction of direct elections for the DC secretary general) and to the interplay between coalition choices and faction payoffs (left-wing DC factions could be assured of proportional representation only in governments embracing the Socialists).

For Christian Democracy as a whole between 1946 and 1992, increases in portfolios offset the office costs of erecting coalitions, as Chapters 5 and 7 made clear. The office benefits that the DC preserved as a party were not distributed equally across its factions. The patterns in the interfactional allocation of offices dovetail with the logic developed in this book.

VARIATIONS IN RATES OF INCREASE
ACROSS OFFICES

If parties and factions manipulate office resources so as to absorb costs and cement coalitions, then the rate of increase in cabinet posts should vary across offices that are recognized as having greater or lesser value. There are firm grounds for believing that Italian politicians have discerned differences in the quality of cabinet posts: Recall from Chapter 4 that the codified guidelines for coalition bargaining in Italy included a four-part ranking of ministries according to prestige. One implication of the hypotheses in this book is that party leaders aiming to gratify legislators and buy loyalty are expected *not* to concentrate the increase in offices among the least prestigious undersecretaryships. As Westefield (1974, 1597) phrases it, "What is the advantage to the leaders of creating new positions ... which are not valued?" Coalition builders should also avoid opening too many junior slots in the ministries at the very top of the hierarchy: "Adding [posts] to the very best [ministries] reduces the value of total resources more than does adding positions to somewhat less prestigious" ministries (ibid., 1599). The increase in undersecretaryships should thus be concentrated within the ministries with above-average prestige.[5]

Westefield (1974) contends that analogous variations in the rate of increase of committee seats should appear in the United States House of Representatives. Compared to other national legislatures, the U.S. House is extremely decentralized and unusually powerful.[6] In addition, of course, in the U.S. presidential system the legislature and the executive are separated, not fused. Yet party leaders have an incentive to strive to secure their legislative followings even where the survival of the executive does not depend on legislative support; indeed, especially in such a setting, party cohesion cannot be taken for granted, since disloyal legislators do not and cannot topple governments (Bowler, Farrell, and Katz 1999; Cox 1987). Given the importance of committees, their powers, and the independence of the legislature and the executive, therefore, majority party leaders in the U.S. House can be expected to "attempt to accommodate member demands for committee positions in order to gain leverage with the members" (Westefield 1974, 1593), and to concentrate the increase in the supply of committee seats "in the middle to upper range of the committee prestige ordering" (ibid., 1595).[7]

In related research, I assess these propositions for Italy and the United States (Mershon 1999b). Again omitting the details, the chief conclusion for the United States is that the reasoning is upheld. Westefield (1974) documents that the data on committee seat additions in the House of Representatives are consistent with the hypotheses for two periods, both 1927–45 and 1947–71. It is straightforward to extend Westefield's analysis to 1991 (using information in Nelson with Benson 1993 and Nelson with Mitchell and Benson 1994). For the 1947–91 period, too, the differential rate of increase in committee size largely conforms to expectations.

In Italy, for 1946–92 and especially for 1946–76, the bulk of the increase in undersecretarial positions was found in the upper-middle range of the prestige hierarchy. From 1976 to 1992, however, the distribution of the increase upsets expectations. In that subperiod, the top-quality ministries witnessed the greatest increment in junior appointments; and the smallest increment appeared not at the very bottom of the scale but in the ministries with below-average prestige. The 1976–92 increase within the least-valued group was almost as great as that within the second-best category. It seems sensible to interpret this pattern as yet another sign of the accentuated competition between the DC and the Socialists (PSI) while the PSI was pivotal— while the Socialists' incumbency (or opposition) guaranteed a legislative majority (or minority) for any DC-based government excluding the Communists. What is the use, though, of rewarding legislators with near-worthless positions? Why would coalition leaders risk depleting the value of the top-notch positions by adding so many of them?

Note that Westefield (1974, 1603) predicts another overhaul of the House committee system "similar to that of 1946." Exploring this prediction is central to understanding the distinctiveness of the 1976–92 period in Italy and provides a way to gauge the long-run consequences of short-run decisions to lower the costs of coalition.

LONG-RUN CONSEQUENCES
OF SHORT-RUN STRATEGIES

An essential component of Westefield's logic is the notion that the value of each single office is eroded as the number of offices rises overall. "As currency becomes more and more plentiful, the basis of exchange is impaired. The leaders must revalue the currency or turn to another medium of exchange" (Westefield 1974, 1601). Accordingly, Westefield interprets the Legislative Reorganization Act of 1946 as a revaluation of the currency of committee positions in the U.S. House. The 1946 act imposed a drastic reduction in the number of committee seats (ibid., 1596). The next retrenchment to attain these proportions was carried out by the Republican Party soon after it won a House majority in 1994 (Deering and Smith 1997, 50, 98–100).

No such revaluation occurred in Italy between 1976 and 1992. Instead, I believe, Italian coalition leaders began to rely on another medium of exchange. Recall a question raised by the 1976–92 distribution of the increase in junior ministerial slots: Why would coalition leaders reward legislators with apparently near-worthless positions? The answer, in a word, is corruption. Once the PSI acquired pivotal status in 1976 and until the corruption scandal broke open in 1992, the value of cabinet offices came more and more to be measured in terms of access to, and discretion over, illegal flows of funds. Even low-prestige ministries presented rich possibilities for collecting kickbacks and bribes.

Admittedly, this interpretation is both cautious and bold. It is cautious, for I do not mean to suggest that corruption occurred only at the apex of the Italian political system or only between 1976 and 1992. And bold, for I have no systematic way of measuring access to corruption or comparing access across ministries. All the same—as investigations, arrests, confessions, and trial evidence have mounted since 1992—a consensus has emerged that the 1980s saw corruption of unprecedented scale and reach in Italy.[8] It is difficult to escape the inference that in Italy short-run decisions to manipulate offices—efforts to diminish the costs of coalition, repeated and refined over time, and intensified when the DC competed against a pivotal PSI—had the long-run consequence of favoring the spread of corruption.[9]

Equally important, in Italy short-run decisions to contain the costs of coalition had the long-run consequence of entrenching the Christian Democrats in government. When the DC first acquired the premiership in December 1945, the party's leaders did not know that it would dominate Italian politics for almost fifty years (on the DC's uncertainty, see, e.g., Chapter 4 and Pasquino [1986]). The DC spearheaded experiments designed to facilitate the immediate management of coalition processes: reach-

ing agreement with many allies, restricting information, delegitimizing opponents, and so forth. The experiments, when successful, evolved into
repertoires of strategic behavior that in the long run helped to cement the
DC in power (cf. Mershon 1994).

The three classes of implications developed here illustrate but obviously
do not exhaust the possibilities for further research. The illustrations lead
naturally to discussing what is often viewed as the "small-N problem" characteristic of empirical research on coalitions. The problem, in a nutshell, is
that empirical analyses chase after the "same rather small fixed universe of
post-war European governments" (Laver and Schofield 1990, 9).

Lessons

The lessons that this book seeks to convey can be grouped under two
rubrics, the methodological and the epistemological. One methodological
lesson is that the existence and severity of a small-N problem hinge on how
cases are understood; put differently, hypotheses about coalitions can be
evaluated in more ways than is commonly imagined.

ON CASES AND DATA COLLECTION

Empirical research on coalitions typically proceeds as follows. The
scholar defends the utility of the party-as-unitary-actor assumption, and
then moves to a quantitative investigation in which the government is the
unit of analysis. Governments are categorized according to whether they
command a parliamentary majority, include the core party, join parties adjacent to each other on the left–right spectrum, last three years or three
months, and so forth. Tables 2.1, 2.2, and 4.3 in this book exemplify such a
strategy. So, too, do the landmark studies conducted by Dodd (1976), King
et al. (1990), and Laver and Schofield (1990), among others. Alternatively,
a few researchers criticize the unitary actor assumption and perform quantitative analyses in which the object under scrutiny is the individual politician who has served in government and responded to a questionnaire (e.g.,
Downs 1998; Müller-Rommel 1994). One virtue of this approach, of course,
is that it increases the number of cases available for analysis (Downs 1998,
6, 274). One drawback is that it is capable of generating only recall data for
past events; and the more distant the past, the more troublesome the data.

There are other ways to conceive of cases in the study of coalitions, however. Governing parties provide empirical observations relevant to hypotheses about coalitions. Across the ten countries in this data set, a total
of fifty-nine parties have ruled for at least half of the span between any two

consecutive elections. It can be instructive to examine aggregated attributes of those parties, as in Table 7.2 (on policy costs) or Table 7.6 (on electoral costs). The analysis of parties can also be disaggregated, so that the dependent variable is some attribute of a party each time it participates in government or competes in parliamentary elections. Thus, for instance, the inquiry into the office costs of breaking coalitions in Chapter 8 rested on 700 cases. Additional observations relevant to my hypotheses were just assessed above. Plainly, this sort of research design does much to alleviate the small-N problem. (For a further look at the large-N subsets of data in my study, see Appendix E. For another study that defines units of analysis so as to obtain relatively large N's, see Laver and Shepsle [1996].)

The second methodological lesson has to do with how data sets are compiled, documented, and disseminated within the scholarly community. In one sentence: Evaluating theories of coalitional behavior entails challenges in data collection that deserve more attention than they have so far received. To elaborate, the longest footnote in this book (in Chapter 3) dissects differences across data sets in governments identified. As it remarks, even scholars who ostensibly use the same criteria to define governments come up with different lists of governments, because subsidiary rules of thumb are needed to implement any set of criteria and because explicit discussion of such rules and judgment calls is rare within the field of coalition studies. Yet, precisely such discussion is essential if we are to enhance the replicability and cumulation of research on coalitions.

The field of judicial politics illustrates how important cooperative work on challenges in data collection can be within a scholarly community. Spaeth completed the *United States Supreme Court Judicial Database* in 1990 and has updated it nine times since then. (The most recent version available is Spaeth 1999.) The *Supreme Court Database* offers a readily accessible, standardized, extraordinarily rich source of data on the decisions of the Court since 1953. It has been subjected to multiple reliability checks and efforts at cross-validation (Djupe and Epstein 1998; Epstein 1995; Gibson 1997; Segal and Spaeth 1993). The researcher who retrieves the Spaeth (1999) codebook from the archives of the Inter-University Consortium for Political and Social Research (ICPSR) will find a 101-page record featuring repeated discussions of reliability and extensive guidelines for investigators wishing to conduct their own analyses of the data. Judicial specialists are also fortunate to be able to consult the 700 pages of data printed in *The Supreme Court Compendium* (Epstein et al. 1996, 2001).

Despite the wealth of empirical research on government coalitions, the field lacks a database comparable to that compiled by Spaeth and colleagues. Published data sets on the composition and duration of governments include Lane, McKay, and Newton (1991) and Woldendorp, Keman, and Budge (1993, 1998). Data sets available in electronic form include those created by Laver and Shepsle (1996) and Tsebelis (1999). All of these are valuable and all signal new possibilities for multi-investigator research. Yet none can claim a comprehensiveness akin to that of Spaeth's *Supreme Court Database*. None gathers in one location anything like the range of dependent and independent variables, with governments and parties-in-government as units of analysis, examined in the research for this book. Granted, my database on coalition politics does not (yet!) match the meticulous documentation (Djupe and Epstein 1998, 1012) or the frequent updating that distinguishes the *Supreme Court Database* archived with the ICPSR. And making my database publicly available is sure to lead to the detection (and correction) of errors. All the same, I hope that the database I have compiled and discussed, and have begun to document and disseminate, might represent a step forward in collaborative, cumulative empirical research on coalitions and within comparative politics.[10]

EPISTEMOLOGICAL LESSONS

Epistemological is a big word, but it aptly describes the second kind of lesson I hope to communicate. What is the nature of our knowledge about coalitional behavior, and how do we advance it? In my view, the answer to that question must entail an attempt to bring theoretical and empirical research into closer conversation with each other. Game-theoretic research needs to be more creative in, and attentive to, identifying propositions capable of being tested against the real world of coalition politics. Theorists should consider seriously the notion that thinking through how a theory might be evaluated empirically might teach them something about the theory. It is possible for empirical research to guide the development of theory, as some natural scientists have emphasized (Keller 1983; Levi Montalcini 1987). Empirical research can be theory informing as well as theoretically informed. The "conversation" between theoretical and empirical research is likely to be clearer and more fruitful if the empirical research insists on the importance of tapping and tracing causal mechanisms. It is time to move beyond empirical evaluations of coalition theories that merely count the observed frequency of expected outcomes without seeking to ascertain whether it is the causal mechanisms posited in the theory that generate the outcomes (cf. Laver and Schofield 1990, 102).

One way to explore causal mechanisms is to organize research around anomalies. After all, science depends on an appreciation of what is *and is not yet* explained (cf. Franzosi 1995, 375). I started this project by puzzling over the combination of instability and stability in Italian government. I have probed the implications of this puzzle for coalition politics outside of

Italy. I have drawn a picture of strategic behavior—of deliberate attempts to manipulate the costs of coalition, carried out under spatial and institutional constraints—that I believe makes sense both of Italy's extremes and the degrees of stability registered in other parliamentary democracies. The variety of evidence I have marshaled bears out my hypotheses and indicates the promise of my approach.

Bates, de Figueiredo, and Weingast (1998, 606) argue that political scientists need to travel both ways on a "two-way street between the [interpretive and rational choice] approaches." As they put it,

Game-theoretic accounts require detailed and fine-grained knowledge of the precise features of the political and social environment within which individuals make choices and devise political strategies. To construct a coherent and valid rational choice account, then, one must 'soak and poke' and acquire much the same depth of understanding as that achieved by those who offer 'thick' descriptions. (ibid., 628; cf. Ferejohn 1991)

I agree, and I urge political scientists to take full advantage of the two-way street between empirical and theoretical research on coalitions.

Trade-offs in, and Contributions to, Political Science

I must confess, again, that I am both cautious and bold. Cautious, because I am very much aware that this book is based on trade-offs. And bold, because, as just suggested, I hope to contribute to a rethinking of the relationship between formal theory and empirical research in political science.

Perhaps the most salient trade-off in this book is between breadth and depth. As already underscored, Part II attains depth at the expense of breadth, whereas Part III exchanges depth for breadth across ten countries. Each trade-off is designed to balance the other.

Another trade-off is between simplicity and detail in the presentation and analysis of evidence. Not only did the treatment of Italian politics immerse the reader in detail; so, too, did the overviews of electoral institutions in Table 6.2, policy costs in Table 7.2, and office payoffs in Table 8.2, to cite just a few examples. On the other hand, I have taken for granted and "for good" some measures devised by others (in particular, those derived from the coding of party and government statements) instead of engaging in the complexities of inventing my own. The detail might have seemed at times unwieldy. But it was vital in the effort to capture causal mechanisms, and it laid the foundation for the simpler models of Chapter 8.

A third trade-off is between formalization of theory and innovation in empirical research. It is in the study of legislative behavior and government coalitions that game theory has made some of its chief contributions. I have not framed a novel formal theory, however. Instead, I have sought innovation in theoretically informed empirical research. In the conclusion to their recent book on the U.S. Supreme Court, Epstein and Knight (1998, 185, 186) admit that

many may be surprised that a book on strategic analysis of the Supreme Court contains no game-theoretic, or formal, models. But that reaction would reflect a misunderstanding of the nature of our enterprise. Our goal has been to develop a picture of judicial choice, a conception of the mechanisms of strategic behavior that characterize decision making on the Court.... The benefits of formal analysis should not be underestimated. The basic point here is that the degree of formalization of the analysis depends on the nature of the explanation that is desired.

My goal has been to develop a picture of party choice, a conception of the mechanisms of strategic behavior underlying the building and breaking of coalitions.

I should acknowledge not only trade-offs but also leaps of faith. One criticism often leveled at empirical research in political science is that it "tends to deduce preferences from outcomes" (Spruyt 1994, 84). I have done my best to escape that criticism. I have tried hard, for instance, to demonstrate intention and foresight sufficient to lead the reader to reject the idea that Italian parties inadvertently reduced the costs of coalition. Nonetheless, a caveat must be kept in mind. Like Lupia and McCubbins (1998, 99), I deem it crucial to stress that "all empirical science . . . require[s] an *inductive leap*. This leap is the assumption that our method of . . . observation is a faithful analogy to our theory. . . . *All* scientists make this leap when they use empirical research to evaluate theoretical explanations" (emphases in original). We can never know for sure whether what we want to believe is in fact right. We can only know when it is wrong. As Bates and colleagues observe, "we are more certain when theories fail than when they fit the case materials" (Bates et al. 1998, 17; cf. Bates 1997; Collier 1999). No theory is ever proven, and any successful theory merely escapes disconfirmation, to paraphrase Campbell and Stanley (1966, 35).

A book, like many journeys, comes to a stopping place instead of an end. Arriving at the stopping place marks an achievement, to be sure. Yet something always remains to be seen the next time around. And one of my aims in this book has been to advocate, illustrate, and prepare the way for a new approach in theoretically informed and theoretically informing empirical research on coalitions. If I have succeeded, this book will have one of the first words, not the last, in its subfield. Even more broadly, achievement and imperfection are inescapably linked in human life and scientific work. It is the incomplete match between theory and data that tells us what to do next and inspires us to do more. The effort to interrogate the imperfection we perceive is what moves science forward and makes life interesting.

Abbreviations

AN	Alleanza Nazionale, National Alliance—Italy
AP	Action Paysanne, Peasant Action—France IV
ARP	Anti-Revolutionaire Partij, Anti-Revolutionary Party—Netherlands
ARS	Action Républicaine et Sociale, Dissident Gaullists (Republican and Social Action)—France IV
BSP	Belgische Socialistische Partij, Belgian Socialist Party—Belgium [Flemish]
CCD	Centro Cristiano Democratico, Christian Democratic Center—Italy
CD	Centrum-Demokraterne, Center Democrats—Denmark
CDA	Christen Democratisch Appèl, Christian Democratic Appeal (electoral alliance of ARP, CHU, KVP in 1977, complete merger in 1980)—Netherlands
CDU	Cristiani Democratici Uniti, United Christian Democrats—Italy
CDU/CSU	Christlich Demokratische Union/Christlich Soziale Union, Christian Democratic Union/Christian Social Union—Germany
CHU	Christelijke Historische Unie, Christian Historical Union—Netherlands
CONS	Conservative bloc—PRL, RI, AP, and peasant parties other than AP—France IV
CP	Centerpartiet, Center Party—Sweden
CP	Clann na Poblachta, Children of the Republic—Ireland
CT	Clann na Talmhan, Children of the Land—Ireland
CVP	Christelijke Volkspartij, Christian People's Party—Belgium [Flemish]
D66	Democraten '66, Democrats '66—Netherlands

DC	Democrazia Cristiana, Christian Democracy—Italy
DIR	Radicaux Dissidents, Dissident Radicals—France IV
DL	Democrazia del Lavoro, Democratic Labor—Italy
DNA	Det Norske Arbeiderparti, Norwegian Labor Party—Norway
DP	Democrazia Proletaria, Proletarian Democracy—Italy
DP	Deutsche Partei, German Party—Germany
DS70	Democratisch-Socialisten '70, Democratic Socialists '70—Netherlands
FDF	Front Démocratique des Francophones, Francophone Democratic Front—Belgium
FDP	Freie Demokratische Partei, Free Democratic Party—Germany
FF	Fianna Fáil, Soldiers of Destiny—Ireland
FG	Fine Gael, Tribe of the Gael—Ireland
FI	Forza Italia, Go Italy!—Italy
FP	Folkpartiet, Liberals (People's Party)—Sweden
FVP	Freie Volkspartei, Free People's Party—Germany
GAUL	Gaullist parties—RPF, RS, URAS—France IV
GB/BHE	Gesamtdeutscher Block/Bund der Heimatvertriebenen und Entrechtcten, Pan-German Bloc/Bloc of Expellees and Disenfranchised—Germany
GDE	Gauche Démocratique, Democratic Left—France IV
Greens	Verdi, Greens—Italy
H	Høyre, Conservatives—Norway
IOM	Indépendents d'Outre Mer, Overseas Independents—France IV
KDS	Kristdemokratiska Samhällspartiet, Christian Democrats—Sweden
KF	Konservative Folkeparti, Conservatives—Denmark
KK	Kansallinen Kokoomus, National Coalition Party—Finland
KP	Maalaisliitto, renamed Keskustapuolue in 1965, Center Party—Finland
KRF	Kristeligt Folkeparti, Christian People's Party—Denmark

KRF	Kristelig Folkeparti, Christian People's Party—Norway
KVP	Katholieke Volkspartij, Christian Democrats (Catholic People's Party)—Netherlands
KVP/CDA	Katholieke Volkspartij/Christen Democratisch Appèl, Catholic People's Party, since 1977 Christian Democratic Appeal—Netherlands
LAB	Labour—Ireland
League	Lega Lombarda/Lega Nord, Lombard League, since 1991 Northern League—Italy
LKP	Liberaalinen Kansanpuolue, Liberal Party—Finland
M	Moderata Samlingspartiet, Moderates/Conservatives—Sweden
MRP	Mouvement Républicain Populaire, Popular Republican Movement (Christian Democrats)—France IV
MSI	Movimento Sociale Italiano, Italian Social Movement (Neo-Fascists)—Italy
NL	National Labour—Ireland
PCB/KPB	Parti Communiste de Belgique/Kommunistische Partij van België, Belgian Communist Party—Belgium
PCF	Parti Communiste Français, French Communist Party—France
PCI	Partito Comunista Italiano, Italian Communist Party—Italy
PD	Progressive Democrats—Ireland
PDS	Partito Democratico della Sinistra, Democratic Party of the Left—Italy
PDUP	Partito di Unità Proletaria, Party of Proletarian Unity—Italy
PLI	Partito Liberale Italiano, Italian Liberal Party—Italy
PLP	Parti pour le Progrès et la Liberté, Party of Liberty and Progress—Belgium [Francophone]
PLP/PVV	Parti pour le Progrès et la Liberté/Partij voor Vrijheid en Vooruitgang, Liberals—Belgium
PNM	Partito Nazionale Monarchico, National Monarchist Party (with slight variations in name over time)—Italy
PPI	Partito Popolare Italiano, Italian Popular Party—Italy
PPR	Politieke Partij Radikalen, Radical Party—Netherlands

PRad	Partito Radicale, Radical Party—Italy
PRI	Partito Repubblicano Italiano, Italian Republican Party—Italy
PRL	Parti Réformateur Libéral, Liberal Reformist Party—Belgium [Francophone]
PRL	Parti Républicain de la Liberté, Republican Party of Liberty—France IV
PSB	Parti Socialiste Belge, Belgian Socialist Party—Belgium [Francophone]
PSB/BSP	Parti Socialiste Belge/Belgische Socialistische Partij, Socialists—Belgium
PSC	Parti Social Chrétien, Christian Social Party—Belgium [Francophone]
PSC/CVP	Parti Social Chrétien/Christelijke Volkspartij, Christian Socials—Belgium
PSDI	Partito Socialista Democratico Italiano, Italian Social Democratic Party—Italy
PSI	Partito Socialista Italiano, Italian Socialist Party—Italy
PSIUP	Partito Socialista Italiano di Unità Proletaria, Italian Socialist Party of Proletarian Unity—Italy
PvdA	Partij van de Arbeid, Labor Party—Netherlands
PVV	Partij voor Vrijheid en Vooruitgang, Party of Liberty and Progress—Belgium [Flemish]
RAD	Radicaux, Radicals—France IV
RC	Rifondazione Comunista, Communist Refoundation—Italy
RF	Retsforbund, Justice Party—Denmark
RGR	Rassemblement des Gauches Républicains, Rally of Left Republicans—France IV
RI	Républicains Indépendents, Independent Republicans—France IV
RPF	Rassemblement du Peuple Français, Gaullists (Rally of the French People)—France IV
RS	Républicains Sociaux, Gaullists (Social Republicans)—France IV
RV	Radikale Venstre, Radical Liberals—Denmark
RW	Rassemblement Wallon, Walloon Rally—Belgium

SAP	Socialdemokraterna, Social Democrats—Sweden
SD	Socialdemokratiet, Social Democracy—Denmark
SFIO	Section Française de l'Internationale Ouvrière, Socialists (French Section of the Workers' International)—France IV
SFP	Svenska Folkpartiet, Swedish People's Party—Finland
SKDL	Suomen Kansan Demokraattinen Liitto, Communists (Finnish People's Democratic League)—Finland
SKL	Suomen Kristillinen Liitto, Finnish Christian League—Finland
SMP	Suomen Maaseudun Poulue, Finnish Rural Party—Finland
SP	Senterpartiet, Center Party—Norway
SPD	Sozialdemokratische Partei Deutschlands, Social Democratic Party—Germany
SSDP	Suomen Sosialidemokraattinen Poulue, Finnish Social Democratic Party—Finland
SVP	Sudtiroler Volkspartei, South Tyrol People's Party—Italy
TPSL	Työväen ja Pienviljelijäin Sosialidemokrattinen Liitto, Social Democratic League—Finland
UD	Unione Democratica, Democratic Union—Italy
UDC	Unione di Centro, Centrist Union—Italy
UDSR	Union Démocratique et Socialiste de la Résistance, Democratic and Socialist Union of the Resistance—France IV
URAS	Union Républicaine d'Action Sociale, Gaullists (Republican Union of Social Action)—France IV
V	Venstre, Liberals—Denmark
V	Venstre, Liberals—Norway
VU	Volksunie, People's Union—Belgium
VVD	Volkspartij voor Vrijheid en Democratie, Liberals (People's Party of Freedom and Democracy)—Netherlands

ABBREVIATIONS OF GOVERNMENT TYPES

MAJ1   One-party majority government
MCW   Minimal connected winning coalition
MIN   Minority government
MW   Minimal winning coalition
S   Surplus coalition

OTHER ABBREVIATIONS

DDM   Dimension-by-dimension median
MP   Member of parliament
PR   Proportional representation
SEE   Standard error of the estimate
STV   Single transferable vote

Scope of Data Sets in Coalition Studies

The argument and the evidence examined in this book build on the research of other scholars. My argument is informed by spatial theories of voting, as made clear in Chapters 2 and 3, among others. My collection and analysis of data have been guided by the data sets compiled, the findings reported, and the questions raised by political scientists who began empirical work on coalitions before I did. I have assumed throughout this enterprise that my data and my manipulation of data would be "better"—that is, my measures would be more reliable, more valid, and more precise, and my results more robust and just plain more worth producing—if I studied coalitional systems where fairly substantial research had already been conducted. In other words, I thought it valuable to check my judgment calls against those made for other data sets and to refer to others' findings in generating and interpreting my own. The data set I have constructed thus embraces what might be called the "data-rich" countries.

Table B.1 illustrates the wealth of information available on these countries. It also shows that although coalition politics is somewhat less thoroughly documented for Finland and Fourth Republic France than for the most studied nations, those two systems have been covered in several important research projects. (Newly democratized Greece, for example, looks like "uncharted territory" compared to Finland and France.) I include Finland and France in this data set to increase the number of multipolar party systems and ensure wide variation in spatial and institutional conditions.

TABLE B.I.

Countries Covered in Major Data Sets Used in Coalition Studies

	Strøm	Woldendorp	Laver–Schofield	Laver–Budge	Laver–Hunt	Laver–Shepsle	Franklin
PARLIAMENTARY DEMOCRACIES							
Most studied coalitional systems							
Belgium	•	•	•	•	•	•	•
Denmark	•	•	•	•	•	•	•
Germany	o	•	•	•	•	•	•
Ireland	•	•	•	•	•	•	•
Italy	•	•	•	•	•	•	•
Netherlands	•	•	•	•	•	•	•
Norway	•	•	•	•	•	•	•
Sweden	•	•	•	•	•	•	•
Less studied but analyzed in this book							
Finland	•	•	•	o	•	•	o
France IV	•	•	o	•	•	o	o
Least studied coalitional systems							
Australia	o	•	o	o	•	o	•
Austria	o	•	•	o	•	•	o
Greece	o	o	o	o	•	o	•
Iceland	•	•	•	o	•	•	o
Israel	•	•	o	•	•	o	o
Japan	o	•	o	o	•	o	o
Luxembourg	o	•	•	•	•	•	o
Malta	o	o	o	o	•	o	o
Portugal	•	o	o	o	•	o	o
Spain	•	o	o	o	•	o	•
Systems where coalitions have not governed							
Canada	•	•	o	o	•	o	•
New Zealand until 1996	o	•	o	o	o	o	•
U.K.	•	•	o	o	•	o	•

TABLE B.1. (*Continued*)

	Strøm	Woldendorp	Laver-Schofield	Laver-Budge	Laver-Hunt	Laver-Shepsle	Franklin
NON-PARLIAMENTARY SYSTEMS							
France V	○	●	○	○	●	○	●
Switzerland	○	●	○	○	●	○	○
U.S.	○	○	○	○	●	○	●

SOURCES AND TIME COVERAGE: (1) Data sets on governments: Strøm (1990b) covers the first postwar election to 1987. Woldendorp, Keman, and Budge (1993) cover 1945 to 1990. Laver and Schofield (1990) cover 1945 to 1987. Laver and Shepsle (1996) cover 1945 to roughly 1991 (but vary by country).(2) Data sets on parties' and/or governments' positions in policy space: Laver and Schofield (1990) report manifesto-based data for 1945 to 1987. Laver and Budge (1992) report manifesto-based data for 1945 to roughly 1989 (but vary by country). Laver and Hunt (1992) report expert judgments for the late 1980s. (3) Data on voters: Franklin, Mackie, and Valen (1992) concentrate on the post-1960 period.

NOTE: A filled circle indicates that the data set includes the country in question, and a blank circle indicates exclusion. Countries included in this book's data set are italicized.

Governments Included in This Study

This book not only builds on others' research. It also seeks to equip and encourage other scholars to build *on it*—to try to replicate the findings here, to criticize the choices made in data collection and analysis, to use measures discussed in the book in new applications, and so forth. Appendices C and D are designed to help achieve that aim.

I take special care in clarifying just which entities are included as governments in this study because, as Chapter 3 noted, the identification of governments is a trickier business than it might at first seem. For example, one specialist in German and comparative politics remarked to me that "Germanists would scratch their heads a bit" when they saw what I considered to be the governments ruling in Germany between 1949 and 1993. He added, "I hate to say it, but according to your criteria they [Erhard III and Schmidt IV] should be separate governments" (Christopher Anderson, personal communication, July 21, 1995). Comments like these convince me that, for the sake of replicability and cumulation in empirical research, Appendix C belongs in the book.

I isolate a new government with each change of party composition, parliamentary election, change of prime minister, and accepted resignation of the cabinet. To apply the criterion of changes in party composition, I need subsidiary rules of thumb to distinguish between "mere" phases of coalition crisis and "real" shifts in the partisan makeup of governments. In this data set, a "real" shift is signaled by no immediate move to call elections; replacement of all resigning ministers with ministers from another party; and, in addition to the appointment of personnel, some move to affirm that the old executive no longer exists.

Implementing these criteria and subsidiary rules, I identify a total of 291 governments in office in ten countries between the first post–World War II elections to January 1, 1993. For each government, six items of information are listed in the pages that follow:

Name of the government (the name of the prime minister or chancellor
    and, if s/he has headed more than one government, a number
    indicating the temporal sequence of the multiple governments)

Date formed (month and year)

Days spent in forming the government (the number of days separating

the demise of a government and the rise of its successor, except when
elections intervene; for governments launched after parliamentary
elections, I count the number of days separating election day and
the announcement of a cabinet)

Party composition, with the prime minister's party listed first (note that
party abbreviations are defined in Appendix A)

Type of government, with acronyms as follows:

MAJ1 One-party majority

MIN   Minority

MW   Minimal winning coalition

S   Surplus coalition

Number of ministers, senior and junior, named when the government
formed (notwithstanding the various titles attached to the position of
junior minister, e.g., in Ireland parliamentary secretary [before 1978]
and ministers of state [since 1978]). Whenever one individual holds two
positions, s/he is counted as one minister (or one junior minister), for
the key attribute of interest here is the number of politicians per party
who enter office. Since not all ministers (or junior ministers) are always
named on the same day, I count appointments within one month of the
official announcement or the investiture of the government in question.

For each table, dotted lines indicate that a parliamentary election was
held in the interval between the fall of one government and the formation
of another. The sources for each table are included in Appendix D. Readers
who wish to see the full data set may consult my home page on the Web:
http://www.faculty.virginia.edu/cmershon/.

Belgium

Government	Date Formed	Days to Form	Party Composition	Type	MINISTERS Sr	MINISTERS Jr
Spaak I	3/46	25	PSB/BSP	MIN	17	0
van Acker II	3/46	10	PSB/BSP + PLP/PVV + PCB/KPB	MW	19	0
Huysman	8/46	24	PSB/BSP + PSC/CVP + PCB/KPB	MW	19	0
Spaak II	3/47	7	PSB/BSP + PSC/CVP	MW	19	0
Spaak III	11/48	7	PSB/BSP + PSC/CVP	MW	17	0
Eyskens I	8/49	15	PSC/CVP + PLP/PVV	MW	17	0
Duvieusart	6/50	4	PSC/CVP	MAJ1	15	0
Pholien	8/50	4	PSC/CVP	MAJ1	16	0
van Houtte	1/52	6	PSC/CVP	MAJ1	16	0
van Acker III	4/54	11	PSB/BSP + PLP/PVV	MW	16	0
Eyskens II	6/58	24	PSC/CVP	MIN	16	0
Eyskens III	11/58	2	PSC/CVP + PLP/PVV	MW	19	0
Lefevre	4/61	30	PSC/CVP + PSB/BSP	MW	17	3
Harmel	7/65	66	PSC/CVP + PSB/BSP	MW	20	7
Vanden Boeynants I	3/66	38	PSC/CVP + PLP/PVV	MW	19	4
Eyskens IV	6/68	79	CVP + PSC + PSB/BSP	S	27	2
Eyskens V	1/72	74	CVP + PSC + PSB/BSP	S	19	10
Leburton	1/73	61	PSB/BSP + PLP + PSC + CVP + PVV	S	22	14
Tindemans I	4/74	45	CVP + PSC + PLP + PVV	MIN	19	6
Tindemans II	6/74	14	CVP + PSC + PLP + PVV + RW	MW	21	6
Tindemans III	3/77	3	CVP + PSC + PLP + PVV	MIN	25	3
Tindemans IV	6/77	47	CVP + PSC + PSB/BSP + FDF + VU	S	23	7
Vanden Boeynants II	10/78	9	PSC + CVP + PSB/BSP + FDF + VU	S	22	9

(Continued on next page)

Belgium (*Continued*)

Government	Date Formed	Days to Form	Party Composition	Type	MINISTERS Sr	Jr
Martens I	4/79	107	CVP + PSC + PSB + BSP + FDF	S	25	8
Martens II	1/80	7	CVP + PSC + PSB + BSP	S	24	8
Martens III	5/80	39	CVP + PSC + PSB + BSP + PVV + PRL	S	27	9
Martens IV	10/80	15	CVP + PSC + PSB + BSP	S	25	7
Mark Eyskens	4/81	6	CVP + PSC + PSB + BSP	S	25	7
Martens V	12/81	36	CVP + PSC + PVV + PRL	MW	15	10
Martens VI	11/85	46	CVP + PSC + PVV + PRL	MW	15	13
Martens VII	10/87	6	CVP + PSC + PVV + PRL	MW	15	13
Martens VIII	5/88	141	CVP + PSC + PSB + BSP + VU	S	19	13
Martens IX	10/91	0	CVP + PSC + PSB + BSP	S	17	10
Dehaene I	3/92	73	CVP + PSC + PSB + BSP	MW	15	1

Denmark

Government	Date Formed	Days to Form	Party Composition	Type	MINISTERS Sr	Jr
Kristensen	11/45	9	V	MIN	13	0
Hedtoft I	11/47	17	SD	MIN	17	0
Hedtoft II	9/50	10	SD	MIN	14	0
Eriksen I	10/50	1	V + KF	MIN	13	0
Eriksen II	4/53	4	V + KF	MIN	13	0
Hedtoft III	9/53	8	SD	MIN	14	0
Hansen I	2/55	3	SD	MIN	13	0
Hansen II	5/57	13	SD + RV + RF	MW	16	0
Kampmann I	2/60	0	SD + RV + RF	MW	17	0
Kampmann II	11/60	3	SD + RV	MIN	17	0
Krag I	9/62	3	SD + RV	MIN	17	0
Krag II	9/64	4	SD	MIN	18	0
Krag III	11/66	6	SD	MIN	19	0
Baunsgaard	2/68	9	V + KF + RV	MW	17	0
Krag IV	10/71	18	SD	MIN	19	0
Jorgensen I	10/72	2	SD	MIN	19	0
Hartling	12/73	15	V	MIN	12	0
Jorgensen II	2/75	35	SD	MIN	16	0
Jorgensen III	2/77	10	SD	MIN	18	0
Jorgensen IV	8/78	21	SD + V	MIN	21	0
Jorgensen V	10/79	3	SD	MIN	18	0
Jorgensen VI	12/81	22	SD	MIN	20	0
Schluter I	10/82	7	KF + V + CD + KRF	MIN	21	0
Schluter II	1/84	1	KF + V + CD + KRF	MIN	21	0
Schluter III	9/87	2	KF + V + CD + KRF	MIN	22	0
Schluter IV	6/88	24	KF + V + RV	MIN	21	0
Schluter V	12/90	6	KF + V	MIN	19	0

NOTE: Alone among these ten democracies, Denmark has not instituted the position of junior minister.

Finland

Government	Date Formed	Days to Form	Party Composition	Type	MINISTERS Sr	MINISTERS Jr
Pekkala	3/46	15	SKDL + KP + SFP + SSDP	S	8	4
Fagerholm I	7/48	27	SSDP	MIN	13	3
Kekkonen I	3/50	16	KP + SFP + LKP	MIN	11	3
Kekkonen II	1/51	0	KP + LKP + SFP + SSDP	S	11	6
Kekkonen III	9/51	79	KP + SFP + SSDP	S	11	6
Kekkonen IV	7/53	12	KP + SFP	MIN	11	3
Tuomioja	11/53	12	Nonpartisan	—	11	5
Torngren	5/54	58	SFP + KP + SSDP	S	11	3
Kekkonen V	10/54	6	KP + SSDP	MW	10	3
Fagerholm II	3/56	17	SSDP + KP + LKP + SFP	S	10	4
Sukselainen I	5/57	5	KP + SFP + LKP	MIN	11	3
Sukselainen II	7/57	0	KP + LKP	MIN	12	2
Sukselainen III	9/57	0	KP + LKP	MIN	12	2
von Fieandt	11/57	42	Nonpartisan	—	11	3
Kuuskoski	4/58	8	Nonpartisan	—	11	3
Fagerholm III	8/58	55	SSDP + KP + KK + LKP + SFP	S	11	4
Sukselainen IV	1/59	40	KP	MIN	11	4
Miettunen I	7/61	16	KP	MIN	10	4
Karjalainen I	4/62	67	KP + KK + LKP + SFP	MW	11	4
Lehto	12/63	1	Nonpartisan	—	11	4
Virolainen	9/64	0	KP + KK + LKP + SFP	MW	11	4
Paasio I	5/66	6	SSDP + KP + SKDL + TPSL	S	11	4
Koivisto I	3/68	21	SSDP + KP + TPSL + SFP + SKDL	S	9	6
Aura I	5/70	59	Nonpartisan	—	12	1
Karjalainen II	7/70	37	KP + LKP + SFP + SKDL + SSDP	S	12	4
Karjalainen III	3/71	9	KP + LKP + SFP + SSDP	S	12	5
Aura II	10/71	0	Nonpartisan	—	12	3
Paasio II	2/72	51	SSDP	MIN	12	5
Sorsa I	9/72	47	SSDP + KP + LKP + SFP	S	12	4
Liinamaa	6/75	9	Nonpartisan	—	11	5

Finland (*Continued*)

Government	Date Formed	Days to Form	Party Composition	Type	MINISTERS Sr	Jr
Miettunen II	11/75	69	KP + LKP + SFP + SKDL + SSDP	S	12	6
Miettunen III	9/76	12	KP + SFP + LKP	MIN	12	4
Sorsa II	5/77	4	KP + LKP + SFP + SKDL + SSDP	S	12	3
Sorsa III	3/78	12	KP + LKP + SKDL + SSDP	S	12	3
Koivisto II	5/79	68	KP + SFP + SKDL + SSDP	S	11	6
Sorsa IV	2/82	29	SSDP + KP + SFP + SKDL	S	12	5
Sorsa V	12/82	0	SSDP + KP + SFP	MIN	12	5
Sorsa VI	5/83	46	SSDP + KP + SMP + SFP	S	12	5
Holkeri I	4/87	45	KK + SMP + SFP + SSDP	S	13	5
Holkeri II	8/90	4	KK + SFP + SSDP	S	13	4
Aho I	4/91	40	KP + KK + SFP + SKL	S	14	3

France

Government	Date Formed	Days to Form	Party Composition	Type	MINISTERS Sr	MINISTERS Jr
Gouin	1/46	3	SFIO + PCF + MRP	S	20	1
Bidault I	6/46	7	MRP + SFIO + PCF	S	23	1
Blum	12/46	15	SFIO	MIN	17	1
Ramadier I	1/47	5	SFIO + PCF + MRP + RAD + UDSR + RI	S	26	0
Ramadier II	5/47	5	SFIO + MRP + RAD + UDSR + RI	S	24	1
Ramadier III	10/47	1	SFIO + MRP + RAD + RI	S	12	1
Schuman I	11/47	3	MRP + SFIO + RAD + UDSR + RI	S	15	8
Marie	7/48	5	RAD + SFIO + MRP + RI	MW	19	9
Schuman II	8/48	4	MRP + SFIO + RAD + RI	MW	15	9
Queuille I	9/48	3	RAD + SFIO + MRP + UDSR + PRL	S	15	14
Bidault II	10/49	21	MRP + SFIO + RAD + UDSR + RI	S	18	11
Bidault III	2/50	3	MRP + RAD + UDSR + RI	MIN	17	9
Queuille II	6/50	6	RAD + MRP + UDSR + RI	MIN	21	12
Pleven I	7/50	7	UDSR + SFIO + MRP + RAD + RI	S	22	11
Queuille III	3/51	9	RAD + SFIO + MRP + UDSR + RI	S	22	13
Pleven II	8/51	29	UDSR + MRP + RAD + RI + AP	MIN	24	13
Faure I	1/52	10	RAD + MRP + UDSR + RI + AP	MIN	26	14
Pinay I	3/52	6	RI + MRP + RAD + UDSR + AP	MIN	17	12
Mayer	1/53	15	RAD + MRP + UDSR + RI + AP + ARS	MW	23	14
Laniel	6/53	36	RI + MRP + RAD + UDSR + AP + ARS + URAS	S	22	16
Mendès-France	6/54	5	RAD + UDSR + RI + URAS + IOM	MIN	16	13
Pineau	2/55	13	SFIO + MRP + RAD + UDSR + RS	S	16	0
Faure II	2/55	4	RAD + MRP + UDSR + RI + AP + ARS + RS	S	19	7

France (*Continued*)

Government	Date Formed	Days to Form	Party Composition	Type	MINISTERS Sr	Jr
Mollet I	2/56	7	SFIO + RAD + UDSR + RS	MIN	15	19
Bourges-Manoury	6/57	22	RAD + SFIO + UDSR + RGR + DIR	MIN	14	25
Pinay II	10/57	16	RI + RAD + UDSR + RGR + DIR + GDE	MIN	15	0
Mollet II	10/57	10	SFIO + MRP + RAD + UDSR +RGR + RS	MIN	22	0
Gaillard	11/57	7	RAD + SFIO + MRP + UDSR + RI + RGR + RS	S	17	17
Pflimlin	5/58	28	MRP + SFIO + RAD + UDSR +RI + RGR + DIR + GDE	S	22	0
de Gaulle	6/58	1	GAUL + SFIO + MRP + RAD + UDSR +RI + RS + DIR	S	24	0

Germany

Government	Date Formed	Days to Form	Party Composition	Type	MINISTERS	
					Sr	Jr
Adenauer I	9/49	31	CDU/CSU + FDP + DP	MW	14	0
Adenauer II	10/53	31	CDU/CSU + FDP + DP + GB/BHE	S	19	0
Adenauer III	7/55	0	CDU/CSU + FDP + DP	S	21	0
Adenauer IV	10/56	10	CDU/CSU + DP + FVP	S	20	0
Adenauer V	10/57	37	CDU/CSU + DP	S	18	0
Adenauer VI	7/60	0	CDU/CSU	MAJ1	17	0
Adenauer VII	11/61	51	CDU/CSU + FDP	MW	21	0
Adenauer VIII	12/62	22	CDU/CSU + FDP	MW	21	0
Erhard I	10/63	5	CDU/CSU + FDP	MW	21	0
Erhard II	10/65	31	CDU/CSU + FDP	MW	22	0
Erhard III	10/66	0	CDU/CSU	MIN	18	0
Kiesinger	12/66	29	CDU/CSU + SPD	MW	20	7
Brandt I	10/69	23	SPD + FDP	MW	16	15
Brandt II	12/72	25	SPD + FDP	MW	18	19
Schmidt I	5/74	10	SPD + FDP	MW	16	20
Schmidt II	12/76	73	SPD + FDP	MW	16	20
Schmidt III	11/80	31	SPD + FDP	MW	17	20
Schmidt IV	9/82	0	SPD	MIN	13	16
Kohl I	10/82	11	CDU/CSU + FDP	MW	17	24
Kohl II	3/83	23	CDU/CSU + FDP	MW	17	25
Kohl III	3/87	45	CDU/CSU + FDP	MW	19	27
Kohl IV	1/91	46	CDU/CSU + FDP	MW	20	28

Ireland

Government	Date Formed	Days to Form	Party Composition	Type	MINISTERS Sr	Jr
Costello I	2/48	14	FG + LAB + CT + CP + NL	MIN	13	3
de Valera II	6/51	13	FF	MIN	12	5
Costello II	6/54	14	FG + LAB + CT	MW	13	7
de Valera III	3/57	15	FF	MAJ1	12	4
Lemass I	6/59	6	FF	MAJ1	14	4
Lemass II	10/61	7	FF	MIN	14	3
Lemass III	4/65	14	FF	MAJ1	14	6
Lynch I	11/66	1	FF	MAJ1	13	6
Lynch II	7/69	14	FF	MAJ1	14	7
Cosgrave	3/73	14	FG + LAB	MW	15	7
Lynch III	7/77	19	FF	MAJ1	15	7
Haughey I	12/79	6	FF	MAJ1	15	15
Fitzgerald I	6/81	19	FG + LAB	MIN	14	14
Haughey II	3/82	19	FF	MIN	15	12
Fitzgerald II	12/82	20	FG + LAB	MW	15	15
Haughey III	3/87	21	FF	MIN	15	15
Haughey IV	7/89	27	FF + PD	MW	15	15
Reynolds I	2/92	5	FF + PD	MW	15	15

Italy

Government	Date Formed	Days to Form	Party Composition	Type	MINISTERS Sr	MINISTERS Jr
De Gasperi II	7/46	41	DC + PCI + PSI[a] + PRI	S	19	27
De Gasperi III	2/47	23	DC + PCI + PSI + DL[b]	S	15	24
De Gasperi IV	5/47	18	DC	MIN	17	7
De Gasperi V	12/47	5	DC + PSDI[a] + PRI + PLI	S	21	19
De Gasperi VI	5/48	35	DC + PSDI + PRI + PLI	S	20	27
De Gasperi VII	11/49	7	DC + PRI + PLI	S	17	23
De Gasperi VIII	1/50	15	DC + PSDI + PRI	S	19	30
De Gasperi IX	4/51	1	DC + PRI	S	16	25
De Gasperi X	7/51	10	DC + PRI	S	17	38
De Gasperi XI	7/53	39	DC	MIN	17	30
Pella	8/53	20	DC	MIN	19	31
Fanfani I	1/54	13	DC	MIN	19	30
Scelba	2/54	11	DC + PSDI + PLI	MW[c]	21	37
Segni I	7/55	14	DC + PSDI + PLI	MW[c]	21	37
Zoli	5/57	13	DC	MIN	20	32
Fanfani II	7/58	37	DC + PSDI	MIN	20	34
Segni II	2/59	20	DC	MIN	21	43
Tambroni	3/60	30	DC	MIN	22	38
Fanfani III	7/60	7	DC	MIN	24	38
Fanfani IV	2/62	19	DC + PSDI + PRI	MW	25	38
Leone I	6/63	54	DC	MIN	23	29
Moro I	12/63	29	DC + PSI + PSDI + PRI	S	26	42
Moro II	7/64	26	DC + PSI + PSDI + PRI	S	26	42
Moro III	2/66	33	DC + PSI + PSDI + PRI	S	26	46
Leone II	6/68	36	DC	MIN	23	46
Rumor I	12/68	23	DC + PSI-PSDI + PRI	S	27	56
Rumor II	8/69	31	DC	MIN	25	55
Rumor III	3/70	48	DC + PSI + PSDI + PRI	S	27	56
Colombo I	8/70	31	DC + PSI + PSDI + PRI	S	27	58
Colombo II	3/71	7	DC + PSI + PSDI	S	26	56
Andreotti I	2/72	33	DC	MIN	25	32

Italy (*Continued*)

Government	Date Formed	Days to Form	Party Composition	Type	Ministers Sr	Ministers Jr
Andreotti II	6/72	40	DC + PSDI + PLI	MW[c]	27	59
Rumor IV	7/73	25	DC + PSI + PSDI + PRI	S	27	58
Rumor V	3/74	12	DC + PSI + PSDI	S	26	42
Moro IV	11/74	51	DC + PRI	MIN	25	43
Moro V	2/76	36	DC	MIN	22	39
Andreotti III	7/76	39	DC	MIN	22	47
Andreotti IV	3/78	54	DC	MIN	22	47
Andreotti V	3/79	48	DC + PSDI + PRI	MIN	21	49
Cossiga I	8/79	62	DC + PSDI + PLI	MIN	25	54
Cossiga II	4/80	16	DC + PSI + PRI	S	28	57
Forlani	10/80	21	DC + PSI + PSDI + PRI	S	27	57
Spadolini I	6/81	33	PRI + DC + PSI + PSDI + PLI	S	28	57
Spadolini II	8/82	16	PRI + DC + PSI + PSDI + PLI	S	28	57
Fanfani V	12/82	18	DC + PSI + PSDI + PLI	S	28	51
Craxi I	8/83	39	PSI + DC + PSDI + PRI + PLI	S	30	59
Craxi II	8/86	35	PSI + DC + PSDI + PRI + PLI	S	30	61
Fanfani VI	4/87	45	DC	MIN	25	33
Goria	7/87	44	DC + PSI + PSDI + PRI + PLI	S	30	61
De Mita	4/88	33	DC + PSI + PSDI + PRI + PLI	S	32	65
Andreotti VI	7/89	64	DC + PSI + PSDI + PRI + PLI	S	32	68
Andreotti VII	4/91	44	DC + PSI + PSDI + PLI	S	30	69
Amato I	6/92	83	PSI + DC + PSDI + PLI	MW	25	35
Ciampi	4/93	6	DC + PSI + PSDI + PLI	MW	20	35
Berlusconi	5/94	43	FI [+ CCD[d]] + League + AN	MW[d]	26	38
Dini	1/95	26	Nonpartisan		20	35

[a]This table always designates the Socialists as the PSI and the Social Democrats as the PSDI, despite brief changes of name.

[b]The Democratic Labor Party (DL) won just one Assembly seat in 1946 and did not survive the 1948 elections.

[c]Exactly half of seats controlled by coalition.

[d]The CCD allied with Forza Italia in the 1994 elections, but then constituted a separate parliamentary group. If parliamentary parties are counted as the units comprising the Berlusconi coalition, it has surplus status.

Netherlands

Government	Date Formed	Days to Form	Party Composition	Type	MINISTERS Sr	MINISTERS Jr
Beel I	7/46	47	KVP + PVDA	MW	14	0
Drees I	8/48	30	PVDA + KVP + CHU + VVD	S	14	0
Drees II	3/51	49	PVDA + KVP + CHU + VVD	S	15	6
Drees III	9/52	67	PVDA + KVP + CHU + ARP	S	16	5
Drees IV	10/56	121	PVDA + KVP + CHU + ARP	S	13	7
Beel II	12/58	10	KVP + ARP + CHU	MW	10	4
de Quay	5/59	7	KVP + CHU + VVD + ARP	S	13	7
Marijnen	7/63	69	KVP + CHU + VVD + ARP	S	14	5
Cals	4/65	45	KVP + PVDA + ARP	S	14	7
Zijlstra	11/66	38	ARP + KVP	MIN	13	8
de Jong	4/67	47	KVP + ARP + CHU + VVD	MW	14	10
Biesheuvel I	7/71	69	KVP + ARP + CHU + VVD + DS70	MW	16	3
Biesheuvel II	7/72	19	KVP + CHU + VVD + ARP	MIN	14	11
den Uyl	5/73	163	PVDA + KVP + ARP + D66 + PPR	S	15	17
van Agt I	12/77	205	CDA + VVD	MW	16	15
van Agt II	9/81	108	CDA + PVDA + D66	S	16	17
van Agt III	5/82	17	CDA + D66	MIN	14	8
Lubbers I	11/82	57	CDA + VVD	MW	14	16
Lubbers II	7/86	54	CDA + VVD	MW	14	11
Lubbers III	11/89	185	CDA + PVDA	MW	14	10

Norway

Government	Date Formed	Days to Form	Party Composition	Type	MINISTERS	
					Sr	Jr
Gerhardsen I	11/45	23	DNA	MAJ1	11	3
Gerhardsen II	10/49	8	DNA	MAJ1	14	5
Torp I	11/51	3	DNA	MAJ1	13	5
Torp II	10/53	3	DNA	MAJ1	13	6
Gerhardsen III	1/55	8	DNA	MAJ1	13	6
Gerhardsen IV	10/57	3	DNA	MAJ1	15	8
Gerhardsen V	9/61	20	DNA	MIN	15	7
Lyng	8/63	5	H + KRF + SP + V	MIN	15	9
Gerhardsen VI	9/63	5	DNA	MIN	15	6
Borten I	10/65	29	H + KRF + SP + V	MW	15	7
Borten II	9/69	1	H + KRF + SP + V	MW	15	10
Bratteli I	3/71	15	DNA	MIN	15	16
Korvald	10/72	11	V + KRF + SP	MIN	15	17
Bratteli II	10/73	36	DNA	MIN	15	18
Nordli I	1/76	6	DNA	MIN	16	19
Nordli II	9/77	7	DNA	MIN	16	19
Brundtland I	2/81	5	DNA	MIN	17	20
Willoch I	10/81	30	H	MIN	17	19
Willoch II	6/83	14	H + KRF + SP	MW	18	21
Willoch III	9/85	15	H + KRF	MIN	17	22
Brundtland II	5/86	7	DNA	MIN	15	20
Syse I	11/89	35	H + KRF + SP	MIN	19	23
Brundtland III	11/90	5	DNA	MIN	19	23

Sweden

Government	Date Formed	Days to Form	Party Composition	Type	MINISTERS Sr	MINISTERS Jr
Hansson V	7/45	0	SAP	MAJ1[a]	15	m.d.
Erlander I	10/46	5	SAP	MAJ1[a]	14	m.d.
Erlander II	9/48	39	SAP	MIN	14	m.d.
Erlander III	10/51	1	SAP + CP	MW	16	m.d.
Erlander IV	9/52	0	SAP + CP	MW	16	m.d.
Erlander V	9/56	0	SAP + CP	MW	16	m.d.
Erlander VI	10/57	4	SAP	MIN	15	m.d.
Erlander VII	6/58	0	SAP	MIN	15	m.d.
Erlander VIII	9/60	0	SAP	MIN	15	12
Erlander IX	9/64	0	SAP	MIN	16	12
Erlander X	9/68	0	SAP	MAJ1	18	12
Palme I	10/69	5	SAP	MAJ1	19	13
Palme II	9/70	0	SAP	MIN	19	12
Palme III	9/73	5	SAP	MIN	18	15
Falldin I	10/76	18	CP + FP + M	MW	20	18
Ullsten	10/78	8	FP	MIN	19	19
Falldin II	10/79	26	CP + FP + M	MW	21	19
Falldin III	5/81	18	CP + FP	MIN	18	18
Palme IV	10/82	19	SAP	MIN	19	22
Palme V	10/85	19	SAP	MIN	21	23
Carlsson I	3/86	12	SAP	MIN	20	20
Carlsson II	10/88	16	SAP	MIN	20	18
Carlsson III	2/90	11	SAP	MIN	22	m.d.
Bildt I	10/91	18	M + CP + FP + KDS	MIN	21	m.d.

NOTE: m.d., missing data.

[a]Controlled exactly half of seats.

Data Sources

Many, though not all, of the sources named in Appendix D are cited elsewhere in this book. At the bottom of every table in the book there appears a note on sources of information. The endnotes in the various chapters discuss data sources with some frequency and in some detail.

Yet I wish to make the origins of the data set compiled for this book as transparent and as easily available as possible for the reader. It is thus crucial to organize in one place the references to the entire body of primary sources I have consulted. By listing my sources in this Appendix, I hope to contribute to replicability and cumulation in empirical research on government coalitions. Put differently, the next several pages help me to drive home the methodological message conveyed in Chapter 9.

The sources I used to construct the ten-nation data set for this book can be divided into two categories: Europe-wide and country-specific. For all countries in my data set, with few exceptions, I relied on the following sources for such basic information as electoral results and government composition.

Electoral and parliamentary institutions: Döring 1995; Gallagher, Laver, and Mair 1995; Herman 1976; Laver and Schofield 1990; Lijphart 1994; Strøm 1990b.

Policy positions of governments and parties, and characterizations of policy space: Budge, Robertson, and Hearl 1987; Laver and Budge 1992; Laver and Schofield 1990; Volkens 1995. See Chapter 6, Notes 3 and 4.

Electoral results (votes and seats): Mackie and Rose 1991, with corrections in Lijphart 1994 and updates from *Keesing's Contemporary Archives* and the *Political Data Handbooks* published annually (1992–) by the *European Journal of Political Research*.

Party composition of governments: *Keesing's*, with checks against Lane, McKay, and Newton 1991; Strøm 1990b; Woldendorp, Keman, and Budge 1993; and the *Political Data Handbooks* of the *European Journal of Political Research*.

Dates of government formations and falls: *Keesing's* and newspapers listed in the References.

Circumstances surrounding government falls: *Keesing's* and newspapers and newsweeklies listed in the References.

Personnel (ministers and junior ministers) within governments: *Keesing's*, as supplemented and corrected by the country-specific sources noted below.

Most of the single-country sources named below identify personnel within governments or cover the circumstances surrounding government falls. Several works on France detail the distribution of seats in the National Assembly (which changed frequently, given the fluidity of political parties in the Fourth Republic).

Belgium. Deruette 1994; "Guide des Ministères/Gids der Ministeries," undated document provided by the Institut Belge d'Information et de Documentation, Brussels, Belgium; Lemaître 1982; "Sommaire: Le Gouvernement Fédéral," June 25, 1993, document provided by the Institut Belge d'Information et de Documentation; Ysebaert 1995.

Denmark. "Ministerierne," undated document provided by the Archives and Information Department, Library of the Folketing, Copenhagen, Denmark; Nannestad 1989; "Regeringens Medlemmer 1992–93," and "Regeringens Medlemmer 1993–94," November 7, 1994, documents provided by the Archives and Information Department, Library of the Folketing.

Finland. Arter 1987; Hakovirta and Koskiaho 1973; "Hallituksen Kokoonpano," August 12, 1993, document provided by the Office of the Prime Minister, Helsinki, Finland; Mylly and Berry 1984; Nyholm 1972; Puntila 1975; Thibaut 1990; *Valtioneuvoston Viikko* 1975–, excerpts provided by the Information Office, Library of Parliament; Zelterburg 1991.

France. Arné 1962; MacRae 1967; Pétry 1987, 1992a, 1992b; Williams 1966.

Germany. Akalin 1992; Braunthal 1994; Hiscocks 1966; Prittie 1972; Schindler 1984, 1988.

Ireland. Farrell and Farrell 1987; FitzGerald 1991; "Ministers and Ministers of State, 1948–1993," undated document provided by the Government Secretariat, Department of the Taoiseach, Dublin, Ireland; Walsh 1986.

Italy. Andreotti 1981; Camera dei Deputati 1998a, 1998b, 1999a, 1999b, 2000; Nocifero and Valdini 1992; Novacco 1971, 1978; Pallotta 1964; Petracca 1980; Pollio Salimbeni 1989; Venditti 1981.

Netherlands. Huygen 1986; "Tabel van de ministeries sedert 1945," undated document provided by the Press and Cultural Section, Royal Netherlands Embassy, Washington, DC.

Norway. Nordby 1985; "The Norway Council of State 1905–1994," 1994, document provided by the Office of the Prime Minister, Oslo, Norway; Torp 1990.

Sweden. Andrén 1968; "The Government 1989," *Klara-Posten*, Stockholm, November 1989; *Cabinet Ministers 1990*, Central Services Office, Stockholm, 1991; *Statsråden 1992*, Central Services Office, Stockholm, 1992; Norberg, Tjerneld, and Asker 1985; Riksdagen 1973–1981, 1982–1987; "Statsråd," in Departementshistoriekommittén 1990; "Statssekreterare, Konsultativa statsråd," December 14, 1988, document provided by the Archive and Information Department, Central Services Office for the Ministries, Stockholm, Sweden.

Subsets of Data in This Database

The database constructed for this book is composed of multiple sub-sets of data. Appendix E provides an overview of the subsets of data, so that the reader can access the data available at my Web site (http://www.faculty .virginia.edu/cmershon/) having in mind ahead of time what the Web site holds.

The easiest way to distinguish the subsets of data here is to identify how a case is defined in each. The ten-country data set with the smallest number of cases (63) has the *governing party* as the unit of analysis, where govern-ing party is operationalized as a party that has governed for at least half of the span between any two consecutive elections, and where a party ruling in Denmark's unipolar system (before 1973) and its multipolar system (since 1973) is treated as constituting two cases. Examples of analyses of this sub-set of data include models 7.4 and 7.5, which explore the electoral costs of incumbency and for which the results are reported in Table 7.6. In another data set, the unit of analysis is the *national legislature after each election* (n = 136), and the key data are the percentage shares of seats won by each party gaining representation in the legislature; with these data, I calculated the ef-fective number of parliamentary parties, assessed as an independent variable in models 7.1 and 7.2 (on bargaining costs). The two models just cited, along with Appendix C of course, point to a third data set: that in which *govern-ments* constitute the cases under scrutiny (n = 291).

There are two additional subsets of data available in this database. They are compared with the governmental data set in Table E.1, which also sorts the number of cases by country. In one data set, the unit of analysis is the *party-in-an-election* (n = 624). This is the data set under study in models 7.6, 8.5, and 8.6, which weigh different influences on electoral payoffs. The largest data set is the one that defines the case as the *party-in-government* (n = 794). In models 8.1 and 8.2 (on office costs) and 8.3 (on policy costs), I analyze this last data set. A look at the country-by-country entries and the ten-country total on the bottom line of each column reveals that none of the three data sets is unduly dominated by observations from any one country. In particular, Fourth Republic France supplies 19.0 percent of all observa-tions in the party-in-government data set, which is the highest percentage for any country across the three data sets.

TABLE E.I.

Number of Cases for Three Subsets in This Database,
by Country and Definition of Case

| | DEFINITION OF CASE | | |
	Government	Party-in-election	Party-in-government
Belgium	34	74	109
Denmark	27	94	50
Finland	41	95	121
France	30	22	151
Germany	22	36	46
Ireland	18	53	29
Italy	52 (58)[a]	54	148
Netherlands	20	71	65
Norway	23	60	40
Sweden	24	65	35
Ten-country total	291	624	794

[a]Between parentheses is the number of governments when the Italian data extend to 1998, as in Chapter 5.

Evidence on Feedback Effects

As Chapter 9 noted, one way to appraise the long-run consequences of short-run decisions to limit the costs of coalition is to reconsider the direction of causality (cf. King, Keohane, and Verba 1994, 185–96). Throughout this study, I have understood short cabinet duration and restricted alternation as products of low costs, which, in turn, result from the successful pursuit of cost-reduction strategies and from certain spatial and institutional conditions, such as one party's long-standing dominance of a party system, electoral laws that foster intraparty competition, and provisions for secret ballots in parliamentary voting. It is also conceivable, however, that over time short duration might depress the costs of coalition, through feedback effects. The recurrence of short-lived governments might induce expectations among politicians that attempts to curtail costs further would be very likely to succeed. In the long run, then, abbreviated durations might encourage cost-reduction strategies and thus might yield ever lower costs of coalition.[1]

This notion, whatever its intuitive appeal, finds little indirect or direct empirical support. No long-run trend toward ever-shorter governments appears in Italy—or France or Finland, or indeed any of the countries included in this book's data set.[2] Moreover, no clear trend toward ever-lower costs appears in any country. The system most likely to evince ever-lower costs, if feedback effects were at play, would be Italy. (The reasoning is that feedback effects would have more time to unfold in Italy than in the French Fourth Republic; and feedback would have a stronger impetus in Italy than in Finland or Belgium, given shorter mean cabinet duration in Italy.) Revisiting the Italian evidence detailed in Chapter 5 casts some doubt on the existence of feedback effects, however. The costs of bargaining over Italian governments have fairly steadily increased, not decreased, over time. The electoral costs of ruling in coalition were slightly more substantial for the DC, not less so, between 1976 and 1992 than for the 1946–76 period; likewise, the electoral costs of rupturing governments were slightly more substantial for the DC between 1976 and 1992. The policy costs incurred by the DC in building executives, as indexed by the distance between DC platforms and government programs, show no discernible trend over time. Nor does a time trend in such policy costs emerge when attention narrows to those governments whose predecessor was a cabinet the DC helped to topple. The PSI did score electoral gains from governing, and also pulled public policy relatively close to its ideals, between 1976 and 1992; but these results could be attributed to the PSI's successful exploitation of its pivotal status as much as to any feedback effect.[3]

Can feedback effects be detected with regard to office payoffs? Chapter 5 documented that the total number of ministers and junior ministers in Italy increased from 1946 to 1992. So, too, did the number of DC junior ministers.[4] In addition, Chapter 5 tracked variations in the number of offices across Italian governments with different numbers of component parties. The task now is to separate out analytically the impact on office payoffs exerted by time and by number of allies in government. This task is a little tricky, since all of Italy's five-party governments ruled after 1980 and while the PSI had pivotal status. One reasonable way to tackle the problem is to regress the number of offices (O) on a series of variables (starting with the number of governing parties, GP_g) and then to inspect the residuals for trends over time. The following equations were thus estimated:

$$O = a + b_1 GP_g + e \tag{F.1}$$
$$O = a + b_1 GP_g + b_2 CL_g + e \tag{F.2}$$
$$O = a + b_1 GP_g + b_2 CL_g + b_3 PV_g + e \tag{F.3}$$

where CL_g is a dummy coded 1 for any government formed after the 1963 elections (which marked the advent of the center-left formula), and PV_g is a dummy coded 1 for any government formed after the 1976 elections (which made the PSI pivotal).

Table F.1 reports the coefficients, standard errors, and adjusted R^2 values resulting from these computations. Part A confirms that, as Italian governments expanded to include additional parties, the total number of ministers and junior ministers rose, whereas the portfolios controlled by the DC declined. Note that the intercepts for the two estimates of DC posts are greater than the intercepts for the corresponding estimates of total posts, and the slopes are smaller for the two estimates of DC posts than they are for the corresponding estimates of total posts; these figures testify to the DC's ability to curb the office costs of building coalitions. The R^2 values in part A are far from spectacular, though, and the SEEs are relatively high. Part B establishes that the R^2 values are boosted, and the SEEs reduced, with the addition of the dummy variable marking post-1963 governments. In contrast, the addition of the dummy variable for pivotal status of the PSI yields virtually no improvement in explanatory power, as shown in part C. The greatest differences between model F.2 (in part B) and model F.3 (part C) appear in the estimations for all junior ministers and DC junior ministers, where the coefficient for pivotal status attains near-significance and the SEEs decline slightly.

TABLE F.1.

Number of Governing Parties and Time Period as Determinants of the
Number of Cabinet Offices in Italy, 1946–92

	Adj. R^2	a	b_1	b_2	b_3	SEE
A. All ministers	0.35	18.60†	1.82†			3.51
All junior ministers	0.27	28.93†	5.17†			11.99
DC ministers	0.31	20.89†	−1.54†			3.25
DC junior ministers	0.06	36.63†	−1.89**			9.16
B. All ministers	0.73	16.94†	1.17†	5.76†		2.28
All junior ministers	0.63	23.60†	3.09***	18.14†		8.57
DC ministers	0.54	19.68†	−2.01†	4.11†		2.64
DC junior ministers	0.41	33.06†	−3.28†	12.17†		7.26
C. All ministers	0.73	17.07†	1.10†	5.46†	0.71	2.29
All junior ministers	0.64	24.67†	2.61***	15.77†	5.71*	8.36
DC ministers	0.54	19.50†	−1.93†	4.50†	−0.94	2.65
DC junior ministers	0.44	33.97†	−3.69†	10.14†	4.88*	7.08

NOTE: N=52 in all analyses. Regression models: Part A: $O = a + b_1GP_g + e$. Part B: $O = a + b_1GP_g + b_2CL_g + e$. Part C: $O = a + b_1GP_g + b_2CL_g + b_3PV_g + e$.
$* p \approx .07$. $** p < .05$. $*** p < .01$. $† p < .001$.

Figure F.1 plots the residuals from the three sets of computations for DC junior ministers, arraying the residuals against the counter for time. (Figure F.1 focuses on the dependent variable for which the improvement in predictive capacity from model F.1 to F.2 to F.3 is most pronounced, but the analogous plots of residuals from the other estimates [of DC ministers, all ministers, and all junior ministers] exhibit roughly the same pattern.) As Figure F.1 shows, model F.1 consistently and substantially overestimates numbers of offices for the late 1940s and early 1950s; the overestimation is more limited for models F.2 and F.3. Otherwise, there are no obvious time trends to indicate feedback effects.[5]

Figure F.2 complements Figure F.1 by charting the actual values for DC junior ministers and the estimated values from the three models. (The lines drawn in the latter figure are based on locally weighted scatterplot smoothing [Cleveland 1979; Wilkinson and Hill 1992; Wilkinson 1998].) In both figures, model F.3 registers a better fit than model F.2. Overall, the evidence portrayed in the two figures and in Table F.1 buttresses the findings on Italian cabinet offices presented earlier.

A final way to probe feedback effects is to regress the change in the num-

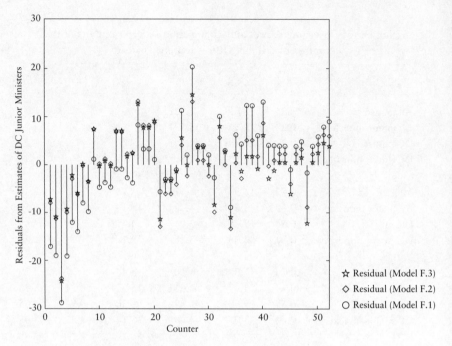

FIGURE F.1. Residuals from Estimates of Number of DC Junior Ministers, by Time

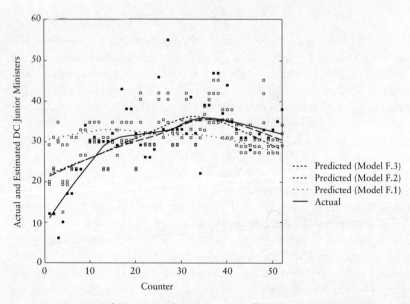

FIGURE F.2. Actual Versus Predicted Number of DC Junior Ministers, by Time
Note: Actual values of DC junior ministries are illustrated in solid boxes; estimated values are in hollow boxes.

ber of offices ($O_g - O_{g-1}$, or ΔO) on the number of governing parties (GP_g), a counter that increases with each successive postwar government (CT_g), and the duration in months of the preceding government (D_{g-1}). For DC ministers and DC junior ministers, respectively:

$$\Delta O_{DC} = 1.83 - 1.17\ GP_g + 0.02\ CT_g + 0.10\ D_{g-1}$$
$$(t = 1.49)\ (t = -3.41)\ (t = 0.73)\ (t = 1.61)$$
$$\text{where adj. } R^2 = .21;\ \text{SEE} = 3.15;\ n = 51$$
$$\Delta O_{DC} = 3.72 - 1.33\ GP_g + 0.03\ CT_g - 0.02\ D_{g-1}$$
$$(t = 1.25)\ (t = -1.60)\ (t = 0.32)\ (t = -0.16)$$
$$\text{where adj. } R^2 = .00;\ \text{SEE} = 7.65;\ n = 51$$

Duration and the counter for time have a small, insignificant impact on changes in the number of DC ministers and junior ministers. To judge from these estimations and from the evidence adduced above, the hypothesis about feedback effects should be rejected.

Glossary

Most entries in this glossary are composed of four elements: a definition of the basic concept in prose, a prose statement of how the concept is measured, an arithmetical operationalization of the measure, and the symbol denoting the measure in the regression equations estimated in Chapters 7 and 8. For some entries (e.g., that on the *conventio ad excludendum*), only the first component is needed.

The overall purpose of the glossary is to make the book more accessible to readers interested in European politics but lacking background in mathematized deductive reasoning. Some of the concepts in formal theory may be rather difficult for some readers, and some of the terminology, rather off-putting. The glossary is designed to alleviate such problems.

BARGAINING COSTS. *Concept*: Negotiating a new government and breaking apart a sitting government require that politicians expend time, effort, and energy. *Measure*: Time. *Operationalization*: For the bargaining costs of building governments, I count the number of days between the fall of one government and the rise of its successor, save for one class of exceptions. For governments launched after a parliamentary election, I count the number of days from the election to the announcement of a cabinet. For the bargaining costs of breaking a government, I count the number of days spent in erecting its replacement; I omit cases before parliamentary elections on the assumption that the ensuing crises are dominated and defined by the election returns. *Symbol*: B_g.

BIPOLAR PARTY SYSTEM. *Concept*: A party system in which a small party can tip the balance of power between two large parties. *Measure*: A bipolar party system is identified by looking at the effective number of parties, their positions in policy space, and their size. *Operationalization*: Effective number of parties, percentage of seats held by parties in the lower house of the legislature, party location in policy space as determined by content analysis of party manifestos; I use that information to identify the bipolar party systems. In this data set, the dummy variable for a bipolar party system is equivalent to a dummy marker for Germany. *Symbol*: BI_g.

CHAOS THEOREMS. *Concept*: The body of mathematical, game-theoretic research that shows that, under simple majority rule, voting games in multidimensional policy space are very likely to "cycle"—that is, voting is very likely to generate a chaotic sequence of outcomes, in which one majority approves a decision and is overthrown by a second majority endorsing a second decision, that decision yields to a third, then to a fourth, and on and on. *Measure*: Observation of cyclical voting majorities and instability in government. *Operationalization*: Not usually measured in the extant literature, but often a short average cabinet duration (average number of months that governments last) is taken as an indicator of chaotic outcomes. *Symbol*: Not used in this study.

COALITION FORMULA. *Concept*: In some parliamentary systems, such as Italy, a recurring pattern in the party composition of government is commonly identified and recognized as a "master plan" or formula for governing alliances, which, even though it may not be implemented in every instance of government formation, is desired by the key players in government formation. In formal theory, the formula would be understood as a commonly viewed focal point in negotiations. *Measure*: Observation of regularities in the party composition of government for some stretch of time, and observation of references to one formula or another (e.g., center–left) in the private and public language used by top politicians. *Operationalization*: A dummy variable coded 1 for any Italian government formed after the 1963 elections (which marked the advent of the center–left formula). *Symbol*: CL_g (used in Appendix F).

'CONVENTIO AD EXCLUDENDUM' (Latin, used in Italy). *Concept*: Agreement to exclude. Commonly used in Italian politics, this phrase refers to the long-standing consensus among center-leaning Italian politicians that the Communist Party should not enter the national executive. Analogous agreements existed about antisystem parties in Belgium and the Netherlands, for example. For formal theories of coalition, such agreements are important in that they turn some arithmetically possible coalitions into politically impossible scenarios. *Measure*: NA. *Operationalization*: NA. *Symbol*: NA.

CORE. *Concept*: In unidimensional or multidimensional policy space, a policy position that cannot be overturned or defeated. Any party that inhabits such a position is termed a core party. *Measure*: In unidimensional space, the median is the core (see the entry on median). In multidimensional space, as in unidimensional space, the core is the party (or legislator) that is a member of all possible majority coalitions. *Operationalization*: Array all parties (or legislators) on all relevant spectra (e.g., left–right, secular–religious), and locate the party (legislator) that contains (is) the "swing" or "tipping" voter on both dimensions, essential to any majority coalition that might form. This task is most easily performed if one imagines a median line drawn in a two-dimensional space that demarcates two alternative majority coalitions: one on the line and to the right, and the other on the line and to the left. If all median lines that can be drawn intersect, the point of intersection is the core of the policy space. *Symbol*: CP_{i_g}, a dummy variable coded 1 when party i occupies the core of the policy space at the time that government g is formed.

DIMENSION-BY-DIMENSION MEDIAN. *Concept*: In Laver and Shepsle's (1994, 1996, 1999) work, the dimension-by-dimension median cabinet is one in which the key ministerial portfolio on each dimension is awarded to the party containing the median legislator on that dimension (e.g., Finance goes to the Christian Democrats, Foreign Affairs goes to the Free Democrats). *Measure*: NA in this study. *Operationalization*: NA. *Symbol*: NA.

DIMENSIONS OF POLICY SPACE. *Concept*: Party competition is channeled along, organized around, and focused on a few major issue clusters, such as the left–right confrontation or the secular–religious divide. *Measure*: Observation of the dominant issue(s) in party competition. *Operationalization*: Number and identity of dimensions of competition, as determined by content analyses of party programs. *Symbol*: NA.

EFFECTIVE NUMBER OF PARTIES. *Concept*: To understand the structure of the policy space, it is important to take into account not only the number but also the relative strength of parties. *Measure*: The number of parties, weighted by the size of their parliamentary contingent. *Operationalization*: Square the total number of seats in the lower house of the legislature (call this S^2); square each party's number of seats in the legislature (S_i^2), and then sum those squares; finally, divide S^2 by the sum of S_i^2 ($N = S^2 / \sum S_i^2$). *Symbol*: N_g.

ELECTORAL COSTS. *Concept*: Political actors who assume governing responsibilities, and who are responsible for the fall of a government, stand to lose or gain votes from having held such responsibilities. *Measure*: Changes in a party's shares of the vote between pairs of consecutive elections to the lower house of parliament. *Operationalization*: Mean change (over the postwar period) in vote share that a party has registered after spending most of the interelectoral period in government; absolute value of the mean shift that a party has seen after incumbency; shift in vote share that a party encounters in election t as compared to election $t–1$. *Symbol*: V_i, $\pm V_i$, ΔV_{it}.

EUCLIDIAN DISTANCE. *Concept*: As used in formal theory, the notion that an actor's preferences can be "reasonably" ordered, so that, for example, the most-preferred outcome or object is first on the actor's preference ranking, and the least-preferred outcome or object is last on the actor's ranking. *Measure*: NA in this study. *Operationalization*: NA. *Symbol*: NA.

FRAGMENTATION (or fractionalization). *Concept*: A fragmented (fractionalized) party system is one in which the effective number of parties is high (see the entry on the effective number of parties). *Measure*: An index that varies from 0 to 1, in which 0 indicates utter fragmentation (a legislature composed of as many parties as seats—e.g., 100 seats and 100 parties), and 1, complete concentration (100 seats all held by one party). *Operationalization*: $N = 1/(1–F)$, so that $F = 1–(1/N)$. *Symbol*: NA in this study.

IDEAL POINT (also bliss point). *Concept*: The notion that an actor's preferences can be "reasonably" ordered, so that the most preferred outcome or object is his or her ideal outcome or object, capable of inducing a state of bliss. *Measure*: NA in this study. *Operationalization*: NA. *Symbol*: NA.

MEDIAN. *Concept*: In unidimensional policy space, the median is a policy position that cannot be overturned or defeated. Any party that inhabits such a position is termed a median party. In one dimension, the median is equivalent to the core.

Measure: Identify the party (or legislator) that is a member of all possible majority coalitions. *Operationalization*: Array all parties (or legislators) on one spectrum (e.g., left–right), and locate the party (legislator) that contains (is) the "swing" or "tipping" voter, essential to any majority coalition that might form on the right or on the left. *Symbol*: CP_{ig}, a dummy variable coded 1 when party i occupies the core of the policy space at the time that government g is formed.

MINIMAL CONNECTED WINNING COALITION. *Concept*: A coalition that joins parties adjacent to each other on a policy spectrum and that would either slip below a legislative majority or stop being connected if any party were to withdraw. *Measure*: Identify the size of each party's parliamentary contingent, the location of each party on the posited spectrum (e.g., left–right), and come up with a list of coalitions that qualify as minimal connected winning. *Operationalization*: Number (or percentage) of seats in the lower house of the legislature held by each party, and the location of each party on the policy spectrum, as determined by content analyses of party programs; use those numbers (or percentages) and locations to identify the coalitions that qualify as minimum connected winning. *Symbol*: MCW.

MINIMAL WINNING COALITION. *Concept*: A coalition that would lose its parliamentary majority if any member party were to withdraw from it. *Measure*: Identify the size of each party's parliamentary contingent, and come up with a list of coalitions that qualify as minimal winning. *Operationalization*: Number (or percentage) of seats in the lower house of the legislature held by each party; use those numbers (or percentages) to identify the coalitions that qualify as minimal winning. *Symbol*: MW.

MINIMUM WINNING COALITION. *Concept*: A minimal winning coalition with the narrowest possible majority in parliament. *Measure*: Identify the size of each party's parliamentary contingent, and come up with a list of coalitions that qualify as minimum winning. *Operationalization*: Number (or percentage) of seats in the lower house of the legislature held by each party; use those numbers (or percentages) to identify the coalitions that qualify as minimum winning. *Symbol*: NA in this study.

MULTIPOLAR PARTY SYSTEM. *Concept*: A party system in which parties face competitors in several directions. *Measure*: A multipolar party system is identified by looking at the effective number of parties, their positions in policy space, and their size. *Operationalization*: Effective number of parties, percentage of seats held by parties in the lower house of the legislature, party location in policy space as determined by content analysis of party manifestos; I use that information to identify the multipolar systems. In this data set, the multipolar systems are Belgium, Finland, Fourth Republic France, Italy, the Netherlands, and post-1973 Denmark. A dummy variable is coded 1 when and where the party system is multipolar. *Symbol*: M_i.

OFFICE COSTS. *Concept*: A political actor entering into coalition (and quitting a coalition) has to share out offices among the actors making up the coalition (and

loses office when it quits a coalition). *Measures*: The offices surrendered by a party
when it governs in coalition, as opposed to governing alone (or when it governs in
many-party coalitions, as opposed to governing in few-party coalitions); the offices
forfeited by a party when it has been responsible for the fall of a government, as opposed to when it has done nothing to contribute to the government's demise.
Operationalization: The number of ministers and junior ministers per party in a
cabinet; the percentage share of all ministerial and junior ministerial posts each
party controls; the ratio between that share and the party's share of the seats in the
lower house that held by a government. *Symbols*: Y_{i_g} (the share of offices held by
party *i* in government *g*), O_{i_g} (the number of offices held).

PIVOTAL PARTY. *Concept*: A party whose addition to a minority government including the core party (or whose withdrawal from a majority coalition including the
core party) would give the executive majority (minority) status in the legislature.
Measure: A pivotal party is identified by looking at the size and position of each
party in the party system. *Operationalization*: Percentage of seats held by parties in
the lower house of the legislature, party location in policy space as determined by
content analysis of party manifestos; that information is used to isolate the pivotal
party. In Italy, the Socialists qualified as pivotal between the 1976 and 1992 elections. *Symbol*: In Appendix F, PV_i is a dummy coded 1 for any Italian government
formed between the 1976 and 1992 parliamentary elections, when the Socialists
were pivotal.

POLARIZATION. *Concept*: A polarized party system is one in which great distances
separate parties. *Measure*: Polarization is an index of the distance separating parties.
Operationalization: The percentage of all parliamentary seats held by extremist parties, where an "extremist party" displays any of three features: "1. a well-developed
non-democratic ideology; 2. a proposal to break up or fundamentally alter the
boundaries of the state; or 3. diffuse protest, alienation and distrust of the existing
political system" (Strøm 1990b, 65). *Symbol*: Not used in this study.

POLICY COSTS. *Concept*: A political actor is very likely to have to compromise his
or her policy preferences when entering into coalition (and when quitting a coalition). *Measures*: The policy costs of building governments are tapped by observing
the extent to which governmental policies deviate from a party's preferences (where
measures of governmental policies and party preferences are derived from content
analyses of, respectively, governmental declarations and party programs). The policy costs of breaking governments are tapped in two ways: (1) by comparing the
measures based on content analyses for governments whose predecessor a party has
helped to topple and for governments whose predecessor ended with no "help"
from the party in question; and (2) by tracking how often parties that bring about
one government's demise prompt a change in incumbent parties and participate in
the next government. (The latter measure rests on the common and common-
sensical assumption that membership in the executive affords parties special opportunities to shape policy.) *Operationalization*: (1) The distance on a 200-point left–

right spectrum between governmental policy and party preferences, as indicated by content analyses. (2) The percentage of the time that the incumbent parties have changed after party i has toppled a government, and the percentage of the time that party i has managed to reenter the executive after having toppled a government. *Symbol*: For the first measure, P_{i_g}. (Recall Note 11 in Chapter 8.)

POLICY SPACE. *Concept*: Parties are assumed to be competing for the support of voters and for control of the executive in a "territory" of policy concerns, structured and organized by one or more overarching policy dimensions (for example, the left–right, socioeconomic divide). Parties are assumed to be positioned (that is, assumed to have preferences) along one or more dimensions in a recognizable spot in the policy space. *Measures*: See the entries on types of party system (bipolar, multipolar, and unipolar), core, median, dimensions of policy space, effective number of parties, pivotal party, and segmentation. *Operationalization*: See the entries just named. *Symbol*: See the entries just named.

RATIONAL FORESIGHT. *Concept*: Political actors are able to look ahead to likely adverse (or acceptable) outcomes, and will thus act to prevent the expected adverse outcome from actually occurring (or hasten the arrival of the expected acceptable outcome). *Measure*: NA in this study. The infrequency of governments' defeats on confidence motions (in Italy and other parliamentary democracies) can, for example, be interpreted as a reflection of politicians' ability to exercise, and act on, rational foresight. *Operationalization*: NA. *Symbol*: NA.

RATIONALITY ASSUMPTION. *Concept*: Political actors have goals, and will make choices that they believe (correctly or not) will help them to reach their goals. The desired goals may involve material benefits, or may involve some other kind of benefit (prestige, the sense of "doing right," and so forth). *Measure*: NA. *Operationalization*: NA. *Symbol*: NA.

SEGMENTATION. *Concept*: The extent to which a national electorate is segmented or subdivided into blocs, with each bloc loyally backing "its" party and securely insulated from the appeals of rival parties. *Measure*: Substantial stability in the electoral alignments supporting parties, and survey evidence indicating that voters of one party or another are impervious to other parties' appeals. *Operationalization*: A rank-ordering devised by Lijphart (1984, 42–45), according to which segmentation is highest in the Netherlands and Belgium (awarded a score of 3), moderate in Finland, France, Germany, and Italy (a score of 2), and low in Denmark, Ireland, Norway, and Sweden (a score of 1). *Symbol*: SG_i.

SPATIAL CONDITIONS. *Concept*: The character and structure of the policy space in which parties compete for voters' support, along with the character and distribution of preferences among voters. *Measure*: The number of dimensions of the policy space, the existence or absence of a core (core party), the degree to which the electorate is segmented into insulated blocs of voters. *Operationalization*: See the entries on types of party systems (bipolar, multipolar, unipolar), core, median, dimensions of policy space, effective number of parties, pivotal party, policy space, and segmentation. *Symbol*: See the entries just named.

SPATIAL THEORY (OR THEORIES) OF VOTING. *Concept*: The body of research in political science and economics that, through mathematized deductive reasoning, examines the outcomes of voting under simple majority rule or under supramajoritarian rules. There are institution-free and institution-focused variants of spatial theory. The basic intuition underlying spatial theory is that the preferences (that is, policy positions) of political actors, along with their relative weight (and, in institution-focused models, certain institutional arrangements), determine the outcomes of voting processes. *Measure*: NA. *Operationalization*: NA. *Symbol*: NA.

STRONG PARTY. *Concept*: In Laver and Shepsle's (1994, 1996, 1999) research, a party able to prevent any majority-preferred government from forming, which, if formed, would constitute an alternative to the government in which the strong party receives all portfolios. *Measure*: NA in this study. *Operationalization*: NA. *Symbol*: NA.

SUPRAMAJORITARIAN RULE. *Concept*: The requirement that certain classes (or all classes) of legislation be approved by a majority that is larger than 50 percent plus 1. Prominent in Belgium and Finland. In spatial theories of voting, supramajoritarian rules are important in that they make a core more likely, even in two or more dimensions (Schofield, Grofman, and Feld 1988). *Measure*: The size of the larger-than-usual majority. *Operationalization*: The percentage weight of the majority required (e.g., 66.7 percent for constitutional amendments). *Symbol*: NA in this study.

SURPLUS COALITION. *Concept*: A majority coalition that is larger than minimal, containing one or several parties not needed to command a legislative majority. *Measure*: Identify the size of each party's parliamentary contingent, and come up with a list of coalitions that qualify as surplus. *Operationalization*: Number (or percentage) of seats in the lower house of the legislature held by each party; use those numbers (or percentages) to identify the coalitions that qualify as surplus. *Symbol*: S.

UNIPOLAR PARTY SYSTEM. *Concept*: A party system in which a single party attracts and orients interparty competition. *Measure*: A unipolar party system is identified by looking at the effective number of parties, their positions in policy space, and their size. *Operationalization*: Effective number of parties, percentage of seats held by parties in the lower house of the legislature, party location in policy space as determined by content analysis of party manifestos; I use this information to identify the unipolar systems. In this data set, the unipolar party systems are Ireland, Norway, Sweden, and pre-1973 Denmark. A dummy variable is coded 1 when and where the party system is unipolar. *Symbol*: U_i.

Notes

1. In Finland and the United Kingdom, convention rather than an explicit formal rule calls for resignation upon a government's defeat in a confidence vote. Under the constructive vote of no confidence used in Germany and Spain, any motion to remove a sitting government must at the same time identify a replacement government. See Gallagher, Laver, and Mair 1995, 29–30; Herman 1976, 829–40; Laver and Schofield 1990, 62–65.

2. Strøm defines the turnover or alternation rate as "the proportion of legislative seats held by parties changing status between government and opposition," averaged across a country's governments (1990b, 125).

3. It is commonly assumed that the costs (or benefits) of coalition include not only the sacrifices of office, policy influence, and votes that parties might incur as a consequence of rupturing coalitions, but also what parties stand to lose (or gain) in terms of office, policy, and votes when they enter into governing coalitions.

4. As discussed later, the central institutions in this argument are electoral laws, legislative rules, and links between the executive and the legislature. Here and throughout the book, I use the phrase "spatial conditions" as a kind of shorthand to refer to the array of parties and voters in policy space or, to elaborate further, the following features of the environment in which parties compete for votes and for control of the executive: the policy dimension(s) dominating interparty competition (such as the left–right dimension); the distribution of voters' preferences along, for example, the left–right spectrum; the degree to which voters are open to, or insulated from, the appeals of a multiplicity of parties; the number of parties engaged in electoral competition; the positions of parties along, again for example, the left–right dimension; and the number of parties represented in Parliament and the size of each parliamentary party. The phrase "spatial conditions" has the obvious virtue of brevity. The phrase also has the advantage of highlighting that my argument is informed by spatial theories of voting.

5. My thanks to Kaare Strøm for providing me with these data. On the measure of alternation (or rate of turnover), see Note 2. Strøm (1990b) used the following criteria to identify the fall of one government and the emergence of another: any change of party composition, parliamentary election, change of prime minister, accepted resignation of the cabinet, and by-election that shifts the government from majority to minority status or vice versa. As detailed in Chapter 3, I use only the first four criteria in the ten-nation data set constructed for this book. The Pearson correlation between alternation and duration is 0.575.

CHAPTER 2

1. The three-party cabinet built by Amintore Fanfani in 1962 controlled 51 percent of the seats in the Chamber of Deputies, whereas three other coalitions held exactly half. The Italian Socialist Party (PSI) abstained on Fanfani's vote of investiture, extending indirect support (and refraining from direct opposition) in a way that a pure search for power would render superfluous. The architects of the Fanfani government saw it as a second-best solution, designed to pave the way for the larger, long-term alliance they preferred, an alliance embracing the PSI. Chapter 5 discusses Italy's other minimal winning coalitions, formed after the 1992 elections.

2. The differences in counts can be consequential, as a look at the rightmost column of Table 2.1 confirms. In particular, note the estimations of the relative success of the minimal winning prediction in Belgium. Chapter 3 discusses the various criteria for defining governments. The figures on France in Table 2.1 require special comment. I have corrected errors in the published version of Strøm's data set, using information in *Keesing's Contemporary Archives* and MacRae (1967), so that my identifications of governing parties and minority governments do not fully duplicate those found in Strøm (1990b, 253−54).

3. In one dimension, the median is the core. Strom (1990) provides an accessible introduction to spatial theories of voting, discussing, for example, the conditions under which the median voter theorem identifies an equilibrium. See also, e.g., Krehbiel 1988; McLean and Urken 1995; Ordeshook 1990; Riker 1990; Schofield, Grofman, and Feld 1988; Shepsle 1986.

4. Note also that the Laver-Schofield study labels the median party prediction as successful when the median party supports the government. Differences in time coverage presumably account for the greatest discrepancy across the two data sets, that involving Ireland. As Tables 2.1 and 2.2 both illustrate, the results produced in tests of coalition theories depend in part on testers' choices.

5. Later chapters expand on this comparison of Italy and the Netherlands. For now, it is enough to observe that empirical research informed by spatial theory classifies Italy and the Netherlands as the only parliamentary democracies with multipolar party systems and strong core parties (e.g., Laver and Schofield 1990; Schofield 1993). As Chapter 6 details, "multipolar" systems have relatively many parties and are often two dimensional, so that parties face competitors in several directions. Chapters 5 and 8 discuss the recent upsets experienced by the Italian and Dutch Christian Democrats: In 1994, after losing core status, both the DC and the CDA went into opposition.

6. If there is a single party that can staff the DDM cabinet, it is almost always a strong party (Laver and Shepsle 1996).

7. Another problem has to do with surplus governments. Laver and Shepsle predict surplus coalitions in three or more dimensions, since a party's control of a particular portfolio may serve as a vital guarantee of government policy, even when that party is superfluous to the government's majority. As Table 2.1 shows, however, surplus coalitions govern in party systems that are routinely characterized as unidimensional (Finland) or two dimensional (Belgium, Israel, Italy, and the

Netherlands), not three dimensional (Budge, Robertson, and Hearl 1987; Laver and Budge 1992).

8. The use of supramajoritarian rules in Belgium and Finland is discussed in Chapter 6.

CHAPTER 3

1. The first three kinds of costs reflect the aims that each actor is assumed to have. Bargaining costs reflect the costs of acquiring and transmitting information among multiple actors.

2. Strøm (1990a) argues that similar conditions influence how parties rank the importance of office, policy, and electoral benefits. Laver and Schofield (1990, ch. 8) discuss how the institutional features I emphasize constrain coalition bargaining.

3. As Katz (1986a, 87) observes, the key feature of a preferential voting system is that it "allow[s] those voting for a party to determine, or at least . . . to influence, the identity of the particular candidates to be elected from among those the party has nominated." Chapter 5 discusses the Italian variant of preference voting, and Table 6.1 presents a cross-national comparison of preference voting. For further details, see Katz 1986a; Katz 1997, 112–14, 206–14.

4. Here my reasoning resembles that of North (1990) and Tsebelis (1990) on one set of cost-reduction strategies, the redesign of institutions.

5. Hence, low expected costs (and spatial and institutional conditions) produce short durations. Yet it is conceivable that over time, as short-lived governments repeatedly collapse at low cost, they induce expectations among politicians that attempts to reduce costs further will succeed. In the long run, then, short durations might encourage cost-reduction strategies and might produce low(er) costs. Appendix F explores the possibility of such feedback effects.

6. The unitary actor assumption may be especially restrictive in thinking about the endogenous management of costs. In particular, the leaders of highly factionalized parties may find increases in cabinet portfolios especially attractive as a means for offsetting the office costs of coalition, since they are concerned to distribute offices among multiple parties and among well-organized intraparty actors. On coalition bargaining as an exercise in intraparty politics, see Luebbert (1986).

7. For an alternative treatment of the costs and benefits involved in coalition government, see Lupia and Strøm (1995). An approach somewhat similar to mine, developed independently, is presented in Grofman and van Roozendaal (1994).

8. Chapter 6 elaborates on this classification of party systems, which is drawn from Laver and Schofield (1990).

9. Strøm also follows a fifth criterion, for he designates a new government with any by-election that shifts the government from majority to minority status or vice versa. This last rule stems from Strøm's special interest in minority governments and seems to be unique to him. I do not adopt it. Its practical effect is confined to one occurrence in one country in my data set: In Ireland the Fitzgerald II government, formed in December 1982, lost its majority in December 1986.

10. Difficult judgment calls are involved in applying whatever criteria are adopted, as episodes from Germany, Ireland, and Italy illustrate. On September 17, 1982, all four Free Democratic (FDP) ministers resigned from a Social Democratic–FDP coalition in Germany. On October 1, 1982, a constructive vote of no confidence was held in the Bundestag, and the Christian Democrats (CDU/CSU) and FDP elected Helmut Kohl as Chancellor (*Keesing's Contemporary Archives* 1982, 31773). In Ireland, a Fine Gael–Labour coalition collapsed on January 20, 1987, when Labour withdrew. Elections took place on February 17, and on March 9, 1987, the Dáil elected Charles Haughey of Fianna Fáil as prime minister (*Keesing's* 1987, 35084–86). In Italy, the Social Democrats withdrew from a four-party coalition (of Christian Democrats [DC], Social Democrats [PSDI], Republicans [PRI], and Liberals [PLI]) on October 31, 1949. New ministerial appointments were announced on November 7, and on November 22, 1949, a DC-PRI-PLI coalition won the confidence of the Chamber of Deputies. That three-party coalition then resigned on January 12, 1950 (*Keesing's* 1950, 10368, 10569).

In all of these episodes the party composition of the government changed. The treatment of these episodes has differed, however, even within the same data set. For example, according to Woldendorp, Keman, and Budge (1993), who use the same four criteria that I do (ibid., 5), a minority SPD-only government ruled Germany from September 17 to October 1, 1982, whereas no FG-only government appeared in Ireland in 1987. According to Woldendorp and colleagues, moreover, the Italian Social Democrats belonged to a four-party coalition from May 1948 through January 1950.

What these episodes and their treatment reveal (apart from an error on Italy in the Woldendorp et al. data set) is that the criterion of changes in party composition cannot be applied without subsidiary rules of thumb that serve to distinguish between "mere" phases of coalition crisis and "real" shifts in the partisan makeup of governments. In this book's data set, again, a real shift is signaled by no immediate move to call elections (which instead was made in the Irish episode); replacement of all resigning ministers with ministers from another party; and, in addition to the appointment of personnel, some move to affirm that the old executive no longer exists (made, e.g., in official party declarations or a parliamentary vote of confidence in a new executive). Hence, I do not exclude all caretakers (that is, all interim administrations designed to perform routine tasks while waiting to be replaced). I discriminate between, on the one hand, those caretakers existing only as remnants of broken coalitions and, on the other, caretakers having a recognized separate status and more-than-caretaker governments. To complete the illustration begun above, I count a separate SPD-only government in Germany and a separate DC-PRI-PLI coalition in Italy, and instead regard Haughey's Fianna Fáil government as the successor to the Fine Gael–Labour coalition in Ireland.

11. As far as I know, the French Fourth Republic is the only parliamentary democracy where parties have repeatedly contributed junior ministers to the government without contributing ministers. Most analysts (e.g., Arné 1962; Strøm 1990b; Williams 1966; Woldendorp, Keman, and Budge 1993) do not consider France's "exclusively junior ministerial parties" to be governing parties.

12. The identification of parties is also a little tricky in Belgium from 1968 to

1978, when linguistic conflicts split what were once three parties into six. I discuss judgment calls on French and Belgian parties further in Part III, as part of the cross-national analysis.

13. *Keesing's* is authoritative, standardized, and available over the entire postwar period. Because it summarizes contemporary newspaper records, the information it reports is very likely to be highly salient to politicians and known to well-informed voters. My designation of responsibility for a government's fall was generally straightforward. For example, in October 1954, the two largest parties in the Finnish government, the Agrarians (renamed the Center Party, KP, in 1965) and Social Democrats (SSDP), publicized their differences over economic policy. The KP pushed for prices for farm products higher than those proposed in Prime Minister Ralf Törngren's anti-inflation package, whereas the SSDP urged lower food prices. Törngren then submitted his resignation. Responsibility for his government's collapse lay with the KP and SSDP.

CHAPTER 4

1. In nine of the fifty governments formed between 1947 and 1992, the same individual headed two of these ministries, which reduced redundancies. Equally important, however, is that since 1947 no one has ever directed all three ministries simultaneously. In twenty-seven of the thirty-four coalitions between 1947 and 1992, the three ministries were headed by politicians from at least two different parties; a Christian Democrat always held at least one of the three portfolios.

2. The designation of ministers without portfolio demands no action on the part of Parliament. Italy's constitution states that legislation is required to establish and organize ministries (article 95).

3. In Table 4.1 and throughout the book, I count the so-called second ministers in Finland as junior ministers. As explained in Chapter 7, experts on Finnish politics disagree on how to define the status of the second ministers, who are appointed to a ministry in which *another* minister has the formal responsibility of heading the governmental unit (Nousiainen 1988, 214; cf. Arter 1987). The classification of cabinet posts in Table 4.1 is not the only one imaginable, of course, and policy is not the only criterion for classification. The former head of the Christian Democratic (DC) group in the Italian Chamber of Deputies has sorted ministries into five categories (e.g., patronage ministries) according to their "utility . . . in maintaining or reinforcing DC power" (Cazzola 1985, 202). A ranking of ministries according to prestige is discussed later in the chapter.

4. Chapter 5 examines just how loose the correspondence was. In fact, in coalition the DC was almost always undercompensated, in the sense that its share of ministers and undersecretaries was smaller than its share of the parliamentary seats controlled by the coalition. To judge from the computations preserved in published memoranda (Venditti 1981), DC politicians took such undercompensation for granted during negotiations over new cabinets.

5. Imagine what would be required to estimate the percentage of public employees—for a given year, at all levels, in the civil service and parastate agencies,

country by country—who owed their jobs to a party's nomination, recommendation, pressure, and/or repayment for a vote: interviews. No matter how ingenious the question wording and how carefully trained the questioners, estimates based on interview responses would be riddled with error.

6. On the definition of "party government," see Katz 1986b, 1987. Note also that in Italy alone, out of eleven countries surveyed between the early 1970s and the late 1980s, a sizable increase in party staff coincided with a sizable *decrease* in official party income (Katz and Mair 1992; discussion in Mair 1994, 6-7). It seems logical to ascribe this discrepancy in part to the Italian parties' unusual access to state resources and corruption—even though it is impossible to disentangle the relative importance of patronage and corruption for party finance in this case.

7. Would-be civil servants typically circumvent the examination system as follows: "Candidates are employed on a temporary basis, normally in a peripheral field office; more and more people are hired; after a given time, usually five years, a law is passed by Parliament that changes the employment contract, making it permanent for thousands or hundreds of thousands of employees. Seniority from the first contract is usually granted" (Cassese 1993, 325). Parliament approved twelve such laws on civil service employment between 1973 and 1990.

8. This statement overlooks variations—within the DC, among the centrist parties, and over time—in evaluations of the PCI and MSI. Most observers have found the antisystem label straightforward in the case of the MSI (Ignazi 1989, 1994a, 1994b) and inapplicable to the PSI since at least the mid-1950s. Analysts have disagreed instead on how to characterize the PCI and its evolution since World War II (compare Farneti 1983; Sartori 1976). As discussed in Chapter 5, the renamed MSI entered government after the 1994 elections, and the renamed PCI, after the 1996 elections.

9. Detailed results for national elections in Italy between 1946 and 1992 appear in Table 5.1.

10. To be more precise, out of the three parties, it was the PCI that dominated the Resistance and the DC that won the most votes in June 1946. De Gasperi twice postponed the elections to the Constituent Assembly; he calculated that the longer the interval between Resistance enthusiasms and nationwide elections, the weaker the Left would be (Ginsborg 1989, 117-19; Pasquino 1986, 62-64).

11. For simplicity, I refer to the Italian Social Democrats as the PSDI here and throughout the book. The party was known as the Italian Socialist Workers' Party (PSLI) from 1947 to 1951, however. Similarly, I always refer to the Italian Socialists as the PSI, even though they carried the name of the Italian Socialist Party of Proletarian Unity before 1947. The Socialists and Social Democrats were reunited under the name of the Unified Socialist Party (PSU) from 1966 to 1969.

12. As noted later in the chapter, the Italian constitution requires that governments obtain the confidence of both chambers of Parliament. The DC fell short of a majority of Senate seats during the 1948-53 legislature.

13. The standing orders of the Chamber of Deputies required use of the secret ballot on final votes from 1948 until 1988. On use of the secret ballot in pre–World War II Italy, see Hine 1993, 190-93; Manzella 1991, 218-26; Traversa 1989, 473-76.

14. Obviously, the existence of four formulae indicates that they are not impervious to change. I treat the shift from centrism to center–left coalitions later in the chapter. On other changes, see Mershon 1994.

15. To be precise, the winning alliance would have received 380 of the 590 seats (or 64.4 percent) then available in the Chamber of Deputies. The decision to assign 380 seats to the majority electoral bloc seems to have reflected two calculations. First, the DC alone would probably have earned a majority in the Chamber in 1953 if the centrist alliance had won more than half of the votes (Ginsborg 1989, 189). In addition, the centrist parties aimed to ensure the selection of jurists they preferred for the Constitutional Court, which was stipulated in the 1948 constitution, under discussion in 1953, and finally established in 1955 (Floridia 1995, 12). According to the rules in force from 1953 to 1967, the five members of the court chosen by Parliament had to earn the support of a three-fifths majority of both houses of Parliament in joint session. See also Note 23.

16. Chapters 5 and 7 discuss the criteria I use to identify the length of government crises. The adoption of different criteria (as in Pollio Salimbeni 1989) yields different figures for average crisis duration during the 1958–63 and 1963–68 legislatures (17.4 days and 31 days, respectively), but the bottom line remains the same. Government crises became more protracted with the inclusion of the PSI in center–left coalitions.

17. Disputes over recent implementation of the guidelines (in negotiations over Andreotti VII) appear in *Corriere della Sera*, April 15 and 21, 1991. Chapter 5 discusses the 1995 Dini government, which abandoned the manual.

18. Despite what I say here about government programs in Italy, in Chapter 5 I use content analyses of them to measure the policy costs and benefits of building coalitions. Why? In brief: Like the Laver-Budge research team, I recognize that few alternatives are available. For further discussion, see Chapters 5 and 7.

19. This classification differs from the one adopted by Strøm (1990b, 118–23), but produces findings that are consistent with his findings for Italy (179–81). For narratives of the resignations of Italian governments, I rely on *Keesing's Contemporary Archives*. On the advantages of this source, see Chapter 3, Note 13.

20. Francesco Cossiga scheduled a vote of confidence for mid-March 1980 in the hope of subduing pressures from the Socialists, who were urging Communist participation in government. Both the PSI and PRI announced that they would vote against the government on the motion, however, which led Cossiga to resign before a vote was held (*Keesing's* 1980, 30341–43). Aldo Moro resigned in January 1966 after the Chamber of Deputies rejected a bill that would have established public nursery schools and kindergartens. The outcome hinged on the behavior of DC deputies, more than fifty of whom voted against the bill. Even though the bill engaged the legislature's confidence, it aroused opposition within the DC, for it would have encroached on the Catholic Church's traditional control of early childhood education (*Keesing's* 1966, 21365–66).

21. De Gasperi XI and Fanfani I fell, respectively, just before and just after the 1953 elections, amid controversy over the majoritarian electoral law. The defeats of Andreotti I (1972), Andreotti V (1979), and Fanfani IV (1987) precipitated early elections. The defeat of Andreotti I was expected and even intended by Andreotti

and the DC (*Keesing's* 1972, 25179–80; Ginsborg 1989, 453–54; Gianfranco Pasquino, personal communication, August 1999).

22. In stark contrast, regularly scheduled elections marked the end of 52.2 percent of postwar governments in Norway and 58.3 percent in Sweden. Chapter 8 expands on such cross-national comparisons.

23. The 1953 legislation was modified in 1967, so that on the first three ballots in the joint session of the Chamber and Senate, a 67 percent majority was required for the election of the five justices, and on any subsequent ballots the required majority dropped to 60 percent. Interestingly, sources differ somewhat in their accounts of the passage in 1953 of the initial enabling legislation for the court (cf. Adams and Barile 1961, 128; Allum 1973, 93; Bonini 1996, 98; Cole 1959, 969; Floridia 1995, 12). My thanks to Mary Volcansek for her help in sorting through the disagreements.

CHAPTER 5

1. A pivotal party is a party whose addition to a minority government including the core party (or whose withdrawal from a majority coalition including the core party) would give the executive majority (minority) status. For this use of the term "pivotal," see Schofield 1986, 1993; also see Rémy 1975.

2. The electoral earthquakes of the early 1990s, moreover, prompted some political scientists to debate the existence of old–new and ideological–pragmatic dimensions in Italy (D'Alimonte and Bartolini 1995; Ricolfi 1993a, 1993b, 1995).

3. Fully twenty-four parties won Chamber seats on at least two occasions between 1947 and 1994. These counts are based on data reported in Buonadonna and Ginex 1994, 28–29; Caciagli and Spreafico 1990, 380; *Corriere della Sera*, April 8, 1992; and Farneti 1983, 36–39.

4. In the penultimate section of the chapter, I discuss the impact of this change as well as the radical overhaul of electoral laws that Parliament approved in 1993.

5. This distinction is most useful after 1968; since then (save in 1992) very short-lived cabinets have ushered in early elections. Strøm and I use the same measure of electoral performance but different units of analysis, for Strøm examines the set of incumbent parties in the aggregate. Thus, the analysis here and in Chapter 7 extends Strøm's work on electoral costs (1990b, 123–25, 165–76).

6. Qualitative compensations exist too. From 1946 to 1994, the DC maintained almost uninterrupted direction of the Interior, Treasury, Posts/Telecommunications, and Education ministries. The first two ministries cover crucial policy jurisdictions, the latter two are rich in patronage, and Education oversees religious instruction in public schools. For further discussion, see Mershon 1989.

7. In particular, appointments of new undersecretaries (and of ministers without portfolio) require no action on the part of Parliament, whereas legislation must be approved to establish new ministries.

8. This example also suggests that competition among DC factions, together with competition between the DC and the PSI, drove portfolio inflation (cf. Chapter 3, Note 6). Chapter 9 briefly treats factional politics.

9. See the sources just named in the text for a detailed discussion of the coding categories, the documents chosen for analysis, and other procedures followed in developing these measures. On the plus side, these data facilitate intertemporal comparisons, have seen broad use, and have been generated for all but one of the countries (Finland) in this study. As I have noted elsewhere (Epstein and Mershon 1996), however, reliance on these data is not unproblematic. Scholars who use the party manifesto data accept parties' statements of intention at election time as true preferences. They assume that political parties do not act strategically in presenting policy packages to the electorate, that parties do not modulate, moderate, or in any way misrepresent their statements of policy intention in order to win votes or enter government. Similarly, reliance on the government program data entails the assumption that governments act sincerely in presenting policy packages to the legislature whose confidence they must have in order to govern. On further critiques of the data on party manifestos and government programs, see Chapter 6, Note 3.

10. The nature of the available evidence leads me to restrict attention here (and in Chapter 7) to distances on the left–right scale, even though two dimensions underpin the party systems of Italy, Belgium, post-1973 Denmark, France, Ireland, and the Netherlands. For those systems, the use of the one-dimensional estimates of policy distance is a less-than-fortunate, but forced, choice. To elaborate: Laver and Budge (1992) and their colleagues track party and governmental positions on the left–right dimension. They also give distances in a twenty-dimensional space, but interpretation of those data is less than straightforward. The published data thus do not permit computation of distances between party and government policies on two dimensions.

11. The separate variances t test yields a p-value of less than 0.001. The PSI issued relatively centrist election manifestos in the 1976, 1979, and 1983 elections (Mastropaolo and Slater 1992).

12. Data source identified in personal communication from Michael Laver, May 1998. The Italian data were collected and analyzed by the team headed by Klingemann, but not reported in published form by Klingemann, Hofferbert, and Budge (1994). On the political business cycle in Italy, see Radaelli 1991; Santagata 1991, 1995. See also Kreppel 1997.

13. As noted in Chapter 3, this identification relies primarily on *Keesing's Contemporary Archives*. In the few cases where *Keesing's* supplied inadequate information on government falls, I coded the *Corriere della Sera* and/or *L'Espresso*. Even when an Italian cabinet has resigned after defeat on a secret ballot, insiders have speculated to journalists about the vote and estimated how many deputies from each governing party defected from the governing majority (*L'Espresso*, July 6, 1986, 9, 11).

14. Table 5.5 does not analyze responsibility for collapses immediately before elections because that variable varies so little: Before 1968, no party was ever responsible for the fall of a cabinet on election eve.

15. The DC's drop when not responsible for cabinet collapses rests on one datum alone: the difference between 1948, when voters rallied around the DC at the onset of the Cold War, and 1953, when controversy over the majoritarian electoral law repulsed some voters.

16. Granted, these measures have shortcomings. For instance, as the data derived from content analyses suggest, two DC-only governments may have distinct policy colorations, and not all governing parties influence policy to the same extent. I look at the data on party manifestos and government programs later in the chapter.

17. The Social Democrats withdrew from several coalitions in the late 1940s and 1950s, however, precisely because they wanted to abstain from governing power. Their withdrawals yielded the desired result.

18. One answer, regarding the pivotal PSI, has already been implied: not much. As noted earlier, there was a relatively close match between government programs and Socialist predilections between 1976 and 1983. And as just emphasized, the PSI terminated every government installed between 1976 and 1992.

19. As shown in Chapter 7, the former scenario characterizes the average Dutch government from 1946 to 1992, and the latter, the average Swedish government (calculated from data in *Keesing's Contemporary Archives*).

20. One advantage of this decision rule is that the measure of bargaining costs, so constructed, is not "contaminated" by cross-national variations in the length of electoral campaigns. Note that no party-specific measure of bargaining costs is available, whereas it is possible to distinguish the different electoral, office, and policy costs of coalition that different parties have incurred. I know of no source furnishing reliable and valid data on the length of time one party or another devoted to negotiations during the interregna between governments.

21. The separate variances t test yields a p-value of less than 0.005. Analyses of variance also reveal that, for entries in each row of Table 5.9, the differences in mean crisis duration across subperiods are statistically significant ($p < 0.05$).

22. The demise of the five-party coalition headed by Ciriaco De Mita (DC) in May 1989 illustrates the difficulties involved in tracking time devoted to sabotaging governments. On May 18, 1989, the Socialist Party's vice secretary addressed the forty-fifth PSI National Congress and, with a rhetorical flourish, warned De Mita that the PSI intended to abandon the government: "When the tram reaches the end of the line, everyone gets off, including the driver" (Claudio Martelli, as quoted in Pasquino 1990, 51). De Mita resigned on May 19. But De Mita's position within the DC was gravely weakened at the eighteenth DC National Congress (February 18–22, 1989), and afterward rival DC leaders probably began plotting against De Mita's premiership. Indeed, the Italian media gave great play to the confidential meetings held in a trailer between the PSI secretary and the newly elected DC secretary at the margins of the PSI Congress (Caciagli 1990, Pasquino 1990). But it is impossible to move from these events, colorful though they may be, to a systematic counting of the time devoted to maneuvering to produce the fall of the De Mita government.

23. I do not pretend to give here an exhaustive analysis of the events and upheaval in Italy since 1992. Relevant sources include D'Alimonte and Bartolini 1995, 1997; Hine and Vassallo 1999; Ignazi 1996, 1997; Katz and Ignazi 1996; Mershon and Pasquino 1994; Pasquino 1995a, 1995b, 1998; Tucciarelli 1998; Vesperini 1998.

24. Even though a PRI Senator was undersecretary to the premier, the PRI did

not consider itself a member of the coalition and abstained on the cabinet's investiture. *Corriere della Sera*, April 29–May 13, 1993.

25. Readers who are not Italianists would probably appreciate some indication of the amazing pervasiveness of corruption in Italy. Consider this telling fact: Between the elections of April 6, 1992, and the date of December 31, 1992, fully 282 deputies and senators (out of 945 total) were the subject of one or more "requests for authorizations to proceed" (known in Italian by the acronym RAP) in investigations on criminal activity by lifting parliamentary immunity (Ricolfi 1993b, 21). Gentle reader: Imagine that 29.8 percent of the national-level legislators were under investigation for corruption in the country where you live or where you were born. (On the probability that almost all RAP in 1992 involved the suspicion of corruption, rather than other types of illegalities, see Ricolfi 1993b.) Consider, too, that Luca Ricolfi, an econometrician, has estimated that if the Parliament had served its full five-year term, between 51.5 percent and 56.5 percent of the MPs elected in 1992 risked being named in a RAP by 1997 (ibid., 117).

26. The Berlusconi government qualifies as minimal winning if electoral alliances (the Freedom Alliance and the Good Government Alliance) are counted as its component units. If parliamentary parties are counted as the units comprising the coalition, it has surplus status and a superfluous member in the CCD.

27. The League went so far as to introduce a motion of no confidence, which MPs from the PPI co-signed. The PDS presented a motion of no confidence of its own. Anticipating defeat, Berlusconi resigned before voting on either motion could begin. This outcome was unprecedented in postwar Italy, as Table 4.3 shows.

28. All the same, the aggregate shift in parties' vote shares (or aggregate electoral volatility) on the PR ballot was lower in 1996 than it was in 1994. The degree of volatility registered in Italy's 1994 elections was among the highest ever seen in twentieth-century parliamentary democracies. For details, see Cartocci 1997. Competition in the single-member districts was decisive for the Olive Tree's victory in 1996.

29. More recently, two other cabinets based on the Olive Tree have ruled: D'Alema II (December 1999 to April 2000) and Amato II (April 2000 to May 2001). In some respects, these governments might seem to signal a return to previous patterns of coalition politics in Italy. Obviously, both cabinets, especially D'Alema II, were short-lived. D'Alema II contained a total of ninety-three positions, senior and junior, which might look like an effort to offset costs of coalition. In other ways, however, all of the executives in power between 1996 and 2001 mark a break with the past. For one thing, in all four executives, nonparliamentarians were numerous. Relatedly, in all four, the largest party obtained relatively few office benefits: The PDS's mean weighted share of senior slots (the ratio of its share of cabinet posts to its share of the government's delegation in the lower house) stood at 0.62 across the four governments; its mean weighted share of junior positions was 0.69. (To discern the size of parliamentary parties at each government formation, I consulted Camera dei Deputati 1999a, 2000; Ignazi 1997. Some nonparliamentarians had a clear partisan affiliation, which the count of cabinet personnel recognized.) Note, too, that in Amato II total portfolios were trimmed to seventy-six. The Olive Tree parties found that incumbency carried electoral costs in the May 2001 elections:

The reunited center–right (the electoral alliance of Forza Italia, the National Alliance, and the Northern League) won comfortable majorities in both houses of Parliament; and, whereas Forza Italia expanded its vote share on the Chamber PR ballot to 29.5 percent, the PDS retreated to 16.5 percent (Ministero dell'Interno 2001). Three lists on the center or left competed independently of the Olive Tree, which in part reflected politicians' experiences—and disappointments—with center–left government. As this book goes to press, the center–right is poised to govern with Berlusconi as premier.

30. Gordon Tullock chose this question as the title for his well-known article in *Public Choice* (1981), and that journal subsequently published several direct responses to Tullock (Niemi 1983; Shepsle and Weingast 1981). For overviews of the much broader scholarly debate, see, e.g., Ordeshook 1986; Shepsle 1986; Strom 1990; and Part I of this book.

CHAPTER 6

1. Following Lijphart (1994), I use a 20 percent criterion for identifying "major" changes in district size, thresholds, and assembly size. Table 6.1 excludes reforms that never took effect, such as Italy's controversial majoritarian electoral law of 1953 (discussed in Chapter 4). For the dates and contents of electoral reforms, I rely not only on Lijphart (1994) but also on the following sources: Gladdish 1991, 95–100; Mackie and Rose 1991, 156–59; Storing 1963, 59–72; Urwin 1974, 136–42; Williams 1966, 321–35, 533–37.

2. Indeed, of all the countries in Strøm's (1990) data set that feature relatively strong committees (scoring a 4 or 5 on the index in Table 6.2), Belgium fits Strøm's argument about minority cabinets least well.

3. The Laver and Budge (1992) series of data ends in the late 1980s. (The data can also be found in Volkens 1995, which includes a detailed and extremely valuable codebook.) Efforts to update the data have led to searching debates within the scholarly community about the most appropriate ways to measure party preferences (e.g., Budge 2000; Gabel and Huber 2000; Kim and Fording 1998; Laver and Garry 2000). Publicly available reanalyses that build on these methodological debates and employ new schemes for coding party manifestos have so far estimated party positions for a few countries and a few elections only (e.g., de Vries 1999 on the 1998 Dutch elections; Laver and Garry 2000 on the 1992 and 1997 British and Irish elections). A comprehensive updating of manifesto-based data on party policy awaits publication (Budge et al. n.d.; Laver n.d.). Thus, despite some shortcomings in the Laver and Budge (1992) data set (see Chapter 5, Note 9), it is the largest, most widely used, and most thoroughly documented and assessed source on party positions publicly available at the time this book goes to press.

4. The discussion of dimensions and core parties in this and the following paragraphs—and thus in Part III overall—relies primarily on Schofield's publications (Laver and Schofield 1990; Schofield 1987, 1993), with supplementary sources as noted in the text. Where discrepancies appear across sources, I adopt the judgment that seems most consistent with the available evidence. For example, some sources

describe one dimension of party competition in Denmark before the "earthquake elections" of 1973, and other sources identify two dimensions. The most detailed published data on Danish party positions (Schou and Hearl 1992) lead me to conclude that the one-dimensional characterization is most apt before 1973. For data on dimensions and party positions in Europe, Schofield draws on content analyses of parties' election manifestos (Budge, Robertson, and Hearl 1987; Laver and Budge 1992). Pétry on France (1987, 1992a, 1992b) also uses manifesto data.

5. The "effective number" of parties, a well-known index, takes into account not only the number but also the relative strength of parties (e.g., Lijphart 1984, 120–23; Lijphart 1994, 67–72; Taagepera and Shugart 1989, 77–91).

6. The second most salient dimension in the Fourth Republic pitted proregime and antiregime forces against each other.

7. The Mannheimer and Sani study (1987) cited in Chapter 5 used composite measures for subcultural belonging that included reports of behavior (e.g., attendance at mass) and attitudinal items (sympathy toward the church).

8. It is worth noting that relatively limited survey data exist for the Fourth Republic and that analysts differ in interpreting the available data. For example, in a carefully reasoned piece, Lewis-Beck (1984) argues against the widely held view that party identification was relatively weak during the Fourth Republic.

CHAPTER 7

1. Figure 7.1 covers the 1946–88 period and excludes the few governments formed when the KVP/CDA did not occupy the core of Dutch policy space: den Uyl (installed in 1973 after the November 1972 elections), van Agt I (1977), and Lubbers I (1982) and II (1986). Although manifesto data on parties' positions in the Dutch 1989 elections are not yet available (see Chapter 6, Note 3), my guess is that the CDA did not occupy the core in 1989; inclusion of the single government formed between the 1989 and 1994 elections (Lubbers III) only slightly alters the results exhibited in Figure 7.1.

2. On the KVP/CDA's time out of the core during the 1970s and 1980s, see note 1. The KP did not control the median legislator in the Parliaments elected in 1958 and 1966. This judgment is based on seat data and a comparison of Laver and Schofield 1990, 117–18; Mylly and Berry 1984; and Soikkanen 1981.

3. To be specific, Figure 7.2 excludes the seven nonpartisan cabinets just noted and excludes four party-based governments: Fagerholm I (formed in 1948), Paasio II (1972), and Holkeri I and II (1987 and 1990). In all postwar Finnish cabinets, at least a few important ministries are assigned two ministers, with one of the two "formally considered as the [single] head of the entire ministerial unit" (Nousiainen 1988, 214). Analysts differ as to whether the so-called "second ministers" (those *not* identified as heads) are to be viewed as junior ministers (Arter 1987) or as full ministers (Nousiainen 1988). Figure 7.2 portrays them as junior ministers. No matter how the definitional question is settled, the bottom line stays the same: The KP sacrifices posts when it builds coalitions.

4. These results are all the more reassuring since, for Norway, the comparisons

across coalitions of three and four parties—which are Norway's only coalitions—
are "contaminated" by both the SP's median status and time. There are only three
four-party coalitions that include the SP, and all of them governed from the early
1960s to the early 1970s, when the SP was not the median party. Two of the three-
party coalitions including the SP governed in the 1980s, when the SP was located at
the median. Hence, the comparison of the SP's officeholders in three- and four-party
coalitions is almost equivalent to a comparison between the SP as a median and
nonmedian governing party and is almost equivalent, still further, to a comparison
between the 1980s and 1960s. The greater range of variation afforded cross-nationally (in the record of the People's Party in Sweden, for example) helps to disentangle such factors. For further treatment of time and cabinet size, see the discussion
of the "bureaucratic accretion" hypothesis later in this section of the chapter.

5. Linguistic conflicts have created such disarray in the Belgian party system
that scholars differ as to just when two *parties* emerged out of the long-standing
language-based *wings* of the Christian Socials. The issue is complicated by separate
but simultaneous congresses for the wings, joint programs, and so forth. I identify
two distinct Christian Social parties starting in 1968, the first split of the Liberals
in 1972, and the split of the Socialists into the Flemish SP and the French PS in 1978
(Covell 1981, 1982; De Ridder and Fraga 1986; Dewachter 1987; Fitzmaurice 1983;
Keesing's Contemporary Archives, various issues; Lemaître 1982; Mabille 1992;
Mughan 1992).

6. The Pearson correlation between 1991 government spending (as a percentage
of gross domestic product [GDP]) and the number of ministers in 1991 is .24; that
between 1991 government spending and 1991 junior ministers is –.10. Data on 1991
government spending and 1960–90 growth in spending are drawn from Gallagher,
Laver, and Mair 1995, 10.

7. The Spearman correlation between date of government formation and number of ministers is .15 for Belgium, –.32 for Fourth Republic France, .20 for Germany, and .20 for the Netherlands. Spearman's r ranges from .63 in Finland to .90
in Norway. Spearman's statistic is most appropriate here, for it is based on the rank
orders of the two sets of observations.

8. The organization of Table 7.1 deserves two additional comments. First, given
the available evidence, I restrict attention here and in Figure 7.7 (as in Table 5.4 and
Figure 5.3) to distances on the left–right scale (cf. discussion in Chapter 5, Note 10,
and Chapter 6, Note 3). Second, I include the Danish SD in the leftmost column of
Table 7.1 so as to facilitate comparisons with Social Democrats in Norway and
Sweden. Discerning a "typical" core party in Denmark is somewhat troublesome,
however, for between 1945 and 1971 the Danish Radical Liberals sat at the left–
right median slightly more often than the SD did (Schou and Hearl 1992, 157).

9. The Pearson correlation between mean distance from government policy (on
the left–right scale) and a party's frequency at the left–right median is –.39. In a
regression model, frequency at the median does a poor job of predicting mean distance (adjusted R^2 = .13, standard error of the estimate = 8.063).

10. Figure 7.7 is based on 153 governments (out of 291 in the entire ten-nation
data set), since the only governments under scrutiny here are those containing long-
standing core parties and those for which policy measures are available.

11. The record of the Gaullists as members of French coalitions during the Fourth Republic also points to the salience of issues not captured in the left–right dimension. In particular, the three governments whose official policies stood furthest from the Gaullists' ideals on the left–right spectrum were Mendès-France (installed in June 1954 in the wake of the French defeat at Dien Bien Phu), the ephemeral Pineau, and Faure II (the latter two formed in February 1955, not long after the outbreak of terrorism in Algeria). Gaullists served in each of these coalitions. The inference obviously is that colonial policy, not left–right policy, held the key to Gaullist participation in government. (When Mendès-France, Pineau, and Faure II are omitted from the computations performed for Table 7.2, the mean for the Gaullists in government changes from 44.4 to 35.8.)

12. I use the following data to identify minimal connected winning coalitions and minimal winning coalitions made up of the fewest parties possible: seat data in Mackie and Rose 1991 (for all countries but France) and MacRae 1967 (on France); manifesto-based data on party positions in Budge and Laver 1992 (for all countries but Finland and Ireland); and expert judgments of party positions in Laver and Schofield 1990 (for Finland and Ireland).

13. Analyses of variance reveal that the means of crisis duration differ strikingly across the ten countries here ($F = 13.5$, $p < .0001$), and slightly less strongly across the five types of governments listed in Table 7.3 ($F = 6.8$, $p < .0001$). The table reports the results of analyses of variance conducted separately for each country.

14. Analyses of variance uncover moderate differences in the means of crisis duration across governments made up of different numbers of parties ($p \approx .01$). With the Netherlands omitted, the differences in means are attenuated ($p < .05$). When analyses of variance are performed for each country, the differences in means across governments containing different numbers of parties are usually small.

15. On the effective number of parties, see Chapter 6, especially Note 5. In Fourth Republic France, parliamentary parties were so fluid that computation of the effective number of parties on the basis of the preceding election was misleading; I used the data in MacRae (1967) to compute the figures specific to each government formation.

16. I used standard OLS (ordinary least squares) estimation procedures. No signs of multicollinearity emerged, and the correlation matrices of regression coefficients revealed relatively low correlations among the estimates. There is some autocorrelation (d-statistic ≈ 1.4–1.7, also indicated by visual inspection of the residuals), which is understandable given the weight of the Netherlands dummy and a few other country dummies, discussed below. The high standard error of the estimate (SEE) reflects the fact that in this data set the dependent variable ranges from 0 to 205, whereas the effective number of parties ranges from 2.2 to 8.4, the index of committee strength varies between 1 and 5, and all other independent variables are dummies.

For all subsequent regression analyses reported in the book, I used standard OLS estimation procedures. Discussions of subsequent regressions mention multicollinearity and autocorrelation only when problems appear.

17. Incorporating the dummy for post-1973 Denmark does little to reduce the standard error of the estimate, which stands at 17.25 in this regression. With the

Danish dummy added, the R^2 moves to 0.40. Recall that the variable denoting a bipolar system is equivalent to a dummy for Germany.

18. The effective number of parties (N) is related to Rae's index of fractionalization (F) as follows:

$$N = 1/(1 - F)$$

On this relationship and on reasons for preferring N to F, see Taagepera and Shugart 1989, 77–81. For the development of F, see Rae 1967. Re-running models 7.1 and 7.2 with F in the place of N produces results similar to those reported in Table 7.4. For the 1965–76 period, mean polarization (average percentage of the national vote won by extremist parties) was 13 in the Netherlands, as opposed to 25 and 37 in Finland and Italy, respectively (Powell 1982, 232).

19. In other words, Table 7.5—unlike Table 5.2—does not distinguish between incumbency on election eve and a party's role in all governments formed between two successive elections. The reason is that, outside Finland (where nonpartisan caretakers are common before elections) and Italy (where DC-only cabinets recur), a party's governing status immediately before an election is usually the same as its dominant interelectoral status. Two points on France should also be noted. First, the analysis here excludes data on the 1958 French elections, which were called six months after the end of the Fourth Republic and rendered a verdict on the regime inaugurated by Charles de Gaulle. Second, the French electoral data included pertain to blocs, for those are the only data available in 1951 and 1956, given the introduction of *apparentement* in 1951.

20. The Radical bloc campaigned from the ranks of the opposition in the June 1946 and November 1946 elections, and so its performance on those occasions is omitted from Table 7.5. After moving to habitual incumbency, the Radical bloc saw its vote share sag in 1951 (as compared to November 1946) and rise in 1956 (from 1951). Soon after the 1956 elections, the Radical bloc suffered severe fragmentation: In particular, in October 1956, the Dissident Radicals emerged as a separate party (MacRae 1967, 169–73, 197–204; Williams 1966, 122–41).

21. Along with Irish single transferable vote and French *panachage*, the two ballots used in Germany create opportunities for cross-party voting, as discussed in Chapter 6. For purposes of this analysis, I overlook the fact that German voters did not cast two votes in 1949 and that the Fourth Republic did not provide for *panachage* until 1951. Later in the chapter, I return to such changes in laws.

22. I borrow the rank-ordering devised by Lijphart (1984, 42–45), according to which segmentation is highest in the Netherlands and Belgium (assigned a score of 3 here), moderate in Finland, France, Germany, and Italy (a score of 2), and low in Denmark, Ireland, Norway, and Sweden (a score of 1). For criticism of this classification (in particular, the place it accords France), see Bartolini and Mair 1990, 226–49. On the lack of party-specific measures of segmentation (which would gauge the degree to which party i's electorate approximates a subcultural bloc), see Chapter 6, Note 7.

23. The lines in Figure 7.9A and B show the predicted values for the number of governing parties from a weighted average of nearby values of the mean shift in

vote share. On the smoothing method, called LOWESS (locally weighted scatter-plot smoothing), see Cleveland 1979, 1981; Wilkinson and Hill 1992; Wilkinson and Balasanov 1998. Figure 7.9B omits the French Gaullists and the Irish Clann na Poblachta; a figure including those outliers would exhibit a more pronounced downward trend.

24. I also examined the impact of three events not listed in Table 6.1: the 1990 German elections incorporated easterners and applied the 5 percent threshold separately to east and west; the 1953 elections in Italy were held under the short-lived majoritarian electoral law, as noted in Part II; and compulsory voting was abolished in the Netherlands in 1970. When these reforms are taken into account, the pattern displayed in Figure 7.10 remains roughly the same.

25. For all countries, the first election in the second period is the first one held after 1973. As Anderson (1995, 90) has observed, many scholars agree that 1973 marks a watershed in European electoral behavior.

26. Despite the overall Italian datum, moreover, Italian Christian Democracy became more vulnerable at the polls after the early 1970s, as stressed in Chapter 5. Figure 7.11 does not consider the 1994 Dutch and Italian elections. Chapter 8 discusses the dramatic losses that the Dutch CDA and the Italian DC suffered in 1994.

27. Elections in the latter half of the 1990s (not covered in this data set) evince higher volatility, however. For an updated cross-national overview, see Gallagher, Laver, and Mair 2001, 262–4.

28. To be sure, time is a rough proxy for declining segmentation, and the scores for cross-national differences in segmentation may be imperfect as well (see Note 22).

29. The parties assessed in model 7.6 are those that qualify as governing parties, that is, that have governed for at least half of the span between any one set of two successive elections.

30. Indeed, the d-statistic (≈ 2.01) and visual inspection of the residuals for the nine-variable version of model 7.6 listed earlier (without the previous vote share and previous vote swing) do not indicate any problem with serial autocorrelation.

31. I also performed the regression using the former strategy, but do not detail the findings here. In that analysis, as in the one depicted in Table 7.7, once salient outliers were removed, incumbency and the dummy identifying long-standing core parties had significant influences on shifts in vote share. The R^2 attained was even lower than that in Table 7.7, however.

This analysis is challenging not only because the data pool cross-sectional and time-series variation. The structure of the data set (where the parties' vote shares at each election in each country must total 1.0) also raises questions about heteroskedasticity—the situation in which the error terms in regression models do not have constant variance (Berry and Feldman 1985, 73–88; Glejser 1969; Goldfeld and Quandt 1965; White 1980). The models estimated in Chapter 8 share the possible problem. Visual inspection of the studentized residuals and other diagnostics I have performed show that the problem is limited for model 7.6 and the others I estimate and, thus, that the findings reported here are robust.

32. The two outliers are the French MRP in 1951 and the French Gaullists in 1956, whose vicissitudes have already been noted.

33. Running separate single-country regressions for the nine other countries yields a negative and statistically significant coefficient for the incumbency dummy in Belgium, Finland, and Ireland. Other than Italy, the only country for which the incumbency coefficient is positive is Denmark; but in Denmark that coefficient is puny and has a *t*-statistic of .07.

34. My thanks to Shawn Aaron for assistance in data collection. Data on inflation were drawn from IMF 1997; figures on unemployment and gross domestic product are from OECD 1997.

CHAPTER 8

1. Appendix D names the other sources I consulted to corroborate or supplement *Keesing's*. For two governments (Hansen I, Denmark, and Sorsa III, Finland) out of the 291 in this data set, I was unable to locate detailed information on the sequence of events and party actions leading to the government's termination. I coded missing data for Hansen I and Sorsa III rather than assume that no party moved to trigger those falls.

2. The Pearson correlation between mean government duration and percentage of governments ended by one or more parties is –0.62.

3. In Table 8.2, the time frame extends to the early 1990s, so that the findings for Finland, Ireland, the Netherlands, and Norway differ slightly from those reported in Mershon 1999a. For almost all parties, the findings for junior ministers roughly resemble those for ministers. One exception is the Belgian Socialists, who suffer a significant sacrifice in junior ministerial offices after they have toppled a government. On the other hand, the differences in weighted shares of junior offices for the French Independent Republicans and Norwegian Center Party do not attain statistical significance.

4. Fine Gael (FG) and Labour ruled four times during the period covered in Table 8.2. The entries in the *no* column for FG and Labour reflect their participation in one cabinet, Costello II, which was also Ireland's only three-party coalition. Naturally, the third ally in Costello II (Clann na Talmhan, literally "People of the Land") obtained some offices. And comparing the division of posts in Ireland's one three-party coalition and three FG–Labour coalitions is equivalent to comparing FG and Labour as incumbents when they held, as opposed to lacked, responsibility for the preceding government's fall.

For the Center Party (SP), two of the three weighted shares averaged in the *yes* column pertain to the party's experience during the 1980s when it contained the median legislator and took part in three-party coalitions; three of the four data points averaged in the *no* column reflect the SP's lack of median status and its membership in four-party coalitions during the 1960s. See also Note 4 in Chapter 7.

5. Like other analysts, I exclude one-party governments because allowing X to equal 1.0 and Y to approach 1.0 (nonpartisan experts are rare in one-party cabinets) would confound the results.

6. The differences in the two estimates can presumably be attributed to differences in country coverage. Unlike Browne and Franklin (1973), I include Fourth

Republic France and exclude Austria, Iceland, Israel, and Luxembourg. Reestimating the model without France brings the *a* and *b* coefficients somewhat closer to the values found by Browne and Franklin (1973).

As observed in Chapter 7 (Note 31), regression analyses of data such as these raise questions about heteroskedasticity (the situation in which the error term does not have constant variance). The diagnostics I have performed dispose of the questions: The problem of heteroskedasticity is limited for the model just reported and for models 7.1 through 7.6 and 8.1 through 8.6.

7. Again, the differences in the two estimates can be attributed to differences in country coverage. Reestimating this model without France brings the *a* and *b* coefficients very close to the values found by Browne and Frendreis (1980).

Two additional comments are in order. First and most important, as a shortcut here I analyze unrounded values for the Gamson prediction and thus ignore the "lumpiness" of the data. As Schofield and Laver (1985, 154) note, "In the real world, of course, it is just not possible for a party to receive, say, 1.87 cabinet seats, *whatever* a theory might predict." In analogous computations on offices received by Christian Democratic factions in Italy (Mershon 2001), I analyze integer values for the Gamson prediction, using the rounding method of Browne and Frendreis (1980). As the faction-level study illustrates, the R^2 values in an analysis with rounded values of the Gamson prediction would be even higher than those reported here for the unrounded values.

The second point regards notation. Since referring to the Gamson prediction as G is very common, I leave it as G in my notation. Nonetheless, here as in Chapter 7, the lower-case g and $g-1$ as subscripts denote attributes of particular governments.

8. The number of observations in the first column of Tables 8.3 and 8.4 is 669 (rather than the 700 cited earlier) since data are missing on the lagged responsibility variable for the first postwar government in each country. The number in the fourth column is smaller still since not all governments have junior ministers.

9. Interestingly, the outlier is Swedish Social Democracy (SAP) in Erlander III, a majority coalition instituted in 1951 after the SAP and the Agrarians (now Center Party) agreed amicably to end SAP minority rule. The SAP obtained an unusually high share and number of offices in this coalition, at the same time that it made unusually substantial policy concessions to the Agrarians in crafting the government's program, as discussed in Note 12 below. In other words, in Erlander III the Social Democrats apparently offset policy losses with office gains.

10. The following parties in Table 8.5 may be defined as "antisystem" or extremist, according to Powell 1982 and Strøm 1990b: the VU and FDF in Belgium; the Communists (SKDL) in Finland; and the PCF and Gaullists in France. Another prominent party often classified as extremist, the Italian Communist Party, governed for less than half of one interelectoral period and thus does not appear in this table.

11. Readers appreciative of the nuances of this notation might consider an alternative label for the dependent variable in model 8.2: O_{ink}, denoting the number of offices that incumbent party *in* receives in coalition *k*.

12. The following cases qualify as outliers: the Gaullists in Mendès-France and Pineau (see Note 11 in Chapter 7); the Belgian Socialists in Vanden Boeyants II,

which embraced the Volksunie and the FDF and were installed as an explicit caretaker after the Flemish Christian Socials (CVP) defected from the Egmont Pact on regionalization (*Keesing's* 1978, 29376-77); and the Swedish Social Democrats in Erlander III, which was the SAP's first postwar coalition with the Center Party (*Keesing's* 1951, 11780).

There are signs of autocorrelation in this estimation (*d*-statistic = 1.38, first-order autocorrelation = 0.31). Inspection of the residuals suggests, however, that the problem reflects country attributes (the interactive terms for the structure of the party system) more than time trends. The same inference is supported when the model is estimated separately for each country, as in the rightmost column of Table 8.7.

13. In the cross-national analysis here I do not use the leading value of crisis duration (with cases before elections omitted) as an indirect measure of the bargaining costs of breaking coalitions. I did use that measure in Chapter 5, however. For Italy, omitting cases before parliamentary elections results in a non-negligible subset of governments that have fallen due to party choice. For no other country in this study, save France, does that statement hold true.

14. Again, note that the variable marking a bipolar system is equivalent to a dummy for Germany.

15. I sorted early elections into the two categories by coding contemporary media commentary found in *Keesing's* and the subsidiary sources named in Appendix D. Seeking to circumvent the most difficult judgment calls in coding (cf. Smith 1996, 106), I looked for explicit mentions of transparent maneuvers for advantage. Such "transparency" is exemplified in the following coverage: In spring 1989 the Irish Premier Charles Haughey dissolved the Dáil and called early elections "in an attempt . . . to take advantage of his Fianna Fáil party's high standing in the opinion polls and to secure a working majority in the Dáil, a feat that has eluded him in four previous elections" (*The Times*, May 26, 1989).

16. Article 51 of the Fourth Republic's constitution "allowed the cabinet to dissolve [the Assembly] . . . when two crises had occurred within eighteen months, provided: first that both governments were constitutionally defeated under Article 49 or 50 by an absolute majority on a vote of confidence or censure; secondly, under Article 45, that they were more than two weeks old; and thirdly that the Assembly that defeated them was over eighteen months old" (Williams 1966, 250). Article 52 required that a caretaker govern between the dissolution and early elections and specified that the caretaker be headed by the president of the Assembly and be composed of "new ministers without portfolio from all groups unrepresented in the [outgoing] government" (ibid.). These caretaker requirements were removed in the November 1954 constitutional amendments.

17. Early elections were also held in June 1951, after the National Assembly had voted its own premature dissolution in May (MacRae 1967, 85-87). The widely shared expectation that the executive would not dissolve the legislature in the Fourth Republic may have been reinforced by the informal rule against early dissolutions that developed in the Third Republic (Williams 1966, 249).

18. The omitted category is of course composed of governments not taking office in the wake of an election.

CHAPTER 9

1. For information on the party composition of the legislature and of governments during the Second Republic, I consulted not only Linz (1978b) but also Payne (1993), Preston (1994), Ruiz Manjón (1976), Tusell (1982), and Varela Díaz (1978). Incredible as it may seem, definitive data on the 1931–36 composition of the Spanish legislature (the *Cortes*) do not exist, given the extreme fluidity of the Second Republic's party system and the spotty official record-keeping characteristic of the *Cortes* at the time. My thanks to Gerard Alexander and Kerstin Hamann for guiding me through the relevant literature.

2. Even such a sharp-eyed observer of Italian politics as Stephen Hellman has affirmed that in "Italian cabinets . . . there are roughly thirty ministers [and] . . . two subministers (undersecretaries) for each [ministerial] portfolio" (Hellman, 1992b, 390). Figure 5.1 shows just how wrong that statement is. Note also that I differ with Sartori on several salient points, in part because I have the advantage of writing in 2000, not 1976. I emphasize the long-standing electoral (and governmental) stability of the DC, rather than centrifugal drives. In my view, the categorization of the Communists (PCI) as an antisystem party was inaccurate by the 1970s. I believe it useful to characterize the Italian party system, along with the Dutch and several others, as two dimensional.

3. On the failures of the Bicameral Committee on Constitutional Reform in the late 1990s, see Pasquino 1999. It is of course beyond the scope of this book to probe the sources of change in democratic party systems.

4. The details can of course be found in the works just cited in the text. It is worth specifying here that, due to data limitations, my study of factional politics is restricted to the nineteen governments that ruled Italy between 1963 and 1979.

5. Note that for this logic to work, politicians must be assumed not only to perceive qualitative differences among cabinet posts but also to view the aggregate value of the cabinet as fixed. As Chapter 5 discussed, memoranda surviving from coalition negotiations suggest that Italian politicians used two yardsticks to measure the aggregate value of the cabinet; they understood the value of the cabinet to be both variable (counting up the value added by new portfolios) and fixed (computing cabinet shares, in which new posts dilute the worth of old ones).

6. For classic studies in the vast literature on the U.S. Congress and its committees, see Polsby (1968); Polsby, Gallagher, and Rundquist (1969); Shepsle (1978); and Wilson (1885 [1958]); for recent overviews and assessments, see Deering and Smith (1997) and Dodd and Oppenheimer (1997); for comparisons between the United States and other countries, see Polsby (1975) and Steinmo (1993).

7. As Cox and McCubbins (1993, 22) observe, to embrace these expectations is to "*assume* that the party leadership has substantial influence over appointments and is interested in securing the loyalty of members" (emphasis in original). Cox and McCubbins defend just these assumptions.

8. On corruption in Italy, see, e.g., Cazzola 1992; della Porta 1992, 1993, 1997; Ricolfi 1993b; on corruption in the 1980s as unusually extensive, see Barca 1994; Barca and Trento 1994; della Porta and Vannucci 1995, 1996.

9. A second way to appraise long-run consequences is to reconsider the direc-

tion of causality and probe for feedback effects. Appendix F shows that the hypothesis about feedback effects should be rejected for all of the countries under examination here.

10. The updated and revised data sets on parties' policy positions mentioned in Chapter 6 are not yet available as this book goes to press (Budge et al. n.d.; Laver n.d.). They also promise to make vital contributions.

APPENDIX F

1. My thanks to an anonymous reviewer for the *American Political Science Review* for pushing me on this point.

2. To elaborate: Regressing government duration on a counter (CT_g) that increases with each successive postwar government produces insignificant coefficients for CT_g for all ten countries, positive coefficients for CT_g for five countries (including Italy), relatively high standard errors of the estimate for all ten countries, and very low R^2 values for all ten countries. (The *highest* R^2 produced by this model, for Norway, was 0.087.)

3. For details confirming these statements, readers can refer to Table 5.9 (on bargaining costs), Tables 5.2 and 5.5 (electoral costs), and Figure 5.3 (policy costs). It is also worth noting that regressing crisis duration (B_g, bargaining costs in days) on a counter (CT_g) that increases with each successive postwar Italian government yields the result

$$B_g = 15.7 + 0.5 \ CT_g$$
where $R^2 = .24$; $n = 52$; coefficient for CT_g significant at the .001 level.

Regressing the distance between DC platforms and government programs (P_{DC}, policy costs for the DC) on the counter yields the result

$$P_{DCg} = 10.8 - 0.13 \ CT_g$$
where $R^2 = .04$; $n = 38$.

Adding to this model a dummy variable coded 1 when the government whose predecessor was a cabinet the DC helped to topple (RF_{DCg-1}) produces insignificant coefficients and an even lower R^2:

$$P_{DCg} = 10.5 - 0.13 \ CT_g + 0.64 \ RF_{DCg-1}$$
where adj. $R^2 = .01$; $n = 38$.

4. To continue the logic of notes 2 and 3, regressing the number of Christian Democratic ministers (O_{DCg}), DC junior ministers (o_{DCg}), all ministers (O_g), and all junior ministers (o_g) on the now-familiar counter gives the following results:

$$O_{DCg} = 14.9 + 0.06 \ CT_g$$
where $R^2 = .04$; $n = 52$

$$o_{DCg} = 22.5 + 0.33 \ CT_g$$
where $R^2 = .27$; $n = 52$; coefficient for CT_g significant at the .001 level

$O_g = 17.3 + 0.25\ CT_g$
where $R^2 = .72$; $n = 52$; coefficient for CT_g significant at the .001 level

$o_g = 23.0 + 0.77\ CT_g$
where $R^2 = .69$; $n = 52$; coefficient for CT_g significant at the .001 level.

5. A clear diagonal band (for model F.1) or several diagonal bands (for models F.2 and F.3) in the array of residuals, with the higher values appearing to the right of the band(s), would constitute plausible evidence of feedback effects.

References

Adams, John Clarke, and Paolo Barile. 1961. *The Government of Republican Italy.* Boston: Houghton Mifflin.

Akalin, Oguz. 1992. *Die Bundesregierung Wird Vorgestellt. Staatsminister, Parlamentarische Staatssekretäre und Staatssekretäre der Bundesregierung sowie des Bundespräsidialamtes.* Bonn: Inter Nationes Press.

Alexander, David. 1990. "L'inquinamento e le politiche per l'ambiente." In Raimondo Catanzaro and Filippo Sabetti, eds., *Politica in Italia. I fatti dell'anno e le interpretazioni. Edizione 90.* Bologna: Il Mulino.

Allum, P. A. 1973. *Italy — Republic Without Government?* New York: Norton.

Anckar, Dag. 1992. "Finland: Dualism and Consensual Rule." In Erik Damgaard, ed., *Parliamentary Change in the Nordic Countries.* Oslo: Scandinavian University Press.

Anderson, Christopher. 1995. *Blaming the Government: Citizens and the Economy in Five European Democracies.* Armonk, N.Y.: M. E. Sharpe.

Andeweg, Rudy B. 1988. "The Netherlands: Coalition Cabinets in Changing Circumstances." In Jean Blondel and Ferdinand Müller-Rommel, eds., *Cabinets in Western Europe.* New York: St. Martin's.

Andeweg, Rudy B., and Wilma Bakema. 1994. "The Netherlands: Ministers and Cabinet Policy." In Michael Laver and Kenneth A. Shepsle, eds., *Cabinet Ministers and Parliamentary Government.* Cambridge: Cambridge University Press.

Andeweg, Rudy B., and Galen A. Irwin. 1993. *Dutch Government and Politics.* London: MacMillan.

Andrén, Nils. 1968. *Modern Swedish Government.* 2nd ed. Stockholm: Almqvist and Wiksell.

Andreotti, Giulio. 1981. *Diari 1976–1979. Gli anni della solidarietà.* Milan: Rizzoli.

Arné, Serge. 1962. *Le Président du Conseil des Ministres sous la Quatrième République.* Paris: Librairie Générale de Droit et de Jurisprudence.

Arter, David. 1987. *Politics and Policy-Making in Finland.* New York: St. Martin's.

Austen-Smith, David, and Jeffrey Banks. 1988. "Elections, Coalitions, and Legislative Outcomes." *American Political Science Review* 82, no. 2 (June): 405–22.

———. 1990. "Stable Governments and the Allocation of Policy Portfolios." *American Political Science Review* 84, no. 3 (September): 891–906.

Axelrod, Robert. 1970. *Conflict of Interest: A Theory of Divergent Goals with Applications to Politics.* Chicago: Markham.

Baker, Kendall L., Russell J. Dalton, and Kai Hildebrandt. 1981. *Germany Transformed: Political Culture and the New Politics.* Cambridge: Harvard University Press.

Balboni, Enzo. 1988. "I nodi istituzionali di una difficile crisi di governo." In Piergiorgio Corbetta and Robert Leonardi, eds., *Politica in Italia. I fatti dell'anno e le interpretazioni. Edizione 88.* Bologna: Il Mulino.

Baldassarre, Antonio. 1985. "Le 'performances' del Parlamento italiano nell'ultimo quindicennio." In Gianfranco Pasquino, ed., *Il sistema politico italiano.* Bari: Laterza.

Barca, Luciano. 1994. "La patologia degli anni Ottanta." In Luciano Barca and Sandro Trento, eds., *L'economia della corruzione.* Bari: Laterza.

Barca, Luciano, and Sandro Trento, eds. 1994. *L'economia della corruzione.* Bari: Laterza.

Barnes, Samuel H. 1974. "Italy: Religion and Class in Electoral Behavior." In Richard Rose, ed., *Electoral Behavior: A Comparative Handbook.* New York: Free Press.

———. 1977. *Representation in Italy: Institutionalized Tradition and Electoral Choice.* Chicago: University of Chicago Press.

———. 1984. "Secular Trends and Partisan Realignment in Italy." In Russell J. Dalton, Scott C. Flanagan, Paul Allen Beck, eds., *Electoral Change in Advanced Industrial Democracies.* Princeton: Princeton University Press.

Baron, David P. 1991. "A Spatial Theory of Government Formation in Parliamentary Systems." *American Political Science Review* 85, no. 1 (March): 137–64.

Baron, David P., and John A. Ferejohn. 1989. "Bargaining in Legislatures." *American Political Science Review* 83, no. 4 (December): 1181–206.

Barrera, Pietro. 1989. "La prima riforma istituzionale. La nuova disciplina dell'attività di governo." In Raimondo Catanzaro and Raffaella Y. Nanetti, eds., *Politica in Italia. I fatti dell'anno e le interpretazioni. Edizione 89.* Bologna: Il Mulino.

Bartolini, Stefano, and Peter Mair. 1990. *Identity, Competition, and Electoral Availability: The Stabilization of European Electorates 1885–1985.* Cambridge: Cambridge University Press.

Bates, Robert H. 1997. "Comparative Politics and Rational Choice: A Review Essay." *American Political Science Review* 91, no. 3 (September): 699–704.

Bates, Robert H., Rui J. P. de Figueiredo, and Barry Weingast. 1998. "The Politics of Interpretations: Rationality, Culture, and Transition." *Politics and Society,* 26, no. 4 (December): 603–42.

Bates, Robert H., Avner Greif, Margaret Levi, Jean-Laurent Rosenthal, and Barry R. Weingast. 1998. *Analytic Narratives.* Princeton: Princeton University Press.

Beccaria, Gian Luigi. 1988. *Italiano. Antico e nuovo.* Milan: Garzanti.

Bellucci, Paolo. 1984. "The Effect of Aggregate Economic Conditions on the Political Preferences of the Italian Electorate, 1953–1979." *European Journal of Political Research* 12, no. 4 (December): 387–401.

———. 1985. "Economic Concerns in Italian Electoral Behavior: Toward a Rational Electorate?" In Heinz Eulau and Michael S. Lewis-Beck, eds., *Economic Conditions and Electoral Outcomes: The United States and Western Europe.* New York: Agathon.

———. 1991. "Italian Economic Voting: A Deviant Case or Making a Case for a Better Theory?" In Helmut Norpoth, Michael Lewis-Beck, and Jean-Dominique

Lafay, eds., *Economics and Politics: The Calculus of Support*. Ann Arbor: University of Michigan Press.

Bergman, Torbjörn. 1995. *Constitutional Rules and Party Goals in Coalition Formation: An Analysis of Winning Minority Governments in Sweden*. Umeå, Sweden: Umeå University.

Berry, William D., and Stanley Feldman. 1985. *Multiple Regression in Practice*. Sage University Paper Series on Quantitative Applications in the Social Sciences, 07–050. Newbury Park, Calif.: Sage.

Black, Duncan. 1948. "On the Rationale of Group Decision Making." *Journal of Political Economy* 56, no. 1 (February): 23–34.

———. 1958. *The Theory of Committees and Elections*. Cambridge: Cambridge University Press.

Blais, André, Donald Blake, and Stéphane Dion. 1993. "Do Parties Make a Difference? Parties and the Size of Government in Liberal Democracies." *American Journal of Political Science* 37, no. 1 (February): 40–62.

———. 1996. "Do Parties Make a Difference? A Reappraisal." *American Journal of Political Science* 40, no. 2 (May): 514–20.

Boix, Carles. 1997. "Political Parties and the Supply Side of the Economy: The Provision of Physical and Human Capital in Advanced Economies, 1960–90." *American Journal of Political Science* 41, no. 3 (July): 814–45.

Bonaccorsi, Marina. 1979. "Gli enti pubblici del settore della sicurezza sociale." In Franco Cazzola, ed., *Anatomia del potere DC. Enti pubblici e 'centralità democristiana'*. Bari: De Donato.

Bonini, Francesco. 1996. *Storia della Corte Costituzionale*. Rome: La Nuova Italia Scientifica.

Borre, Ole. 1984. "Critical Electoral Change in Scandinavia." In Russell J. Dalton, Scott C. Flanagan, and Paul Allen Beck, eds., *Electoral Change in Advanced Industrial Democracies*. Princeton: Princeton University Press.

———. 1992. "Denmark." In Mark N. Franklin, Thomas T. Mackie, and Henry Valen, eds., *Electoral Change: Responses to Evolving Social and Attitudinal Structures in Western Countries*. Cambridge: Cambridge University Press.

Bottiglieri, Bruno. 1984. *La politica economica dell'Italia centrista (1948–1958)*. Milan: Edizioni di Comunità.

Bowler, Shaun, David M. Farrell, and Richard S. Katz, eds. 1999. *Party Discipline and Parliamentary Government*. Columbus: Ohio State University Press.

Braunthal, Gerard. 1994. *The German Social Democrats Since 1969: A Party in Power and Opposition*. 2nd ed. Boulder, Colo.: Westview.

Browne, Eric C. 1973. *Coalition Theories: A Logical and Empirical Critique*. Beverly Hills: Sage.

Browne, Eric C., and Mark Franklin. 1973. "Aspects of Coalition Payoffs in European Parliamentary Democracies." *American Political Science Review* 67, no. 2 (June): 453–69.

Browne, Eric C., and John P. Frendreis. 1980. "Allocating Coalition Payoffs by Conventional Norm: An Assessment of the Evidence from Cabinet Coalition Situations." *American Journal of Political Science* 24, no. 4 (November): 753–68.

Browne, Eric C., John P. Frendreis, and Dennis W. Gleiber. 1986. "The Process of

Cabinet Dissolution: An Exponential Model of Duration and Stability in West-ern Democracies." *American Journal of Political Science* 30, no. 3 (August): 628–50.

———. 1988. "Contending Models of Cabinet Stability: Rejoinder." *American Political Science Review* 82, no. 3 (September): 930–41.

Browne, Eric C., Dennis W. Gleiber, and Carolyn S. Mashoba. 1984. "Evaluating Conflict of Interest Theory: Western European Cabinet Coalitions, 1945–80." *British Journal of Political Science* 14, no. 1 (January): 1–32.

Budge, Ian. 2000. "Expert Judgements of Party Policy Positions: Uses and Limita-tions in Political Research." *European Journal of Political Research* 37, no. 1 (January): 103–13.

Budge, Ian, and Hans Keman. 1990. *Parties and Democracy: Coalition Formation and Government Functioning in Twenty States*. Oxford: Oxford University Press.

Budge, Ian, Hans-Dieter Klingemann, Andrea Volkens, and Judith Bark. n.d. *Map-ping Policy Preferences: Estimates for Parties, Electors, and Governments 1945–98*. Oxford: Oxford University Press, forthcoming.

Budge, Ian, and Michael Laver. 1992. "The Relationship between Party and Coali-tion Policy in Europe: An Empirical Synthesis." In Michael Laver and Ian Budge, eds., *Party Policy and Government Coalitions*. London: St. Martin's.

Budge, Ian, David Robertson, and Derek Hearl, eds. 1987. *Ideology, Strategy and Party Change: Spatial Analyses of Post-War Election Programmes in 19 Democ-racies*. Cambridge: Cambridge University Press.

Buonadonna, Sergio, and Roberto Ginex. 1994. *Guida alla Seconda Repubblica*. Palermo: Edizioni Arbor.

Caciagli, Mario. 1985. "Il resistibile declino della Democrazia cristiana." In Gian-franco Pasquino, ed., *Il sistema politico italiano*. Bari: Laterza.

———. 1988. "Quante Italie? Persistenza e trasformazione delle culture politiche subnazionali." *Polis* 2 (December): 429–57.

———. 1990. "Il XVIII congresso della Dc. La fine del settennato di De Mita e l'af-fermazione del neodoroteismo." In Raimondo Catanzaro and Filippo Sabetti, eds., *Politica in Italia. I fatti dell'anno e le interpretazioni. Edizione 90*. Bologna: Il Mulino.

Caciagli, Mario, and Alberto Spreafico, eds. 1990. *Vent'anni di elezioni in Italia. 1968–1987*. Padua: Liviana.

Calise, Mauro, and Renato Mannheimer. 1982. *Governanti in Italia. Un trentennio repubblicano, 1946–1976*. Bologna: Il Mulino.

Camera dei Deputati, Servizio Studi. 1998a. "Modifiche nella composizione del Governo Prodi." http://www.camera.it/camera/composiz/governo/modcomp .htm. Last accessed May 13, 1998.

———. 1998b. "I [Primo] Governo D'Alema (21 ottobre 1998)." http://www.camera .it/camera/composiz/governo/composiz.htm. Last accessed October 23, 1998.

———. 1999a. "Composizione della Camera. Modifiche nella composizione dei grup-pi." http://www.camera.it/deputati/composizione/01.camera/gruppiparlamentari _modifiche.asp. Last accessed September 17, 1999.

————. 1999b. "Il rapporto con il Governo: Crisi del Governo Prodi." http://
www.camera.it/attivita/rapporto/governoecamera_crisiprodi.asp. Last accessed
July 15, 1999.

————. 2000. "Composizione della Camera. Modifiche nella composizione dei grup-
pi." http://www.camera.it/deputati/composizione/01.camera/gruppiparlamentari_
modifiche.asp. Last accessed August 7, 2000.

Cameron, David R. 1978. "The Expansion of the Public Economy: A Comparative
Analysis." *American Political Science Review* 72, no. 4 (December): 1243–61.

Campbell, Donald T., and Julian C. Stanley. 1966. *Experimental and Quasi-
Experimental Designs for Research*. Chicago: Rand McNally.

Caprara, Maurizio. 1989. "Le cinque correnti del mare Dc." *Corriere della Sera*,
February 14.

Cartocci, Roberto. 1994. *Fra Lega e Chiesa. L'Italia in cerca di integrazione*.
Bologna: Il Mulino.

————. 1997. "Indizi di un inverno precoce. Il voto proporzionale tra equilibrio e
continuità." In Roberto D'Alimote and Stefano Bartolini, ed., *Maggioritario per
caso*. Bologna: Il Mulino.

Cassese, Sabino. 1980. "Is There a Government in Italy? Politics and Administration at the Top." In Richard Rose and Ezra N. Suleiman, eds., *Presidents and
Prime Ministers*. Washington, D.C.: American Enterprise Institute.

————. 1983. *Il sistema amministrativo italiano*. Bologna: Il Mulino.

————. 1985. "Esiste un governo in Italia?" In Gianfranco Pasquino, ed., *Il sistema
politico italiano*. Bari: Laterza.

————. 1988. "Italy." In Donald C. Rowat, ed., *Public Administration in Developed Democracies: A Comparative Study*. New York: M. Dekker.

————. 1993. "Hypotheses on the Italian Administrative System." *West European
Politics* 16, no. 3 (July): 316–28.

Casstevens, Thomas W. 1989. "The Circulation of Elites: A Review and Critique of
a Class of Models." *American Journal of Political Science* 33, no. 1 (February):
294–317.

Castles, Francis G., and Rudolf Wildenmann, eds. 1986. *Visions and Realities of
Party Government*. Berlin: de Gruyter.

Catanzaro, Raimondo, and Raffaella Y. Nanetti, eds. 1989. *Politica in Italia. I fatti
dell'anno e le interpretazioni. Edizione 89*. Bologna: Il Mulino.

Cazzola, Franco. 1976. "I pilastri del regime. Gli enti pubblici di sicurezza sociale."
Rassegna italiana di sociologia 17 (July–September): 421–47.

————, ed. 1979. *Anatomia del potere DC. Enti pubblici e 'centralità democristiana'*. Bari: De Donato.

————. 1985. "Struttura e potere del Partito socialista italiano." In Gianfranco
Pasquino, ed., *Il sistema politico italiano*. Bari: Laterza.

————. 1992. *L'Italia del pizzo. Fenomenologia della tangente quotidiana*. Turin:
Einaudi.

Cazzola, Franco, and Elio Rossitto. 1979. "Introduzione. Per un'analisi dell'ege-
monia democristiana." In Franco Cazzola, ed., *Anatomia del potere DC. Enti
pubblici e 'centralità democristiana'*. Bari: De Donato.

Cerase, Francesco Paolo. 1990. *Un'amministrazione bloccata. Pubblica amministrazione e società nell'Italia di oggi*. Milan: Franco Angeli.

Ceri, Paolo. 1987. "Dopo Cernobyl. Il 'nucleare' come nuova frattura nella politica e nella società italiana." In Piergiorgio Corbetta and Robert Leonardi, eds., *Politica in Italia. I fatti dell'anno e le interpretazioni. Edizione 87*. Bologna: Il Mulino.

Chassériaud, Jean-Paul. 1965. *Le Parti Démocrate Chrétien en Italie*. Paris: Armand Colin.

Cheli, Enzo. 1978. *Costituzione e sviluppo delle istituzioni in Italia*. Bologna: Il Mulino.

Cioffi-Revilla, Claudio. 1984. "The Political Reliability of Italian Governments: An Exponential Survival Model." *American Political Science Review* 78, no. 2 (June): 318–37.

Cleveland, William S. 1979. "Robust Locally Weighted Regression and Smoothing Scatterplots." *Journal of the American Statistical Association* 74, no. 368 (December): 829–36.

———. 1981. "LOWESS: A Program for Smoothing Scatterplots." *American Statistician* 35, no. 1 (February): 54.

Cole, Taylor. 1959. "Three Constitutional Courts: A Comparison." *American Political Science Review*, 53, no. 4 (December): 963–84.

Collier, David. 1999. "Letter from the President: Data, Field Work, and Extracting New Ideas at Close Range." *APSA-CP* 10, no. 1 (Winter): 1–2, 4–6.

Colombo, Gherardo. 1990. "Il nuovo codice di procedura penale." In Raimondo Catanzaro and Filippo Sabetti, eds. *Politica in Italia. I fatti dell'anno e le interpretazioni. Edizione 90*. Bologna: Il Mulino.

Corbetta, Piergiorgio, Arturo M. L. Parisi, and Hans M. A. Schadee. 1988. *Elezioni in Italia. Struttura e tipologia delle consultazioni politiche*. Bologna: Il Mulino.

Cotta, Maurizio. 1988. "Italy: A Fragmented Government." In Jean Blondel and Ferdinand Müller-Rommel, eds., *Cabinets in Western Europe*. New York: St. Martin's.

———. 1994. "The Rise and Fall of the 'Centrality' of the Italian Parliament: Transformations of the Executive-Legislative Subsystem after the Second World War." In Gary W. Copeland and Samuel C. Patterson, eds., *Parliaments in the Modern World: Changing Institutions*. Ann Arbor: University of Michigan Press.

———. 1995. "Il Parlamento nella Prima Repubblica." In Gianfranco Pasquino, ed., *La politica italiana. Dizionario critico 1945–95*. Rome: Laterza.

Covell, Maureen. 1981. "Ethnic Conflict and Elite Bargaining: The Case of Belgium." *West European Politics* 4, no. 3 (October): 197–218.

———. 1982. "Agreeing to Disagree: Elite Bargaining and the Revision of the Belgian Constitution." *Canadian Journal of Political Science* 15, no. 3 (September): 451–69.

Cox, Gary W. 1987. *The Efficient Secret: The Cabinet and the Development of Political Parties in Victorian England*. Cambridge: Cambridge University Press.

Cox, Gary W., and Matthew McCubbins. 1993. *Legislative Leviathan: Party Government in the House*. Berkeley: University of California Press.

Criscitiello, Annarita. 1993. "Majority Summits: Decision-Making Inside the Cabinet and Out: Italy, 1970–1990." *West European Politics* 16, no. 4 (October): 518–94.

———. 1994. "The Political Role of Cabinet Ministers in Italy." In Michael Laver and Kenneth A. Shepsle, eds., *Cabinet Ministers and Parliamentary Government*. Cambridge: Cambridge University Press.

Daalder, Hans. 1966. "The Netherlands: Opposition in a Segmented Society." In Robert A. Dahl, ed., *Political Oppositions in Western Democracies*. New Haven: Yale University Press.

———. 1987. "The Dutch Party System: From Segmentation to Polarization—and Then?" In Hans Daalder, ed., *Party Systems in Denmark, Austria, Switzerland, the Netherlands and Belgium*. New York: St. Martin's.

D'Alimonte, Roberto, and Stefano Bartolini. 1995. "Il sistema partitico italiano. Una transizione difficile." In Stefano Bartolini and Roberto D'Alimonte, eds., *Maggioritario ma non troppo*. Bologna: Il Mulino.

———, eds. 1997. *Maggioritario per caso*. Bologna: Il Mulino.

Dalton, Russell J. 1984. "The West German Party System Between Two Ages." In Russell J. Dalton, Scott C. Flanagan, and Paul Allen Beck, eds., *Electoral Change in Advanced Industrial Democracies*. Princeton: Princeton University Press.

Dalton, Russell J., Paul Allen Beck, and Scott C. Flanagan. 1984. "Electoral Change in Advanced Industrial Democracies." In Russell J. Dalton, Paul Allen Beck, and Scott C. Flanagan, eds. *Electoral Change in Advanced Industrial Democracies*. Princeton: Princeton University Press.

———. 1988. *Citizen Politics in Western Democracies*. Chatham, N.J.: Chatham House.

Damgaard, Erik. 1992. "Denmark: Experiments in Parliamentary Government." In Erik Damgaard, ed., *Parliamentary Change in the Nordic Countries*. Oslo: Scandinavian University Press.

———. 1994. "The Strong Parliaments of Scandinavia: Continuity and Change of Scandinavian Parliaments." In Gary W. Copeland and Samuel C. Patterson, eds., *Parliaments in the Modern World: Changing Institutions*. Ann Arbor: University of Michigan Press.

De Cecco, Marcello. 1989. "Keynes and Italian Economics." In Peter A. Hall, ed., *The Political Power of Economic Ideas: Keynesianism across Nations*. Princeton: Princeton University Press.

Deering, Christopher J., and Steven S. Smith. 1997. *Committees in Congress*. 3rd ed. Washington, D.C.: Congressional Quarterly Press.

della Cananea, Giacinto. 1996. "Administrative Reform in Italy." *West European Politics* 19, no. 2 (April): 321–39.

della Porta, Donatella. 1992. *Lo scambio occulto. Casi di corruzione politica in Italia*. Bologna: Il Mulino.

———. 1993. "La capitale immorale. Le tangenti di Milano." In Stephen Hellman and Gianfranco Pasquino, eds., *Politica in Italia. I fatti dell'anno e le interpretazioni. Edizione 93*. Bologna: Il Mulino.

———. 1997. "The Vicious Circles of Corruption in Italy." In Donatella della Porta and Yves Mény, eds., *Democracy and Corruption in Europe*. London: Pinter.

della Porta, Donatella, and Alberto Vannucci. 1995. "Politics, the Mafia, and the Market for Corrupt Exchange." In Carol Mershon and Gianfranco Pasquino, eds., *Italian Politics: Ending the First Republic*. Boulder, Colo.: Westview.

———. 1996. "Controlling Political Corruption in Italy: What Did Not Work, What Can Be Done." *Res Publica* 38 (2): 353–70.

Della Sala, Vincent. 1987. "Governare per decreto. Il governo Craxi e l'uso dei decreti-legge." In Piergiorgio Corbetta and Robert Leonardi, eds., *Politica in Italia. I fatti dell'anno e le interpretazioni. Edizione 87*. Bologna: Il Mulino.

De Mucci, Raffaele. 1990. "L'area dei partiti laici fra flussi e riflussi." In Mario Caciagli and Alberto Spreafico, eds., *Vent'anni di elezioni in Italia. 1968–1987*. Padua: Liviana.

Dente, Bruno, ed. 1990. *Le politiche pubbliche in Italia*. Bologna: Il Mulino.

———. 1991. "Politica, istituzioni e deficit pubblico." *Stato e Mercato*, no. 33 (December): 339–70.

Dente, Bruno, and Gloria Regonini. 1987. "Politica e politiche in Italia." In Peter Lange and Marino Regini, eds., *Stato e regolazione sociale. Nuove prospettive sul caso italiano*. Bologna: Il Mulino.

Departementshistoriekommittén. 1990. *Att styra riket. Regeringskanliet 1840–1990*. Stockholm: Uddevalla Bohuslähgen.

De Ridder, Martine, and Luis Ricardo Fraga. 1986. "The Brussels Issue in Belgian Politics." *West European Politics* 9, no. 3 (July): 376–92.

Deruette, Serge. 1994. "Belgium." *European Journal of Political Research* 26, no. 3/4 (December): 247–54.

De Swaan, Abram. 1973. *Coalition Theories and Cabinet Formations*. Amsterdam: Elsevier.

de Vries, Miranda W. M. 1999. "Computer-Based Content Analysis on the Party Manifestos of the 1998 Dutch Elections." Paper presented at the 1999 Joint Sessions of the European Consortium for Political Research, Mannheim, Germany.

Dewachter, Wilfried. 1987. "Changes in a Particratie: The Belgian Party System form 1944 to 1986." In Hans Daalder, ed., *Party Systems in Denmark, Austria, Switzerland, the Netherlands and Belgium*. New York: St. Martin's.

Di Palma, Giuseppe. 1977. *Surviving Without Governing*. Berkeley: University of California Press.

———. 1979. "The Available State: Problems of Reform." *West European Politics* 2, no. 3 (October):149–65.

Di Scala, Spencer M. 1988. *Renewing Italian Socialism: Nenni to Craxi*. Oxford: University of Oxford Press.

Djupe, Paul A., and Lee Epstein. 1998. "From Schubert's *The Judicial Mind* to Spaeth's *U.S. Supreme Court Judicial Data Base*: A Crossvalidation." *American Journal of Political Science* 42, no. 43 (July): 1012–19.

Dodd, Lawrence C. 1974. "Party Coalitions in Multiparty Parliaments: A Game-Theoretic Analysis." *American Political Science Review* 68, no. 3 (September): 1093–117.

———. 1976. *Coalitions in Parliamentary Government*. Princeton: Princeton University Press.

Dodd, Lawrence C., and Bruce I. Oppenheimer, eds. 1997. *Congress Reconsidered*. 6th ed. Washington, D.C.: Congressional Quarterly Press.

Dogan, Mattei. 1984. "Come si diventa ministro in Italia. Le regole non scritte del gioco politico." In Centro studi P. Farneti, ed., *Il sistema politico italiano tra crisi e innovazione*. Milan: Franco Angeli.

Donolo, Carlo. 1980. "Social Change and Transformation of the State in Italy." In Richard Scase, ed. *The State in Western Europe*. London: Croom Helm.

Donovan, Mark. 1988. "The 1987 Election in Italy: Prelude to Reform?" *West European Politics* 11, no. 1 (January): 126–32.

———. 1996. "A Turning Point that Turned? The April 1996 General Election in Italy." *West European Politics* 19, no. 4 (October): 805–12.

Döring, Herbert, ed. 1995. *Parliaments and Majority Rule in Western Europe*. New York: St. Martin's.

Downs, William M. 1996. "Federalism Achieved: The Belgian Elections of May 1995." *West European Politics* 19, no. 1 (January): 168–75.

———. 1998. *Coalition Government Subnational Style: Multiparty Politics in Europe's Regional Parliaments*. Columbus: Ohio State University Press.

Elia, Leopoldo. 1973. "La forma di governo dell'Italia repubblicana." In Paolo Farneti, ed. *Il sistema politico italiano*. Bologna: Il Mulino. First published in *Enciclopedia del Diritto*, Vol. 19 (Milan: Giuffré, 1969).

Epstein, Lee. 1995. "Conducting Research on Law and Courts: Sources of Data." Appendix C in Lee Epstein, ed., *Contemplating Courts*. Washington, D.C.: CQ Press.

Epstein, Lee, and Jack Knight. 1998. *The Choices Justices Make*. Washington, D.C.: Congressional Quarterly Press.

Epstein, Lee, and Carol Mershon. 1996. "Measuring Political Preferences." *American Journal of Political Science* 40, no. 1 (February): 261–94.

Epstein, Lee, Jeffrey A. Segal, Harold J. Spaeth, and Thomas G. Walker. 1996. *The Supreme Court Compendium: Data, Decisions, and Developments*. 2nd ed. Washington, D.C.: CQ Press.

———. 2001. *The Supreme Court Compendium*. 3rd ed. Washington, D.C.: CQ Press.

Eriksen, Svein. 1988. "Norway: Ministerial Autonomy and Collective Responsibility." In Jean Blondel and Ferdinand Müller-Rommel, eds., *Cabinets in Western Europe*. New York: St. Martin's.

Eulau, Heinz, and Michael S. Lewis-Beck, eds. 1985. *Economic Conditions and Electoral Outcomes: The United States and Western Europe*. New York: Agathon.

Europa Year Book. 1959–. London: Europa Publications.

Farneti, Paolo. 1983. *Il sistema dei partiti in Italia 1946–1979*. Bologna: Il Mulino.

Farrell, Brian. 1994. "The Political Role of Cabinet Ministers in Ireland." In Michael Laver and Kenneth A. Shepsle, eds., *Cabinet Ministers and Parliamentary Government*. Cambridge: Cambridge University Press.

Farrell, Brian, and David M. Farrell. 1987. "The General Election of 1987." In Howard Penniman and Brian Farrell, eds., *Ireland at the Polls 1981, 1982, and*

1987: A Study of Four General Elections. Durham, N.C.: Duke University Press/American Enterprise Institute.

Ferejohn, John A. 1991. "Rationality and Interpretation: Parliamentary Elections in Early Stuart England." In Kristen Renwick Monroe, ed., *The Economic Approach to Politics.* New York: Harper Collins.

Ferrera, Maurizio. 1982. "Crescita da domanda o crescita da offerta? Un'analisi delle spese sociali in Italia." *Rivista italiana di scienza politica* 12, no. 2 (August): 297–331.

———. 1989. "Le politiche pubbliche." In Leonardo Morlino, ed., *Scienza politica.* Turin: Fondazione Giovanni Agnelli.

FitzGerald, Garret. 1991. *All in a Life.* Dublin: Gill and Macmillan.

Fitzmaurice, John. 1983. *The Politics of Belgium: Crisis and Compromise in a Plural Society.* London: Hurst.

———. 1996. *The Politics of Belgium: A Unique Federalism.* Boulder and London: Westview and Hurst.

Floridia, Giuseppe G. 1995. "La Costituzione." In Gianfranco Pasquino, ed., *La politica italiana. Dizionario critico 1945–95.* Bari: Laterza.

Follini, Marco. 1990. *L'arcipelago democristiano.* Bari: Laterza.

Franklin, Mark N. and Thomas T. Mackie. 1983. "Familiarity and Inertia in the Formation of Governing Coalitions in Parliamentary Democracies." *British Journal of Political Science* 13, no. 3 (July): 275–98.

———. 1984. "Reassessing the Importance of Size and Ideology for the Formation of Governing Coalitions in Parliamentary Democracies." *American Journal of Political Science* 28, no. 4 (November): 671–92.

Franklin, Mark N., Thomas T. Mackie, and Henry Valen, eds. 1992. *Electoral Change: Responses to Evolving Social and Attitudinal Structures in Western Countries.* Cambridge: Cambridge University Press.

Franzosi, Roberto. 1995. *The Puzzle of Strikes: Class and State Strategies in Postwar Italy.* Cambridge: Cambridge University Press.

Frognier, André-Paul. 1988. "Belgium." In Jean Blondel and Ferdinand Müller-Rommel, eds., *Cabinets in Western Europe.* New York: St. Martin's.

Gabel, Matthew J., and John D. Huber. 2000. "Putting Parties in Their Place: Inferring Party Left–Right Ideological Positions from Party Manifestos Data." *American Journal of Political Science* 44, no. 1 (January): 94–103.

Gallagher, Michael, Michael Laver, and Peter Mair. 1995. *Representative Government in Modern Europe.* 2nd ed. New York: McGraw-Hill.

———. 2001. *Representative Government in Modern Europe.* 3rd ed. New York: McGraw-Hill.

Galli, Giorgio. 1978. *Storia della Democrazia cristiana.* Bari: Laterza.

———. 1993. *Mezzo secolo di DC.* Milan: Rizzoli.

Galli, Giorgio, and Alfonso Prandi. 1970. *Patterns of Political Participation in Italy.* New Haven: Yale University Press.

Gamson, William. 1961. "A Theory of Coalition Formation." *American Sociological Review* 26, no. 3 (June): 373–82.

Gibson, James L. 1997. *United States Supreme Court Judicial Data Base, Phase II: User's Guide.* New York: Peter Lang.

Ginsborg, Paul. 1989. *Storia d'Italia dal dopoguerra a oggi. Società e politica 1943–1988.* Turin: Einaudi.

Gladdish, Ken. 1991. *Governing from the Centre: Politics and Policy-Making in the Netherlands.* London and S'Gravenhage: Hurst and Sdu Uitgeverij.

Glejser, H. 1969. "A New Test for Heteroskedasticity." *Journal of the American Statistical Association* 64, no. 325 (March): 316–23.

Goldfeld, Stephen M., and Richard E. Quandt. 1965. "Some Tests for Homoskedasticity." *Journal of the American Statistical Association* 60, no. 310 (June): 539–47.

Gourevitch, Peter. 1980. *Paris and the Provinces: The Politics of Local Government Reform in France.* London: George Allen and Unwin.

Grofman, Bernard. 1989. "The Comparative Analysis of Coalition Formation and Duration: Distinguishing Between-Country and Within-Country Effects." *British Journal of Political Science* 19, no. 2 (April): 291–302.

Grofman, Bernard, and Arend Lijphart, eds. 1986. *Electoral Laws and Their Political Consequences.* New York: Agathon.

Grofman, Bernard, and Peter Van Roozendaal. 1994. "Toward a Theoretical Explanation of Premature Cabinet Termination: With Application to Postwar Cabinets in the Netherlands." *European Journal of Political Research* 26, no. 1 (July): 155–70.

Guarnieri, Carlo. 1989. "Strutture e processi decisionali." In Leonardo Morlino, ed., *Scienza politica.* Turin: Fondazione Giovanni Agnelli.

———. 1992. *Magistratura e politica in Italia. Pesi senza contrappesi.* Bologna: Il Mulino.

Gundle, Stephen. 1995. "Rai e Fininvest nell'anno di Berlusconi." In Piero Ignazi and Richard S. Katz, eds., *Politica in Italia. I fatti dell'anno e le interpretazioni. Edizione 95.* Bologna: Il Mulino.

Gunther, Richard, Giacomo Sani, and Goldie Shabad. 1978. *Spain After Franco: The Making of a Competitive Party System.* Berkeley: University of California Press.

Hakovirta, Harto, and Tapio Koskiaho, eds. 1973. *Suomen hallitukset ja hallitusohjelmat 1945–1973.* Helsinki: Gaudeamus.

Hanushek, Eric A., and John E. Jackson. 1977. *Statistical Methods for Social Scientists.* New York: Academic Press.

Harper, John L. 1986. *America and the Reconstruction of Italy, 1945–1948.* Cambridge: Cambridge University Press.

Hearl, Derek John. 1992. "Policy and Coalition in Belgium." In Michael Laver and Ian Budge, eds., *Party Policy and Government Coalitions.* New York: St. Martin's.

Hellman, Judith Adler. 1987. *Journeys Among Women.* Oxford: Oxford University Press.

Hellman, Stephen. 1977. "The Longest Campaign: Communist Party Strategy and the Elections of 1976." In Howard R. Penniman, ed., *Italy at the Polls: The Parliamentary Elections of 1976.* Washington, D.C.: American Enterprise Institute.

———. 1992a. "La difficile nascita del Pds." In Stephen Hellman and Gianfranco

Pasquino, eds., *Politica in Italia. I fatti dell'anno e le interpretazioni. Edizione 92.* Bologna: Il Mulino.

———. 1992b. "Italian Politics in Transition." In Mark Kesselman and Joel Krieger, eds., *European Politics in Transition.* 2nd ed. New York: D.C. Heath.

Herman, Valentine. 1976. *Parliaments of the World: A Reference Compendium.* Berlin: de Gruyter.

Hicks, Alexander, and Dwayne Swank. 1992. "Politics, Institutions, and Welfare Spending in Industrialized Democracies, 1960–82." *American Political Science Review* 86, no. 3 (September): 658–74.

Hill, Keith J. 1974. "Belgium: Political Change in a Segmented Society." In Richard Rose, ed., *Electoral Behavior: A Comparative Handbook.* New York: Free Press.

Hine, David. 1993. *Governing Italy: The Politics of Bargained Pluralism.* Oxford: Oxford University Press.

Hine, David, and Salvatore Vassallo, eds. 1999. *Politica in Italia. I fatti dell'anno e le interpretazioni. Edizione 99.* Bologna: Il Mulino.

Hiscocks, Richard. 1966. *The Adenauer Era.* Philadelphia: J. B. Lippincott.

Hooghe, Liesbet. 1991. "A Leap in the Dark: Nationalist Conflict and Federal Reform in Belgium." Occasional Paper no. 27, Western Societies Program, Cornell University.

Huber, John D. 1996. *Rationalizing Parliament: Legislative Institutions and Party Politics in France.* Cambridge: Cambridge University Press.

Huygen, Maarten. 1986. "Dateline Holland: NATO's Pyrrhic Victory." *Foreign Policy* 62 (Spring): 167–85.

Ignazi, Piero. 1989. *Il polo escluso. Profilo del movimento sociale italiano.* Bologna: Il Mulino.

———. 1994a. *L'estrema destra in Europa.* Bologna: Il Mulino.

———. 1994b. *Postfascisti? Dal Movimento sociale italiano ad Alleanza nazionale.* Bologna: Il Mulino.

———. 1996. "Italy." *European Journal of Political Research* 30, no. 3–4 (December): 393–98.

———. 1997. "Italy." *European Journal of Political Research* 32, no. 3–4 (December): 417–23.

International Monetary Fund. Statistics Department. 1997. *International Financial Statistics Yearbook.* Washington, D.C.: IMF Publication Services.

Irwin, Galen, and Karl Dittrich. 1984. "And the Walls Came Tumbling Down: Party Dealignment in the Netherlands." In Russell J. Dalton, Scott C. Flanagan, and Paul Allen Beck, eds., *Electoral Change in Advanced Industrial Democracies.* Princeton: Princeton University Press.

Katz, Richard S. 1985. "Preference Voting in Italy: Votes of Opinion, Belonging, or Exchange." *Comparative Political Studies* 18, no. 2 (July): 229–49.

———. 1986a. "Intraparty Preference Voting." In Bernard Grofman and Arend Lijphart, eds., *Electoral Laws and Their Political Consequences.* New York: Agathon.

———. 1986b. "Party Government: A Rationalistic Conception." In Francis G.

Castles and Rudolf Wildenmann, eds., *Visions and Realities of Party Government*. Berlin: de Gruyter.

———. 1987. "Party Government and Its Alternatives." In Richard S. Katz, ed. *Party Governments: European and American Experiences*. Berlin: de Gruyter.

———. 1995. "The 1993 Parliamentary Electoral Reform." In Carol Mershon and Gianfranco Pasquino, eds. *Italian Politics: Ending the First Republic*. Boulder, Colo.: Westview.

———. 1997. *Democracy and Elections*. Oxford: Oxford University Press.

Katz, Richard S., and Piero Ignazi, eds. 1996. *Italian Politics: The Year of the Tycoon*. Boulder, Colo.: Westview.

Katz, Richard S., and Ruud Koole, eds. 1997. *Political Data Yearbook, 1997. (European Journal of Political Research* 32, no. 3-4 [December]). Dordrecht: Kluwer.

———, eds. 1998. *Political Data Yearbook, 1998. (European Journal of Political Research* 34, no. 3-4 [December]). Dordrecht: Kluwer.

———, eds. 1999. *Political Data Yearbook, 1999. (European Journal of Political Research* 36, no. 3-4 [December]). Dordrecht: Kluwer.

Katz, Richard S., and Peter Mair, eds. 1992. *Party Organizations: A Data Handbook on Party Organizations in Western Democracies, 1960–90*. London: Sage.

Keesing's Contemporary Archives. 1945–1986. London: Keesing's Limited. Published as *Keesing's Record of World Events*. 1987–. London: Longman.

Keller, Evelyn Fox. 1983. *A Feeling for the Organism: The Life and Work of Barbara McClintock*. San Francisco: W. H. Freeman.

Keman, Hans. 1995. "I Paesi Bassi. Confronto e fusione in società frammentate." In Josep M. Colomer, ed. *La politica in Europa*. Bari: Laterza.

Kim, HeeMin, and Richard Fording. 1998. "Voter Ideology in Western Democracies: 1946–89." *European Journal of Political Research* 33, no. 1 (January): 73–97.

King, Gary, James E. Alt, Nancy Elizabeth Burns, and Michael Laver. 1990. "A Unified Model of Cabinet Dissolution in Parliamentary Democracies." *American Journal of Political Science* 34, no. 3 (August): 846–71.

King, Gary, Robert O. Keohane, and Sidney Verba. 1994. *Designing Scientific Inquiry: Scientific Inference in Qualitative Research*. Princeton: Princeton University Press.

Kitschelt, Herbert. 1989. *The Logics of Party Formation: Ecological Politics in Belgium and West Germany*. Ithaca: Cornell University Press.

Klingemann, Hans-Dieter, Richard I. Hofferbert, and Ian Budge. 1994. *Parties, Policies, and Democracy*. Boulder, Colo.: Westview.

Klingemann, Hans-Dieter, and Andrea Volkens. 1992. "Coalition Governments in the Federal Republic of Germany: Does Policy Matter?" In Michael Laver and Ian Budge, eds., *Party Policy and Government Coalitions*. New York: St. Martin's.

Knight, Jack. 1992. *Institutions and Social Conflict*. Cambridge: Cambridge University Press.

Kogan, Norman. 1981. *A Political History of Postwar Italy: From the Old to the New Center-Left*. New York: Praeger.

Koole, Ruud, and Richard S. Katz, eds. 1996. *Political Data Yearbook, 1996*.

(European Journal of Political Research 30, no. 3-4 [December]). Dordrecht: Kluwer.

Koole, Ruud, and Peter Mair, eds. 1992. *Political Data Yearbook, 1992. (European Journal of Political Research* 22, no. 3-4 [December]). Dordrecht: Kluwer.

———, eds. 1993. *Political Data Yearbook, 1993. (European Journal of Political Research* 24, no. 3-4 [December]). Dordrecht: Kluwer.

———, eds. 1994. *Political Data Yearbook, 1994. (European Journal of Political Research* 26, no. 3-4 [December]). Dordrecht: Kluwer.

———, eds. 1995. *Political Data Yearbook, 1995. (European Journal of Political Research* 28, no. 3-4 [December]). Dordrecht: Kluwer.

Kopecký, Petr, and Lia Nijzink. 1995. "Party Discipline and the Relations Between Ministers and MPs: A Comparision between the Netherlands and the Czech Republic." Paper presented at the Annual Joint Sessons of Workshops of the European Consortium for Political Research, Bordeaux.

Krehbiel, Kieth. 1988. "Spatial Models of Legislative Choice." *Legislative Studies Quarterly* 13, no. 3 (August): 259–319.

———. 1992. *Information and Legislative Organization.* Ann Arbor: University of Michigan Press.

Kreppel, Amie. 1997. "The Impact of Parties on Legislative Output in Italy." *European Journal of Political Research* 31, no. 3 (April): 327–50.

Kuhn, Thomas S. 1970. *The Structure of Scientific Revolutions.* 2nd ed. Chicago: University of Chicago Press.

Lane, Jan-Erik, David McKay, and Kenneth Newton. 1991. *Political Data Handbook: OECD Countries.* Oxford: Oxford University Press.

Lange, Peter, and Marino Regini, eds. 1987. *Stato e regolazione sociale. Nuove prospettive sul caso italiano.* Bologna: Il Mulino.

Lanza, Orazio. 1979. "Gli enti del settore agricolo." In Franco Cazzola, ed., *Anatomia del potere DC. Enti pubblici e 'centralità democristiana'.* Bari: De Donato.

La Palombara, Joseph. 1987. *Democracy: Italian Style.* New Haven: Yale University Press.

Larsson, Torbjörn. 1988. "Sweden." In Jean Blondel and Ferdinand Müller-Rommel, eds., *Cabinets in Western Europe.* New York: St. Martin's.

———. 1994. "Cabinet Ministers and Parliamentary Goverment in Sweden." In Michael Laver and Kenneth A. Shepsle, eds., *Cabinet Ministers and Parliamentary Government.* Cambridge: Cambridge University Press.

Laver, Michael. 1992a. "Are Irish Parties Peculiar?" In John H. Goldthorpe and Christopher T. Whelan, eds., *The Development of Industrial Society in Ireland.* Proceedings of the British Academy. Vol. 79. Oxford: Oxford University Press.

———. 1992b. "Coalition and Party Policy in Ireland." In Michael Laver and Ian Budge, eds., *Party Policy and Government Coalitions.* New York: St. Martin's.

———. 1997. "In Search of the 'Big' Model of Political Competition. *European Journal of Political Research* 31, no. 2 (February): 179–82.

———. 1998. "Models of Government Formation." In Nelson W. Polsby, ed., *Annual Review of Political Science.* Vol. 1. Palo Alto, Calif.: Annual Reviews.

———., ed. n.d. *Estimating the Policy Position of Political Actors.* London: Routledge, forthcoming.

Laver, Michael, and Ian Budge. 1992. *Party Policy and Government Coalitions.* New York: St. Martin's.

Laver, Michael, and John Garry. 2000. "Estimating Policy Positions for Political Data." *American Journal of Political Science* 44, no. 3 (July): 619–34.

Laver, Michael, and W. Ben Hunt. 1992. *Policy and Party Competition.* London: Routledge.

Laver, Michael, and Norman Schofield. 1990. *Multiparty Government: The Politics of Coalition in Europe.* Oxford: Oxford University Press.

Laver, Michael, and Kenneth Shepsle. 1990a. "Coalitions and Cabinet Government." *American Political Science Review* 84, no. 3 (September): 873–90.

———. 1990b. "Government Coalitions and Intraparty Politics." *British Journal of Political Science* 20, no. 4 (October): 485–507.

———. 1990c. "The Size Principle and Minority Cabinets." Presented at the Conference in Honor of William H. Riker, University of Rochester, October 12–13.

———, eds. 1994. *Cabinet Ministers and Parliamentary Government.* Cambridge: Cambridge University Press.

———. 1996. *Making and Breaking Governments: Cabinets and Legislatures in Parliamentary Democracies.* Cambridge: Cambridge University Press.

———. 1999. "How Political Parties Emerged from the Primeval Slime: Party Discipline, Intraparty Politics, and Government Formation." In Shaun Bowler, David M. Farrell, and Richard S. Katz, eds., *Party Discipline and Parliamentary Government.* Columbus: Ohio State University Press.

Leiserson, Michael. 1968. "Factions and Coalitions in One-Party Japan: An Interpretation Based on the Theory of Games." *American Political Science Review* 62, no. 3 (September): 770–87.

Lemaître, Henri. 1982. *Les gouvernements belges de 1968 à 1980. Processus de crise.* Stavelot: Chauveheid.

Leonardi, Robert. 1981. "The Victors: The Smaller Parties in the 1979 Italian Elections." In Howard R. Penniman, ed., *Italy at the Polls, 1979: A Study of the Parliamentary Elections.* Washington, D.C.: American Enterprise Institute.

Leonardi, Robert, and Douglas Wertman. 1989. *Italian Christian Democracy: The Politics of Dominance.* New York: St. Martin's.

Lepsius, M. Rainer. 1978. "From Fragmented Party Democracy to Government by Emergency Decree and National Socialist Takeover: Germany." In Juan J. Linz and Alfred Stepan, eds., *The Breakdown of Democratic Regimes: Europe.* Baltimore: Johns Hopkins University Press.

Levi Montalcini, Rita. 1987. *Elogio dell'imperfezione.* Milan: Garzanti. Published in English as *In Praise of Imperfection: My Life and Work,* translated by Luigi Attardi (New York: Basic Books, 1988).

Levite, Ariel, and Sidney Tarrow. 1983. "The Legitimation of Excluded Parties in Dominant Party Systems: A Comparison of Israel and Italy." *Comparative Politics* 15, no. 3 (April): 295–328.

Lewin, Leif. 1988. *Ideology and Strategy: A Century of Swedish Politics.* Cambridge: Cambridge University Press.

Lewis-Beck, Michael S. 1980. *Applied Regression: An Introduction.* Beverly Hills: Sage.

————. 1984. "France: The Stalled Electorate." In Russell J. Dalton, Scott C. Flanagan, and Paul Allen Beck, eds., *Electoral Change in Advanced Industrial Democracies*. Princeton: Princeton University Press.

————. 1986. "Comparative Economic Voting: Britain, France, Germany, Italy." *American Journal of Political Science*, 30, no. 2 (August): 315–46.

————. 1988. *Economics and Elections: The Major Western Democracies*. Ann Arbor: University of Michigan Press.

Leyden, Kevin M., Terry J. Royed, Stephen A. Borrelli, and Brad Lockerbie. 1995. "Economic Accountability and Multiparty Government: Who Do Voters Hold Responsible?" Paper presented at the 1995 Annual Meeting of the Midwest Political Science Association, Chicago, April 6–8.

Lijphart, Arend. 1968. *The Politics of Accommodation*. Berkeley: University of California Press.

————. 1984. *Democracies: Patterns of Majoritarian and Consensus Government in Twenty-One Countries*. New Haven: Yale University Press.

————. 1994. *Electoral Systems and Party Systems: A Study of Twenty-Seven Democracies 1945–1990*. Oxford: Oxford University Press.

Linz, Juan J. 1978a. "The Breakdown of Democratic Regimes: Crisis, Breakdown, and Reequilibration." In Juan J. Linz and Alfred Stepan, eds., *The Breakdown of Democratic Regimes*. Baltimore: Johns Hopkins University Press.

————. 1978b. "From Great Hopes to Civil War." In Juan J. Linz and Alfred Stepan, eds., *The Breakdown of Democratic Regimes*. Baltimore: Johns Hopkins University Press.

Luebbert, Gregory M. 1986. *Comparative Democracy: Policymaking and Governing Coalitions in Europe and Israel*. New York: Columbia University Press.

Lupia, Arthur, and Mathew D. McCubbins. 1998. *The Democratic Dilemma: Can Citizens Learn What They Need to Know?* Cambridge: Cambridge University Press.

Lupia, Arthur, and Kaare Strøm. 1995. "Coalition Termination and the Strategic Timing of Parliamentary Elections." *American Political Science Review* 89, no. 3 (September): 648–65.

Maas, P. F. 1986. "Coalition Negotiations in the Dutch Multi-Party System." *Parliamentary Affairs* 39, no. 2 (April): 214–29.

Mabille, Xavier. 1992. *Histoire politique de la Belgique. Facteurs et acteurs de changement*. 2nd ed. Brussels: Centre de recherche et d'information socio-politiques.

Mackie, Thomas T., and Richard Rose. 1991. *The International Almanac of Electoral History*. 3rd ed. Washington, D.C.: Congressional Quarterly Press.

MacRae, Duncan. 1967. *Parliament, Parties, and Society in France 1946–1958*. New York: St. Martin's.

Maddala, G. S. 1971. "The Likelihood Approach to Pooling Cross-Section and Time-Series Data." *Econometrica* 39, no. 6 (November): 939–53.

Maestri, Ezio G. 1984. "Partiti e sistema pensionistico in Italia. Un'analisi dell'azione parlamentare della Dc e del Pci (1953–1975)." *Rivista italiana di scienza politica* 14, no. 1 (April): 125–59.

Mair, Peter. 1987. *The Changing Irish Party System: Organization, Ideology, and Electoral Competition.* London: Pinter.

———. 1992. "Explaining the Absence of Class Politics in Ireland." In John H. Goldthorpe and Christopher T. Whelan, eds., *The Development of Industrial Society in Ireland.* Proceedings of the British Academy. Vol. 79. Oxford: Oxford University Press.

———. 1994. "Party Organizations: From Civil Society to the State." In Richard S. Katz and Peter Mair, eds., *How Parties Organize: Change and Adaptation in Party Organizations in Western Democracies.* London: Sage.

Mannheimer, Renato, and Giacomo Sani. 1987. *Il mercato elettorale. Identikit dell'elettore italiano.* Bologna: Il Mulino.

Manzella, Andrea. 1991. *Il parlamento.* 2nd ed. Bologna: Il Mulino.

Marletti, Carlo. 1988. "Partiti e informazione televisiva. La nomina di Enrico Manca a presidente della Rai." In Piergiorgo Corbetta and Robert Leonardi, eds., *Politica in Italia. I fatti dell'anno e le interpretazioni. Edizione 87.* Bologna: Il Mulino.

Marradi, Alberto. 1982. "From 'Centrism' to Crisis of the Center-Left Coalitions." In Eric C. Browne and John Dreijmanis, eds., *Government Coalitions in Western Democracies.* London: Longman.

Marsh, Michael. 1992. "Ireland." In Mark N. Franklin, Thomas T. Mackie, and Henry Valen, ed., *Electoral Change: Responses to Evolving Social and Attitudinal Structures in Western Countries.* Cambridge: Cambridge University Press.

Mastropaolo, Alfio, and Martin Slater. 1987. "Italy 1947–1979: Ideological Distances and Party Movements." In Ian Budge, David Robertson, and Derek Hearl, eds., *Ideology, Strategy and Party Change: Spatial Analyses of Post-War Election Programmes in 19 Democracies.* Cambridge: Cambridge University Press.

———. 1992. "Party Policy and Coalition Bargaining in Italy, 1948–87: Is There Order Behind the Chaos?" In Michael Laver and Ian Budge, eds., *Party Policy and Government Coalitions.* New York: St. Martin's.

Mattson, Ingvar, and Kaare Strøm. 1995. "Committee Power in European Parliaments." Paper presented at the Annual Joint Sessions of Workshops of the European Consortium for Political Research, Bordeaux.

Mazzoleni, Gianpietro. 1994. "La Rai tra ristrutturazione e risanamento." In Carol Mershon and Gianfranco Pasquino, eds., *Politica in Italia. I fatti dell'anno e le interpretazioni. Edizione 94.* Bologna: Il Mulino.

McCarthy, Patrick. 1992. "The Referendum of 9 June." In Stephen Hellman and Gianfranco Pasquino, eds. *Italian Politics: A Review.* Vol. 7. London: Pinter.

McKelvey, Richard D. 1976. "Intransitivities in Multidimensional Voting Models and Some Implications for Agenda Control." *Journal of Economic Theory* 12, no. 3 (June): 472–82.

———. 1979. "General Conditions for Global Intransitivities in Formal Voting Models." *Econometrica* 47, no. 5 (September): 1085–1112.

McKelvey, Richard D., and Norman Schofield. 1987. "Generalized Symmetry Conditions at a Core Point." *Econometrica* 55, no. 4 (July): 923–33.

McLean, Iain, and Arnold B. Urken. 1995. "General Introduction." In Iain McLean and Arnold B. Urken, eds., *Classics of Social Choice*. Ann Arbor: University of Michigan Press.

Mény, Yves. 1993. *Government and Politics in Western Europe: Britain, France, Italy, West Germany*. Oxford: Oxford University Press.

Mershon, Carol. 1989. "Government Coalitions in Postwar Italy: The Logic of Sudden Death and Sure Resurrection." Typescript. Washington University, St. Louis.

————. 1994. "Expectations and Informal Rules in Coalition Formation." *Comparative Political Studies* 27, no. 1 (April): 40–79.

————. 1996a. "The Costs of Coalition: Coalition Theories and Italian Governments." *American Political Science Review* 90, no. 3 (September): 534–54.

————. 1996b. "The Costs of Coalition: The Italian Anomaly." In Norman Schofield, ed., *Collective Decision-Making: Social Choice and Political Economy*. Boston: Kluwer.

————. 1998. "Party Factions and Coalition Government: A Re-Assessment." Paper presented at the Conference on Party Politics in Japan and Europe, European Consortium for Political Research and Japanese Political Science Association, Kumamato, Japan.

————. 1999a. "The Costs of Coalition: A Five-Nation Comparison." In Shaun Bowler, David M. Farrell, and Richard S. Katz, eds., *Party Discipline and Parliamentary Government*. Columbus: Ohio State University Press.

————. 1999b. "Party Leaders' Manipulation of Office Rewards: A Comparison of the U.S. House of Representatives and the Italian Executive." Manuscript. University of Virginia.

————. 2001. "Contending Models of Portfolio Allocation and Office Payoffs to Party Factions: Italy, 1963–79." *American Journal of Political Science* 45, no. 2 (April): 277–93.

————. n.d. "Party Factions and Coalition Government: Portfolio Allocation in Christian Democracy." Forthcoming in *Electoral Studies*.

Mershon, Carol, and Gianfranco Pasquino, eds. 1994. *Politica in Italia. I fatti dell'anno e le interpretazioni. Edizione 94*. Bologna: Il Mulino.

Ministero dell'Interno. 2001. "Elezioni della Camera dei Deputati." http://www.cittadinitalia-elezioni2001.it/camera/C000000.htm and http://www.cittadinitalia-elezioni2001.it/camera/C000000_compl.htm. Last accessed May 28, 2001.

Molitor, André. 1988. "Belgium." In Donald C. Rowat, ed., *Public Administration in Developed Democracies: A Comparative Study*. New York: M. Dekker.

Montalenti, Paolo. 1978. "Stato democratico e sistema delle Partecipazioni statali nel dibattito giuridico e politico dal dopoguerra ad oggi." In Gastone Cottino, ed., *Ricerca sulle Partecipazioni statali*. Turin: Einaudi.

Morlino, Leonardo. 1994. "Italy: Tracing the Roots of the Great Transformation." In Richard S. Katz and Peter Mair, eds., *How Parties Organize: Change and Adaptation in Party Organizations in Western Democracies*. London: Sage.

Motta, Riccardo. 1985. "L'attività legislativa dei governi (1948–83)." *Rivista italiana di scienza politica* 15, no. 2 (August): 255–92.

Mughan, Anthony. 1992. "Belgium." In Mark Franklin, Tom Mackie, and Henry

Valen, eds., *Electoral Change: Responses to Evolving Social and Attitudinal Structures in Western Countries*. Cambridge: Cambridge University Press.

Müller-Rommel, Ferdinand. 1994. "The Role of German Ministers in Cabinet Decision Making." In Michael Laver and Kenneth A. Shepsle, eds., *Cabinet Ministers and Parliamentary Government*. Cambridge: Cambridge University Press.

Mylly, Juhani, and R. Michael Berry. 1984. *Political Parties in Finland: Essays in History and Politics*. Turku: University of Turku.

Nannestad, Peter. 1989. *Reactive Voting in Danish General Elections 1971–1979*. Aarhus: Aarhus University Press.

Nelson, Garrison, with Clark H. Benson. 1993. *Committees in the United States Congress 1947–1992, Volume 1: Committee Jurisdictions and Membership Rosters*. Washington, D.C.: Congressional Quarterly Press.

Nelson, Garrison, with Mary T. Mitchell and Clark H. Benson. 1994. *Committees in the United States Congress 1947–1992, Volume 1: Committee Histories and Member Assignments*. Washington, D.C.: Congressional Quarterly Press.

Niemi, Richard. 1983. "Why So Much Stability? Another Opinion." *Public Choice* 41, no. 2: 261–70.

Nocifero, Nicolò, and Sergio Valdini. 1992. *Il palazzo di vetro. Il lavoro dei deputati italiani nella decima legislatura*. Florence: Vallecchi.

Nohlen, Dieter. 1984. "Choices and Changes in Electoral Systems." In Arend Lijphart and Bernard Grofman, eds., *Choosing an Electoral System*. New York: Praeger.

Norberg, Anders, Andreas Tjerneld, and Björn Asker. 1985. *Tvåkammarriksdagen 1867–1970: Ledamöter och valkretsar*. Stockholm: Sveriges Riksdag.

Nordby, Trond, ed. 1985. *Storting og regjering 1945–1985*. Oslo: Kunnskapsforlaget.

Norpoth, Helmut, Michael Lewis-Beck, and Dominique Lafay, eds. 1991. *Economics and Politics: The Calculus of Support*. Ann Arbor: University of Michigan Press.

North, Douglass C. 1990. *Institutions, Institutional Change and Economic Performance*. Cambridge: Cambridge University Press.

Nousiainen, Jaako. 1971. *The Finnish Political System*. Translated by John H. Hodgson. Cambridge: Harvard University Press.

———. 1988. "Finland." In Jean Blondel and Ferdinand Müller-Rommel, eds., *Cabinets in Western Europe*. New York: St. Martin's.

———. 1994. "Finland: Ministerial Autonomy, Constitutional Collectivism, and Party Oligarchy." In Michael Laver and Kenneth A. Shepsle, eds., *Cabinet Ministers and Parliamentary Government*. Cambridge: Cambridge University Press.

Novacco, Domenico, ed. 1971. *La prima legislatura del Parlamento della Repubblica*. Vol. 14 of *Storia del Parlamento italiano*. Palermo: Flaccovio.

———, ed. 1978. *La seconda legislatura della Repubblica (1953–58)*. Vol. 15 of *Storia del Parlamento italiano*. Palermo: Flaccovio.

Nyholm, Pekka. 1972. *Parliament, Government and Multi-Dimensional Party Relations in Finland*. Series Commentationes Scientiarum Socialium. Helsinki: Societas Scientiarum Fennica.

Ordeshook, Peter C. 1986. *Game Theory and Political Theory: An Introduction.* Cambridge: Cambridge University Press.

———. 1990. "The Emerging Discipline of Political Economy." In James E. Alt and Kenneth A. Shepsle, eds., *Perspectives on Positive Political Economy.* Cambridge: Cambridge University Press.

Orfei, Ruggero. 1976. *L'occupazione del potere. I democristiani '45–'75.* Milan: Longanesi.

Organization for Economic Cooperation and Development (OECD). 1990. *Public Management Developments: Survey 1990.* Paris: OECD Publications.

———. 1993. *Public Management Developments: Survey 1993.* Paris: OECD Publications.

———. 1997. *OECD Statistical Compendium.* Computer file. Rheinberg (Germany): DSI Data Service and Information, Department CD-ROM; Paris: OECD/OCDE, Electronic Editions.

———. 2000. *OECD Historical Statistics 1970–1999.* Paris: OECD Publications.

Ozinga, James R., Thomas W. Casstevens, and Harold T. Casstevens. 1989. "The Circulation of Elites: Soviet Politburo Members, 1919–1987." *Canadian Journal of Political Science* 22, no. 3 (September): 609–17.

Pallotta, Gino. 1964. *Dizionario della politica italiana.* Isola del Liri: Pisani.

Panebianco, Angelo. 1988. *Political Parties: Organization and Power.* Cambridge: Cambridge University Press.

Parisi, Arturo, and Gianfranco Pasquino. 1979. "Changes in Italian Electoral Behavior: The Relationships Between Parties and Voters." *West European Politics* 2, no. 3 (October): 6–30.

Pasquino, Gianfranco. 1972. "Le radici del frazionismo e il voto di preferenza." *Rivista italiana di scienza politica* 2, no. 2 (August): 353–68.

———. 1977. "Per un'analisi delle coalizioni di governo in Italia." In Arturo Parisi and Gianfranco Pasquino, eds., *Continuità e mutamento elettorale in Italia.* Bologna: Il Mulino.

———. 1980. "Italian Christian Democracy: A Party for All Seasons?" In Peter Lange and Sidney Tarrow, eds., *Italy in Transition: Conflict and Consensus.* London: Frank Cass.

———. 1981. "The Italian Socialist Party: Electoral Stagnation and Political Indispensability." In Howard R. Penniman, ed., *Italy at the Polls, 1979: A Study of the Parliamentary Elections.* Washington, D.C.: American Enterprise Institute.

———. 1986. "The Demise of the First Fascist Regime and Italy's Transition to Democracy: 1943–1948." In Guillermo O'Donnell, Philippe C. Schmitter, and Laurence Whitehead, eds., *Transitions from Authoritarian Rule: Southern Europe.* Baltimore: Johns Hopkins University Press.

———. 1987a. "Party Government in Italy: Achievements and Prospects." In Richard S. Katz, ed., *Party Governments: European and American Experiences.* Berlin: de Gruyter.

———. 1987b. "Regolatori sregolati. Partiti e governo dei partiti." In Peter Lange and Marino Regini, eds., *Stato e regolazione sociale. Nuove prospettive sul caso italiano.* Bologna: Il Mulino.

———. 1988. "La politica al posto di comando: Le fonti del mutamento in Italia." *Polis* 2, no. 2 (August): 459–82.

———. 1990. "La crisi del governo De Mita e i poteri del presidente della Repubblica, ovvero: Quale forma di governo?" In Raimondo Catanzaro and Filippo Sabetti, eds. *Politica in Italia. I fatti dell'anno e le interpretazioni. Edizione 90.* Bologna: Il Mulino.

———. 1995a. "I governi." In Gianfranco Pasquino, ed., *La politica italiana. Dizionario critico 1945–95.* Bari: Laterza.

———. 1995b. "La partitocrazia." In Gianfranco Pasquino, ed., *La politica italiana. Dizionario critico 1945–95.* Bari: Laterza.

———. 1998. "New Government, Old Party Politics." *South European Society and Politics* 3, no. 2 (Autumn): 124–33.

———. 1999. "Autopsia della Bicamerale." In David Hine and Salvatore Vassallo, eds., *Politica in Italia. I fatti dell'anno e le interpretazioni. Edizione 99.* Bologna: Il Mulino.

Payne, Stanley G. 1993. *Spain's First Democracy: The Second Republic, 1931–1936.* Madison: University of Wisconson Press.

Pedersen, Mogens N. 1974. "Political Development and Elite Transformation in Denmark." Typescript. Institute of History and Social Sciences, Odense University.

———. 1979. "The Dynamics of European Party Systems: Changing Patterns of Electoral Volatility." *European Journal of Political Research* 7, no. 1 (January): 1–26.

———. 1983. "Changing Patterns of Electoral Volatility in European Party Systems, 1948–1977: Explorations in Explanation." In Hans Daalder and Peter Mair, eds., *Western European Party Systems: Continuity and Change.* London: Sage.

———. 1987. "The Danish 'Working Multiparty System': Breakdown or Adaptation?" In Hans Daalder, ed., *Party Systems in Denmark, Austria, Switzerland, the Netherlands and Belgium.* New York: St. Martin's.

Pempel, T. J., ed. 1990. *Uncommon Democracies: The One-Party Dominant Regimes.* Ithaca: Cornell University Press.

Petracca, Orazio M. 1980. *Storia della prima repubblica.* Milan: Mondo Economico.

Pétry, François. 1987. "France 1958–1981: The Strategy of Joint Government Platforms." In Ian Budge, David Robertson, and Derek Hearl, eds., *Ideology, Strategy and Party Change: Spatial Analyses of Post-War Election Programmes in 19 Democracies.* Cambridge: Cambridge University Press.

———. 1992a. "Coalition Bargaining in the French Fourth Republic, 1946–58." In Michael Laver and Ian Budge, eds., *Party Policy and Government Coalitions.* New York: St. Martin's.

———. 1992b. "Government Coalition Payoffs in the French Fourth Republic." Typescript. University of Manitoba.

Pierce, Roy. 1995. *Choosing the Chief: Presidential Elections in France and the United States.* Ann Arbor: University of Michigan Press.

Political Data Yearbook. 1992–. *European Journal of Political Research*, December. Dordrecht: Kluwer.

Pollio Salimbeni, Antonio. 1989. "Presidente per la sesta volta." *L'Unità.* 23 July.

Polsby, Nelson W. 1968. "The Institutionalization of the U.S. House of Representatives." *American Political Science Review* 62, no. 1 (March): 144–68.

———. 1975. "Legislatures." In Fred I. Greenstein and Nelson W. Polsby, eds., *Handbook of Political Science.* Vol. 5. Reading, Mass.: Addison-Wesley.

———. 1998. "Social Science and Scientific Change: A Note on Thomas S. Kuhn's Contribution." *Annual Review of Political Science* 1: 199–210.

Polsby, Nelson W., Miriam Gallagher, and Barry Spencer Rundquist. 1969. "The Growth of the Seniority System in the U.S. House of Representatives." *American Political Science Review* 63, no. 3 (September): 787–807.

Powell, G. Bingham, Jr. 1982. *Contemporary Democracies: Participation, Stability, and Violence.* Cambridge: Harvard University Press.

Powell, G. Bingham, Jr., and Guy D. Whitten. 1993. "A Cross-National Analysis of Economic Voting: Taking Account of the Political Context." *American Journal of Political Science* 37, no. 2 (May): 391–414.

Preston, Paul. 1994. *The Coming of the Spanish Civil War: Reform, Reaction and Revolution in the Second Republic.* 2nd ed. London: Routledge.

Pridham, Geoffrey. 1988. *Political Parties and Coalitional Behaviour in Italy.* London: Routledge.

Prittie, Terence C. F. 1972. *Konrad Adenauer, 1876–1967.* London: Tom Stacey Ltd.

Przeworski, Adam, and John Sprague. 1986. *Paper Stones: A History of Electoral Socialism.* Chicago: University of Chicago Press.

Przeworski, Adam, and Henry Teune. 1970. *The Logic of Comparative Social Inquiry.* New York: Wiley.

Puntila, L. A. 1975. *The Political History of Finland 1809–1966.* Translated by David Miller. Heinemann: London.

Pustetto, Maria Bruno. 1991. *Il manuale del candidato politico.* Milan: Bridge.

Putnam, Robert D. 1995. "Bowling Alone: America's Declining Social Capital." *Journal of Democracy* 6, no. 1 (January): 65–78.

———. 2000. *Bowling Alone: The Collapse and Revival of American Community.* New York: Simon and Schuster.

Putnam, Robert D., with Robert Leonardi and Raffaella Y. Nanetti. 1993. *Making Democracy Work: Civic Traditions in Modern Italy.* Princeton: Princeton University Press.

Radaelli, Claudio Maria. 1991. "Il controllo politico dell'economia. Gli studi sul ciclo politico-economico." *Rivista Italiana di Scienza Politica* 21, no. 2 (August): 315–41.

Rae, Douglas W. 1967. *The Political Consequences of Electoral Laws.* New Haven: Yale University Press.

Regini, Marino, and Gloria Regonini. 1981. "La politica delle pensioni in Italia. Il ruolo del movimento sindacale." *Giornale di diritto del lavoro e di relazioni industriali* 3, no. 10: 217–42.

Rémy, Dominique. 1975. "The Pivotal Party: Definition and Measurement." *European Journal of Political Research* 3, no. 3 (September): 293–301.

Rhodes, Martin. 1988. "Craxi e l'area laico-socialista: terza forza o tre forze?" In Piergiorgio Corbetta and Robert Leonardi, eds., *Politica in Italia. I fatti dell'anno e le interpretazioni. Edizione 88.* Bologna: Il Mulino.

Ricolfi, Luca. 1993a. "La geometria dello spazio elettorale in Italia." *Rivista italiana di scienza politica* 23, no. 3 (December): 433–74.

———. 1993b. *L'ultimo Parlamento. Sulla fine della prima Repubblica.* Rome: La Nuova Italia Scientifica.

———. 1995. "Il voto proporzionale e il nuovo spazio politico italiano." In Stefano Bartolini and Roberto D'Alimonte, eds., *Maggioritario ma non troppo.* Bologna: Il Mulino.

Riker, William H. 1962. *The Theory of Political Coalitions.* New Haven: Yale University Press.

———. 1980. "Implications from the Disequilibrium of Majority Rule for the Study of Institutions." *American Political Science Review* 74, no. 2 (June): 432–46.

———. 1990. "Political Science and Rational Choice." In James E. Alt and Kenneth A. Shepsle, eds., *Perspectives on Positive Political Economy.* Cambridge: Cambridge University Press.

Riksdagen. 1973–1981. *Förteckning över riksdagens ledamöter, riksdagens utskott, m.fl.* Stockholm: Ridsdagens förvaltningskontor.

Riksdagen. 1982–1987. *Riksdagen.* Stockholm: Riksdagens förvaltningskontor.

Robertson, John D. 1983. "Inflation, Unemployment, and Government Collapse: A Poisson Application." *Comparative Political Studies* 15, no. 4 (January): 425–44.

Rose, Richard, and Thomas T. Mackie. 1983. "Incumbency in Government: Asset or Liability?" In Hans Daalder and Peter Mair, eds., *Western European Party Systems: Continuity and Change.* London: Sage.

Rudd, Chris. 1984. "Coalition Formation in Belgium 1965–81." Essex Papers in Politics and Government, no. 17. University of Essex, Department of Government.

Ruiz Manjón, Octavio. 1976. *El partido republicano radical 1908–1936.* Madrid: Ediciones Giner.

Sabetti, Filippo. 2000. *The Search for Good Government: Understanding the Paradox of Italian Democracy.* Montreal: McGill–Queen's University Press.

Sainsbury, Diane. 1990. "Party Strategies and the Electoral Trade-Off of Class-Based Parties." *European Journal of Political Research* 18, no. 1 (January): 29–50.

Salvati, Michele. 1980. "Muddling Through: Economics and Politics in Italy 1969–1979." In Peter Lange and Sidney Tarrow, eds., *Italy in Transition: Conflict and Consensus.* London: Frank Cass.

———. 1981. "May 1968 and the Hot Autumn of 1969: The Responses of Two Ruling Classes." In Suzanne D. Berger, ed., *Organizing Interests in Western Europe.* Cambridge: Cambridge University Press.

———. 1985. "The Italian Inflation." In Leon N. Lindberg and Charles S. Maier, eds., *The Politics of Inflation and Economic Stagnation.* Washington, D.C.: Brookings Institution.

Sanders, David, and Valentine Herman. 1977. "The Stability and Survival of Governments in Western Democracies." *Acta Politica* 12: 346–77.

Sani, Giacomo. 1975. "Mass-Level Response to Party Strategy: The Italian Electorate and the Communist Party." In Donald L. M. Blackmer and Sidney Tarrow, eds. *Communism in Italy and France*. Princeton: Princeton University Press.

––––. 1977. "The Italian Electorate in the Mid-1970s: Beyond Tradition?" In Howard R. Penniman, ed., *Italy at the Polls: The Parliamentary Elections of 1976*. Washington, D.C.: American Enterprise Institute.

––––. 1991. "Church Attendance and the Vote for the DC: Evidence from the 1980s." *Italian Politics and Society* 34 (Fall): 13–18.

––––. 1994. "Il verdetto del 1992." In Renato Mannheimer and Giacomo Sani, eds., *La rivoluzione elettorale. L'Italia tra la prima e la seconda repubblica*. Milan: Anabasi.

Sani, Giacomo, and Giovanni Sartori. 1983. "Polarization, Fragmentation, and Competition in Western Democracies." In Hans Daalder and Peter Mair, eds., *Western European Party Systems: Continuity and Change*. London: Sage.

Santagata, Walter. 1991. "Ideologia, opportunismo e pluralismo. Il ciclo politico della spesa pubblica." *Stato e Mercato*, no. 33 (December): 371–412.

––––. 1995. *Economia, elezioni, interessi. Tra economia e scienza politica: Una analisi dei cicli economici elettorali in Italia*. Bologna: Il Mulino.

Sartori, Giovanni. 1966. "European Political Parties: The Case of Polarized Pluralism." In Joseph LaPalombara and Myron Weiner, eds., *Political Parties and Political Development*. Princeton: Princeton University Press.

––––. 1976. *Parties and Party Systems*. New York: Cambridge University Press.

Sayrs, Lois W. 1989. *Pooled Time Series Analysis*. Newbury Park, Calif.: Sage.

Schindler, Peter, ed. 1984. *Datenhandbuch zur Geschichte des Deutschen Bundestages 1949 bis 1982*. Baden-Baden: Nomos.

––––, ed. 1988. *Datenhandbuch zur Geschichte des Deutschen Bundestages 1980 bis 1987*. Baden-Baden: Nomos.

Schofield, Norman. 1983. "Generic Instability of Majority Rule." *Review of Economic Studies* 4, no. 153 (October): 695–705.

––––. 1986. "Existence of a 'Structurally Stable' Equilibrium for a Noncollegial Voting Rule." *Public Choice* 51 (3): 267–84.

––––. 1987. "Coalitions in West European Democracies: 1945–1987." *The European Journal of Political Economy* 3: 555–91.

––––. 1993. "Political Competition and Multiparty Coalition Governments." *European Journal of Political Research* 23, no. 1 (January): 1–33.

Schofield, Norman, Bernard Grofman, and Scott L. Feld. 1988. "The Core and the Stability of Group Choice in Spatial Voting Games." *American Political Science Review* 82, no. 1 (March): 195–211.

Schofield, Norman, and Michael Laver. 1985. "Bargaining Theory and Portfolio Payoffs in European Coalition Governments 1945–83." *British Journal of Political Science* 15, no. 2 (April): 143–64.

Schott, Kerry. 1984. *Policy, Power, and Order: The Persistence of Economic Problems in Capitalist States*. New Haven: Yale University Press.

Schou, Tove-Lise, and Derek John Hearl. 1992. "Party and Coalition Policy in Denmark." In Michael Laver and Ian Budge, eds., *Party Policy and Government Coalitions*. London: St. Martin's.

Scibilia, Salvo. 1979. "L'amministrazione per enti. Sviluppo e uso politico." In Franco Cazzola, ed., *Anatomia del potere DC. Enti pubblici e 'centralità democristiana.'* Bari: De Donato.

Scoppola, Pietro. 1995. "La Democrazia cristiana." In Gianfranco Pasquino, ed., *La politica italiana. Dizionario critico 1945–95.* Bari: Laterza.

Segal, Jeffrey A., and Harold J. Spaeth. 1993. *The Supreme Court and the Attitudinal Model*. Cambridge: Cambridge University Press.

Shepsle, Kenneth A. 1978. *The Giant Jigsaw Puzzle: Democratic Committee Assignments in the Modern House*. Chicago: University of Chicago Press.

———. 1979. "Institutional Arrangements and Equilibrium in Multidimensional Voting Models." *American Journal of Political Science* 23, no. 1 (February): 27–59.

———. 1986. "Institutional Equilibrium and Equilibrium Institutions." In Herbert F. Weisberg, ed., *Political Science: The Science of Politics*. New York: Agathon.

Shepsle, Kenneth A., and Barry R. Weingast. 1981. "Structure-Induced Equilibrium and Legislative Choice." *Public Choice* 37, no. 3: 503–19.

———. 1987. "The Institutional Foundations of Committee Power." *American Political Science Review* 81, no. 1 (March): 85–104.

Smith, Alistair. 1996. "Endogenous Election Timing in Majoritarian Parliamentary Systems." *Economics and Politics* 8, no. 2 (July): 85–110.

Soikkanen, Timo. 1981. "The Structure and Development of the Political Party Spectrum in Finland." Helsinki: Ministry for Foreign Affairs.

Spaeth, Harold J. 1999. "United States Supreme Court Judicial Database, 1953–1997 Terms." Computer file. 9th ICPSR version. East Lansing, Mich.: Michigan State University, Department of Political Science [producer], 1998. Ann Arbor, Mich.: Inter-University Consortium for Political and Social Research [distributor], 1999.

Spanò, Piero. 1979. "Gli enti del settore creditizio. Aspetti economici e politici dello sviluppo del credito speciale all'industria nel secondo dopoguerra." In Franco Cazzola, ed., *Anatomia del potere DC. Enti pubblici e 'centralità democristiana'.* Bari: De Donato.

Spotts, Frederic, and Theodor Wieser. 1986. *Italy: A Difficult Democracy*. Cambridge: Cambridge University Press.

Spreafico, Alberto, and Franco Cazzola. 1970. "Correnti di partito e processi di identificazione." *Il Politico* 35: 695–715.

Spreafico, Alberto, and Joseph La Palombara. 1963. *Elezioni e comportamento politico in Italia*. Milan: Comunità.

Spruyt, Hendrik. 1994. *The Sovereign State and Its Competitors: An Analysis of System Change*. Princeton: Princeton University Press.

Steinberg, Dan. 1998. "Two-Stage Least Squares." In Leland Wilkinson, ed., *SYSTAT 8.0: Statistics*. Chicago: SPSS.

Steinmo, Sven. 1993. *Taxation and Democracy*. New Haven: Yale University Press.

Stimson, James A. 1985. "Regression in Space and Time: A Statistical Essay." *American Journal of Political Science* 29, no. 4 (November): 914–47.

Storing, James A. 1963. *Norwegian Democracy*. Boston: Houghton Mifflin.

Strom, Gerald S. 1990. *The Logic of Lawmaking: A Spatial Theory Approach*. Baltimore and London: Johns Hopkins University Press.

Strøm, Kaare. 1985. "Party Goals and Government Performance in Parliamentary Democracies." *American Political Science Review* 79, no. 3 (September): 738–54.

———. 1990a. "A Behavioral Theory of Competitive Political Parties." *American Journal of Political Science* 34, no. 2 (May): 565–98.

———. 1990b. *Minority Government and Majority Rule*. Cambridge: Cambridge University Press.

———. 1994. "The Political Role of Norwegian Cabinet Ministers." In Michael Laver and Kenneth A. Shepsle, eds., *Cabinet Ministers and Parliamentary Government*. Cambridge: Cambridge University Press.

Strøm, Kaare, and Torbjorn Bergman. 1992. "Sweden: Social Democratic Dominance in One Dimension." In Michael Laver and Ian Budge, eds., *Party Policy and Government Coalitions*. New York: St. Martin's.

Strøm, Kaare, Ian Budge, and Michael Laver. 1994. "Constraints on Cabinet Formation in Parliamentary Democracies." *American Journal of Political Science* 38, no. 2 (May): 303–35.

Strøm, Kaare and Jørn Y. Leipart. 1992. "Norway: Policy Pursuit and Coalition Avoidance." In Michael Laver and Ian Budge, eds., *Party Policy and Government Coalitions*. London: St. Martin's.

———. 1993. "Policy, Institutions, and Coalition Avoidance: Norwegian Governments, 1945–1990." *American Political Science Review* 87, no. 4 (December): 870–87.

Sweden. Riksdagen. 1973–1981. *Förteckning över riksdagens ledamöter*. Stockholm.

———. 1982–1987. *Riksdagen. Ledamöter och riksdagsorgan*. Stockholm.

Taagepera, Rein, and Matthew Soberg Shugart. 1989. *Seats and Votes: The Effects and Determinants of Electoral Systems*. New Haven: Yale University Press.

Tamburrano, Giuseppe. 1971. *Storia e cronaca del centro sinistra*. Milan: Feltrinelli.

Tarrow, Sidney. 1990. "Maintaining Hegemony in Italy: 'The Softer They Rise, the Slower They Fall!' " In T. J. Pempel, ed., *Uncommon Democracies: The One-Party Dominant Regimes*. Ithaca: Cornell University Press.

Taylor, Michael. 1972. "On the Theory of Government Coalition Formation." *British Journal of Political Science* 2: 361–73.

Taylor, Michael, and Valentine Herman. 1971. "Party Systems and Government Stability." *American Political Science Review* 65 (March): 28–37.

Taylor, Michael, and Michael Laver. 1973. "Government Coalitions in Western Europe." *European Journal of Political Research* 3: 205–48.

Thibaut, Françoise. 1990. *La Finlande. Politique intérieure et neutralité active*. Paris: Librairie Générale de Droit et de Jurisprudence.

Timmermans, Arco. 1994. "Cabinet Ministers and Policy-Making in Belgium: The Impact of Coalition Constraints." In Michael Laver and Kenneth A. Shepsle, eds., *Cabinet Ministers and Parliamentary Government*. Cambridge: Cambridge University Press.

Tops, Pieter, and Karl Dittrich. 1992. "The Role of Policy in Dutch Coalition Building, 1946–81." In Michael Laver and Ian Budge, eds., *Party Policy and Government Coalitions*. London: St. Martin's.

Törnudd, Klaus. 1969. "Composition of Cabinets in Finland 1917–1968." In *Scandinavian Political Studies*. Vol. 4. New York: Columbia University Press.

Torp, Olaf. 1990. *Stortinget i navn og tall*. Oslo: Universitetsforlaget.

Traversa, Silvio. 1989. *Il Parlamento nella Costituzione e nella prassi*. Milan: Giuffré.

Tsebelis, George. 1990. *Nested Games: Rational Choice in Comparative Politics*. Berkeley: University of California Press.

———. 1999. "Veto Players Data." Located at http://www.sscnet.ucla.edu/polisci/faculty/tsebelis/vpdata.html. Last accessed on July 5, 1999.

Tucciarelli, Claudio. 1998. "Il rapporto Parlamento-Governo, tra attività legislative e funzione di controllo nella prassi della XII e della XIII legislatura." In Silvio Traversa and Antonio Casu, eds., *Il parlamento nella transizione*. Milan: Giuffré.

Tullock, Gordon. 1981. "Why So Much Stability?" *Public Choice* 37 (2): 189–202.

Tusell, Javier. 1982. *Las Constituyentes de 1931*. Madrid: Centro de Investigaciones Sociológicas.

Uleri, Pier Vicenzo, and Roberto Fideli. 1996. "I referendum non piovono dal cielo. La consultazione referendaria di giugno." In Mario Caciagli and David I. Kertzer, eds., *Politica in Italia. I fatti dell'anno e le interpretazioni. Edizione 96*. Bologna: Il Mulino.

Urwin, Derek W. 1974. "Germany: Continuity and Change in Electoral Politics." In Richard Rose, ed., *Electoral Behavior: A Comparative Handbook*. New York: Free Press.

Van der Eijk, Cees, and Kees Niemöller. 1992. "The Netherlands." In Mark N. Franklin, Thomas T. Mackie, and Henry Valen, eds., *Electoral Change: Responses to Evolving Social and Attitudinal Structures in Western Countries*. Cambridge: Cambridge University Press.

Van Roozendaal, Peter. 1992. *Cabinets in Multi-Party Democracies: The Effect of Dominant and Central Parties on Cabinet Composition and Durability*. Ph.D. dissertation, University of Groningen. Amsterdam: Thesis Publishers.

Varela Díaz, Santiago. 1978. *Partidos y parlamento en la II República española*. Madrid: Fundación Juan March.

Vassallo, Salvatore. 1994. *Il governo di partito in Italia (1943–1993)*. Bologna: Il Mulino.

Venditti, Renato. 1981. *Il manuale Cencelli*. Rome: Editori Riuniti.

Vesperini, Giulio, ed. 1998. *I governi del maggioritario. Obiettivi e risultati*. Rome: Donizelli.

Volkens, Andrea. 1995. *Dataset CMP95: Comparative Manifestos Project: Programmatic Profiles of Political Parties in Twenty Countries, 1945–1988*. Comparative Manifestos Project, Science Center Berlin, Research Unit: Institutions and Social Change (Director H.-D. Klingemann) in cooperation with the Manifesto Research Group (Chairman I. Budge).

Walsh, Dick. 1986. *The Party: Inside Fianna Fáil*. Dublin: Gill and Macmillan.

Warwick, Paul. 1979. "The Durability of Coalition Governments in Parliamentary Democracies." *Comparative Political Studies* 11, no. 4 (January): 465–98.

————. 1992a. "Ideological Diversity and Government Survival in West European Parliamentary Democracies." *Comparative Political Studies* 25, no. 3 (October): 332–61.

————. 1992b. "Rising Hazards: An Underlying Dynamic of Parliamentary Government." *American Journal of Political Science* 36, no. 4 (November): 857–76.

————. 1994. *Government Survival in Parliamentary Democracies*. Cambridge: Cambridge University Press.

Warwick, Paul, and Stephen T. Easton. 1992. "The Cabinet Stability Controversy: New Perspectives on a Classic Problem." *American Journal of Political Science* 36, no. 1 (February): 122–46.

Wertman, Douglas. 1977. "Government Formation in Italy." In Howard R. Penniman, ed., *Italy at the Polls, 1983: A Study of the Parliamentary Elections*. Durham: Duke University Press/The American Enterprise Institute.

Westefield, Louis P. 1974. "Majority Party Leadership and the Committee System in the House of Representatives." *American Political Science Review* 68, no. 4 (December): 1593–604.

White, Halbert. 1980. "A Heteroskedasticity-Consistent Covariance Matrix Estimator and a Direct Test for Heteroskedasticity." *Econometrica*, 48, no. 4 (May): 817–38.

Whyte, J. H. 1974. "Ireland: Politics Without Social Bases." In Richard Rose, ed., *Electoral Behavior: A Comparative Handbook*. New York: Free Press.

Wilkinson, Leland, ed. 1998. *SYSTAT 8.0: Statistics*. Chicago: SPSS.

Wilkinson, Leland, and MaryAnn Hill. 1992. *FASTAT: Easy-to-Use Statistics for Real-World Analyses*. Evanston, IL: SYSTAT, Inc.

Wilkinson, Leland, and Yuri Balasanov. 1998. "Time Series." In Leland Wilkinson, ed., *SYSTAT 8.0: Statistics*. Chicago: SPSS.

Williams, Philip M. 1966. *Crisis and Compromise: Politics in the Fourth Republic*. Garden City, N.Y.: Anchor.

Wilson, Woodrow. 1885. *Congressional Government*. Reprint, Gloucester, Mass.: Peter Smith.

Woldendorp, Jaap, Hans Keman, and Ian Budge. 1993. "Political Data 1945–1990: Party Government in 20 Democracies." *European Journal of Political Research* 24, no. 1 (July): 1–120.

————. 1998. "Party Government in 20 Democracies: An Update (1990–1995)." *European Journal of Political Research* 33, no. 1 (January): 125–64.

Ysebaert, Clair. 1995. *Politicographe: Mémento Politique/Politiek Zakboekje*. Zaventem: Kluwer.

Zariski, Raphael. 1993. "Italy." In M. Donald Hancock, ed., *Politics in Western Europe*. Chatham, N.J.: Chatham House.

Zelterburg, Seppo. 1991. *Finland After 1917*. Helsinki: Otava.

Zuckerman, Alan. 1979. *The Politics of Faction*. New Haven: Yale University Press.

NEWSPAPERS AND NEWSWEEKLIES CONSULTED

Corriere della Sera, Milan.

Daily Telegraph, London.
The Economist, London.
L'Espresso, Rome.
Financial Times, London.
Le Monde, Paris.
The New York Times.
Nieuwe Rotterdamse Courant, Rotterdam.
Il Popolo, Rome.
La Stampa, Turin.
The Times, London.

Index

Note: Page numbers in **Boldface** refer to definitions in the glossary: pages **229–35**. Political parties are mostly noted by party acronyms grouped by type of party (e.g., Christian Democratic, Social Democratic/Socialists, etc.); otherwise, they are listed by specific party name. A full list of party names and abbreviations can be found in Appendix A, pages 191–96.